RURAL SOCIAL SYSTEMS AND ADULT EDUCATION

Study of Adult Education in Rural Areas

RURAL SOCIAL SYSTEMS

AND

ADULT EDUCATION

A Committee Report by

CHARLES P. LOOMIS
Chairman

J. ALLAN BEEGLE
Editor

OLEN E. LEONARD

T. WILSON LONGMORE

SHELDON G. LOWRY

JOSEPH L. MATTHEWS

FRANK C. NALL

JACK J. PREISS

WAYNE C. ROHRER

ORDEN C. SMUCKER

CARL C. TAYLOR

JOHN F. THADEN

RUTH WARNCKE

AND

EDWARD W. WEIDNER

Resulting from a Study Sponsored by
The Association of Land Grant Colleges and Universities
and
The Fund for Adult Education Established by
The Ford Foundation

THE MICHIGAN STATE COLLEGE PRESS
1953

Copyright 1953 by

THE MICHIGAN STATE COLLEGE PRESS

COMPOSED AND PRINTED BY WAVERLY PRESS, INC.
BALTIMORE, U. S. A.

CONTENTS

Chapter   Page

Foreword   vii

PART I

1. ADULT EDUCATION AND ITS SOCIAL SYSTEMS IN RURAL AMERICA   *by Charles P. Loomis* 1
2. ADULT EDUCATION IN THE PUBLIC SCHOOLS AND THE COMMUNITY   *by John F. Thaden* 24
3. THE COOPERATIVE EXTENSION SERVICE OF THE UNITED STATES   *by Joseph L. Matthews* 51
4. GENERAL FARMERS' ORGANIZATIONS AND COOPERATIVES   *by Carl C. Taylor and Wayne C. Rohrer* 80
5. ADULT EDUCATIONAL PROGRAMS OR ACTIVITIES OF THE GENERAL FARMERS' ORGANIZATIONS AND COOPERATIVES   *by Wayne C. Rohrer and Carl C. Taylor* 100
6. SERVICE, PROFESSIONAL AND OTHER CIVIC CLUBS   *by T. Wilson Longmore and Frank C. Nall* 122
7. SPECIAL AGENCIES WITHIN THE DEPARTMENT OF AGRICULTURE   *by T. Wilson Longmore* 146

PART II

8. PUBLIC LIBRARIES   *by Ruth Warncke* 172
9. ADULT EDUCATION IN THE RURAL CHURCH   *by Orden C. Smucker* 196
10. CONTINUATION EDUCATION IN COLLEGES AND UNIVERSITIES   *by Olen E. Leonard and Sheldon G. Lowry* .. 230
11. INTERNATIONAL EXCHANGE OF PERSONS   *by Olen E. Leonard and Sheldon G. Lowry* 244
12. RURAL LOCAL GOVERNMENT AND POLITICS AND ADULT EDUCATION   *by Edward W. Weidner and Jack Preiss* 271
13. MASS MEDIA OF COMMUNICATION   *by J. Allan Beegle* 295
14. RURAL ADULT EDUCATION—THE OVERALL PICTURE *by Charles P. Loomis* 320

APPENDIX A   THE CONTRIBUTORS 334
APPENDIX B   SCHEDULES USED IN STUDY OF ADULT EDUCATION IN RURAL AREAS 348
APPENDIX C   SAMPLING PROCEDURES UTILIZED 375
APPENDIX D   SUB-COMMITTEE DOCUMENT: ORIENTATION MANUAL FOR STUDY OF ADULT EDUCATION IN RURAL AREAS 390

Foreword

In order to understand the nature of the present report, it is necessary to understand the nature of the various individual and agency contributions. The Fund for Adult Education commissioned the Association of Land Grant Colleges and Universities to make the study and provided most of the financial support for it. However, substantial contributions in the form of professional services were provided without charge by the Division of Farm Population and Rural Life of the Bureau of Agricultural Economics, the Extension Service of the United States Department of Agriculture, and the Agricultural Experiment Station of Michigan State College. Officials of all the organizations cooperated wholeheartedly in the study.

The Association of Land Grant Colleges and Universities employed the director of the project. The Social Research Service of Michigan State College employed the study staff, handled accounts and conducted the statistical analyses.

As indicated in the introductory and concluding chapters of the report, the study was conducted as a combination of team and individual effort. The staff as a committee determined the general policies within the limits set by the sponsoring agencies and developed the research instruments to be used. The staff members, in pairs or as individuals, carried through the investigation, wrote and are responsible for the contents of the separate chapters which deal with the various systems and organizations in rural areas. Chapter 12 was prepared by the Governmental Research Bureau of Michigan State College and Jack J. Preiss as a separate part of the project.

The study staff wishes especially to thank Mr. Russell Thackrey, Executive Secretary of the Association of Land Grant Colleges and Universities and Mr. C. Scott Fletcher, President of the Fund for Adult Education Established by the Ford Foundation, for their wholehearted cooperation and encouragement during the entire conduct of the study.

Special acknowledgment should go to Mrs. Loleta Fyan, President of the American Library Association; Mr. Allan Kline, President of the American Farm Bureau Federation and member of the Board of Directors of the Fund for Adult Education; and three officials of the United States Department of Agriculture, namely, Mr. Oris Wells, Chief of the Bureau of Agricultural Economics, Mr. M. C. Wilson, Division of Field Studies and Training of the Extension Service, and Mr. M. L. Wilson, Director of the Extension Service, for the invaluable advice and time they gave the study. Of the members of the committee, two deserve special recognition. Dr. T. Wilson Longmore served as assistant director of the study and Dr. Allan Beegle served as editor of the report. Also, acknowledgment should go to Professors Wilbur Brookover, Duane Gibson, Charles Hoffer, Paul Miller, Christopher Sower and Gregory Stone, who assisted with the study but did not write chapters. The author of each chapter assumes full responsibility for the content of the chapter.

                        Charles P. Loomis, Director of the Study
                        Social Research Service
                        Michigan State College
                        East Lansing, Michigan

Part One

Chapter 1:

ADULT EDUCATION AND ITS SOCIAL SYSTEMS IN RURAL AMERICA

Introduction

The Nature and Importance of Education—Especially Adult Education.—Education is the process whereby culture is transmitted. The cultural heritage transmitted by education includes skills, ideas, moral values, practices, and factual knowledge. It also includes the interaction and expectancy patterns which make roles—such as those of parent and child, teacher and student, foreman and worker—operative within the society. The attitudes and beliefs which are important components of citizenship and personality are parts of this heritage. All of the components of the cultural heritage are ingredients of our social structure and our value orientation. Traditionally, the educational process has been thought to involve mainly children, beginning with the infant and continuing until he achieves economic independence. Both in the past and present it is correct to consider the child as the chief recipient of education; but it is also true that most adults are also involved in the educational process. All adults are teachers or potential teachers of children, of other adults or both.

Formal and informal adult education in rural and urban areas are important forces in the lives of more people than ever before. According to the United States Office of Education, three million adults in this country participate in educational programs in the public schools.[1] According to the American Institute of Public Opinion, 41 million people either have taken or would be interested in taking some formal classroom adult education courses. This Institute also reports that four million adults in the United States are now engaged in formal classroom study.[2] With a rate of social change unknown before to mankind, with personal and group tensions and with political and international struggles rampant in the world, effective adult educational procedures and organization must be developed. Cultural changes are now occurring so rapidly that no nation, least of all the United States, can afford to wait for the wise people of one generation to teach its culture to the children of the next. Survival requires that all normal adults learn constantly. What should be done in the case of an air raid? Why are prices so high? Should prices be controlled, and if so how? How can the weaknesses of government be overcome? What causes international tension and how can peace be promoted? These and many other questions must be considered by youths and adults if the nation is to survive. Cultural survival requires that the intellectual and cultural attainments of

---

[1] Homer Kempfer, *Adult Education Activities of the Public Schools, 1947–48*, Pamphlet No. 107, Washington: Federal Security Agency, 1949, p. iv.

[2] *Ibid.*, p. 1 and Homer Kempfer, "State Programs of General Adult Education," *Adult Education Journal*, Vol. 7, No. 2, April, 1948, pp. 75–81.

adults be furthered; actual physical survival in a world which may bring attack at any moment requires an adult educational organization with effective and dependable channels of communication.

In the pages to follow, primary emphasis is placed upon non-formalized, non-credit-bearing, and non-vocational adult education directed to those who have finished their formal education. The sponsors of this study have directed that attention be focused on adult education for rural people. Therefore, programs and activities are considered rural in which people living in the open-country or in places of less than 2500 population participate.

Independence and the Job—American Values Inhibiting Adult Education.—The educational program in rural and urban areas is weakest at the adult level. Although there are many reasons for this condition, only some of those related to the subsequent discussion will be stressed. Of prime importance is the fact that the past generations which set our educational patterns did not have to deal with the incredibly rapid cultural changes of today. In all societies, the culture imparted by the past assists the individual in changing his roles by dividing the life cycle into rather distinct periods, separated by *rites of passage.* These periods include those related to birth, graduation from formal schooling, marriage, and death.

In our culture the family and the community have considered it their responsibility to bring the child from birth to independent adulthood. Traditionally the period between birth and adulthood has been the time set aside for education. Education centers first in the family, then in the school. The function of both the family and school is to transform the dependent child into an independent, functional adult. With the attainment of adulthood the individual usually marries—an important *rite of passage* in our society which is generally related to being accepted as an adult. In the middle classes, at least, the termination of school, the beginning of fulltime employment, and/or marriage usually means that adulthood has been reached. The boy or girl having reached adult status is supposed to have achieved independence and is expected to assume the adult role in the family and vocational systems of the culture. For fully occupied adults, adult educational activity for other than occupational requirements is not in great demand. Such a pattern of training was relatively adequate when cultural change was less rapid and when the skills and knowledge necessary for the vocations could be mastered during youth.

Few societies are more vocationally-oriented than our own. At the present time, there is no better single index of social status and position in America than the individual's profession or vocation. All studies demonstrate a remarkable relationship between educational attainment and the occupation in which the person is engaged. With a few exceptions, one's occupation is closely related to such material items as home ownership, possession of radios, or automobiles, and to such non-material items as the stimuli which reach the individual through mass media, organizations, and institutions. As will be shown later, the nature of the occupations in the various regions of rural America have tremendous influence upon the extent and nature of adult education activities. The emphasis here, however, has been the importance of occupation as related to education and "coming of age" in America.

The sponsors of this study have directed that the focus of the inquiry be the following subject-matter fields:[3] (1) international understanding for peace, (2) strengthening of democracy, (3) understanding and strengthening of the economy. It is not necessary to stress the importance of these three fields for the development and preservation of society. The manner in which adult education is related to these fields will be vitally influenced by the attitudes toward education which we have just described. Even today there are many who believe that only the jobless or maladjusted continue education into adulthood.

SPECIAL CONDITIONS OF RURAL ADULT EDUCATION

Ecological Factors—Sparsity of Population and Organizational Efficiency.—In most respects, rural areas are comparatively disadvantaged in the availability of adult education facilities. One reason for this is related to the problem of space and its effect on communication and organization. Everyone is aware that man is a space-bound creature and that no dreams of magic carpets or supermen change this. However, in an age of supersonic speeds and mass media we may forget that organizations, to function effectively, require a minimum number of participants, members or consumers in a relatively small area. Professional standards, for example, require that the trade center community or integrated region, served by a library administrative unit for reasonably good service, should not have less than 25,000 to 50,000 people. An effective public school administrative unit should not have less than 50,000 to 60,000 people.[4] Public health services and public welfare administrative units should not have less than 50,000 people.[5] Interestingly enough, the standards for units of secondary highway administration, so important in the functioning of these and other units in rural areas, require a minimum of 12,000 to 28,000 population.[6]

[3] For the sake of brevity, the three fields will frequently be referred to as "the three fields" and "the three fields of interest" throughout the pages to follow.

[4] Lowell Martin, "The Optimum Size of the Public Library Unit," in *Library Extension: Problems and Solutions*, edited by C. B. Joeckel, Chicago: University of Chicago Press, 1946, pp. 32–46; for discussion of the minimum requirements of various agencies see Zona Kemp Williams, *The Determination of Administrative Units for Library Purposes in Relation to Desirable Administrative Units for Certain Other Governmental Functions*, Chicago: University of Chicago Master's Thesis, 1951, pp. 106 ff; see also National Commission on School District Reorganization, *Your School District*, Washington: National Education Association, Department of Rural Education, 1948, pp. 85–87.

[5] American Public Health Association Committee on Administrative Practice, Subcommittee on Local Health Units, *Local Health Units for the Nation*, a report by Harvey Emerson, New York: The Commonwealth Fund, 1945, pp. 333 ff.

[6] New York State Commission to Revise Tax Laws, *Depression Taxes and Economy Through*

A large segment of the rural population of the United States lives in natural service units or trade center communities which have fewer people than these minima prescribe. Obviously, the minimum population required for effective service is related to many factors involving the economic status, cultural homogeneity, accessibility, day-to-day interaction and movements of the people. But the disadvantaging factors of low population densities and long distances to services in many rural areas of the United States need no emphasis for adult education workers with experience in the sparsely settled areas. The county agricultural agent, vocational agriculture teacher, extension librarian, and rural minister have very different problems in the Range-Livestock or Wheat Areas of the Great Plains than do adult educators in large cities[7] or in thickly settled rural areas. Some of the difficulties of providing services in the most rural parts of the nation could be overcome if incomes for all rural sections were comparable. As will be indicated later, however, incomes are generally lower in the more rural and less densely populated areas.

Economic Base for Services—The Rich have the Money, the Poor the Children.— Among the important reasons for the lack of adult educational facilities in rural as compared with urban areas is the lower income of the rural people. In general, the more rural the county the lower the average farm family's income will be. In 1946, the per capita net income of persons living on farms was $779, as compared with $1288 for persons not living on farms. In 1940 almost twice as large a proportion of non-farm as farm residents paid income tax (19 percent compared with 11 percent).

From Table 1, it is easy to discern the effect of rurality on income as reflected in income taxes paid, per capita bank deposits, and purchase of government bonds. The larger the proportion of rural-farm population in a county, other things being equal, the lower the income will be. In 1940 the buying power of non-farm families was estimated to exceed that of farm families by more than one-half.[8] Figure 1 shows additional indices in which the farm, compared with the non-farm population is deficient. The most complete annual expenditure study for families in the United States, made in 1935–36, reveals

---

Reforms of Local Government, Albany: 1933, pp. 127–128; Princeton Local Government Survey, *Readjusting Local Services and Areas*, Princeton: Princeton University Press, 1937, pp. 16, 51; Brookings Institution, Institute for Government Research, *Report on Survey of Administration in Iowa, Submitted to the Committee on Reductions of Government Expansions*, Des Moines: State of Iowa, 1933, p. 308; R. S. Ford and M. A. Bacon, *Michigan Highway Finances*, Ann Arbor: Bureau of Government of the University of Michigan, 1943.

[7] We have not attempted to deal here with the disadvantages of units too large for optimum service. Obviously such problems should be handled by those dealing with adult education in urban areas. For example, governmental expenditures per capita for units from 30,000 to 300,000 are about the same. However, such expenditures for units from 300,000 up increase rapidly with the size of the unit. See William Anderson, "The Units of Government in the United States," Chicago: *Public Administration Service Publication, No. 83*, 1942, p. 42.

[8] Carl C. Taylor and others, *Rural Life in the United States*, New York: Alfred Knopf and Co., 1949, p. 299.

TABLE 1
*Proportion of Persons 21 Years of Age and Over Who Paid Income Taxes in 1940, Per Capita E Bond Purchases in 1944, and Per Capita Savings Deposits (Time) in 1944**

Residence and Region	Proportion of Persons 21 and Over Paying Income Tax	Per Capita Bank Deposits	Per Capita E Bond Purchases
	%	$	$
TOTAL	18	323	90
North	21	434	101
South	10	112	61
West	21	346	115
Rural-Farm	11	143	61
North	15	257	83
South	6	55	41
West	17	203	91
Non-Farm (Rural-Nonfarm plus Urban)	19	376	98
North	21	466	104
South	12	148	74
West	22	375	120
Counties: 0–24.9% Rural-Farm	22	459	111
North	23	521	110
South	17	234	102
West	24	453	132
Counties: 25–49.9% Rural-Farm	11	132	64
North	13	205	74
South	7	50	46
West	13	111	79
Counties: 50–74.9% Rural-Farm	6	60	47
North	9	103	72
South	4	39	35
West	10	43	50
Counties: 75–100% Rural-Farm	2	21	22
North	4	23	50
South	2	20	21
West	—	—	—

* Based on county information prepared by Walter C. McKain and Grace L. Flagg in *Differences between Rural and Urban Levels of Living*, Part II, Washington, USDA, June, 1948.

the following differences in expenditures: farm families, $1215; rural-nonfarm families, $1409; and urban families, $1855.[9] This study reveals the following

[9] National Resources Planning Board, *Family Expenditures in the United States*, Washington: Government Printing Office, 1941. The significance of income levels is brought out by a detailed analysis of expenditures at various income levels for farm families. For example, for the four income levels: I, under $500; II, $1000–$1250; III, $2500–$3000; and IV, $5000–$10,000, expenditures for education were $2, $11, $30, and $57, respectively; for reading $3, $7, $12, and $20, for savings minus $208, minus $10, plus $777, and plus $3,463.

average annual expenditures for education: for farm families, $11; for rural-nonfarm, $18; and for urban families, $16. The comparable expenditures for reading were $6, $12, and $16, respectively. In 1940 urban teachers were paid salaries fully twice as high as those paid rural teachers, and the average value of school equipment per pupil was more than twice as large for urban as for rural schools.[10] The significance of these differences becomes obvious in view of the fact that 51 percent of the nation's children 6 to 15 years of age live on farms or in rural territory, and only approximately 37 percent of all moneys expended on primary and secondary education go to rural schools.[11] For education of children the close relationship between rurality and low income is par-

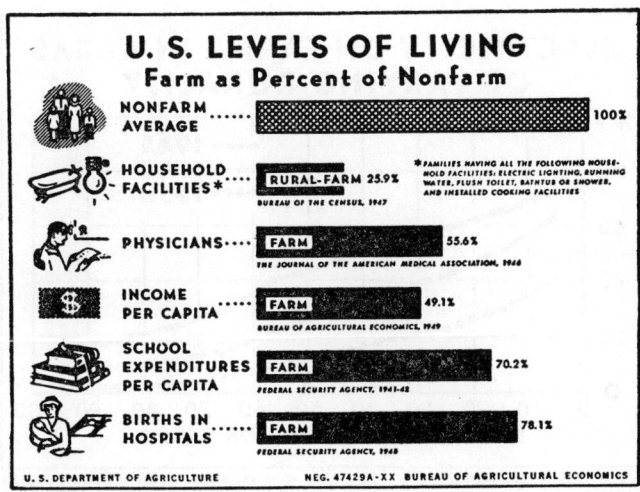

FIG. 1. Rural-farm areas of the United States are disadvantaged as compared with the non-farm areas of the nation.

ticularly serious because rural and low-income areas have higher birth rates than less rural, higher income areas. Since many children born and reared in low income rural areas must migrate to the cities, the problem is a national one. It is estimated that in 50 years, 80 percent of all urban people will have come out of a farm background.[12]

That rural people place education very high in the scale of values is demonstrated by the proportion of state income which the various states devote to education. South Dakota, a rural state, contributes the largest proportion of its income to education; Delaware, an industrial state, the smallest proportion.

[10] C. P. Loomis and J. Allan Beegle, *Rural Social Systems*, New York: Prentice-Hall, Inc., 1950, p. 479 and Taylor, *op. cit.*, pp. 300–301.
[11] Loomis and Beegle, *Ibid.*, p. 479.
[12] Joseph Ackerman and Marshall Harris, *Family Farm Policy*, Chicago: The University of Chicago Press, 1946, p. 399, and *American Country Life Conference*, Report of Committee I, 1946.

All the states in the upper half of the array are rural and most of those below are industrial. In relation to their incomes, rural people make far greater sacrifices in payment of taxes for education than do urban people.[13] When the states are ranked according to their accomplishment in formal education, a few rural states rank above such urban states as New York or Massachusetts, but unfortunately many, mostly in the South, rank at the bottom.[14]

Although more farm families now have radios and access to various other types of mass media than in earlier decades, the more rural counties of the nation continue to be disadvantaged. Figure 2 demonstrates that the more rural the county the less likely are farm families to have electricity, necessary

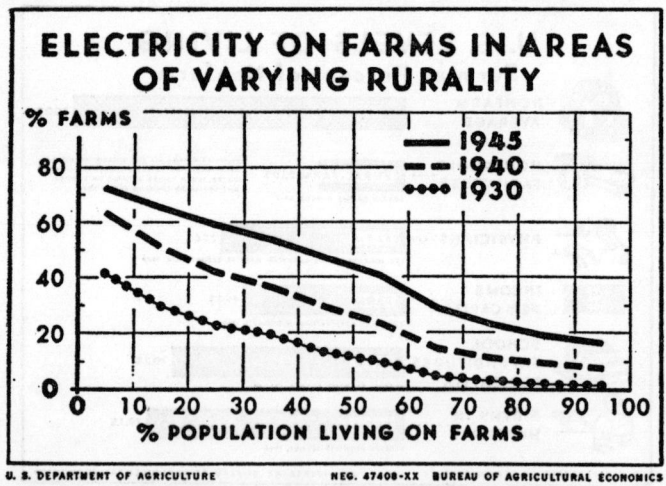

FIG. 2. The proportion of farms having electricity decreases with increased rurality. As may be noted from 1945 data, many farms are still without electricity.

for the reception of such mass media as television and radio. Such differences demonstrate the cumulative effects of low incomes and sparse populations as disadvantaging factors for all formal organizations and social systems discussed in this report.

DEMOGRAPHIC FACTORS

Age and Vital Processes.—The farms of the United States are not solely the producers of the food and fiber consumed by the nation. They also produce far more than their share of the children.

The growth of urban centers is probably the most important change in the last century. In 1850, 15 percent of our population was urban; in 1950, 64 per-

[13] R. M. Hughes and W. H. Lancelot, *Education—America's Magic*, Ames, Iowa: State College Press, 1946, p. 70.
[14] Loomis and Beegle, *op. cit.*, pp. 475 ff.

cent was urban and the remainder, or 36 percent, was rural. Less than half of the rural population, however, lived on farms. More than 40 percent of our population now live in cities of 25,000 or more, and 29 percent live in cities of at least 100,000. The growing centralization has been accompanied by a rationalization of farming and industry. For example, in 1820 the amount of food and fiber produced by an agricultural worker was sufficient to feed and clothe five persons; in 1940 each agricultural worker produced enough for 15 persons.[15] More and more of the processing of agricultural products has moved from the rural areas to the cities.[16]

Anyone interested in adult education must be concerned with the dynamics of population. Over half of the potential consumers of adult education are in the cities, whereas over half of the children of school age are living in rural areas. The median age of the urban population in 1950 was 31.5; that of the farm population, 26.0. The nature of the "center" activities, or those carried on in cities, require young adults, especially females. The farm areas retain relatively large proportions of children and males. Since the cities have not been reproducing themselves, they have had to rely upon migration from the rural areas or from abroad.

The rural-farm segment of the population contains smaller percentages of foreign born, but larger percentages of Negroes, than the urban segment. While less than 3 percent of the farm population in 1950 was born abroad, nearly 9 percent of the urban population reported foreign birth. Slightly more than 14 percent of the farm population was reported as Negro in 1950 but slightly under 10 percent of the urban population was Negro.

Although this is not the place to discuss the specific effects of the great population adjustments necessary to produce and maintain our industrial culture, one fact not unrelated to the need for adult education may be mentioned. Rapid movement and imbalance in sex and age groups can be calculated to produce an instability which is incompatible with a healthy democracy. Several scholars have reported that rapid industrialization and secularization were related in a causal manner to the development of Nazism in Germany.[17] In all parts of the world most types of suicide indicate frustrations and maladjustments. They were extremely prevalent in Germany. In the United States a high positive correlation exists between the rate of growth of cities of 100,000 or more and the suicide rate.[18] Recent findings in Michigan revealing high suicide rates in rural areas, contrary to expectation on the basis of past studies, are also significant indications of stress. The suicide rates in Michigan are particularly high in the Cut-over Area, a long-time problem area, and one experiencing high rates of

[15] Loomis and Beegle, *op. cit.*, p. 206.
[16] Loomis and Beegle, *op. cit.*, p. 206.
[17] Charles P. Loomis and J. Allan Beegle, "The Spread of German Nazism in Rural Areas," *American Sociological Review*, Vol. XI, No. 6, December, 1946, pp. 724–734.
[18] Loomis and Beegle, *op. cit.*, p. 406.

out-migration.[19] Certainly adult education has a responsibility in assisting in adjustments necessitated by changes in residence required by our culture.

Actual and Potential Back-to-the-Land Movements.—On the whole, Americans are an optimistic people. For them the process of urbanization and the movement of rural people to cities is closely linked with belief in progress. Only twice during the 27-year period between 1920 and 1947 did the movement of urban people to farm areas exceed the reverse movement, namely during the depression years, 1931 and 1932, and the post World War II years, 1945 and 1946. In fact, during the 27-year period under consideration, there was an average net migration from farms of 600,000 per year. Urban population increased from 51 percent of the total to 59 percent and rural-farm population decreased from nearly 30 percent to 19 percent. It should be noted, however, that rural people not living on farms actually increased from 19 to nearly 22 percent during the period. These figures reflect the feelings of many city dwellers who, even during normal times, long for the independence they believe a home and a plot of ground will give them. Undoubtedly such sentiments play a part in the current growth of suburban and fringe populations. This population development, especially around the fringes of the cities, is neither urban nor rural. It is not effectively reached by adult education facilities designed either for the city or the farm families.

Probably in part because of our inherent optimism, many have forgotten the misery and deprivation which the last depression brought. During 1932 alone, a total of 1,777,000 persons left towns and cities for farms. Although many moved back onto unoccupied farms in poor land areas or into the homes of relatives on occupied farms, the vast majority moved only a short distance from towns and cities. Characteristically, they settled on small tracts of land in the dual hope that they could escape urban rents and bread lines, and that they could produce subsistence products for home consumption. Back-to-the-land was once again revived as a panacea for those caught in the complexities of industrial cities.

The records prove that during depressions, urban adult education facilities, especially those which might help in finding a job are heavily used. Almost none of these facilities are available to those participating in the back-to-the-land movement, during normal or depression periods. The facilities are either not available or the participants are too poor or isolated to be able to use them.[20]

Those who worked in rural areas surrounding the bombed-out cities of England and Germany after World War II were reminded of back-to-the-land movements in the United States during the last great depression. What, we may ask, would happen in America if three or four of our major cities were bombed

---

[19] William W. Schroeder, *Suicide Differentials in Michigan*, East Lansing: Michigan State College, Master's Thesis, 1951.

[20] For a general description of back-to-the-land movements and one attempt to deal with the phenomenon, see Charles P. Loomis, *Studies of Rural Social Organization in the United States, Latin America and Germany*, East Lansing: Michigan State College Press, 1945, Chapter 3.

tomorrow? A political scientist who knows the results of the German bombardment writes what he thinks would happen.[21] With the first bombardment, the rural areas would be snarled into hopeless knots; serious food, shelter, relief, and fire problems would arise immediately. The spectre of millions of frightened, starving, and dispossessed city people, plodding through the rural areas after the initial bombardment, should remind adult educators of the reciprocity of the rural and urban populations. He who is interested in strengthening democracy cannot confine his attention in this age to any one population segment.

RURAL REGIONS—MAJOR TYPES OF FARMING AREAS

Obviously, the adult educator will have different problems in different parts of the country. For example, the Dairy Areas, with relatively constant work loads from month to month, may be expected to pose different problems than the Cotton Belt, in which almost one-half of the total man hours of labor fall in September and October. Since this report is organized around the various systems through which adult education programs of the rural areas are carried and since these are all in a large measure structured and influenced by the way people make a living, we shall briefly describe the major types of farming areas.[22] Figure 3 shows the major types of farming areas of the nation and the sample counties used in this study.

The Cotton Belt contains approximately 33 percent of the farm population of the nation and is characterized by high birth rates, low levels of living, high proportions of native American stock, and except in the western portion, high proportions of non-whites and non-owners. It is the most rural of the regions. Cotton is king throughout this area. The pulsation of activities required in growing and harvesting cotton determine school vacations, social events, business activities, and church revivals. The extremely heavy work period, during the picking season in September and October, stands in contrast to the slack period in winter and early spring. During the latter period, farmers are not too busy for adult education programs. The plantation organization is the pacesetter in much of the area. For generations, the plantation system has permitted only a relatively few to initiate action, to make important decisions, or to engage in concerted community action. Interaction in groups is largely informal, with traditional and sacred activities dominant. Rural religion is generally fundamentalistic. Discussion meetings are relatively uncommon. Traditionally, a rather high value is placed on oratory and speeches. The Farm Bureau is the strongest of the general farmers' organizations and the cooperative movement is particularly weak in the area. Some of the most solidary neighborhoods in the entire country, often organized around a church, are found in the Cotton Belt. This is particularly true of Negro neighborhoods. In contrast to the

---

[21] A. W. Bromage, "Public Administration in the Atomic Age," *American Political Science Review*, Vol. LI, No. 5, October, 1947, pp. 947–955.

[22] For a more detailed description, see Loomis and Beegle, *op. cit.*, Chapter 8.

family farm, however, the plantation is the important entrepreneurial unit. The area is not, therefore, as family oriented as some of the other areas.

In many respects the *Wheat Areas*, containing approximately 4 percent of the farm population of the nation, stand in sharp contrast to the Cotton Belt. Levels of living and income are high, relatively little of the produce is consumed by the family, the birth rate is low, and proportions owning a tractor are high. The Wheat Areas, like the Cotton Belt, are highly rural. Neighborhoods are weak, however, with proportionately few open-country churches. The trade centers are relatively important structuring points for economic and social life. The rate of tenancy is comparatively high even though farm enterprises are managed by families. Tenants, however, have relatively high status. The

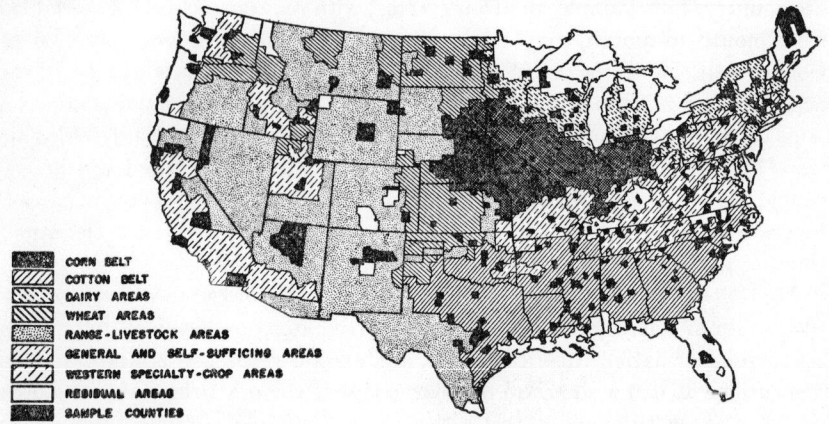

FIG. 3. The types of farming areas in the United States and the sample counties used in the study.

Farmers' Union is strongest in these areas, particularly in the northern part which was settled in large part by northern Europeans. Over three-fourths of the work is concentrated in four months. Spring, winter, and early summer are idle months—a period when adult education may be furthered.

In the *Corn Belt*, containing approximately 14 percent of the nation's farmers, less reliance is placed upon a single crop than in the Cotton or Wheat Areas. Even though activities such as hog breeding and feeding are also important, the growing of corn and the corn market exerts a tremendous effect upon the lives of the people. This area is characterized by high levels of living and large incomes, coupled with low birth rates. The one-room neighborhood school is still important but in other social and economic activities the trade center is very important and neighborhoods located near the center are dying out. Rural churches are more frequently located in the trade centers than in the Cotton Belt. Special interest groups are organized around commodities, and farms are highly mechanized. The Farm Bureau is strongest in this area. Heaviest work loads usually come in April, May, June, September and October. Other months would be better for most adult education activities.

The *Dairy Areas*, accounting for approximately 12 percent of the farm population, include several cultural regions. In the west the Scandinavian-American stocks are dominant; in the east the Old American and Canadian stocks predominate. The value of products consumed at home is high and a high rate of farm operator ownership prevails. The farms in this area are highly mechanized and the work loads are relatively stable thorughout the year. The New England heritage is more important in this region than in other areas of the United States. Many special interest groups exist and producer's cooperatives are strong. The strongest farm organization is the Grange in much of this area. West of New England, the trade-centered village settlement pattern which grew up in the border areas such as New York State, is common. Few farmers are more closely bound to their work routine, season in and season out, than the dairy farmer. The adult educator will find few slack periods here.

The *General and Self-Sufficing Areas* contain approximately 19 percent of the farmers of the country. Family-oriented activities are dominant in this region. Lower levels of living, average machinery inventories, and relatively high birth rates characterize this area. Neighborhood, informal friendship or clique groups, churches, and other organizations support the informal family-centered life. The families of the area produce for home use to a larger extent than elsewhere. There are few non-whites and foreigners. The family farm is dominant and the ownership rate is relatively high. In this area there is considerable time for non-work activities especially during the winter.

In the *Range-Livestock Areas* the nature of the economic enterprise demands that farmers travel long distances. This area embraces approximately four percent of the farm population, the largest land area, and the most diverse cultural groups. The neighborhoods are relatively weak and population density is generally sparse. Birth rates are low except for the areas inhabited by Indians, Spanish-Americans, and Mormons. Outside the Indian and Spanish-speaking areas incomes are relatively high. The livestock industry dominates the lives of the people everywhere, and the traditions of the "wild and woolly West" are kept alive through such events as rodeos. The dominant industry is well organized and constitutes a social, economic, and political power to be reckoned with. There are few open-country churches. There is perhaps more leisure time in this area than others, but distances and population sparsity make most adult education activities very difficult.

The *Western Specialty-Crop Areas* comprise about three percent of the farm population. These areas are small and are scattered through other types of farming areas, except for the California portion. Factory farms are found in the California area, where labor-management cleavages are important. The family farm prevails elsewhere, especially in the Mormon areas. The foreign population is large and the area is characterized by strong peasant traditions. High levels of living, high incomes and low birth rates are characteristic of this area. Harvest seasons in these regions require much labor and often pose special problems, especially when transient labor is necessary.

There are several smaller areas, when lumped together are called *Residual Areas*. The Lakes States Cut-over Area is characterized by low incomes, relatively high birth rates, and large proportions of foreign-born. This section contains a large proportion of rural-nonfarm inhabitants who depend upon off-farm work, especially in the mines. In many respects, the Lakes States Area is like the General and Self-Sufficing Areas. Additional sources of income are being opened up by tourist and recreation industries. This was one of the six problem areas during the depression.[23]

The tobacco-growing counties of Kentucky, Tennessee, Virginia, and North Carolina stand out as major sections not included in the seven major types of farming areas. In these areas, people are dependent upon the intensive cultivation of a cash crop that requires a great deal of carefully directed labor. The associational life of the people is not unlike that of the General and Self-Sufficing Farming Areas.

The Atlantic Seaboard, although not a large area, is an important vegetable-producing section. The largest district outside of the seven major types of farming regions is the Gulf Coast Fringe, including much of Florida. Sugar cane, citrus fruits, and vegetables are grown here. The Gulf Coast Areas are similar to the Western Specialty-Crop Areas in some respects, especially in the need for transient labor. In the former, however, the small family operator is more common.

Northern Maine is noted for its potato and timber production. Also outside the seven major types of farming regions is a part of the northern Pacific coast which includes many dairy enterprises, commercial orchards and part-time farming operations of rural-nonfarm dwellers.

INFORMAL GROUPS AS SYSTEMS AND CHANNELS FOR ADULT EDUCATION

While most rural areas may have insufficient population and financial support for the formal social systems that provide health, educational, welfare and road services, such areas are not disadvantaged in all the requirements for effective adult education.

The Family and Kinship Groupings.—In most farming and ranching areas, the family functioning as a unit occupationally is an effective means of communication. Families, as groups, usually operate the farms and ranches of the United States. A family enterprise, whether a two-acre truck farm or a 1500-

---

[23] The six problem areas of the United States in the mid-30's were: (1) the Appalachian-Ozark area; (2) the eastern cotton belt; (3) the Texas and Oklahoma cotton areas; (4) the Great Lakes cut-over area; (5) the spring wheat area of the Northern Plains; and (6) the winter wheat area of the Central Plains. See Taylor, *op. cit.*, p. 310.

acre cattle ranch, ties the members into a team relationship which no effective adult educator fails to consider in his work. Thus, a 4-H Club leader or a Vocational Agriculture teacher may find that a boy's father, who at first scoffed at his son's crop or livestock project, upon seeing the advantages, adopts the improvements.

Outside the immediate family, the kinship or family system is an important communication network and mutual-aid system in all rural areas. In some rural areas studied by the author, 80 percent of the day-to-day contacts off the farm are with relatives. Such communities are rather unusual, and are largely ethnic groupings, such as the Spanish-Americans in the southwest and Dutch groups

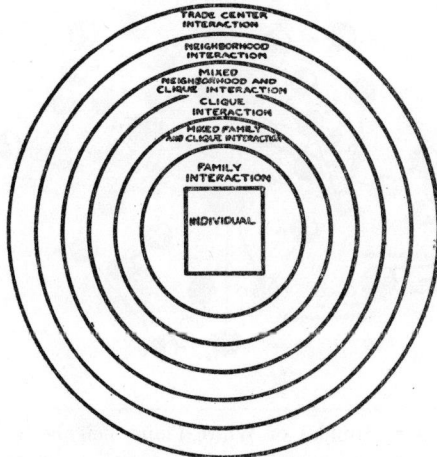

FIG. 4. Schematic diagram of the interaction of the individual in rural society.

in the north. But in all parts of rural America, particularly in the older settlements, family ties are important.

Cliques or Friendship Groups.—As indicated by Figure 4, the clique ranks next to the family in the intimacy it provides participating members. Within the communities the clique groupings are referred to by various terms, depending upon who is doing the evaluation. Thus, in a small village a member of lower-class groupings may refer to his clique as "our gang." A middle-class person might refer to this same clique as the "town toughs." The matter of social status and stratification will be discussed later. Only the relation of cliques to communication needs to be pointed out here. For purposes of this report, the clique or friendship group is regarded as a small, non-family group, consisting of two to about thirty persons, in association, and possessing a feeling of unity. Such groups are described as "informal" because there are no formally elected officials, constitutions, by-laws or other formal structuring elements. The intensity, frequency and significance of social interaction of rural people in such groupings is great.

Neighborhoods.—The neighborhood may be defined as an area in which people "neighbor together." Except in the most sparsely settled areas, the rural parts of the nation have the strongest neighborhoods.[24] It may be observed that since the invention of the motor car and modern road system, the small neighborhood of from 15 to 150 families who "neighbor together" is lessening in importance, whereas the trade center community made up of several to a dozen or so neighborhoods is becoming more important.

Figure 5 describes the visiting relations among families in a rural neighbor-

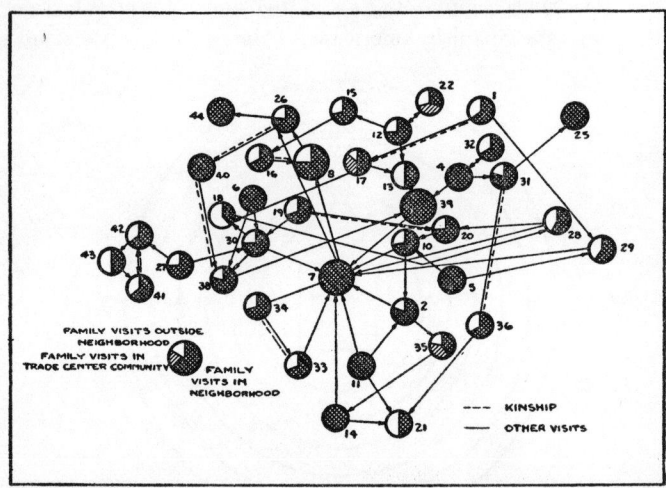

FIG. 5. Visiting among families of White Plains neighborhood, Charles County, Maryland. Such networks are important in the spread of information. For example, few would expect dissemination of information to be as rapid if imparted to family No. 22, at the top of the chart, as if imparted to family No. 7, the key family, in the center. There are many reasons for this, some of which may be noted from the chart. Thus, family No. 22 directs two-thirds of its visits outside the neighborhood and is relatively isolated within the neighborhood, while No. 7 is a key figure in a "clique" of families, namely, Nos. 33, 14, 11, 2, 10, 8, 7, and 34, who interact directly with one another.

hood. The inter-relationship between cliques and the neighborhood and the trade center community may be noted. In this figure the circles represent families and the lines indicate the amount, direction, and type of visiting. The importance of such interaction in the spread of information and learning to adult education is generally accepted.[25]

[24] Loomis and Beegle, *op. cit.*, Chapter 6.
[25] Perhaps the most complete documentation for rural society is to be found in Loomis and Beegle, *op. cit.*, Chapter 5. For an interesting discussion of the importance of such groups in a depressed section of New York City, see Hurley H. Doddy, *Informal Groups and the Community*, Institute of Adult Education, Teachers College, 1951, cited in Paul L. Essert and Coolie Verner, "Education for Active Adult Citizenship," *Teachers College Record*, Vol. 53, No. 1, pp. 16–31.

Informal Groups and Communication.—Whether they be organized about the neighborhood or the trade-center, inter-personal relations such as those described in Figures 5 and 7, are far more important in communication and in adult education than is generally recognized. Unfortunately, there is not much information concerning the function of such groupings in the performance of the social organizations. Neither are there many data to indicate their function in communication. It would be interesting to inquire of the families represented in Figure 5 shortly after some event such as the Pearl Harbor attack, how many knew about the event and how they had heard about it. Even on a college campus, in a random sample of 143 students interviewed the morning after Franklin D. Roosevelt's death, all but 16 had heard the news first by word of mouth. The original 16 who had heard of the event by radio thus activated an enormous amount of word of mouth communication.[26] These data are presented in support of the belief that the informal clique and neighborhood relationships are important to the adult educator.

The operation of interpersonal relations in the communication system for the spread of news, of course, may not be the same as that for changing attitudes. Unfortunately, concrete and objective information concerning the optimum social situation for the change of attitudes is not available. The information and research available stresses the importance of the informal group and the group member whose judgment is respected, thus providing a friendly atmosphere in which one may influence attitudes. Involvement of the individual through discussion and other means of eliciting participation is also considered important.[27] Thus, what is now known indicates that the cliques and rural neighborhoods in which people are acquainted and interact verbally with great frequency and intensity are settings in which adult education may be carried on effectively. Revolutionary changes brought about by shock procedures that disrupt the individual's relations to his group, such as those advocated by Communist leaders, follow entirely different principles and are not discussed here.

Since the interaction networks which maintain the family, clique, neighborhood, and community in rural areas, are extremely important for effective adult education, they will be described briefly. Two figures (6 and 7) will be useful in this discussion. Figure 6 depicts the locality groups of Livingston county, a rural county between Lansing and Detroit, Michigan; Figure 7 shows the leadership choices of families within one of the neighborhoods in this county.

For those interested in adult education there are several important facts

---

[26] Delbert Miller, "A Research Note on Mass Communication," *American Sociological Review*, Vol. X, No. 5, October, 1945, pp. 691–694.

[27] See Kurt Lewin, "The Relative Effectiveness of a Lecture Method and a Method of Group Decision for Changing Food Habits," Iowa City: Child Welfare Research Station, Preliminary Report, 1942; and Bryce Ryan and Neal C. Gross, "The Diffusion of Hybrid Seed Corn in Two Iowa Communities," *Rural Sociology*, Vol. VIII, No. 1, March, 1943, pp. 15–24.

presented in Figure 6. First there is a large area devoid of neighborhood activity—a kind of no-man's land. At one time there were active neighborhoods in this area, but urbanization with concomitant high mobility dissolved them. However, the families living in this area do belong to clique or friendship groups, and their interaction in such systems as farmers organizations, schools, and churches, is important to the life of the communities.

A second fact portrayed in Figure 6, important to those interested in adult education, is the significance of the district school where neighborhoods or extended districts exist. Various systems or organizations in the past have served as the chief integrating interest for rural neighborhoods. Churches,

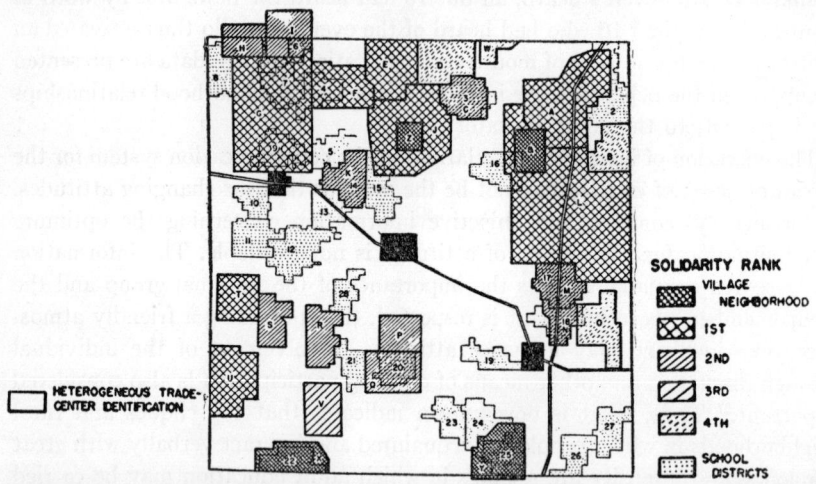

FIG. 6. Social organizations of Livingston County, Michigan. Twenty-eight active school district neighborhoods are shown as well as twenty-six extended neighborhoods. The extended neighborhoods are rated by degree of solidarity.

stores, and active family interaction, neighboring, and cooperation are also important. School and church reorganization, whether conducted to improve services or to adjust to population decline affects the vitality of rural neighborhoods.

A third feature of interest for adult educators in Figure 6 is the importance of highways. The so-called "checker-board" system of land division, in which each unit is one mile square and bounded by roads running north and south, and east and west, gives the locality groups straight line boundaries. Only the eighteen states settled before 1785, when the ordinance establishing the "checker-board" system of land division passed Congress, are not influenced by it. The changes along the highways and around the cities, including the development of filling stations, stores, and the development of fringe residences explain, in large measure, the decline of the neighborhood and the rise of the trade-center as the chief focus of influence in rural areas. The neighborhood-less areas shown in Figure 6 are primarily fringe areas around cities and along the highways,—areas which previous to the automobile and good roads had strong neighborhoods, district schools, and in some instances, churches or other integrative agencies.

A Neighborhood under Stress.—Figure 7 shows the leadership pattern of a small extended neighborhood, one of the neighborhoods depicted in Figure 6 which is losing services to the growing trade centers to the north and south.

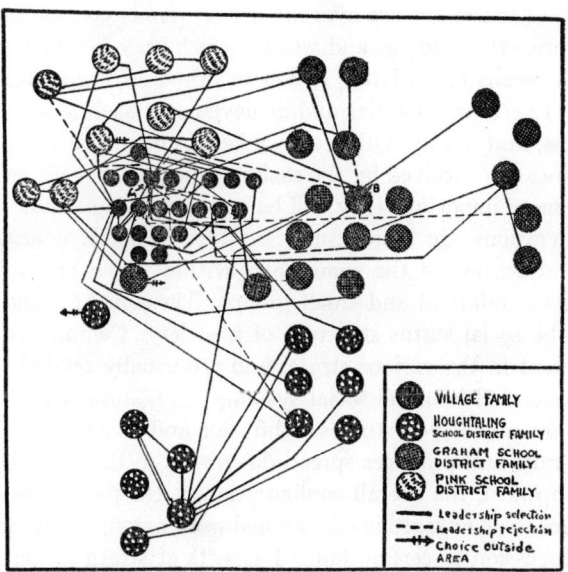

FIG. 7. Leadership choices and rejections in Cohoctah, Michigan. The village residents, the group in favor of the school consolidation, tend to make leadership choices within the village. Members of each of the school districts, most of whom are opposed to consolidation, tend to select persons from the district in which they live.

This neighborhood is torn with strife between those who want to close their schools and send the children to the larger center, and those who wish to maintain local schools. If the past is a guide to the future, this neighborhood may become less important in the lives of the people and the larger trade centers more important. Those interested in adult education in rural areas must plan and execute their programs for such neighborhoods with the pertinent facts in mind. In fact, the data for both Figures 6 and 7 were gathered at the request of the local agricultural extension agent. The extension service and other agencies for a number of years had been unable to get locals of farm organizations, 4-H club work, and similar activities to thrive. The strife over the school and the loss of services to larger centers, in part, is the explanation.

STRATIFICATION PATTERNS

In no society do all individuals have equal rights, authority, privileges, responsibilities and prestige. Normal individuals, in most situations will be given different treatment and will be evaluated differently, to say nothing of the different kinds of treatment given such abnormal individuals as the feebleminded, insane, and the outlaws.[28] The status accorded individuals is determined by the values of the group. Different societies and groups stress different criteria but the following are often important in ranking individuals: (1) the authority and/or power one has over others, (2) family connections and family prestige, (3) property holdings and wealth which may function as symbols of status or as a means of initiating action to others or exercising control over others, and (4) personal qualities and achievements such as age, sex, beauty, skill, politeness, and ability. Other things being equal, the greater the utility of these qualities as conceived by the society generally and the less widespread they are, the more important they will be in determining status.

Few considerations are more important for the adult educator than the pattern of stratification of the community within which he works. We have already discussed informal and small groups. These are the most important supports for the social status structure of a society. Communication systems are very different in the various strata, and are usually related to the nature of family, clique, and informal social systems or organization patterns.

Since most anthropological studies of diffusion and social change have demonstrated that traits and practices spread downward in the class structure more rapidly than upward, the overall configuration of the pattern of stratification is of importance to all engaged in educational work among adults. Here we must confine our discussion to certain limited aspects of stratification as related to adult education in rural areas. In general the studies available indicate that farming areas in which the family farm predominates (all areas except the Cotton belt and the Western Specialty-Crop areas) contain larger proportions in the middle stratum than do the cities. The proportion in the middle stratum also exceeds that of the farming areas where the large estates are worked by many sharecroppers or wage hands.

A study of Yankee City, an urban center located in New England, revealed a very different stratification pattern than did a comparable study of a Corn belt community in the midwest which contained 6,000 people in the center and 4,000 more in the service area surrounding the trade center.[29] The so-called

---

[28] For a more complete treatment of the subject see Loomis and Beegle, *op. cit.*, Chapters 10 and 11.

[29] W. Lloyd Warner and Paul S. Lunt, *The Social Life of a Modern Community*, New Haven: Yale University Press, 1941, p. 82; W. Lloyd Warner and Associates, *Democracy in Jonesville*, New York: Harper and Brothers, 1949; A. B. Hollingshead, *Elmtown's Youth*, New York: John Wiley and Sons, Inc., 1949; and Robert H. Havighurst and Hilda Taba, *Adolescent Character and Personality*, New York: John Wiley and Sons, Inc., 1949.

middle classes in the former community comprised slightly over 38 percent of the population and accounted for a relatively large proportion of the memberships in the organizations of the community. In the Corn belt trade center community, from 41 to 48 percent of the people were classified as being in the middle classes. The upper middle class was composed of professional men, officials in local industries, "better" business men and a few leading farmers. Among them were those considered "pillars of the church," "the people you go to if you want to get anything done,"—persons who placed much emphasis on high moral standards. Such people made up 6 to 8 percent of the town families. In the rural areas, the upper middle class was found to include the "squire farmers," who were outstanding agriculturalists and lived in large, modern farm homes. Squire farmers supervise rather than farm, and their social participation is almost exclusively urban.[30]

Although adequate data are not available to outline the stratification patterns of the various types of farming areas of the nation, it is important to note that it is the middle groups who may most conveniently be reached by the various organizations and facilities described in the following sections.[31] A single notable exception is the program of the Farmers' Home Administration, whose program, not primarily educational, is designed for low income families. To reach the 12 to 15 percent of the families in the lowest stratum in the Corn belt community or the 25 percent of the families in the lowest stratum in Yankee City, the many hundreds of organizations and agencies in the United States may not be effective. Adult education programs are in general designed for and most easily reach the middle stratum of our society. Most members of the various strata, however, are tied into the clique and family groupings described in Figure 5. The increasing importance of trade centers for rural sub-areas has been mentioned.

Urbanization and Trade Center Influence on the Status Structure in Rural Areas.
—Few trends in the last generation are more important than the increasing importance of the trade center community with its middle-class dominated town and its farming hinterland. In general, the more rural the county, the less it is bombarded by the stimuli of the middle classes of the trade centers and cities and the various systems described in this report. To understand the differences in rural and urban life one must understand the processes whereby the two are increasingly intermingled. Over-simplified explanations abound and there are those who believe the differences have vanished. The absence or presence of electricity, for example, will be related to the possession of such mass media receivers as radios and television sets, and to the use of printed matter. That this one item is related to the many facets of the whole urbanization process is indicated since the proportion of farms having electricity is very

[30] Havighurst and Taba, *Ibid.*, pp. 15–19.
[31] Perhaps the most complete data available on rural stratification by major type of farming areas is to be found in Loomis and Beegle, *op. cit.*, Chapters 10 and 11.

high, but negatively related to the birth rate, which is almost universally higher in the rural and lower in the urban areas.[32] The coming of the automobile, electricity, the development of the trade center community, the decline in the importance of the rural neighborhood, the increasing educational level of farm people, and the increasing control of the environment and related rationality, are part of the process whereby rural people are taking on the ways of the middle classes of the cities.

FORMAL ORGANIZATIONS IN RURAL AREAS—SOCIAL SYSTEMS PROVIDING THE MAIN CHANNELS OF COMMUNICATION FOR ADULT EDUCATION

Schools, churches, farmers' organizations, libraries, and similar organizations we call formal organizations because they have formally elected, appointed, or employed officials and definite rules, such as constitutions, procedure manuals, organization charts and similar written or agreed upon ways of operating. Such characteristics enable us to differentiate them from groups we call informal, such as cliques and friendship groupings. Until recently, informal rather than formal organizations dominated the social life of farmers and ranchers in the United States.

Few farmers and ranchers have not heard first hand accounts of life on the frontier from their fathers or grandfathers. Some of the older farmers in the Range-Livestock and Wheat areas can remember the frontier first hand. From the point of view of time, no great nation on earth is so close to unbroken plains, virgin forests, and dry deserts. The conquest of the frontier in America was completed without many of the formal organizations we know today, as for example, the various federal bureaus, the national farmers' organizations, and the Land-Grant College and University systems. Security during the frontier era depended mostly upon small and informal groupings, although frontier settlements were rarely without their school and church. Rural life, as compared with urban life however, has always been characterized by fewer formal, large-scale organizations.

When security was no longer to be found in small informal groups, formal organizations began to appear. Large farmers' organizations grew from local, protective societies and other similar small-scale groups. The farmers' movement resulting in the development of the three major farmers' organizations—the Grange, Farm Bureau, and Farmers' Union—together with the cooperative movement, represented the farmers' attempt to adjust to the price and market regime. These movements and collateral developments brought a host of government bureaus and educational institutions with which farmers have frequent

[32] For Michigan, the correlation coefficient expressing the relationship between the percentage of the homes having electric lights and the fertility ratio is −.66. See J. Allan Beegle, *Differential Birth Rates in Michigan*, East Lansing: Michigan Agricultural Experiment Station Bulletin 346, February 1947, pp. 23–25.

contact. As American farmers and ranchers moved from a self-sufficient, family economy, to an industrialized and commercialized economy based upon scientific agriculture, their need for formal organizations comparable to those in the cities increased rapidly. The increasing participation of farmers in the many occupational and civic groups in order to meet special interests, is a part of the general quest for security and fellowship common among the urban middle classes of the western world.

The following pages attempt to summarize the present status of the main formal organizations in rural areas with respect to adult educational activities. Primary consideration will be given to these organizations as channels of communication.

Charles P. Loomis, Director of Study
Social Research Service
Michigan State College
East Lansing, Michigan

BIBLIOGRAPHY

Benedict, Ruth, "Transmitting our Democratic Heritage in the Schools," *American Journal of Sociology*, Vol. XLVIII, No. 6, May 1943.
Chapple, Eliot D. and Coon, Carleton S., *Principles of Anthropology*, New York: Henry Holt, 1942.
Landis, B. Y. and Willard, J. D., *Rural Adult Education*, New York: The Macmillan Company, 1933.
Loomis, Charles P. and Beegle, J. Allan, *Rural Social Systems*, New York: Prentice-Hall, Inc., 1950.
Loomis, Charles P., *Studies of Rural Social Organization*, East Lansing: State College Book Store, 1945.
Malinowski, Bronislaw, "The Pan-African Problem of Culture Contact," *American Journal of Sociology*, Vol. XLVIII, No. 6, May 1943.
Mead, Margaret, *Coming of Age in Samoa*, New York: William Morrow and Company, 1939.
Murdock, G. P., *Social Structure*, New York: The Macmillan Company, 1949.
Parsons, Talcott, *The Social System*, Glencoe, Illinois: The Free Press, 1951.
Sherif, Muzafer, *An Outline of Social Psychology*, New York: Harper and Brothers, 1948.
Sorokin, P. A., Zimmerman, Carle C., and Galpin, Charles J., *A Systematic Source-Book in Rural Sociology*, Minneapolis: The University of Minnesota Press, 1932.
Warner, W. Lloyd, Havighurst, Robert J., and Loeb, Martin B., *Who Shall Be Educated?*, New York: Harper and Brothers, 1944.
Warner, W. Lloyd et al., *Social Class in America*, Chicago: Science Research Associates, Inc., 1949.
Warner, W. Lloyd et al., *Democracy in Jonesville*, New York: Harper and Brothers, 1949.

Chapter 2:

ADULT EDUCATION IN THE PUBLIC SCHOOL AND THE COMMUNITY*

The School and Community on the Frontier.—No social system offering a public service of any magnitude is as subject to local control as the public school system in the United States. The American farmer who established the original pattern of the school system on the frontier, wove the principle of local autonomy firmly into the social fabric of our life. Even today the teachers and curriculum in both rural and urban areas are the responsibility of the local people. Of course, this local control is subject to the norms and standards of the state accrediting agencies, but the control of the school is local, not state or national. Schools in the rural areas are even more subject to local neighborhood and community influence than are city schools.

Several generations ago the rural school in many respects was an extension of the families on the farms and ranches. It was an integral part of the neighborhood and community. The teacher either roomed and boarded with a local farmer or rancher and thereby became a family member, or in many cases she was the wife, daughter or other relative of a local farm family. Families knew all of the children in school and almost every act of the teacher. Everything occurring at school was made public property through the conversation of the families in the neighborhood or community. With this background, it is not surprising that leading educators consider the community school which serves as the center of all educational activities for children and adults, as the ideal for rural America. Such schools would serve as headquarters for most of the adult activities discussed in this volume. But to understand the nature and dynamics of the community school movement, we must realize that our roots, particularly those of the farmers and ranchers of the country, only a few decades ago grew in a soil, the chief components of which were a relatively integrated life centered in the family, neighborhood, and community.

Background of the Neighborhood and Community and the Relation to the School.—There are many definitions of neighborhood and community in use, but for our purposes both neighborhood and community consist of interacting persons, among whom there is a feeling of solidarity. The neighborhood usually consists of fewer persons than the community and is organized around incomplete services. Particularly in the last generation, but even today in portions of the Corn Belt and Wheat Areas, the one-room district school is often a neighborhood agency. The community, is ordinarily larger than the neighborhood, is

---

* *Editor's Note:* This chapter has been reviewed and amplified by the Director of this study. Therefore, the present version of this chapter is not identical with that originally submitted to the Fund for Adult Education.

often composed of neighborhoods and is organized around relatively complete institutional services. When termed a trade-center community, the center of that community usually provides the most important social and economic services for the people living in the area. Most progressive school plans advocate that high schools be located in trade-centers and that the school system serve the trade-center community.

Formerly, most of the social life of American families took place in the neighborhood. The hard-surfaced road and the automobile have changed this so that the neighborhood is no longer important in many areas of the nation. In most areas of the United States, the trade-center is now the pace-setter, in terms of the life style and activity of rural people. The middle class values of the whole society come to the rural people from the trade-center. Numerous sociological and anthropological studies have shown that one of the most important characteristics of the middle classes of the United States is their activity in the infinite variety of formal organizations.

This volume deals with many of these formal organizations as systems and channels of communication for adult education. We wish to emphasize here that rural life has changed since the time when the "team haul" determined the size of the community, not only due to the automobile and better roads but also because rural life has become more organized and bureaucratized. These great changes, coupled with population decreases, have weakened the importance of the small district and neighborhood school in the life of rural people. Such changes also brought a segmentation of life which has extended from the cities to the country. Not only is there likely to be competition for the time of those who may participate in different events, but many agencies are likely to be competing for financial support.

As will be indicated in Chapter 9 dealing with the rural church, secularization has also been a consequence of this development. "From all evidence at hand, it can be concluded that no young people in our history have been so detached from their culture, so thwarted in normal processes of community identification as those maturing in the immediate past and current present."[1] Furthermore, there are no indications that adults are any more integrated into their communities than youths. It is the hypothesis of the author that the rapidity with which we have changed has led to a feeling of insecurity associated in many instances with an irrational compulsion to hold to or to return to that which represents the past.[2] If this is true, it would account for some of the opposition to consolidation and reorganization of rural schools. This rather

---

[1] Lloyd Allen Cook and Elaine Forsyth Cook, *A Sociological Approach to Education*, New York: McGraw-Hill Book Company, 1950, p. 280. The Cooks cite Howard Wilson, *Educating for Citizenship*, New York Regents Inquiry: McGraw-Hill, 1938, pp. 41–49. In a test of "community knowledge" given to 3,500 New York State high-school students, reported here, one in five seniors could not give the approximate size of his home town; one in three the number of churches; and less than half, the size of the average family.

[2] C. P. Loomis and J. A. Beegle, "The Spread of German Nazism in Rural Areas," *American Sociological Review*, Vol. XI, No. 6, December, 1946, pp. 724–734.

sketchy statement has been introduced as a background for our discussion of the community.

The Community as an Ideal.—We have attempted to use the concept of community and its relation to the school as something empirical and objective. There is a wide-spread romanticization of the community which identifies it with that which would, it is hoped, eliminate the frustrations and insecurities brought about by increasing changes and segmentation of life and activities.[3] The authors sympathize with many elements of this view. When the original structure and values which gave integration to rural life disappeared, when bureaus and organizations became engaged in struggles for the time and money of the people, and when families and communities became torn by conflicting interests, it may be natural to idealize the neighborhood or the district school. However, we believe it is wishful thinking to attempt to turn back the hand of time. Community life which will satisfy the whole of man's nature must be created, but this will not be accomplished by dreaming and yearning for past forms.

Community Agencies as a Way Out.—Hitler did not have difficulty in winning the support of millions of Germans with his promises of security and integration.[4] But the integration and security he provided came from one agency, namely, the government. On the other hand, the community council and similar movements rest upon the principle that integration and security can be achieved by the same kind of cooperation that produced the old neighborhood and community, in which all families and organizations worked together for defense against danger, for mutual-aid, and for social life. Unfortunately, up to now, the forces of segmentation seem to be stronger than those of integration. The community council and similar movements have not been notably successful in providing integration in rural society.

The Community Council and Adult Education as Integrative Efforts.[5]—The importance of integration for adult education programs is expressed in the following summary statement made by the National Education Association in its recent study of adult education in the cities of the nation: "Cooperation seems to be a key word in the development of a large percentage of existing adult education activities. Adult education councils or advisory committees are in operation..." in from one-third to over half of the cities. "The councils help to integrate programs and provide a medium for exchange of ideas and information while advisory committees give representation from other community groups so that the school program is planned in cooperation with other agencies."[6]

---

[3] Baker Brownell, *The Human Community—Its Philosophy and Practice for a Time of Crisis*, New York: Harper and Brothers, 1950.

[4] Loomis and Beegle, *op. cit.*

[5] Cook and Cook, *op. cit.*, p. 413.

[6] Gordon L. Lippitt and Helen L. Allion, *A Study of Urban Public School Adult Education Programs of the United States*, Washington: Division of Adult Education Service, National Education Association, 1952, p. x.

Adult Education in Public Schools

In our study of the agencies and social systems carrying on adult education in the 263 county sample of the major type of farming areas of the nation, it was found that the school works extensively with farm organizations, parents' organizations, schools, colleges and universities, civic and service organizations, churches, and a great variety of other agencies. (See footnote, Table 1.) Nearly three-fifths of all school administrators reporting indicated that they worked with farm organizations and parents' organizations. See Table 1.

Homer Kempfer[7] found that of the 2,684 school districts (both rural and urban) reporting educational activities for adults and out-of-school youth, 6.4 percent involve community councils. Only 4.1 percent of the 316 districts in rural places (under 2,500 population), however, reported community councils. Community center activities were reported by 12.4 percent of all districts, while 12.0 percent of those in rural places reported such activities. McClusky describes 89 organizations and activities which communities can have or do. These range from community councils to services for baby sitters. Considering the great need for integration of agencies in the same line of service today, the reader will no doubt be impressed by the lack of use in adult education of various means of integrating services. Where there is active effort to organize integrating services the mortality is great and where no such effort is made their numbers are few.

In view of this difficulty, the penetrating analysis of Adult Education Councils by Glen Burch[8] should be mentioned. The development of the Adult Education Council movement after the first unit was organized in Cleveland in 1925 is traced. He indicates the council objectives and states that these objectives are seldom attained, especially in larger centers. The following four reasons for failure are offered: First, the marginal character of adult education itself handicaps community-wide efforts at co-ordination. Few agencies consider adult education their prime reason for existing. Second, the representatives on the councils from the various agencies seldom have the authority to act. Third, councils are poorly supported and often are organized on a volunteer basis. Fourth, ineffectiveness among most adult education councils is due to their separatist character and the fact that they are often not related to other efforts at over-all community organization. In concluding, Burch indicates that urban adult education councils have often included professional and semi-professional adult educators, and few lay citizens. A plea is made to keep adult education close to the people, both in urban and rural areas.

As a solution to the difficulties, Burch offers three suggestions. First, in larger communities a coordinating council such as the Social Welfare Council or a Metropolitan Planning Council should carry on the work and accomplish the

---

[7] Homer Kempfer, *Adult Education Activities of the Public Schools*, Washington: Federal Security Agency, Office of Education, 1947–48, Pamphlet No. 107, p. 8.

[8] Glen Burch, "Community Organization for Adult Education," Mary L. Ely, ed. *Handbook of Adult Education*, New York: Institute of Adult Education, Teachers College, Columbia University, 1948, pp. 284 ff.

TABLE 1

Percentage of School Respondents Working with or through Specified Organizations, According to Rank Order, in their Educational Work with Adults; and Percentage of Specified Organizations Working with or through Schools, According to Rank Order, in their Educational Work with Adults

Organizations on questionnaire	Organizations used as channels by *School* personnel — Percent responding	Rank order	Use of schools as a channel by *other* organizations — Rank order	Percent reporting	Organizations reporting
Farm organizations	57	1	1	97	Weekly newspapers
Parent's organizations	57	1	2	92	Radio stations
Schools	52	3	3	90	Cooperative Extension Service
Colleges and universities	44	4	4	81	Parent-Teachers Association
Civic and service organizations	43	5	4	81	Soil Conservation Service
			6	69	Civic and service org. (all *)
Churches and religious organizations	42	6	7	63	Continuation Education Depts.
Cooperative Extension Service	36	7	8	58	General Federated Women's Clubs
Federal and/or state gov't. bureaus	31	8	8	58	Chamber of Commerce
Libraries	28	9	10	57	Libraries
Women's clubs	25	10	11	55	Business and professional women's clubs
Community councils	21	11	12	53	Churches (all ***)
Professional organizations	21	11	12	53	Protestant churches
Patriotic and veterans' organizations	18	13	12	53	Rotary
Welfare councils	14	14	15	52	Government bureaus (all **)
Fraternal organizations	9	15	15	52	Schools[1]
Elected or appointed gov't. bodies	8	16	17	50	Grange
			18	47	Kiwanis
Labor unions	5	17	19	45	Farm organizations (All ****)
Other organizations	5	17	19	45	Farm Bureau
UNESCO organizations	3	19	21	43	Farmers' Union
Political parties and/or organizations	2	20	22	42	Catholic churches
Inter-agency councils	2	20	23	40	Lions
			24	34	Farmers Home Administration
			25	31	Cooperatives
			26	24	Production & Marketing Assoc.
			27	20	Supervisors
			28	13	County Medical Society

objectives of coordination and development which Adult Education Councils have attempted through a division of adult education. Cleveland and New Orleans are given as examples of this approach. In smaller communities he indicates the community council can accomplish the task. Another suggestion involves arranging adequate financial support to make the adult education councils function effectively. The Denver Council for Adult Education is given as an example of a solution of the problem along this line. A third solution offered is that of "making the provision of facilities for community-wide coordination and promotion of adult education activities a function of an existing publicly supported institution, such as the public schools or the public library."[9] Examples of this approach in which the schools take the lead include the rural community of Sac City, Iowa; Schenectady, New York; Springfield, Massachusetts; Philadelphia, Pennsylvania; Baltimore, Maryland; and Des Moines, Iowa. Examples in which the library takes the lead are Detroit, Newark, Oakland, Grand Rapids, and Washington, D. C.

The School as the Central Adult Education Agency for Community Integration.—When Burch suggested that the coordinating of adult education activities might properly be the function of an existing publicly supported institution such as the public schools, he admitted that this seems "to violate one of the cardinal principles of community organization—that no agency operating a program in a given field should attempt to coordinate the efforts of other agencies and organizations in that field."[10] Kempfer and Wright make no such apologies for their pleas that the school take the lead. "Over a period of years the school . . . can develop a set of educational services for community groups which will make it what it is basically intended to be—the recognized central agency concerned with education in the community."[11] They attempt to back

[9] *Ibid.*, p. 286.
[10] *Ibid.*, p. 286 and 287.
[11] Homer Kempfer and Grace S. Wright, *Selected Approaches to Adult Education*, Federal Security Agency Bulletin, 1950, No. 16, p. 6.

---

[1] School administrators responding to this question and checking "schools" probably meant to indicate work with other school systems and other levels of school organization. Undoubtedly many administrators, through modesty, refrained from checking "schools."

* All Civic and service organizations refer to a combination of the following: Lions, Rotary, Kiwanis, Optimist, Civitan, Altrusa, Quota, G.F.W.C., B. & P.W., A.A.U.W., League of Women Voters, PTA., Chamber of Commerce, N.A.A.C.P. and County Medical Society. These organizations are listed separately in the Table only if there are 50 or more returns.

** All Government Bureaus refer to a combination of Soil Conservation Service, Production & Marketing Association, and Farmers Home Administration.

*** All Churches refer to a combination of Protestant ministers and Catholic Rural Life Leaders.

**** All Farm Organizations refer to a combination of Farm Bureau, Farmer's Union, Grange, and Cooperatives.

up this contention by stating that the school is the agency which, when adequately supported, has the responsibility of making services available to the whole community. Further, the school represents the largest concentration of specialized personnel familiar with educational methods, techniques, and materials. More people can be reached with less cost for housing, promotion, and similar expenditures through the school than would be the case if other facilities were used. Then the following statement which justifies Burch's hint of skepticism is made: "In addition, if community groups know that they can turn to the schools for competent help in their educational work, there will come into being a general strengthening of public attitude favorable towards the schools."[12] More recently the National Education Association study of adult education in urban areas reports that "the value of adult education in promoting general good will for the whole public school system was mentioned repeatedly."[13] Of course, this same principle would hold for the Farm Bureau, Cooperative Extension Service, or the other systems we will describe. Each might plan to improve its own public relations without concern for the whole community.

In justifying the school role as the prime mover in adult education in the community we may recall, as indicated earlier, the rural school grew out of the rural neighborhood where the family and friendship groups were originally the chief educational agencies. Because the school is the custodian of our children in the formative years, no agency outside the family, not even the church, is as close to the central values of the people, as the local school. Few families in America will sacrifice their children's welfare and learning for any of the other agencies we shall study in this report.

Teachers in Rural Areas.—The teacher is the key to the effectiveness of the rural school in education, whether for children or adults. Unfortunately, the better salaries in the cities attract many of the better teachers. The turn-over of teachers, for example, has been as much as four times as high in rural schools as in city schools.[14] In view of such circumstances, a high positive correlation between the economic status of counties and the number of years of education beyond high school possessed by teachers is to be expected. Teachers in the lowest tenth of the counties have completed slightly less than a year of college work, whereas those in the top tenth averaged a little less than four years of college.[15]

When schools are considered as a central agency for adult education in communities, a resource of great importance is frequently overlooked. This resource is the tremendous amount of participation of teachers in other social systems of the community. One study reveals that 95 percent of teachers are members of one or more community groups, exclusive of school clubs. This

---

[12] *Ibid.*, p. 6.
[13] Lippitt and Allion, *op. cit.*, p. x.
[14] J. H. Kolb and E. deS. Brunner, *A Study of Rural Society*, Boston: Houghton-Mifflin, 1952, p. 328.
[15] *Ibid.*

study revealed that teachers belong to a modal number of five non-school, community groups. Four-fifths gave money to one or more such groups. The specific activities listed in the order of their frequency for the 9,122 Ohio teachers were as follows: Church, PTA, Sunday School, Red Cross, Alumni Association, Lodge, Church Youth, Social Club, Bridge Club, YMCA-YWCA. These are typical middle class organizations and a teacher is expected to belong to such organizations.[16]

Teachers in the United States are predominantly young, rural teachers being somewhat younger than urban teachers. Only about one-fourth of all women teaching in 1940 were married. The percentage of married men teachers is higher, approximately 72 percent. The typical elementary school teacher in rural areas is a young, unmarried girl, only recently graduated from a teachers' college. She accepts a relatively low salary and is often more interested in finding a husband than in her job. Nonetheless, the rural teacher is of tremendous importance in the lives of adults and children in the schools and community agencies they serve.

Ways in which the School Supports the Central Value System.—In rural areas no agency is as effective in assisting the process of advancing middle class values as the school system. Warner, Havighurst, and Loeb estimate that 90 percent of the teachers in this country come from the upper and lower middle classes. As representatives of the middle classes, teachers embody middle class values. Not only do teachers tend to teach these values, but they also tend to select for advancement those pupils who more nearly represent their own feelings and beliefs. One brief quotation states the problem lucidly: "Teachers represent middle-class attitudes and enforce middle-class values and manners. In playing this role, teachers do two things. They train or seek to train children in middle class manners and skills. And they select those children from the middle and lower classes who appear to be the best candidates for promotion in the social hierarchy. Two groups of children escape this influence in part. Children of upper-class parents often do not go to the public schools or drop out after a few years of public-school attendance. These children attend private schools or have private tutors. . . . Many children of lower-class parents also escape the influence of teachers through being recalcitrant in school and through dropping out of school just as early as possible."[17] Social status is much more important in many ways in determining whether one will continue education in the school system than is intellectual ability. Of two groups of comparable intelligence, 57 percent in the upper status group attended college while only 13 percent of those in the low status group attended.[18] Warner and his asso-

---

[16] Cook and Cook, *op. cit.*, p. 445.

[17] W. Lloyd Warner, R. J. Havighurst, and Martin B. Loeb, *Who Shall Be Educated?* New York: Harper and Brother, 1944, p. 101. For a more complete development of this theme see J. Allan Beegle and C. P. Loomis, "Orientation of School Administrators to Social Groups," in C. P. Loomis's *Studies in Applied and Theoretical Social Science,* East Lansing, Michigan State College Press, 1950, Ch. 6.

[18] *Ibid.*, p. 52.

ciates[19] use dramatically presented and plausible facts to demonstrate that the lower-class child is treated by the teacher in ways which prevent him from continuing his education. Obviously, the various studies involving social status indicate that one of the school's functions at present is that of selecting those having the traits which the middle-class feels should be rewarded. This point should be of interest to adult educators who decry the fact that only 1 out of 8 schools in the United States reports education for adults when 9,420,000 people aged 14 and above had no more than 4th grade education.[20] Apparently, upward mobility for adults as well as children is hindered both by lack of desire of those with little education and the channels through which they must pass.

The Rural School as an Actual and Potential System of Adult Education.—

TABLE 2
Comparison of Rural and Urban Public Schools, 1939–40

	Urban	Rural
Population 1940	74,423,702	57,245,573
Population 5–17 years	14,703,957	15,041,289
Percent of total	20.0	26.2
Pupils enrolled	13,309,547	12,123,995
Number school buildings	37,700	189,062
Number teaching positions	441,852	469,983
Number pupils per teacher	31.7	26.6
Average length school term	181.7	167.6
Average number days attended by each pupil	158.2	144.5
Average salary of teachers	$1,955	$959
Estimated value school property per pupil enrolled	$ 405	$185
Current expense per pupil	$ 105	$ 70

Table 2 indicates how rural areas in the United States are disadvantaged in school facilities. Rural people make relatively greater sacrifices in terms of tax payments to educate their children than do urban people. This is indicated by Figure 1. When outlay for schooling is related to income, the agricultural states make the greatest contributions to education. Although it is the rural families who suffer most from these disadvantages, the total national welfare is also affected. This point is well stated in the following: "Lest anyone think that the lack of high school opportunities is a matter that concerns only the people in rural communities, it is pointed out that about half of the young people migrate from rural areas to urban centers to make their homes and accept employment in business and industry . . . through failure of the schools in many rural areas to meet their educational obligations these urban residents are placed

[19] W. Lloyd Warner and Associates, *Democracy in Jonesville*, New York: Harper and Brothers, 1949, p. 9, ff.
[20] Kempfer, *op. cit.*

under such serious handicaps that the social structure of American life may be materially weakened."[21]

Many educators believe the small school, particularly the one or two-room school in many rural areas is the most important single disadvantaging element in rural education. Some 50,000 one-room schools are located in the rural areas of Illinois, Iowa, Missouri, Minnesota, Kansas, Nebraska, Wisconsin, Michigan, and Pennsylvania. The small school not only sends relatively fewer students on

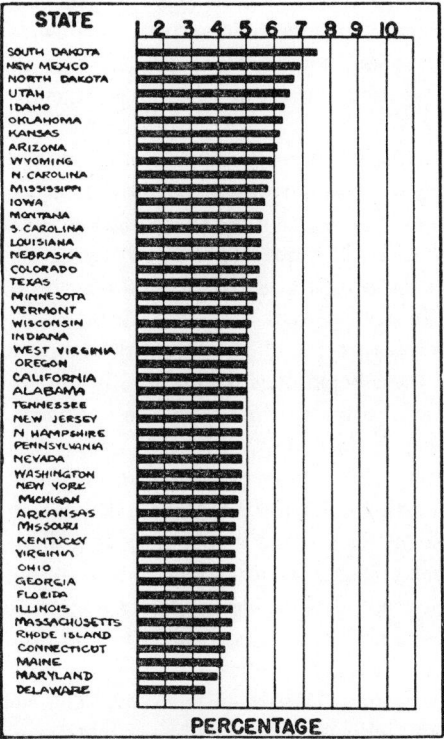

FIG. 1. Rank of the states in percentage of income devoted to education. (Source: Hughes and Lancelot, *Education—America's Magic*, 1946, p. 70).

to high school and college than the larger school, but the larger school is more likely to have an adult education program. It cannot be expected that teachers handling all the students and classes of a one-room school will have time for an extensive adult education program in any field. A large number of rural school districts in the wealthiest agricultural states of the middle west where the small school district is more frequently found may have less than half of the youth 16 and 17 years of age in school.[22]

[21] *Your School District*, Washington: The Report of the National Commission on School District Reorganization, Department of Rural Education, National Educational Association of the United States, 1948, pp. 17 and 18.

[22] *Ibid.*, p. 17 concerning dropouts and p. 33, concerning the lack of adult education in small schools.

With all its weakness—insufficient support, frequent inconvenient or distant location, and poorly paid teachers, inadequate size and curriculum and shorter school term—the school in the rural areas, when compared with other agencies, has the greatest potential as a channel of communication for adult education. Rural people attend more than 189,000 schools. It is difficult to exaggerate the potential role of the local school in times of crisis. In the event of a widespread airborne attack, meetings in the schools of the nation could be called in a matter of hours. If telephone communications were severed, Cooperative Extension personnel and vocational teachers could activate neighborhood leaders throughout the nation. The school houses might well serve as the meeting place for most of the nation's farmers and ranchers for emergency instruction and organization.

Extent of Rural Adult Education Programs and Activities Carried on by Public Schools.—Adult education as an organized movement is little more than a quarter of a century old.[23] Wisconsin began establishing its schools of vocational and adult education in 1911. A quarter of a century ago, California and Pennsylvania established the principle of free general education for adults and out-of-school youth as an integral part of public education. Until recently only a few states moved in this direction.[24] The tremendous strides which adult education has made from these beginnings is indicated by the fact that the National Education Association estimates that there are now over three and one-half million adults engaged in formal and informal adult education programs and activities conducted by the schools of the nation in places of 2,500 and over. If we add to this an estimated 1,100,000 adults who are engaged in educational activities conducted by the schools in places of less than 2,500 people, there are 4,140,000 persons engaged in adult educational activities in the nation.[25] Of this total, almost one-fourth reside in the state of California.

The approximate number of adults enrolled in vocational classes and other reimbursable courses, is readily determined. Annual reports give the number of persons enrolled in evening classes of federally-aided vocational courses in agriculture, trades and industry, distributive occupations and home economics. The financial cost of conducting such courses is partly reimbursable from federal funds under the Smith-Hughes and George Barton Acts. Funds are allotted to states, dollar for dollar, with state or local funds or both. The number of persons who were enrolled in such courses totalled 1,466,968 in 1950–51. Slightly more females than males were enrolled. The number enrolled in the different kinds of federally-aided vocational evening classes is as follows:[26]

[23] Kempfer, *op. cit.*
[24] *Ibid.*, p. 2, and Walter H. Gaumitz and H. S. Stanton, *Supervision of Education of Out-of-School Youth and Adults as a Function of State Departments of Education*. Washington: Office of Education Bulletin, No. 6, Monograph, No. 12.
[25] Lippitt and Allion, *op. cit.*, p. 4.
[26] *Digest of Annual Reports of State Boards of Vocational Education, Fiscal Year Ended June 30, 1951*, Washington: United States Office of Education, pp. 88–89.

	Male	Female
Vocational agriculture	318,009	—
Vocational trade and industry	245,556	20,550
Vocational distributive occupations	122,677	101,767
Vocational home economics	40,842	617,567
Total	727,084	739,884

Of the men, over two-fifths, mostly farmers, were enrolled in agriculture, while of the women, over two-fifths were enrolled in home economics. The enrollment, by rural and urban residence, is unknown.[27]

Texas schools have a total adult enrollment of 56,214 in agriculture, followed by Georgia and South Carolina, each with 42,000. California leads all states in adult enrollment in each of the other three fields—trade and industry, distributive occupations, and home economics, with 51,366, 54,247, and 163,781 enrolled respectively. California has a total enrollment in all four fields of 274,939, followed by Texas with 181,743, and South Carolina with 79,579. Other states with over 50,000 adults enrolled in the different types of federally-aided vocational evening classes are Georgia, New York, and Washington.

Even on the basis of total potential adult enrollees, four of the five states mentioned above rank high. Enrollment in federally-aided vocational evening classes as a percentage of total adult population[28] indicates that there are a total of 27 states with from one to seven percent of their adults enrolled.

The ranking of states is based upon those enrolled in vocational evening classes that are reimbursed from federal funds; therefore, the number of enrollees is available at a central source. The evening class is the major type of educational service offered adults by the public school. However, many public schools with evening adult classes also provide other types of more informal

[27] *Ibid.*, pp. 88–89. The number of persons, nominally adults, who are enrolled in federally-aided vocational agriculture, trade and industry, distributive occupations, and home economics evening classes in 1950–1951, is available by states. These enrollments do not include all-day classes and part-time classes which are normally composed largely of youngsters of school age.

[28] U. S. Census, *Current Population Reports*, Series P-25, No. 63, August 31, 1952 gives estimates of the civilian population of voting age for states, as of November 1, 1952, as used in these calculations. These percentages and rank of states are as follows:

South Carolina	7.22	Iowa	1.65	Nevada	1.08	New York	.62
Utah	4.30	Florida	1.50	Michigan	1.07	New Hampshire	.60
Washington	3.83	Wisconsin	1.47	Missouri	1.02	Kansas	.57
Texas	3.75	Nebraska	1.44	Wyoming	.94	Vermont	.56
California	3.74	Kentucky	1.33	North Dakota	.89	Ohio	.54
Mississippi	3.69	Massachusetts	1.30	Tennessee	.88	Illinois	.48
Georgia	3.47	Oregon	1.19	Indiana	.83	Montana	.43
Arkansas	2.63	Louisiana	1.15	Idaho	.79	South Dakota	.43
Virginia	2.39	Alabama	1.15	North Carolina	.75	Pennsylvania	.36
West Virginia	2.29	Delaware	1.14	Dist. of Col.	.72	New Mexico	.33
Oklahoma	1.95	Arizona	1.14	Maryland	.65	Maine	.28
Colorado	1.81	Minnesota	1.10	Connecticut	.63	New Jersey	.28
						Rhode Island	.21

educational activities for adults and out-of-school youth. The same is also true of many school systems that do not have evening classes. That is, in some states adults are enrolled in classes which receive no federal reimbursements and therefore such enrollments are not included in the federal reports. In most states rural adult education is predominantly vocational education and, as a rule, general adult education attains importance in states in which vocational education for adults is also important.[29]

Enrollments of adults outside of the vocational fields of public schools are considerable, especially in some states, but their numbers are unknown except where enrollments in such programs are financed in whole or in part by state aid. Even in such states much general adult education in the public schools may take place because such programs do not fulfill all requirements of the school code, and other reasons.

State Aid for General Adult Education.—Twenty-one states now provide some form of financial subsidy or reimbursement for public school programs of general adult education. In 1949-50, the figure amounted to ten million dollars in California; in New York it totalled a little over two million dollars. It is difficult to determine the exact amount of state aid expended for adult education in Pennsylvania since state aid for this purpose is an integral part of the state aid formula. However, state officials estimate it to be approximately $510,000. Ranking fourth in this respect is Michigan which allocated $300,000 for this purpose. This figure amounts to $154,000 in Washington, $110,000 in South Carolina, $105,000 in Virginia and lesser amounts in other states. In general, enrollment in general adult education is high or low depending on availability of state aid. However, several states have considerable numbers enrolled in general adult education although local school districts are not reimbursed for this program from state sources. New Jersey, the outstanding exception, offers general adult education in most of the larger schools,

Adult Education in Rural and Urban Areas of Michigan.—Data regarding adult enrollment in either vocational or general adult education classes separately for rural and urban areas are not readily available by state. However, data on this basis of classification has been compiled for Michigan.

Only 14 percent of the 390 high schools in rural areas have general adult education classes as compared with 77 percent of those in urban centers. The fact that six-sevenths of the rural high schools have no general adult education programs indicates that the public school policy of free instruction is not generally observed in the area of adult education, especially in rural areas. The

---

[29] *Ibid.* p. 19. Correlation by the rank difference method between states in percent of adults enrolled in federally aided vocational evening classes in 1951 and Homer Kempfer's rank of states in percent of total population involved in total adult education activities is .78 with a probable error of .04. This correlation indicates a high degree of association between the two rankings. If the data were for identical years and the percentages were based on adult population in both instances, a higher relationship might have resulted.

smallness of rural high schools tends to militate against expansion of the regular curriculum.

All types of federally aided vocational classes are more prevalent in urban than rural high schools except in the area of adult agriculture classes and in the area of trade and industry classes. Between one-fourth and one-fifth of the rural high schools have adult education programs in the area of veteran on-farm training, trade and industry, and adult agriculture. In the veteran on-farm training program, 23 percent of the rural high schools have it. Even in the young farmer program, urban high schools exceed the rural high schools by a narrow margin.

Rural high schools which are two and one half times as numerous as urban high schools in Michigan, have a somewhat larger total adult enrollment in adult agriculture, in young farmer classes, and in veteran on-farm training classes than do urban high schools.

In rural Michigan, adults are principally enrolled in vocational education classes and urban people in general education. For example, of the 21,094 rural adults enrolled in the various kinds of classes for adults, three-fourths are enrolled in federally aided vocational classes and one-fourth in general education. Almost the reverse prevails in urban centers where 29 percent of the 176,022 enrolees are in federally aided vocational classes and 71 percent are in general education classes. The number of adults who are enrolled in general adult education could be readily doubled or tripled by determined action on the part of superintendents and school boards of the larger rural districts. Reorganization which increases the size of schools and school districts increases adult education enrollments, as will be noted later. At present about 1.7 percent of the approximate 1,245,000 adult rural population of Michigan is enrolled in adult education classes while 5.8 percent of the approximate 3,000,000 urban population is enrolled in adult education classes. The difference between rural and urban areas in adult enrollment of people in adult education classes is less than these percentages indicate since more urban centers have tributary rural populations many of whom attend adult education classes in urban centers. Actual percentages are probably more nearly 2.0 and 5.6 respectively.

Lippitt and Allion[30] estimate the number of adults in urban areas who are enrolled in adult education classes to total 3,344,256. This number would comprise seven percent of the total urban adult population, or a slightly higher percentage than that for urban Michigan. On this basis, an estimate of the enrollment of rural people in adult education classes in the United States may be made. On the assumption that the ratio of adult enrollments in rural areas to the total adult population in urban areas bears the same relationship as the enrollment of adults in rural Michigan to the total adult population in rural Michigan, over one million adults in rural areas of the United States are enrolled in general and vocational classes.

[30] Lippitt and Allion, *op. cit.*, p. 4.

The National Education Association[31] reports that the subjects in which programs and activities have increased most in the cities (places of 2,500 and above) during the last five years are the following: (1) civic and public affairs forums, informal classes and other groups, reported as available in 30 percent of the schools in 1950–51, increased in enrollment by 428 percent. (2) Safety and driver education, reported as available in 44 percent of the schools, increased in enrollment by 535 percent. (3) Remedial and special education, reported by 16 percent of the schools, increased in enrollment by 228 percent. (4) Health and physical education, reported by 36 percent of the schools, increased by 166 percent. No doubt the on-farm training of veterans in the regions of these cities explained in large part the increase in vocational adult education courses reported.

Differences in both the amounts and the quality of adult education for rural people is due, in part, to variations related to support for the work under public funds from state legislation and in part to the nature of school district structure. Thus, institutional groups in Michigan must be of such size and organization as will meet sound educational principles. The National Education Association study of adult education in urban areas reports that almost half of all public school adult education programs are underwritten by state aid in states where such aid is provided.[32]

More and more rural people are requesting adult education from their schools and it is gradually being supplied. In 1924, Brunner found that in 140 village centers servicing rural areas throughout the United States, only 9 high schools offered courses for adults. In 1936 when the villages were re-surveyed, three out of ten had such offerings.[33] The United States Office of Education, on the basis of a mailed questionnaire survey made of school districts in all parts of the nation in 1947–48, estimate that 3,000,000 adults are being served in rural and urban communities by our public schools. The National Adult Education study of urban adult education, previously cited, shows an increase of 1,744,256 for the school year 1950–51 as compared with the year 1947–48. Interestingly enough, the increases were three times as great for the smaller cities as for the larger.[34] When rural and urban school districts are considered together, 81 percent of those reporting indicated that they were conducting educational activities for adults and out-of-school youth. Even if the third of the schools which did not reply to the inquiry had no adult education programs whatever, a condition which is hardly likely, the offerings in adult education available to rural people is considerable. It has certainly increased greatly since 1926. Enrollments are likewise impressive. For populations of 2,500 to 10,000 they

---

[31] Lippitt and Allion, *op. cit.*, p. 20.
[32] Lippitt and Allion, *op. cit.*, p. 38.
[33] Kolb and Brunner, *op. cit.*, pp. 346, 347, and 328.
[34] Lippitt and Allion, *op. cit.*, p. viii.

average 175, for small districts of 2,500 population or less they average 101 and for county-wide systems, 549.[35]

The curriculum or subject matter offerings in these vocational courses has also changed greatly. The survey of 140 villages by Brunner revealed that in 1936 four-fifths of all courses were vocational in nature and were made available through the federally subsidized vocational education program.

The 1947-48 survey revealed that many non-vocational courses were available. Brunner calculated the proportions of districts having various non-vocational offerings to be as follows: Public affairs, 3.5 percent; consumer education 4.3; health education, 6.6; dramatics, 5.2; safety, 7 percent; family life and parent education, 8.7 percent; preparation for marriage, 2.1 percent. It is also interesting to note that this study revealed that 5 percent of the smaller districts which serve rural people are members of community councils and one school in eight was conducting community center activities.[36] Granting the limitations of studies based upon the mailed questionnaire as well as a poor sample of smaller districts, it proves that rural people have available considerable non-vocational education in the three fields of special interest to the present study.

Vocational Training.—Even though by law, agriculture taught under the Smith-Hughes and George-Barden acts must be vocational in nature, some aspects of the three fields of interest, particularly as related to understanding and strengthening of the economy are woven into regular course work. Some of the most remarkable community-centered activities are carried on by vocational teachers. For example, they have helped organize community cooperative canneries, freezing plants, potato storage or drying plants. Sometimes these are located on the school grounds or close to the school. Many times these enterprises are a part of a well-rounded program of community development. The 23,917 teachers and counsellors of federally aided vocational evening schools constitute a potential for rural adult education surpassed only by the Cooperative Extension Service.

The extent to which the people in a small rural community can be actively involved in the adult education program of its high school is exemplified in Olivet, Michigan.

Adult Education in the Olivet Community School.—A diversified adult education program has been carried on by the public school system of Olivet, Michigan for a period of five years. Olivet is a small village of 887 people. About 1100 people reside in its tributary trade and service area of about 41 square miles. Olivet is the only population center in Walton township. In 1928, the various elementary school districts in this township united to form the Walton Township Unit School District, which is coterminous with the township. However,

[35] Kempfer, *op. cit.* p. 8.
[36] *Ibid.* p. 14.

it is slightly smaller than the composite trade and service area of the village of Olivet.

In 1951, enrollments in 22 classes for adults totaled 242. A majority of them met weekly for a period of 10 weeks. There were 8 classes in farm crops, with a total enrollment of 72. There were 19 enrolled in a course in knitting, 17 in a rural electrification course, 15 in a course entitled "What is the trouble in Korea?," 15 in art, 14 in a village firemen's course, 13 in fly-tieing, fly and bait casting, 12 in physical education, 12 in a young farmer class, 11 in a Christmas club, 9 in typewriting, 8 in farm mechanics, 6 in photography, and 5 in drivers training.

In addition to the above regular courses, the Tenth Annual Adult Institute, attended by 135 during the day and by 225 in the evening, was held in 1951. This Institute was sponsored jointly by the Walton Township School and the local Parent Teacher Association. The participants were divided into discussion groups who discussed "action to be taken," "how action is to be taken," and "persons to follow-up on action" on ten problems. The problem areas were selected by a committee of twenty citizens after a series of meetings. The problems taken up by the various discussion groups were: "needed grade school expansion," "provision of an adequate library," "provision of light for an athletic field," "provision of needy shop expansion," "will outside (school) districts want to go to other towns or come to Olivet?" "reading and spelling are not adequately taught," "study High School curriculum," "develop a closer relationship between parents, teachers, and pupils," "how to improve home and family living," and "how to prepare for family living." Only one resource person from outside the community was used. The purpose of the Institute was to apply the democratic processes to the solution of school and community problems.[37]

A course that pertained to international understanding was offered on Wednesday evenings, January 3 to March 7, entitled "What is behind the trouble in Korea?" This course was taught by a professor of Political Science at the local college of Olivet.

Adult Education in Stephenson School.—Stephenson is a rural community in the upper peninsula of Michigan with an unusual amount and variety of adult education in its public schools. Stephenson village has a population 791, and its tributary trade and service area of about 385 square miles, including a number of small neighborhood centers, has a population of about 4,500. Stephenson's 12-grade school district is coterminous with Stephenson township and comprises 41 square miles. It serves a much larger area since approximately

---

[37] Interview with Walter P. Schroeder, Director of Adult and Vocational Education, November 5, 1951. Mr. Schroeder is primarily responsible for the development of the adult education programs and activities of the Olivet school system, and has been director of Adult and Vocational Education during the past 5 years. He still finds his major obstacles to continued growth and expansion, that of getting more local people to understand the importance and value of democratic participation.

two-thirds of the pupils attending Stephenson high school are non-residents. No other high school in Michigan located in a rural village of less than 1000 population has as many different kinds of classes for adults or as many adults enrolled.

During the year 1951–52, 177 adults were enrolled in the following general adult education courses: 41 in state and national affairs; 45 in national affairs; 2 in adult-driver training; 27 in homecrafts; 15 in high-school subjects; 8 in crafts and avocations; and 39 in recreation and leisure time. In addition, 1151 were enrolled in adult agriculture courses, 16 in young farmer courses, 105 in veteran on-farm training classes, and 19 in adult homemaking classes. Thus, a total of at least 1468 persons were enrolled in a variety of general, vocational and veteran courses for adults offered by the Stephenson Public School System.

Stephenson community was one of the five communities selected by the Michigan Department of Public Instruction in 1946 for the development of an experimental program known as the Community School Service Program and was partially subsidized by W. K. Kellogg Foundation. An important initial phase was the discovery and motivation of latent leadership and the formation of an organization known as the Stephenson Community Coordinating Council, of which the school superintendent served as executive secretary. Approximately 175 persons serve on seven problem-study committees which have completed over 50 specific projects. The Community School Service Program operates on the philosophy that when people share, people care—then democracy grows. Dynamic local leaders with a community wide organization can enrich and vitalize all aspects of the community, and in the process the school can be an extraordinary educational agency.

Adult Education in Public Schools of Michigan.—The origin and development of education classes for out-of-school youth and adults in Michigan exhibits an interesting pattern, and in many respects is similar to that of other states. Michigan is among the pioneers in the field of education for adults. It started, as in many states, with attempts to reduce illiteracy among adults and with Americanization programs for aliens. The Michigan alien education law, enacted in 1906, authorized the Superintendent of Public Instruction to cooperate with boards of education of school districts to provide for the education of aliens and native illiterates over the age of 18 years. Adults in urban centers have received the major benefits of this law.

Diversified vocational training was made available to adults in Michigan in 1919 in what is commonly known as the Tufts Acts. This act accepts the provisions of the federal Smith-Hughes Act and provides for financial assitance to boards of education from federal and state funds. Many adults in rural areas are enrolled in this program.

Since 1921 many adults in Michigan who were disabled have been aided in their return to civil employment through a state vocational rehabilitation law. The General School Law of Michigan accepts the provisions of the federal vocational rehabilitation statute whereby federal and state funds are made available for the promotion of vocational rehabilitation. Many more urban people than rural people are affected by this program.

In 1944 the Michigan legislature made provisions for general adult education. This legislation authorized a board of education of any school district, except primary school districts (which are essentially elementary districts), to provide instruction for adults, employ qualified teachers, and provide the necessary equipment. Two hundred and fifty thousand dollars were allocated for the purpose of providing an experimental program in adult education for the school year ending June 1945 and a sum of $235,000 was appropriated for each of the years 1946 and 1947. The appropriations were under the supervision of the Superintendent of Public Instruction and an advisory committee of 15. Forty-five school districts and a number of public colleges and universities shared the funds for general adult education during each of the three years of the experimental program.

Since 1948 the sum of $300,000 has been appropriated each year under the provisions of the State Aid Act for the purpose of assisting public schools in maintaining adult education classes. Each year the number of schools sharing in these funds has increased, or from 109 in 1948–49 to 167 in 1951–52. School districts that are approved for this purpose by the State Superintendent of Public Instruction are reimbursed on the basis of the equated membership year.

The equated membership year, consisting of 720 clock hours of actual attendance (based on 36 weeks of 20 hours per week), has been adopted as the unit of measure in determining state aid. During the year 1951–52, the attendance hours of 230,588 adults enrolled in general adult education classes totaled 2,270,165. Up to the present, reimbursement is unequal for those over 21 and those under 21 years of age. Reimbursement per equated membership year for those under 21 was $155.80; for those 21 years of age and over, $77.95.

In 1951–52 the 167 school districts reported an expenditure of $780,097 for adult education. Of this amount $300,000, or 38 percent, was recovered through state aid. Classes for adults were conducted by boards of education at a cost of approximately 30.9 cents per student hour of instruction. Nearly 12 cents (11.9) per hour was recovered through state aid. A total of 2,970 teachers were employed, of whom 64 percent were professionally trained public school teachers. Thirty-one percent were artisans, technicians and professional practitioners certified to teach in a given subject area in which they had special skill and information, and 5 percent were college teachers. Eleven school districts, all with urban centers, employed full-time directors. During the year 1951–52, 6,301 courses were offered in 19 different content areas. Table 3 lists these areas in order of volume, in attendance hours. Crafts and avocations claim first interest, followed by high school subjects and elementary school subjects. It will be noted that 2,994 persons were enrolled in 146 leadership training courses,

2,156 in 108 national defense courses, 2,584 in 65 community problems courses, 1,163 in 23 international affairs courses, and 3,195 in 20 state and national affairs courses. It should be remembered that these are the courses offered by the 55 rural high schools and by the 112 urban high schools.

TABLE 3
Number of Courses, Enrollment, and Total Attendance Hours by Content Areas in Public Schools of Michigan, 1951–52*

Content area	Number of courses	Enrollment	Total attendance, hours
Total	6,301	130,588	2,520,458
Crafts and avocations	1,232	27,081	644,051
High school subjects	1,312	22,659	494,534
Elementary subjects	478	11,214	358,611
Music, drama, fine arts	554	13,266	228,173
Home crafts	645	10,067	174,356
Recreation and leisure time	495	11,400	163,542
Americanization and citizenship	134	3,193	83,513
Driver training	634	4,728	77,930
Workers' education	210	4,030	75,408
Parent and family education	152	7,968	55,113
Leadership training	146	2,994	39,274
National Defense	108	2,156	28,999
Programs, displaced persons	48	1,124	28,872
Community Problems	65	2,584	22,668
International affairs	23	1,163	11,592
State and national affairs	20	3,195	11,173
Programs for the aging	17	520	8,723
Adult counseling services	19	1,029	8,624
Older youth programs	9	217	5,301

* Annual report of Henry J. Ponitz, Chief, Adult Education Division, Michigan Department of Public Instruction, July, 1952.

SIZE OF HIGH SCHOOL AND ADULT EDUCATION PROGRAMS

A total of 263 sample counties were selected for the purpose of determining the extent and nature of adult education programs and activities offered by public high schools throughout the country. Questionnaires regarding the nature of adult education programs and attendance were sent to the 1,460 superintendents of 12-grade school systems in the counties. A total of 837 superintendents, or 57 percent, responded. Their responses were tabulated on the basis of size of high school, size of town in which high school is located, type-of-farming, rurality of county, and level-of-living index of the county.

A total of 813 school administrators replied to the question, "Does your school district have any educational programs or activities for adults?" and 569 replied to the question, "Was there any program or activity for adults that included (1) international understanding for peace, (2) strengthening of democracy, and (3) understanding and strengthening of the economy, carried on within or by your school district during the past year?" The Directory of Secondary Schools[38] regarding number of high school graduates in 1945-46 was used as the basis of classifying responses.

Slightly less than two-thirds (63 percent) of the respondents said that their school system had some kind of an adult education program. The prevalence of adult education programs increases with the size of the high school as classified by the size of the graduating class. While only about one half (54 percent) of the small high schools, those with less than 20 in their graduating classes, have adult education programs, four-fifths of the largest high schools have such programs. No doubt, these are primary vocational courses. Since small high schools are usually located in small villages, adult education classes are not as readily available to rural people as to urban people. However, since only one-half of the 340 small high schools in the 263 sample counties have an adult education program, it would appear that a great undeveloped potential awaits qualified leadership and effective organization.

Two-fifths of the superintendents reporting claim that they have adult education programs in the three fields of interest. A much larger proportion of the smaller school systems failed to answer this question for the probable reason that many were unable to answer affirmatively. Less than one-half of the schools with less than 100 graduates indicated programs in these three fields, but 60 percent of those with 100 or more indicated having such programs. In the larger systems there are likely to be sufficient people interested as well as qualified teachers to permit such non-vocational courses to materialize.

Of the cities of 2,500 and over reporting to the National Education Association,[39] 27 percent had programs or activities in world affairs and world peace; 35 percent in strengthening of democracy, and 20 percent in studying and understanding the Western economies. The percentages of the total enrollment in adult education programs and activities involved in these three fields as reported were 21, 5, and 2, respectively. Increases in enrollment reported for these three fields in the last five years were 387, 308, and 189, respectively.

The types of organizations that high schools work with are numerous, but farm organizations and parents' organizations were mentioned most frequently. The organizations vary somewhat with the size of the high school. The small

---

[38] United States Office of Education, Circular 250, January 1949. A more recent directory was still in press at the time of this writing.

[39] Lippitt and Allion, *op. cit.*, p. 24.

ones are more likely to cooperate with Parent-Teacher Associations and farm organizations and the largest ones with colleges, libraries, civic and service clubs, such as the Rotary and Kiwanis, and with UNESCO. There are many factors other than size of the graduating class that affect the extent and nature of school cooperation with other organizations in offering adult education programs and activities. Only 38 percent of the smallest high schools cooperate with colleges as compared with 60 percent of the high schools having 100 or more graduating seniors. With respect to cooperation with civic and service clubs the percentages are 35 and 71 percent. Such organizations are few in the smaller communities and therefore, possible cooperation with them is limited. A similar situation exists with respect to libraries, a fact that may explain why only one-fourth of the high schools with less than 30-member graduating classes cooperate with libraries.

From one-fifth to one-seventh of the smaller high schools (less than 40 graduating seniors) answered "yes" to the question, "During the past year did any foreign person appear on your program?" The percentage was 35 for the largest sized high schools, those with graduating classes of 100 or more. One-fifth of all schools, regardless of size, reported using a foreign person on their adult education program. Some 32 high schools claimed to have no adult education programs, yet used foreign persons in their school-community public relations activities.

Mass Media Used by 12-Grade School Systems in Adult Education.—The nature of the mass media used in education programs and activities for adults tends to vary with size of high school, as measured by size of graduating class. A total of 465 of the 510 high schools having adult education programs indicated the type of mass media used. The responses indicate that with an increasing size of high school, the use of the movie decreases from about 70 percent to about 43 percent. The use of newspapers, radio, and television however, increases with size. Television is used in one school in a hundred of those with less than 30 seniors; in one school in fifty with 30 to 99 seniors; and in one school in twenty-five with 100 or more seniors. Of high schools with 30 seniors, one-fifth or less use the radio in connection with adult education programs, but it is used by 29 percent of high schools with 100 or more seniors. As a rule less than one-half of the high schools with less than 30 seniors use the newspaper as a medium in their adult education programs, but it is used by two-thirds of the high schools with a hundred or more seniors.

Forms and Procedures Used by the 12-Grade Systems in Adult Education that Rate "Best."—The administrators of the 12-grade school systems in the 263 sample counties were requested to "... check the form or forms which your best program or activity in the three fields took." The categories, together with the percentages checking them, are as follows: Public Meeting, 68 percent; Conference, 31 percent; Workshop, 28 percent; Demonstration, 28 percent;

Tour, 8 percent; Radio Listening, 6 percent; and Institute, 4 percent.[40] Public Meetings were considered the form of best program by all school systems regardless of size. The Institute is likely to be twice as prevalent in the large schools as in the smaller ones, although it is rarely used by any of them. Demonstrations tend to be used less with increasing size of high school. This tendency may reflect the different types of organizations that high schools cooperate with as they increase in size. Aside from the two associations mentioned, size of school has little effect upon the form of the "best" program.

Respondents also answered the following question: "In conducting the program or activity what procedures were used?" The categories listed and the percentages checking them are as follows: Group discussion, 74 percent; Lecture, 70 percent; Panels, 28 percent; Large groups split into small discussion groups, 14 percent; and other procedures, 14 percent. Thus, we may conclude that the 12-grade schools of the nation rely heavily upon public meeting and conferences and that group discussion and lecture methods predominate. There is a tendency for the smaller high schools to make more frequent use of group discussion and for the larger ones to use the lecture method more often.

Size of High School in Relation to Size of Town.—Although some large cities have rather small graduating classes and some small villages have large graduating classes, there is a tendency for the graduating classes to become larger with an increase in size of the population center in which the high school is located. This relationship is indicated in Table 4. Of 248 towns with less than 500 population, it will be noted that 100 had less than 10 in their graduating classes. At the other extreme, of 74 high schools in cities with over 10,000 population, 47 had 100 or more in their graduating classes. Because of this interdependence, one could expect the extent and nature of adult education to vary with increase in size of the population center in which the high school is located.

Size of Population Center and Prevalence of Adult Education Programs.—Of the 813 high schools in the 263 sample counties responding with regard to their adult education programs, 568 are rural high schools (located in population centers of less than 2,500 population) and 245 are urban high schools. A significantly higher proportion of the high schools in the urban centers than in rural centers have educational programs or activities for adults, 73 percent as compared with 58 percent. Less than one-half, 47 percent, of the high schools in villages of less than 500 population have adult education programs. See Table 5.

The percentages for urban centers are higher than those reported by the

---

[40] The National Education Association study of adult education in urban centers reports the following forms, with percentages of the cities using them: Formal lecture, 46; Teacher pupil recitation, 76; Informal group discussion, 67; Demonstration laboratory, 78; debates, 6; forums, 23; panel discussion, 25; workshop, 44; home study (individual), 14; correspondence, 5. Those forms which have increased most during the last 5 year were forums, panel discussion, workshops, and informal discussion. Lippitt and Allion, *op. cit.*, p. 54.

TABLE 4
Size of High School Graduating Class in Relation to Size of Population Center in which High School is Located

Size of high school graduating class	Under 500	500–999	1000–1499	1500–1999	2000–2999	2500–4999	5000–9999	10,000 & over
Total	248	157	75	62	41	94	86	74
Under 10	100	22	11	4	6	7	7	6
10–19	74	55	24	11	7	7	8	3
20–29	33	44	18	14	6	10	4	2
30–39	18	23	12	17	12	15	2	2
40–59	9	10	7	11	8	26	12	4
60–99	7	3	3	5	1	25	34	10
100 or over	7	0	0	0	1	4	19	47

TABLE 5
Prevalence of General Adult Education Programs and of such Programs in the Three Fields of Interest

Size of town	Number of high schools responding	General adult education program Number	General adult education program Percent	Number of high schools responding	Have adult education programs in three fields Number	Have adult education programs in three fields Percent
All Groups	813	510	63	568	227	40
Rural						
Under 500	238	111	47	148	63	43
500–999	154	99	64	106	35	33
1,000–1,499	75	51	68	57	16	28
1,500–1,999	60	41	68	44	16	36
2,000–2,499	41	30	73	31	9	29
Urban						
2,500–4,999	91	68	75	68	24	35
5,000–9,999	83	55	66	58	32	55
10,000 & over	71	55	66	56	32	57

National Education Association. In the latter study, the size of city and the proportion reporting adult education programs in 1950–51 are as follows: Places over 100,000, 97 percent; 30,000 to 100,000, 86 percent; 10,000 to 30,000, 63 percent; 5,000 to 10,000, 45 percent; and 2,500 to 5,000 42 percent.[41]

High schools with adult education programs in the fields of international understanding for peace, strengthening of democracy, and understanding and

[41] Lippitt and Allion, *op. cit.*, p. 2.

strengthening of the economy, prevail in 36 percent of the rural communities, and in 48 percent of the urban communities, according to reports from school administrators. The only group in which more than one-half of the school systems have programs in these three fields are urban centers—towns in the 5,000–9,999 population class and in those of 10,000 or more.

Influence of Regional Factors.—The extent and nature of adult education programs of the 813 high schools which reported seemed to be influenced less by type of farming, size of community, the rurality of the county and level of living index in which the schools were located than by favorable legislation pertaining to adult education, and possibly, with the nature of the school district organization. For instance, 75 percent of the schools of the Western Specialty-Crop Areas reported adult education as compared with only 63

TABLE 6
Adult Education Classes in Consolidated and Non-Consolidated School Districts of Michigan, by Size of Village, 1951–52

Size of Village	Consolidated School Districts			Non-Consolidated School Districts		
	No. of H. S.	Have adult education classes		No. of H. S.	Have adult education classes	
		Number	Percent		Number	Percent
Total number............	250	140	56	140	65	46
Under 500..............	94	41	45	28	4	14
500–999................	92	50	54	52	19	37
1,000–1,499............	31	24	77	22	15	68
1,500–1,999............	21	17	81	19	14	74
2,000–2,499............	12	8	67	19	13	68

percent of the total. Most of specialty crop areas fall in the state of California where legislation favorable to adult education exists. In the other specialty crop areas of Utah, Washington, Arizona, and Idaho, several have school legislation favorable to the formation of community school districts and to adult education in general. It is interesting to note that of all the areas, the schools of specialty crop area, work most with farmers' organizations, particularly with the Farm Bureau. Eighty-one percent of the schools reported work with or through farm organizations in their adult education programs in this type of farming area.

Comparison of Consolidated with Non-Consolidated Rural School Districts in Prevalence of Adult Education Classes.—Several times in this chapter it has been suggested that reorganization of school districts may encourage adult education. This hypothesis is substantiated as far as Michigan is concerned by the data of Table 6. There are 390 high schools in rural Michigan, 250 of which are consolidated districts and 140 are not. Many of the consolidations center in the smaller villages where adult education is commonly less prevalent than in the larger centers.

Regardless of size of village, adult education classes are more prevalent in consolidated school districts than in non-consolidated ones. During the school year 1951–52 in villages with less than 500 population, adult education classes were offered by 44 percent of the consolidated districts and by only 14 percent of the non-consolidated districts. In villages with 500–999 population, adult education classes were offered by 55 percent of the consolidated districts as compared with 37 percent of the non-consolidated districts. In villages of larger size, the difference between consolidated and non-consolidated school districts becomes increasingly less.

SUMMARY

The fact that the one-teacher school system is still the most prevalent type of school structure in the majority of states, contributes to the comparative rarity of adult education in rural areas. The rapid progress in school district reorganization in recent years in some populous rural states, such as New York, Illinois, Missouri, Michigan, and Texas, can be expected to accelerate the growth of adult education in rural areas, especially when supported by favorable legislation. The growth of adult education in public school systems in many rural communities is contingent in part upon the formation of community school districts and community schools. It is also dependent upon the supply of qualified and adequately trained teachers, supervisors and directors of adult education. When these are buttressed by state aid, community initiative, and resourcefulness the extent and nature of the adult education programs and activities offered by the public school system are largely determined.

From these data it is obvious that there is tremendous variation in the extent to which the various states use the schools for adult education. In some states, such as New York a majority of local 12-grade rural schools are included in the attempt to reach adults with enlightening and helpful programs. In other states where functional illiteracy is high, the rural schools are practically untouched by any general adult education program. Experience demonstrates that if the rural schools are to have effective adult education programs dynamic and effective state leadership is necessary. In most of rural areas of the nation, rural schools as systems and channels of communication for adult education, are a very great potential which remains to be developed. The fields of adult education of interest to our study: (1) international understanding for peace, (2) strengthening of democracy, and (3) understanding and strengthening of the economy, are not being furthered in most of the rural school systems of the nation through systematic programs.

John F. Thaden
Department of Sociology and Anthropology
Michigan State College
East Lansing, Michigan

BIBLIOGRAPHY

American Association of School Administrators, "Extension and Enrichment of Education for Adults" in *The Expanding Role of Education,* Twenty-sixth Yearbook, Washington, D. C.: The Association, a department of the National Education Association, 1948, pp. 79–98.

Anderson, Presco, "In-Service Training for Directors of Adult Education," *Adult Education,* Vol. 1, August 1951, pp. 223–228.

Branz, George G., "Organizing the Adult Curriculum," *The Nation's Schools,* Vol. 39, February 1947, pp. 24–25, and 32.

Brown, Giles T., "Never too Old to Learn: A Gerontological Experiment in General Education," *School and Society,* Vol. 74, November 3, 1951, pp. 279–281.

Caliver, Ambrose, "Problem of Adult Illiteracy," *American Teacher,* Vol. 33, February 1949, pp. 16–19.

Cook, L. A. and Cook, E. F., *A Sociological Approach to Education,* New York: McGraw-Hill Book Company, 1950.

Deans, Stephen R., "Who Seeks Adult Education and Why; A Description of Adult Education Participants," *Adult Education,* Vol. 1, October 1950, pp. 18–25.

Deming, Robert C., "Characteristics of an Adequate Adult Education Program," *Adult Education,* Vol. 1, October 1950, pp. 25–26.

Donahue, Francis J., "Principles of Post-high school Education in Michigan," *School and Society,* Vol. 65, May 10, 1947, pp. 346–347.

Donahue, Wilma T., "Preparation for Living in the Later Years," *Adult Education,* Vol. 1, December 1950, pp. 43–51.

Ely, Mary L., editor, *Handbook of Adult Education in the United States,* New York: Columbia University, Institute of Adult Education, 1948, 555 p.

Essert, Paul L., "The Future of Adult Education," *Teachers College Record,* Vol. 49, November 1947, pp. 87–97.

Essert, Paul L., *Creative Leadership of Adult Education,* New York: Prentice-Hall, Inc., 1951, 333 p.

Fitzwater, Charles O., "Some Guides to a Wider Use of Rural Schools for Adult Education Purposes," *Adult Education Bulletin,* Vol. 13, October 1948, pp. 212–216.

Gaumnitz, Walter H. and Stanton, H. L., "Supervision of Education for Out-of-School Youth and Adults as a Function of State Departments of Education," *Office of Education Bulletin,* 1940, No. 6, Monograph No. 120, Washington, D. C.: Superintendent of Documents, Government Printing Office, 1941, 85 p.

Getsinger, Joseph W., "What Do The California Adult Schools Teach?" *Adult Education Journal,* Vol. 8, October 1949, pp. 231–236.

Hallenbeck, Wilbur C., "Participation in Public Affairs; A Diagnosis of the Problem," *Adult Education,* Vol. 2, October 1951, pp. 8–17.

Holmes, Henry W., editor, *Fundamental Education: Common Ground for All Peoples,* New York; The Macmillan Company, 1947, 325 p.

Jones, Leo, *Handbook on Continuation Education in California,* Sacramento, California: California State Department of Education, March 1950, 42 p.

Kempfer, Homer, *Adult Education Activities of the Public Schools: Report of a Survey, 1947–48,* Office of Education Pamphlet No. 107, Washington, D. C.: Superintendent of Documents, Government Printing Office, 1949, 21 p.

Kempfer, Homer, *Education for a Long and Useful Life,* Office of Education Bulletin, 1950, No. 6, Washington, D. C.: Superintendent of Documents, Government Printing Office, 1950, 32 p.

Kempfer, Homer, *Identifying Educational Needs of Adults,* Office of Education Circular No. 330, Washington, D. C.: Superintendent of Documents, Government Printing Office, 1951, 64 p.

Kempfer, Homer and Wright, Grace S., *100 Evening Schools,* Office of Education Bulletin 1949, No. 4, Washington, D. C.: Superintendent of Documents, Government Printing Office, 1949, 71 p.

Kempfer, Homer and Wright, Grace S., *Selected Approaches to Adult Education,* Office of

Education Bulletin 1950, No. 16, Washington, D. C.: Superintendent of Documents, Government Printing Office, 1950, 48 p.

Knowles, Malcolm S., *Informal Adult Education: A Guide for Administrators, Leaders and Teachers*, New York: Association Press, 1950, 272 p.

Lippitt, G. L. and Allion, H. L., *A Study of Urban Public School Adult Education Programs in the United States*, Washington, National Education Association, 1952.

Maaske, Roben, J., "How to Set Up an Adult Education Program in a Small Community," *National Educational Association Journal*, Vol. 40, April 1951, pp. 252–253.

Mann, George C., *Handbook on Adult Education in California*, Sacramento, California: California State Department of Education, May 1949, 37 p.

McClusky, Howard Y., "Dissemination of Child Development Knowledge Through a Program of Adult Education and Community Action," *Child Development*, Vol. 19, March 1948, pp. 40–51.

Mumma, Richard A., "Trends in Adult Education Offerings in Region II," *Adult Education Bulletin*, Vol. 14, August 1950, pp. 180–186.

Mumma, Richard A., "Barriers to the Development of an Adult Education Program," *Adult Education*, Vol. 1, February 1951, pp. 106–113.

National Education Association, American Education Research Association, and Department of Adult Education, Joint Committee, *Needed Research in Adult Education*, Washington, D. C.: The Association, 1949, 32 p.

Pollard, L. Belle, *Adult Education for Homemaking*, New York: John Wiley and Sons, 1947, 194 p.

Ponitz, Henry, "Competencies Required of Adult Education Teachers and Group Leaders," *Adult Education Bulletin*, Vol. 14, April 15, 1950, pp. 124–125.

Reeves, Floyd W., Fansler, Thomas, and Houle, Cyril O., *Adult Education*, New York: McGraw-Hill Book Company, 1938, 171 p.

Sillers, Robertson, "Education for International Understanding," *Adult Education Journal*, Vol. 8, April 1948, pp. 91–98.

Spence, Ralph B., and Shangold, Benjamin, *Public School Adult Education in New York State, 1944–47*, Albany: New York State Education Department, 1950, 82 p.

Stensland, Per G., "Adult Education Grows to Maturity," *Phi Delta Kappan*, Vol. 32, May 1951, pp. 385–386.

Studebaker, John Ward, *The American Way: Democracy At Work in Des Moines Forums*, New York and London: McGraw-Hill Book Company, Inc., 1935, 206 p.

Thaden, John F., "Adult Education," in Joseph S. Roucek, *Sociological Foundations of Education*, New York: Thomas Y. Crowell Company, 1942, pp. 395–417.

Chapter 3:

THE COOPERATIVE EXTENSION SERVICE OF THE UNITED STATES

Introduction

The Cooperative Extension Service, with a total staff of over 12,000 professional workers,[1] is the largest adult educational organization of its kind in the world. The staff is small in relation to the clientele—a little under seven million fami-

[1] *Report of Cooperative Extension Work in Agriculture and Home Economics, 1951*, Washington: USDA, Extension Service, 1951, p. 47.

lies—divided about 69 percent farm and 31 percent non-farm.[2] The non-farm group is mainly rural but includes many urban people, some in each state. Paid professional workers have the assistance of about one million unpaid voluntary leaders who give an average of over two weeks each to extension work.[3] The help of the voluntary leaders, valued at a rate of pay for unskilled labor, exceeds the amount of the entire 1950 budget. The budget is the largest of any adult education organization supported by public or private funds. From all sources in 1951, 77¼ million dollars were appropriated for cooperative extension work.

In terms of geographical coverage there are 3,107 county extension services[4] in the United States, Hawaii, Puerto Rico, and Alaska. It is the only adult educational organization with a local unit in almost all of the rural counties of the United States.

WHAT THE COOPERATIVE EXTENSION SERVICE IS

The Cooperative Extension Service of the United States aims to teach people, wherever they are, outside school and college classrooms.[5] Teaching is done in which little use is made of books and lectures but there is much observation and doing. Each member of the family participates in learning by doing things in a better way, as viewed by extension workers and farm leaders. The Cooperative Extension Service feels that through doing things in a better way, through use of the latest knowledge and the improved methods, that education takes place.

The first educational responsibility of the Service is to carry to rural people the teaching and results of research of the state agricultural colleges and experiment stations and the United States Department of Agriculture. The purpose is that of helping to apply the teachings and research findings to improve the farm, the home, the community, and the nation. The Cooperative Extension Service does not operate alone on the knowledge and research of the colleges and the USDA. Long ago it learned that the people, through their own experience and study of their own problems, have much to contribute to the improvement of rural life.

The purpose of the Cooperative Extension Service, as conceived by its administrators and workers, is not so much to make two blades of grass grow where one grew before, but to develop self-confident, effective and understanding men, women, and youth who will be capable of meeting leadership responsibilities.

[2] Amelia S. Osmundson, *Extension Activities and Accomplishments 1950*, Washington: USDA, Extension Service Circular 273, June 1951, p. 1.
[3] *Ibid.*, p. 10.
[4] Records of the Federal Extension Service, USDA, Washington.
[5] C. B. Smith, *What Agricultural Extension Is*, Extension Service Leaflet, USDA, Washington: Government Printing Office, 1944.

Local control is exercised at the county level with regard to the selection of extension workers. The decision to have or not to have a county cooperative extension service is made in the county, since the three-way partnership between local people, the state, and the federal government can only exist when the local people elect to participate. This partnership structure has educational implications. Extension agents with the help of local leaders assemble facts about the situation in the county and together develop educational programs based on the needs of the people.[6] In order to introduce the thinking of local people into the program planning processes, it is often necessary for extension workers to develop rural organizations and to work with them when they are present. Through developing and working with organizations of local people, leadership is developed and utilized in promoting social and civic improvement. These are the educational processes that bring satisfaction to the individual.[7]

The Cooperative Extension Service is the product of a series of events that began with the agricultural revolution in England. Along with the social changes which followed the agricultural revolution, scientific bodies such as the American Philosophical Society in 1743 and the Philadelphia Society for the Promotion of Agriculture in 1785, appeared in the United States. The latter was the first of the agricultural societies which reached the peak of their influence nearly seventy years later. The agricultural societies are credited with introducing educational exhibits at fairs and other agricultural events. Farmers' clubs were organized and obtained speakers on agricultural subjects at their meetings. The era of influence of the agricultural societies ended about 1861. A graphic outline of the development of the Cooperative Extension Service is given in Figure 1.

Farmers' cooperative demonstration work was originated in 1904 by Seaman A. Knapp, the leader of the movement that was well established at the time of his death in 1911. Although much of its impetus resulted from the emergency efforts to combat an invasion of cotton boll weevil in Texas, Dr. Knapp conceived cooperative demonstration work as a method of providing informal practical education in agriculture for farm families.

In 1906 the General Education Board became interested in cooperative demonstration work as a means of helping achieve its purposes of improving economic conditions among farm families in the South. By 1908 in eleven states there were 157 agricultural agents, of whom 85 were paid by the General Education Board. The investment of $862,250 in extension work by the Board

[6] Fred C. Jans, *Extension Looks at Program Planning*, Washington: USDA, *Extension Service* Circular 478, March 1952.

[7] Paul J. Leagans, *The Educational Interests of Farm Operators in North Carolina as Related to Work of the Agricultural Extension Service*, Unpublished Doctor's dissertation, Department of Education, University of Chicago, 1949, p. 7.

was an important factor in its rapid development during the nine years preceding the passage of the Smith-Lever Act.[8]

The Smith-Lever act of 1914 established demonstration work on a nationwide basis as a part of the land-grant college system. The law provided that each land-grant college should create a separate extension division under a director and that the federal organization should be a separate office of extension work in the United States Department of Agriculture for administering Smith-Lever funds, coordinating new work, and taking over that already under way.

Thus the Cooperative Extension Service came into existence as the culmination of a series of events and activities covering a period of at least 126 years.

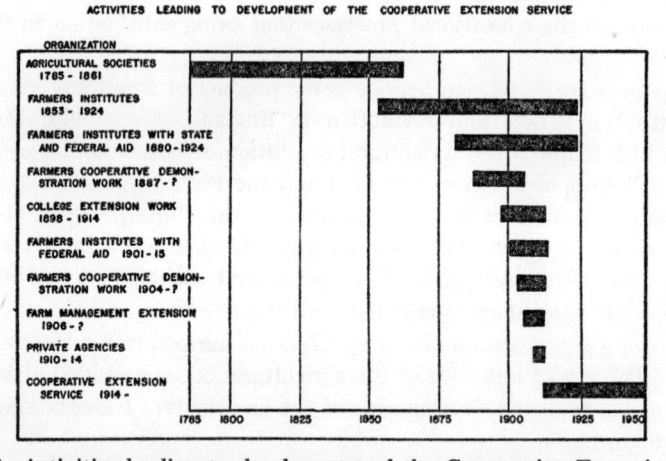

FIG. 1. Activities leading to development of the Cooperative Extension Service Adapted from a talk by C. G. Bauman at the Intra-Regional Conference on Supervision, College Station, Texas, December, 1950.

It would be a mistake to regard the Cooperative Extension Service as an organization that developed to meet the particular needs of the rural people alone. It must be seen as an integral part of the land-grant college movement in the United States.[9] The movement crystallized into the beginnings of a nationwide system of colleges of agricultural and mechanical arts education with the passage of the first Morrill Act in 1862. This law provided grants of land for a college to teach military service, and agricultural and mechanical arts in each state. The Hatch Act of 1887 was the second phase in the development of the land-grant college system and provided for a system of agricultural experiment stations in connection with the land-grant colleges.

[8] Alfred C. True, *A History of Agricultural Extension Work in the United States*, USDA, Miscellaneous Publication No. 15, Washington: Government Printing Office, 1928.

[9] Frederick B. Mumford, *The Land-Grant College Movement*, Columbia: Missouri Agricultural Experiment Station, Bulletin 419, 1946, pp. 117–118.

The three major activities of the land-grant colleges are resident teaching, research, and extension teaching. The Morrill Act contemplated an educational program which would affect agriculture and rural life everywhere. It developed that teaching on the college campus required facts as a basis. The experiment stations were established to provide the facts through programs of research. Once facts were available it became apparent that a means was needed to carry the teachings and research of the land-grant colleges directly to the people living on farms. The Cooperative Extension Service, the third major phase in the land-grant college movement, was established to meet this need.

Objectives of the Service.—The objectives of the Cooperative Extension Service have been set forth in three main ways: (1) in Federal legislation; (2) in official documents and agreements developed by the Secretary of Agriculture, the Cooperative Extension Service, and agencies of the United States Department of Agriculture; and (3) in the philosophies of outstanding early leaders in extension work.

According to federal legislation, the purposes of cooperative extension work are to disseminate and encourage the application of useful and practical information relating to agriculture and home economics among the people of the United States. The work should consist of instruction and practical demonstrations to persons not enrolled in the land-grant colleges, through field demonstrations, publications, and otherwise. Recent legislation extended the scope of cooperative extension work to include marketing and distribution of farm products, 4-H Club work, older youth programs, and other technical and educational assistance.[10]

A memorandum of understanding between the Secretary of Agriculture and the Executive Committee of the Land-Grant College Association has been the basis for extension work of the agricultural colleges and the Department of Agriculture since the passage of the Smith-Lever Act.[11] The colleges agreed to establish a separate and distinct administration for cooperative extension work with a responsible leader selected by the college and satisfactory to the Department of Agriculture. The Department agreed to establish a States Relations Committee, which later became the Extension Service of the U.S.D.A., and that cooperative extension work in the states should be planned jointly by the State Director and the Department. It provided further that all agents should be joint appointees of the colleges and the Department.

The Extension Service Charter, issued in 1942 by Secretary Wickard, was for the purpose of defining the duties of the Cooperative Extension Service and its relation to the work of other agencies. It states that the extension service is responsible for the general education work in agriculture and home economics. In regard to the educational functions of the agencies of the Department of

---

[10] *Federal Legislation, Regulations, and Rulings Affecting Cooperative Extension Work in Agriculture and Home Economics,* Miscellaneous Publication No. 285, USDA, Washington, 1946, p. 9.

[11] True, *op. cit.,* p. 25.

Agriculture, the Charter states: "The Extension Service is recognized as the responsible subject-matter agency that taps the scientific and economic information of this Department and of the State Experiment Stations and uses this information in a practical way in guiding farm people on all phases of farming and homemaking in the most comprehensive sense."[12]

Dr. Seaman A. Knapp, without a doubt, has had the greatest influence on the early development of the Cooperative Extension Service.[13] Almost single-handedly he established extension as we now know it. About 1903 he began his work in the South and continued it until his death in 1911. His concept of extension probably is best expressed by the following quotation from the USDA Yearbook of 1909:

The farmers' cooperative demonstration work may be regarded as a method of increasing farm crops and is logically the first step toward a true uplift, or it may be considered a system of rural education for boys and adults by which a readjustment of country life can be effected and placed upon a higher plane of profit, comfort, culture, influence, and power.

C. B. Smith, a former assistant director of extension work, exercised an important influence on the Cooperative Extension Service. His address before the annual conference of the extension staff in Washington in 1944 contains this summary statement:

... in the United States agricultural extension is what agricultural extension does. Its normal and primary function is that of teacher, counselor and adviser in all matters affecting rural people and rural life ...

The most recent official statement of the purposes and objectives of the Cooperative Extension Service is contained in the *Report of the Committee on the Scope of Extension's Educational Responsibility*.[14] The nine areas of educations' responsibility are listed in Figure 5.

The Cooperative Extension Service has three organizational levels, namely, national, state, and county. The organization at the national level serves to lead but not direct the work of the state organizations. It coordinates the work in the United States, Hawaii, Puerto Rico, and Alaska. In 1950 it administered the expenditure of $33,425,000 of Federal money which represented 43.3 percent of the total extension budget.[15]

The Federal Cooperative Extension Service.—The Federal office of the Extension Service maintains one of the smallest bureau staffs in the United States Department of Agriculture. In 1950 there were 15 specialists in agriculture and

---

[12] USDA Miscellaneous Publication 285, *op. cit.*, p. 25.
[13] Gladys Baker, *The County Agent*, Chicago: The University of Chicago Press, 1939, pp. 25–28.
[14] *Report of the Committee on the Scope of Extension's Educational Responsibilities*, Washington: U.S.D.A., Extension Service, 1946.
[15] *Report of Cooperative Extension Work, op. cit.*, p. 60.

4 specialists in home economics. Subject matter specialists include such areas as animal husbandry, poultry, agronomy, forestry, soil conservation, dairying, horticulture, entomology, plant pathology, agricultural engineering, rural electrification, health and rural sociology, home management, foods and nutrition, clothing, and family relations.

The specialists help relate the work of the bureaus or agencies in the Department of Agriculture to extension educational effort on particular subjects in the states. The specialist also works in liaison capacity with other Federal bureaus, with industry, and with the various agricultural and educational organizations. He transmits information from the federal office to the states, from the states to the federal office, and from state to state. Much of his time is spent working with and helping specialists in the states.

One of the main functions of the federal Cooperative Extension Service is to help all extension workers get information to the people in the most effective ways. This function is carried out by the Division of Extension Information which serves as liaison between the federal office and the states on matters relating to the use of press, radio, television, publications, visual aids, and other public communications media. This Division works closely with state extension editors and their staffs, promoting, facilitating, and teaching effective use of these media.

The staff of professional people in the Division of Field Studies and Training makes field studies and carries on basic extension research. Studies are made to develop more effective use of methods now employed and evaluation studies are carried out with state and county extension workers. The Division makes recommendations and assists with the training of extension workers based on studies of training needs.

To help coordinate cooperative extension work, the nation is divided into four geographical regions. Each region is composed of about 12 states, with an agricultural, home demonstration, and 4-H Club field agent from the federal office assigned to each. The field agents visit and consult with the state directors and others affected by their particular field of work. They hold conferences and workshops, help plan programs and advise on improvement of program development, teaching procedures, administration, and supervision.

State Cooperative Extension Services.—Each state and territory has an Extension Service Division at the land-grant college. All are headed by a Director of Extension appointed by the college governing board and approved by the Secretary of Agriculture. There are many minor differences from state to state, with no two exactly alike. In the main, the differences in types of organization derive from factors such as size of organization, number of counties in the state, method of coordinating subject matter, and organization of the land-grant institution. Figures 2 and 3 are generalized administrative and functional diagrams of extension organization.

The most common state organization consists of one or more assistant directors and state leaders for county agricultural agent work, home demonstration work, and 4-H Club work. The states also have subject-matter specialists for much the same subjects as the federal office, but in varying numbers according to individual need. Specialists keep abreast of the developments in their own particular fields, keep county workers up to date on new developments and research results, and help county agents and home demonstration agents plan and conduct educational programs for rural people. They write bulletins, contribute to journals and newspapers, help prepare educational movies and other

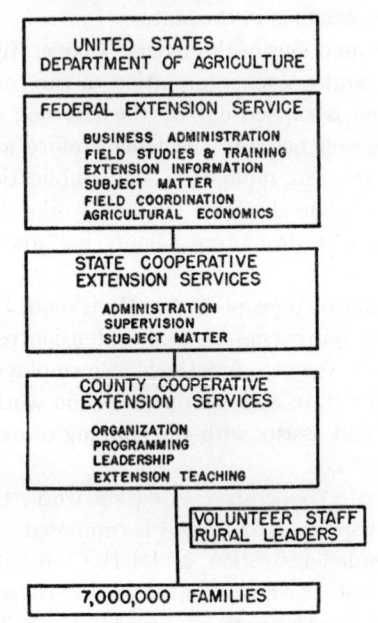

ORGANIZATION CHART
OF THE COOPERATIVE EXTENSION SERVICE

```
UNITED STATES
DEPARTMENT OF AGRICULTURE

FEDERAL EXTENSION SERVICE
    BUSINESS ADMINISTRATION
    FIELD STUDIES & TRAINING
    EXTENSION INFORMATION
    SUBJECT MATTER
    FIELD COORDINATION
    AGRICULTURAL ECONOMICS

STATE COOPERATIVE
EXTENSION SERVICES
    ADMINISTRATION
    SUPERVISION
    SUBJECT MATTER

COUNTY COOPERATIVE
EXTENSION SERVICES
    ORGANIZATION
    PROGRAMMING
    LEADERSHIP
    EXTENSION TEACHING

          VOLUNTEER STAFF
          RURAL LEADERS

7,000,000 FAMILIES
```

FIG. 2. Organization chart of the Cooperative Extension Service.

visual teaching materials, make radio talks, and appear at meetings to present subject-matter materials and lead discussions.

County Cooperative Extension Services.—The basic unit of the Cooperative Extension Service is the county, for it is here that programs are made and extension teaching is done. The federal and state organizations are designed to give the maximum help to county extension agents and local volunteer leaders to enable them to give the greatest aid to the people in the counties.

A typical county is served by a county agricultural agent and usually by a home demonstration agent. In many states, especially in the East, the county has one, and frequently two, 4-H Club agents. In many states there are assistant county agricultural agents and assistant home demonstration agents. In many states 4-H Club work is done by the county agent and home demonstration agent or by assistant county agents or home demonstration agents. The average is about three professional workers per county. In some counties with highly specialized types of agriculture and where the financial resources permit, there are assistant agents and subject-matter specialists on the county staff.

The county extension service offices generally are located in the county-seat town.[16] The county staff is responsible for conducting educational programs

FUNCTIONAL ORGANIZATION OF THE COOPERATIVE EXTENSION SERVICE

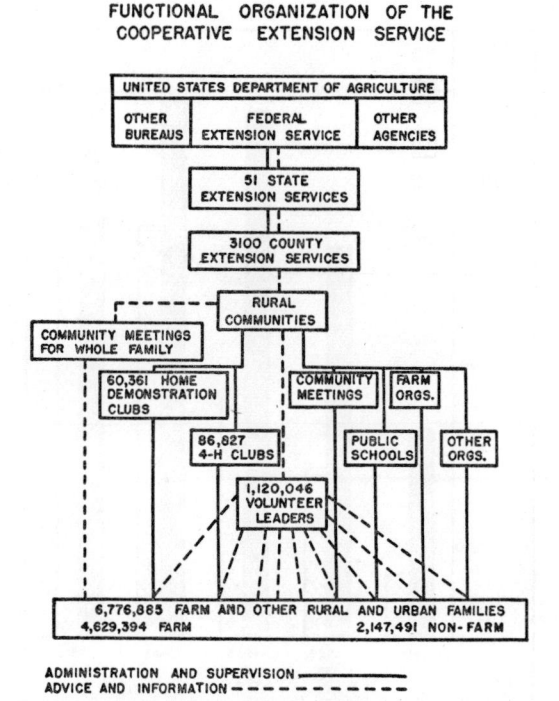

```
UNITED STATES DEPARTMENT OF AGRICULTURE
OTHER BUREAUS | FEDERAL EXTENSION SERVICE | OTHER AGENCIES

51 STATE EXTENSION SERVICES

3100 COUNTY EXTENSION SERVICES

RURAL COMMUNITIES

COMMUNITY MEETINGS FOR WHOLE FAMILY

60,361 HOME DEMONSTRATION CLUBS
COMMUNITY MEETINGS
FARM ORGS.
86,827 4-H CLUBS
PUBLIC SCHOOLS
OTHER ORGS.
1,120,046 VOLUNTEER LEADERS

6,776,885 FARM AND OTHER RURAL AND URBAN FAMILIES
4,629,394 FARM          2,147,491 NON-FARM
```

ADMINISTRATION AND SUPERVISION ———
ADVICE AND INFORMATION — — — — —

FIG. 3. Functional organization of the Cooperative Extension Service. Source: Adapted from Extension Service Circular 393.

related to problems affecting the welfare of the people in the county. It is aided by volunteer local leaders, adult men, women, and youth who help to develop programs, conduct meetings, hold demonstrations, and to help to get information to their neighbors.

County extension workers, as representatives of a land-grant college of agriculture and the United States Department of Agriculture, are responsible to both. In addition, the county workers are employees of the county government, and their tenure in the county is subject to the approval of the sponsoring

---

[16] C. Herman Welch, Jr. and Meredith C. Wilson, *Public Relations Inventory of the Cooperative Extension Service*, Washington: USDA, Extension Service Report, October, 1951, p. 23. (Mimeographed).

organizations or the county governing bodies and the state extension administration. In Chapter 4, the relationship between the Farm Bureau and the county extension services in the states where the Bureau is the local sponsoring agency is discussed.

Tradition.—The influence of tradition is strong in the Cooperative Extension Service. Traditionally, the emphasis has been on obtaining the adoption of farm

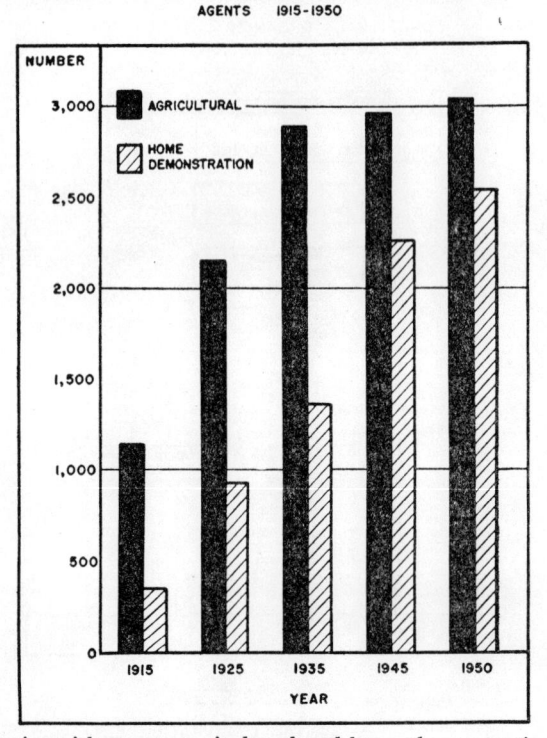

FIG. 4. Counties with county agricultural and home demonstration agents, 1915–1950. Source: Report of Cooperative Extension Work, 1950.

and home practices as a means of improving the welfare of the people.[17] This tradition leads people to think of extension programs largely in terms of agricultural and home economics subject matter. Thus, farm people expect and tend to ask for the things related to the business side of the farm and the home. It has influenced the county extension workers themselves in causing them to appraise their work in such terms. When agents can point to farm families who have adopted new practices, they have concrete and specific results to show

[17] *Joint Committee Report on Extension Programs, Policies, and Goals, USDA, and Association of Land-Grant Colleges and Universities,* Washington: Government Printing Office, 1948, p. 7.

for their efforts. A tradition of counting practices adopted, meetings held, people worked with, and activities of the agents tends to obscure the less tangible social benefits of extension education.

Professional organizations.—Epsilon Sigma Phi fraternity is the Cooperative Extension Service professional fraternity to which all extension workers with ten years or more experience are eligible to belong. This fraternity has chapters in 47 states and a membership of about 4500. Its purpose is to exercise leadership in the professional improvement of extension workers. The National Association of County Agricultural Agents, the National Association of County Home Demonstration Agents, and the National Association of 4-H Club Agents are organizations which promote the interests and give professional recognition to the three groups of county workers. The American Association of Agricultural College Editors is the professional group to which extension editors may belong.

Assets and facilities.—Unlike most educational organizations, the Cooperative Extension Service has no plant and owns no land or buildings. By agreement, the land-grant colleges provide office space for the staff of the state extension office. Office space for the county office may be supplied or paid for by the county governing body or the sponsoring organization. A recent survey[18] indicates that 46 percent of the county offices are located in county courthouses, 14 percent in Federal buildings or U. S. Post Offices, and 17 percent in other rented buildings. Since the Cooperative Extension Service owns no real estate and pays no rent for county offices, its funds are spent mainly for salaries, travel, printing, and supplies.

Extension staff[19] may be categorized as follows:

Directors and assistant directors	119
State leaders, county agent work	31
Assistant state leaders and district agents	179
State leaders, home demonstration work	47
Assistant state leaders, home demonstration work	161
State leaders, 4-H Club work	64
Assistant state leaders, 4-H Club work	183
County agents	3,403
Assistant county agents	1,893
County home demonstration agents	2,902
Assistant county home demonstration agents	756
County 4-H Club agents	549
Assistant county 4-H Club agents	107
Subject-matter specialists	2,248
Total	12,642

Virtually all county extension workers have degrees in agriculture or home economics, many from the land-grant colleges. Many have graduate training

[18] Welch and Wilson, *op. cit.*, p. 23.
[19] *Report of Cooperative Extension Work, 1951, op. cit.*, pp. 46–47.

and all receive in-service training as a regular operational procedure through workshops, special courses, and conferences in the field. Many attend the regular college summer schools or the special regional short-term extension summer schools held annually.

Budget.—Funds from all sources for cooperative extension work for the year ending June 30, 1951, amounted to $77,233,791. Of this amount, 56.7 percent is from state, county, and local sources, and 43.3 percent is from federal funds. Funds for cooperative extension work for the year 1948–49 were 46 percent from the federal government, 28.4 percent from the state governments, 22 percent from the county governments, and 3.6 percent from farmers' organizations and other sponsoring groups.

Expenditures for the year 1948–49 were 1.7 percent in the federal office, 31.8 percent in the state offices, and 66.5 percent in the county offices. Expenditures of Cooperative Extension Service funds according to purposes for which the money was used in 1948–49 were 31.6 million for adult work in the counties, 19.3 million for 4-H Club and youth work, 13.1 million for subject-matter specialists, 2.2 million for administration, and 1 million for publications.

COUNTY EXTENSION WORKERS SURVEYED

Much of the information for this Chapter is based on the records and reports of the county, state, and federal Cooperative Extension Services. Additional information, particularly about current adult education programs and activities, was obtained from a mailed questionnaire. The study design and the sampling plan are described in Chapter 1 and Appendix C. A questionnaire was mailed to all county extension workers in the sample counties by the Directors of the state Cooperative Extension Service. The self-addressed questionnaires were returned direct to the author of this chapter. Completed questionnaires were received from one or more county extension workers in 260 of the 263 counties. Details of the methods used are found in Appendix C.

Clientele.—The emphasis in extension work is on bringing about changes in individual members of families with which work is done. Some of the families are reached through one member of the family, while frequently all members of the family are reached. Most of the objectives and the content of programs are such that through the individual an entire family is affected by the teaching of the county extension workers. In 1950 nearly 7 million families were influenced in one way or another. Among the estimated 6,808,612 families, 68.6 percent were farm and 31.4 percent were nonfarm families.[20]

Sixty percent of the county extension agents responding to the survey question on numbers of people reached indicated that almost all lived in the open country or in centers of less than 2500 people. More than 80 percent of the agents said that three-fourths or more of the people reached live in the open-

[20] Osmundson, *op. cit.*, p. 1.

country. Only about six percent of the agents work with one-fourth or less people from the open country.

Work with youth is carried on mainly through the 4-H Club. In 1950 there were 1,990,932 members enrolled from about 1.4 million different homes, about three-fourths of which were farm homes. The membership included 1,087,191 girls and 903,741 boys enrolled in 86,827 local 4-H Clubs.[21] An essential part is played in the effectiveness of the 4-H Clubs by the 251,550 volunteer local leaders[22] who assist the county extension workers in carrying out the 4-H Club program.

Young men and women between the ages of 18 and 30 years represent a transitional group between the adolescents and the adults. This group has been receiving special attention in recent years. In 1950 the county extension agents worked with 339,859 young men and women who might not have been affected by the regular adult programs.[23]

Negro families are an important part of the clientele of the Cooperative Extension Service. Among the 435,038 Negro families who participated in 1950, 329,241 were farm families and 105,797 were nonfarm and urban families.[24] These figures apply to the 391 counties in the 17 states where 775 Negro county extension agents are employed to work with the Negro population.

Volunteer workers.—The effort of the county extension agents is multiplied by local voluntary leaders who devote time to helping with programs in their own communities. These public-spirited leaders were 56 percent women, 38 percent men, and 6 percent older 4-H Club boys and girls. Altogether, 1,120,046 men, women, boys, and girls gave an average of two weeks each during the year to helping with extension activities.[25] The voluntary leaders held the meetings which were attended by nearly one-fifth (17.7 percent) of those attending extension meetings in 1950. About 24 percent of the leaders devoted their efforts to 4-H Club work and the other 76 percent worked with adults—45 percent women and 31 percent men working with adults.

CONTENT OF PROGRAMS

Historically, agricultural production has received the most attention and will continue to receive much attention in the future because it is basic to the welfare of people on farms and to the nation as a whole. Agricultural commodities represent an important part of national productive capacity. Increasingly higher agricultural production by the most efficient methods is essential to the maintenance of adequate living standards for people living on farms. During the

[21] *Ibid.*, p. 1.
[22] *Ibid.*, p. 10.
[23] *Ibid.*, p. 1.
[24] Records of the Federal Extension Service, USDA, Washington.
[25] Osmundson, *op. cit.*, p. 10.

decade 1940–50, about one-third of the efforts of county extension workers were directed toward more efficient production of crops and livestock.[26]

It can be seen from Figure 5 that county extension workers devote about one-fourth of their time to developing and servicing rural organization and voluntary leadership. Much effort is directed toward improving social relationships, helping make social adjustments, and developing cultural values among rural people.

TIME DEVOTED BY EXTENSION WORKERS TO THE VARIOUS AREAS OF EXTENSION EDUCATIONAL RESPONSIBILITY IN 1950

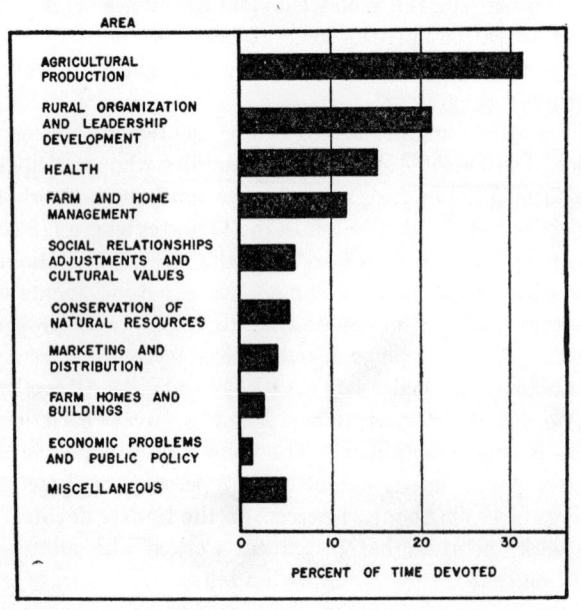

FIG. 5. Time devoted by extension workers to the various areas of extension educational responsibility in 1950. Source: Annual Reports, County Extension Workers, 1950.

Rural organization activities include helping the people to organize themselves for cooperative effort in dealing with their problems in rural living, and in working with established groups to assist in planning and carrying out educational and group action programs to meet the needs of the local people. The most important aspect of working with groups and organizations consists of developing them both as a means and as an end in program building.

Economic problems and public policies deal with the relation of local, national, and international economic problems to the welfare of farm people and the general public. Consideration is given measures that could be adopted to

[26] Figures compiled from annual reports of the Federal Extension Service.

overcome the problems involved. The agents report only a small portion of time devoted to this area, but this does not reflect the true situation for several reasons. Possibly the most important one is that the work in economics and public policy is done largely by the state extension economists whose efforts are not included in county reports. County extension workers carry on much of their work with economic problems in connection with commodity programs and tend to report all related efforts under specific commodity classifications. Matters of public policy frequently are introduced as a part of other programs in such a way that they are a minor part of the whole activity and are obscured in reporting use of time by units of a day or fractional parts of days, or in classifying the kinds of meetings and other events held.

The agricultural phase of extension work is as broad as agriculture itself. It deals with any and all problems of crop and livestock production, soil and water conservation, soil improvement, forestry, wildlife, and the management aspects of farming and rural living. Much attention is given to the business side of farming, including farm accounting, credit, planning, adjustments, and tenancy. Marketing and distribution of agricultural products comes in for a share of attention. Economic phases of farming are taken into account in agricultural outlook work, price and trade policies, land policy, public finance and services.

An estimated 4,661,094 families changed one or more agricultural practices.[27] Eighty percent were farm and twenty percent were nonfarm families. There is wide variation in the extent and nature of county organizations for agricultural extension, depending on such factors as the type of farming and the density of the agricultural population in the county. Many counties have a strong and effective agricultural organization while some have little or no formal organization. In general, agricultural programs are conducted with relatively fewer organized groups than in home demonstration work.

The average home demonstration agent works with 410 homemakers in 17 different home demonstration clubs or other organized groups, and with 560 who are not in an organized group.[28] She works with 970 families, 597 farm and 373 other families. To do this job, she has the help of 146 volunteer leaders. She holds 240 meetings in a year, including 22 on leader training, 151 method demonstrations, 6 result demonstrations, 52 general meetings, and 9 miscellaneous in character. Each year she makes 265 home visits, receives 504 office visitors, writes 96 news articles, and distributes 3,000 bulletins. Her time is spent on the various kinds of work about as follows:

	%
Extension organization and planning.	26
Food selection, preparation, and preservation.	14
House furnishings and equipment.	14
Clothing and textiles.	14

[27] *Ibid.*, p. 1.
[28] Extension Service Annual Statistical Reports, 1950.

Recreation and community activities............................. 7
Other work... 7
Home production of family food supply........................... 4
Marketing and other agricultural economics...................... 4
Home management (family economics)............................. 4
General health and safety work.................................. 3
Family relationships and child development..................... 3

Home economics extension is carried on mainly through organized groups of homemakers. In some states they are known as home demonstration clubs, in some as home bureaus, and in others no one organization is the chief medium for reaching the woman. The sponsoring groups are organized at community, county, and state levels. These organizations with the help of the extension agents develop their own leadership and are an important source of leadership for other community, state, and national programs and activities.

Beginning in World War II greater emphasis has been given to extension work with young men and women. It is an important group numerically since the average agricultural county contains more than 3,000 young men and women between the ages of 18 and 30 years.[29] They need much help because they are often simultaneously starting families, and embarking on farming or other business enterprises. For this reason, a relatively independent program for this age group has been developed and is carried out through organized groups of young men and women. In 1950, 2,312 such groups with a membership of 87,113 were sponsored.[30] An additional 160,351 other young people were assisted through the programs of 5,234 similar groups not organized by the Cooperative Extension Service.

The youth are difficult to reach because they are no longer in school, and they are moving away from their parents' families. The programs of adult organizations generally do not attract them and many are uncertain as to what they want and how they will get it. Outside the church only about 12 percent participate in any kind of organized group. The need of specific training for people who are assigned to work with young men and women was emphasized in the Jackson's Mill Conference.[31] Mothers with children under 10 years of age have been most difficult to reach in home economics extension. A recent study revealed that television has good possibilities as a means of doing effective teaching with mothers of young children.[32]

Extension work with Negroes.—In 17 Southern States Negro extension workers are employed to work with Negro families. These agents are employed largely in counties where there is a large Negro population relative to the number of

[29] E. W. Aiton, *Extension Work with Young Men and Women*, Washington: USDA, PA-73, October, 1949, p. 1.
[30] Osmundsen, *op. cit.*, p. 15.
[31] *Report of the National Extension Young Adult Planning Conference, February 21-25, 1949*, Washington: USDA, Extension Service, p. 1. (Mimeographed).
[32] Meredith C. Wilson and Ed. Mae, *Effectiveness of Television in Teaching Sewing Practices*, Washington: USDA, Extension Service Circular 466, June 1951.

white people. The work of the Negro agents is an important part of the Cooperative Extension Service's contribution to the improvement of living in rural areas.

Dr. E. B. Evans, President of Prairie View A and M College, has been associated with the college since 1913 and served as State Leader of Extension work with Negroes for many years. He and a few members of his staff were asked to give their appraisal of the influence of extension work with Negro people. Their evaluation was in terms of the intangible improvements rather than in terms of agricultural or homemaking practices. Improved practices in farming and homemaking have brought more diversification in farm production, greater stability of income, and larger incomes to Negro farmers. These changes have contributed to improved appearance, resulting from better physical condition that goes with better diets, and better dress made possible with larger and more stable incomes.

In the opinion of President Evans and the other members of the staff, the development of leadership among Negro people in county, community, and neighborhoods has been one of the most impressive contributions of the Cooperative Extension Service. This leadership has developed almost entirely since 1913. The satisfaction that comes from the leadership function is a stabilizing influence among the people. Negro county extension agents are called upon to take the leadership in cooperating with other agencies and organizations more than other individuals, due to the fact that Negro agents are usually the only professional workers on a county-wide basis to develop leadership among Negro people.

The effectiveness of extension work among Negro families is limited in some areas by local attitudes. This applies especially to work with public policy, and the democratic processes. Among Negro farm families, unsatisfactory landlord-tenant relationships are a limiting factor in the improvement of the welfare of tenant families. The present status of training of Negro extension agents and supervisors is a third factor limiting the effectiveness of extension educational programs, particularly with respect to the general adult education phases of extension work.

Extension work in 4-H Clubs.—A discussion of extension programs would be incomplete if it did not describe the 4-H Club program and relate it to adult work. Many of the men and women leaders now helping the county extension agents with adult and 4-H Club work began as members of 4-H Clubs and have continued to work with extension in leadership roles. As boys and girls they learned about agriculture and home economics from 4-H Club projects. As 4-H Club members, many of them held club offices, served on committees, or developed their leadership abilities in other ways. Others accumulated livestock, equipment, land, and capital for an education or to establish themselves in farming or other business enterprise.

Many parents who would not accept the teaching and advice of the extension agent about farming or homemaking were convinced of the value of a new idea by the son or daughter in a 4-H Club project. Studies have shown repeatedly that one of the most important factors in the success of a 4-H Club member is the cooperation and encouragement of the parents.

In 1950 more than one-quarter million local leaders assisted with 4-H Club work. This group includes 80,622 men and 124,367 women who served as leaders

TABLE 1
Other Organizations Extension Agents Work With

Organizations worked with	Agents	First choice	Second choice	Third choice
	%	%	%	%
Farm organizations	96	49	25	12
Schools	90	17	18	7
Colleges and universities	79	11	8	8
Women's clubs	70	6	7	4
Federal and/or State government bureaus	69	2	4	4
Churches and religious organizations	66	1	2	2
Community councils	57	4	7	5
Parents' organizations	56	2	3	3
Elected or appointed government bodies	46	—	—	—
Civic and service organizations	45	3	14	12
Welfare councils	36	—	—	—
Libraries	36	—	—	—
Inter-agency councils	36	—	—	—
Patriotic and veterans' organizations	34	—	—	—
Fraternal organizations	19	—	—	—
UNESCO organizations	13	—	—	—

Source: Survey of county extension agents in 263 sample counties.

for 4-H Clubs. In addition, 30,204 of the older club boys and 39,084 of the older club girls worked as volunteer leaders in their own or other 4-H Clubs.[33]

Community development.—Community improvement and community action are especially important today, because they are a part of helping to preserve democratic ideas and processes. The Cooperative Extension Service, on request, has aided in fitting church programs to community needs, in improving town-country relationships, and in training rural leaders. It has also helped to unite local groups on community-wide projects on such projects as health, recreation, community beautification, conservation, and marketing.

Throughout the country, extension agents assisted 34,100 communities with their recreational facilities, 57,600 community groups with organization prob-

[33] Osmundson, *op. cit.*, p. 10.

lems, nearly 7,000 communities in obtaining library facilities, and 2,266 communities in building community houses.

Today, 25 states have full-time community-relations specialists, and several other states draw upon teaching and research specialists for extension assistance in this field. In addition to working with communities, these specialists carry on other educational activities in the field of organization and rural sociology for improving extension work in its relation to rural life. The emphasis is on increased community spirit and pride, greater teamwork, and stronger feelings of self-reliance on the part of communities in doing things for themselves.

Cooperation with other organizations and agencies.—Extension workers cooperate with many different kinds of organizations, particularly those that are found at the county and community level. County workers who completed survey questionnaires said that they cooperate mainly with 17 different organizations. The frequency of cooperation with different organizations ranges from about 13 to over 95 percent, as shown in Table 1. The extension service cooperates with the agencies of the United States Department of Agriculture such as Farm Credit Administration, Production and Marketing Administration, Soil Conservation Service, Farmers Home Administration, and Rural Electrification Administration. In addition, it cooperates with such Federal agencies as the Employment Service, Social Security, Public Health, Children's Bureau, and Tennessee Valley Authority.[34] Table 1 in Chapter 5 gives the percentage of Farm Bureaus, Granges, Farmers' Unions and Cooperatives that say they work with the Cooperative Extension Service.

CONTRIBUTIONS TO THE THREE FIELDS OF INTEREST

International Understanding for Peace.—Extension Service Administration feels that the Cooperative Extension service has made contributions to international understanding for world peace in a number of ways and over a long period of time. About 77 percent of the county workers in the 263 sample counties have programs or activities dealing with international understanding for peace, strengthening of democracy, or understanding and strengthening of the economy. On the basis of the sample survey, an estimated 9 million people are reached by such programs in the United States. Ninety-six percent of the county workers with programs relating to the three areas are in counties that are mainly rural. Ranked according to percent of agents using them, the various kinds of activities are: public meetings, 82 percent; demonstrations, 51 percent; conferences, 30 percent; tours, 27 percent; radio listening groups, 21 percent; workshops, 16 percent; institutes, 10 percent; and other kinds, 7 percent.

Extension administrators feel that the Cooperative Extension Service has helped relieve the tensions that may arise with minority groups. In addition to the general policy of working with all such groups, there are important special

[34] *Ibid.*, pp. 46–47.

programs aimed at two specific groups, the Negroes and those of Mexican extraction. The work with Negroes has been discussed previously in this chapter.

The problem of working with persons of Mexican extraction, especially in the Southwest, has existed ever since extension work began. In recent years Latin-American migratory workers have been a part of the seasonal agricultural labor force in other areas. Work with this group has consisted of teaching better-homemaking subjects, such as better diets, sanitation, child care, and clothing. In some states, workers have received training under the leadership of Extension workers to increase their efficiency on the job.

The study of other peoples and foreign lands have also been promoted. Materials on the United Nations, UNESCO, and FAO have been distributed throughout the Cooperative Extension Service. In addition, many information releases and other materials have been prepared for use with organizations of rural people and extension leaders. International understanding received more intensive effort with home demonstration groups than with farmer groups.

Many county and state home demonstration councils have promoted study of different foreign countries each year. The purpose and program of UNESCO and FAO have been the subject of discussion by home demonstration groups throughout the country. Other activities include correspondence with people in foreign countries, becoming better acquainted with local foreign-born families, and having people from foreign countries visit the groups and tell about life in their native lands. Nearly half of the county extension workers surveyed had foreign persons appear on one or more of their programs.

In connection with the observance of United Nations Day, October 24, 1950, a nation-wide United Nations flag-making project was organized and about 50,000 flags were made by homemakers in clubs and groups during September and October.[35] This activity was initiated upon the request of a committee from the various farm organizations. The system of home economics groups and local leaders demonstrated its effectiveness by completing the project in a few weeks. In one state, for example, the flag-making project was handled entirely by correspondence with the county organizations and completed in three weeks. As a result, 3,393 flags were made in that state. Flags were presented in 2,790 special programs or ceremonies, 194 radio programs were given on the United Nations flag, 1,204 newspaper stories and 295 pictures were in the newspapers. Flags were presented to the governor of the state, the congressmen, state legislators and to the presidents of four colleges. Many county and city school officials received flags. Flag-making did not end with the special effort in 1950. Some flags are still being made and presented in special ceremonies.

One of the most important contributions to international understanding for world peace is being made through the International Farm Youth Exchange. This project, which is discussed in another chapter, is now in its fourth year.

[35] Extension Service Annual Statistical Reports, 1950.

One hundred and forty-eight 4-H Club members have gone abroad to live and work with farm families in foreign countries. These young people have learned about problems of farm people in foreign countries and carried information about this country to them.

The Foreign Student Training Program of the Cooperative Extension Service is another important contribution to world understanding. In 1950, 521 persons were brought to this country for training in agriculture, home economics, or extension teaching methods. Training consists of four main types, in-service training, young farmer training, visiting technician training, and the International Farm Youth Exchange program described in the previous paragraph. Foreign students are placed according to their training needs on farms where they can observe and receive experience in modern farming practices. The Federal Extension Service is responsible for programming, orientation, placement, training, and supervision of persons who come here for training in agriculture and home economics.

Information on world affairs is released, and discussions on national and international topics are held in the states. Some of the topics which received the most attention were inflation, price stabilization and controls, international relations, the interrelationships of agriculture and other segments of the economy, and agricultural policy.

Certain states provide discussion leaflets for home economics groups with titles like "Let's Understand FAO's Program"; "Our Part in World Peace"; "The Homemaker as a World Citizen"; "Our Ideas for the Post-War World"; and "Food Around the World."[36]

National Home Demonstration Week, observed each year, included many international features in 1950. Such themes as world citizenship were used, with local foreign-born people and displaced persons presenting native dress, songs, dances, and customs. International Farm Youth Exchangees took part in many local programs. In county programs "International Fiestas" or international pageants were organized to help understand foreign countries. In some states the home demonstration clubs met in district-wide meetings for programs related to world understanding for peace.

Some college economics staffs have prepared materials for use in discussion groups which have been widely used by county extension workers and others. One of the series of such publications is a 16-page statement entitled "Understanding Asia."[37]

Possibly the most important contribution of the Cooperative Extension Service to the improvement of relations with other countries has come about through the influence and teaching of experienced extension workers who have

[36] Gertrude Humphreys, *Good Living Series 18*, Lessons 1, 2, and 3, Morgantown: West Virginia, Agricultural Extension Service.
[37] C. Malone and W. Ogg, *Understanding Asia*, Ames: Iowa Agricultural Extension Service, August, 1951.

worked to help establish agricultural education and extension in underdeveloped countries. No statistics are available, but it is safe to say that hundreds of well-trained and experienced extension workers are making such contributions.

Strengthening of democracy.—Extension work, as conceived by the Cooperative Extension Service, is democracy itself. From the beginning its aim has been to improve the people by developing their abilities to analyze problems, to decide upon practical solutions, and to plan and carry out action programs designed to improve farming and rural living. Extension workers try to implement this philosophy by democratic extension teaching activities conducted with the organizations of rural people through which much of their work is done. The county extension services, through their close relationships with the county governing body or other sponsoring organization, are a basic part of our system of local government.

Local ties are made even stronger by the men and women on agricultural advisory and planning committees, the home demonstration councils and organizations, young men and women's groups and committees, and the 4-H Club organization and adult advisory committees that work with it. County extension services usually are closely tied to the neighborhoods and families throughout the county.

As a result of these relationships and the procedures used in extension work, it is believed that a large contribution is made to democratic concepts and procedures, byproducts not directly related to the objectives of improving farming and homemaking. Such intangible byproducts are difficult to measure. It is revealed, however, in growth of leadership and the ability of people to do for themselves.

In addition to the contributions arising out of the procedures used and the organizations with which it works, The Cooperative Extension Service is making an impressive contribution through activities aimed specifically at democratic objectives. The extension service and the home demonstration sponsoring organizations have conducted a four-day annual State conference for officers of the local sponsoring organizations in one state for 13 consecutive years.[38] The conferences deal with the responsibilities of the leaders of extension work and the function of the organization in leadership training.

Another state has held four consecutive two-day citizenship leader-training schools in the last four years. The purpose is to help homemakers become better-informed citizens. Programs deal with such topics as jury systems and the courts, social security insurance, State and Federal taxes, town and county officers, how the government handles your money, voting procedures, and assessment. Visits of both adult and youth groups are made to government institutions like post offices, courthouses, jails, courts, and schools.

Some of the states prepare series of discussion leaflets which are used in local adult and youth group meetings. Leaflets and other duplicated materials have

[38] Extension Service Annual Statistical Reports, 1950.

been prepared and distributed on such topics as "Group Medical Care," "Duties and Privileges of a Voter," "Parents Teach Regard for the Rights of Others," "Training the Child for Good Citizenship," and "Returns from Our Taxes." Youth programs feature such group discussion topics as the philosophical base of democracy, functioning of a democracy, democratic organization, local, state, and national government, duties of officers, program planning, and discussion leadership. See Chapter 5 for the topics discussed in the Citizen Leader Training School of the New York Home Bureau Federation.

Understanding and strengthening of the economy.—Educational work in farm economics in the Cooperative Extension Service has six phases which are currently receiving major emphasis.[39] Outlook and economic information is a program of continuous release of economic information bearing on expected changes or trends in the agricultural situation. Research and extension economists participate in preparing information and using it with county workers, farm leaders, and the general public. Some information is prepared for general distribution, and some is for special groups and for specific purposes. Outlook information usually consists of annual outlook statements, series of current releases, timely statements on special problems, and economic handbooks, charts, and slides for use by all extension workers.

Farm planning and business analysis consists of direct assistance to farmers in improving their ability to make management decisions. Emphasis is on general farm and home plans that will make the best use of resources, and on training in the techniques of making current business decisions regarding capital outlay, use of credit, enterprise adjustments, and so forth. This educational work may be conducted through farm and home accounting and balanced farming associations, demonstration farms, enterprise record cooperators, special farm planning meetings or in various types of farm and home management contacts.

Land tenure and agricultural finance work includes such items as farm leasing arrangements, family operating agreements, credit statements, income tax and social security reports, and investments for farm families. Organizations which service farm people, such as banks, credit agencies, local business firms, lawyers, and government agencies receive considerable aid in this phase of farm economics.

Efforts in labor utilization are designed to result in more efficient use of the agricultural manpower on the farm. Job instruction for seasonal workers, labor relations and management, farm labor housing, camp management, and special activities related to improving the welfare and working conditions of hired labor are all features of this phase of the farm economics work.

Work with area planning and economic development is for the purpose of helping local groups that want to plan for the economic development of the

---

[39] 1950–51 Annual Report of the Farm Management and General Economic Section, Division of Agricultural Economics, Washington: Extension Service.

area in which they live. It includes land use adjustments, soil and water resource development, taxation and local government, rural zoning, schools, roads, and other matters of local concern. This effort may be on community, county, watershed, or some other geographical basis.

The national economic affairs phase is designed to develop in individuals a better understanding of the issues involved in important national and international affairs affecting agriculture. It is designed to create a desire and ability to participate effectively in the solution of problems in this area. This phase includes price policies, reciprocal trade agreements, national debt, and inflation, and usually is done on a discussion basis with small groups of leaders representing various interests and points of view. This work mainly is carried on by the state extension economists who personally do much of the work.

There are great variations in the number of economics workers on the state staffs, the area to be covered, and the number of county workers seeking such help. This means that there are wide variations in the concentration of effort among the six major phases of farm economics. Obviously there is much more to be done than the staff available can possibly do. It is to be expected, therefore, that the emphasis in a particular phase is largely a matter of choice. The scope and nature of the job are limited by the fact that sixty percent of the extension economists are employed in 12 states, 8 of which are in the Middle West, while 17 states have one economist or less in the Cooperative Extension Service.

The lack of an adequate staff of economics specialists in many states is one of the main obstacles to more effective economic programs, particularly with respect to public policy and understanding the economic system. Another obstacle arises out of the need of special training in economics and educational methods in farm economics. The lack of appreciation of the importance of programs in economics and public policy by some state extension administrations is also an obstacle.

PROGRAMMING PROCEDURES

One of the basic principles of extension program planning is that of participation of the people in the planning of programs which affect them.[40] Their participation in making decisions about objectives and activities mean that they understand and feel a part of the process from the beginning. This insures that programs are based on needs and interests that they recognize and which they feel are important. Programs that the people help plan are also more likely to begin at the level of their knowledge and understanding.

In the states, programming policies and procedures are developed and implemented through the supervisory people and subject-matter specialists. Supervisors and specialists are responsible for guiding and assisting county personnel in following effective procedures in program development. Specialists help pro-

[40] Joint Committee Report, *op. cit.*, p. 37.

vide the information which is needed by county program-planning groups, such as major trends, newly discovered problems, and new technical information that is helpful in solving many of the problems with which planning groups must deal.

County extension workers are responsible for developing the organizations of local people and the leadership that is required for program development and execution. They motivate, train, and guide local people in analysing the situation in the county, deciding on objectives, and carrying into action the plans that are made.

How Programs Are Developed.—In 1950 about one-fifth of the counties had integrated county extension programs, usually with a single group or commit-

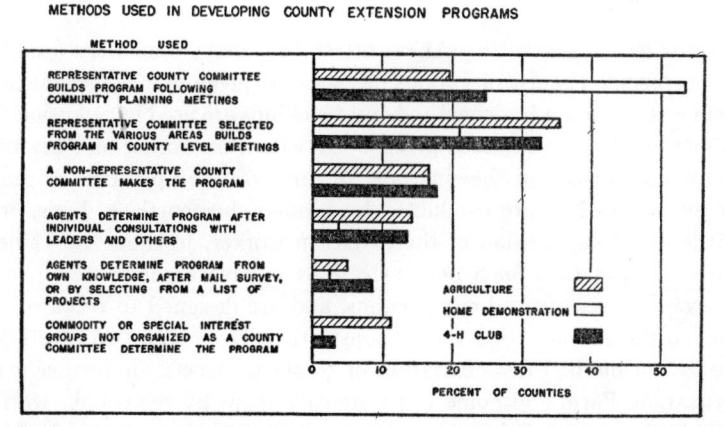

Fig. 6. Methods used in developing county extension programs. Source: Extension Service Circular 477.

tee determining the objectives or content for both agriculture and home economics. In the other counties the three kinds of programs were developed separately.[41]

Six major methods are used in program determination. Methods vary widely in detail, according to the extent to which leadership has been developed in the county, the type of agriculture, and the experience of the county extension workers. The six methods are given below with an indication of the extent to which each was used:

1. A county committee representing the various rural groups and interests plans the county program following community meetings where problems and needs are discussed. This method is used to develop about 32 percent of the county programs.

2. Discussion of problems and drafting of program on county level by selected representatives from townships or communities and representatives from organiza-

[41] Joseph L. Matthews, *National Inventory of Extension Methods of Program Development*, Washington: U.S.D.A., Extension Service Circular 477, January 1952.

tions and agencies, serving as county program-building committees. About 30 percent of all programs are developed by this method.

3. Discussion of problems and drafting of program by a county committee which is non-representative geographically or by major interest. This method is used to determine about 16 percent of the programs.

4. Program largely planned by the county extension agents through personal consultation with leaders and well-informed people of the county, not organized into a program-planning committee. About 10 percent of the county extension programs are determined by this method.

5. Agents plan the program from their own knowledge, after a mail survey, or by selection from a list of projects prepared at the college. About 5 percent of the programs are determined in this manner.

6. Program is determined by commodity or special-interest committees, not organized as a county program-planning group. This method is used to determine about 5 percent of the programs.

Extension teaching methods.—About fifteen principal methods are used by extension workers.[42] The use of various methods are given in averages in Table 2. The demonstration is a basic method and two kinds are used in extension teaching. A method demonstration is given by an extension worker or other trained leader for the purpose of showing how to carry out an operation or practice. Result demonstrations are conducted by farmers, homemakers, boys, or girls under the direct supervision of the extension worker, to show the value of a recommended practice. Such demonstrations involve a substantial period of time, records of results and comparisons, and are designed to teach others in addition to those conducting the demonstration. Demonstration meetings are held to give a method demonstration or to start, inspect, or further a result demonstration. Farm and home visits are calls made by the county worker to give or obtain some definite information relating to extension work. Leader-training meetings are held to train project leaders, local leaders, or committeemen to carry on extension activities. Other methods include general meetings, office calls, telephone calls, correspondence, circular letters, exhibits, posters, news stories, and radio and television shows.

Indirect influences are important in supplementing the influence of the various direct methods used. Indirect influence occurs with the spread of information and practices from neighbor to neighbor.

Almost all, 97 percent, of the county extension workers use newspaper releases as a means of disseminating information. Radio is used by 68 percent, moving pictures by 67 percent, and circular letters are used by 19 percent. Television probably would be used by more than 3.6 percent if local facilities were more widely available. The use of mass media by extension workers tends to increase with the degree of rurality in the counties. Over 75 percent of the county workers who returned questionnaires work in counties which are 50 percent or more rural.

[42] L. D. Kelsey and C. C. Hearne, *Cooperative Extension Work*, Ithaca: Comstock Publishing Company, 1949, p. 234.

TABLE 2
Use of Extension Methods by Agricultural and Home Demonstration Agents in 1950

Item	Average per agent-year — Agricultural agents	Average per agent-year — Home demonstration agents
Farm or home visits made	523	265
Different farms or homes visited	294	158
News articles published	104	96
Bulletins distributed	1,976	3,000
Radio talks broadcast or prepared for broadcasting	18	13
Training meetings held for local leaders (adult work):		
Number	8	14
Attendance: Men	163	10
Women	25	270
Total	188	280
Method demonstration meetings held (adult work):		
Number	21	91
Attendance	529	1,458
Meetings held at result demonstrations: Number	7	6
Attendance	386	200
Tours conducted (adult work): Number	2	2
Attendance	154	50
Achievement days held (adult work): Number	—	2
Attendance	—	297
Other meetings of an extension nature participated in by county or State extension workers and not previously reported (adult work): Number	45	31
Attendance	2,754	1,645
Meetings held by local leaders or committeemen not participated in by county or State extension workers and not reported elsewhere (adult work): Number	14	72
Attendance	386	1,268

Source: 1950 Annual Reports of County Extension Agents.

TABLE 3
Procedures Used in Conducting Programs and Activities Relating to World Peace, Strengthening Democracy and the Economic System

Procedure	All Agents	All Agents Double Checking	County Agricultural Agents	Home Demonstration Agents	4-H Club Agents
	%	%	%	%	%
Group discussion	80	26	80	80	77
Lecture	67	10	74	56	64
Large group split into small groups	26	2	23	23	32
Panels	23	2	28	15	23
Other	24	6	20	26	9

The procedures used in conducting the programs relating to world peace, democracy and the economics system, and the percent of extension workers using them are shown in Table 3.

WHAT GROUPS ARE REACHED?

The Cooperative Extension Service is criticised for working less effectively with low-income groups than with middle and higher-income groups. In 1941 a study was made to determine the extent to which low-income families were being reached.[43] It was found that 77 percent of the tenant families and 81 percent of the farm-owner families were reached in 17 sample areas in 16 states. In 7 sample areas in 7 states, 78 percent of the farmers with eighth-grade schooling were reached in contrast to 88 percent of those with high school but no college education. About 45 percent of the children of tenant farmers and 56 percent of the children of farm owners were in 4-H Clubs. An analysis of family income level and 4-H Club enrollment gave these averages for 3 groups of 14 states each:

Average income per family	Percentage of farm children in 4-H Clubs
Lowest	47
Middle	60
Highest	52

An analysis of participation in home demonstration work indicated only small differences between participants and non-participants. The socio-economic status of participants was somewhat higher than that of the women who did not participate. Generally, slightly more farm families in the average and above-average socioeconomic segments than of relatively disadvantaged farm families in the same areas are participating in extension work.

Some minority groups and the farm laborers and families are the most neglected groups. Migratory families are neglected because the programs of the Cooperative Extension Services are directed primarily at stable families. Many of the stable farm labor families do not have the resources to participate in activities designed to improve family living conditions. Gibson thought more personnel and facilities should be provided to reach additional segments of the population without denying service to those who now use it.[44]

Needs and interests.—A study of the educational interests of 1,017 farm operators[45] revealed that they were as highly interested in learning about many

---

[43] Meredith C. Wilson, *How and to What Extent is the Extension Service Reaching Low-Income Farm Families?*, Washington: U.S.D.A., Extension Service Circular 375, December 1941, p. 12; and Charles P. Loomis and J. Allan Beegle, *Rural Social Systems*, New York: Prentice-Hall, 1950, p. 663.

[44] Duane L. Gibson, "The Clientele of the Agricultural Extension Service", Michigan Agricultural Experiment Station Quarterly Bulletin, Vol. 26, No. 4, May 1944 and *Migratory Labor in American Agriculture*, Report of the President's Commission on Migratory Labor, Washington: U. S. Government Printing Office, 1941, p. 170.

[45] Leagans, *op. cit.*, p. 6.

essentially social or education subjects as those primarily economic in content. The level of interest was not always in proportion to its application to their own particular situation. Interest varied among the different types of farming areas, geographical areas, age, tenure status, race, education, level-of-living status, and size of farm. Education and acres of cropland farmed seemed to be the most influential in shaping the educational interests.

In a survey of the needs and interests of rural people[46], a larger income was considered the greatest need. Next came the need of better management of their time, resources, money, and of better health, including need of better diet, medical and dental care, hospitalization, and better housing. The need for better community life was frequently mentioned. In this they included need of better rural churches and guidance from rural churches, better family life, better opportunity for youth, better recreation, and better rural schools.

SUMMARY

In summary it can be said that the Cooperative Extension Service is an important part of the adult education movement in this country. In terms of size of organization, financial support, geographical coverage, scope of program and clientele, it has the largest program of adult education in rural areas of the United States.

Extension programs give much emphasis to vocational objectives. Non-vocational phases of the extension program for adults generally are closely tied with vocational objectives. Traditionally, emphasis has been on agricultural production, but the trend is toward greater emphasis on community development, rural family living, international understanding, public policy problems, and economics. More attention is being given to the development of lay leadership through democratic procedures.

County extension workers need more education and training in the social sciences and in techniques of dealing with programs with general education objectives. County extension workers' education and training needs are limiting their effectiveness in developing and carrying out programs and activities that deal with international understanding, democracy, and the economy. Financial assistance and more administrative encouragement are needed for the individuals who are willing to study to improve their competence in these areas.

Replies were received from one or more county extension workers in 260 of the 263 sample counties. Two counties did not have county workers at the time of the survey. Workers in three counties indicated that there were no programs or activities dealing with international understanding for peace, strengthening democracy, or understanding and strengthening of the economy, and in three other counties the agents did not reply to this question. In the other 255 counties

[46] Gladys Gallup, *The Effectiveness of the Home Demonstration Program in Reaching Rural People and in Meeting their Needs*, Washington U.S.D.A., Extension Service (Mimeograph), 1944, p. 5.

one or more county workers indicated that the program contained activities related to the three areas. In about eighty percent of the counties more than one agent reported activities related to the three areas. Eight home demonstration agents and 27 county agents indicated that there were no activities relating to the three areas. Generally more programs and activities relating to the three areas are carried on in county home demonstration programs than in agricultural programs. The presence or absence of activities related to the three areas does not appear to be associated with the degree of rurality or the level of living in the county.

>Joseph L. Matthews, In Charge
>Educational Research Section,
>Division of Field Studies and Training
>Extension Service, Washington, D. C.

BIBLIOGRAPHY

A Selected List

Bailey, Joseph C., Seaman A. Knapp, *Schoolmaster of American Agriculture*, New York: Columbia University Press, 1948.

Baker, Gladys, *The County Agent*, The University of Chicago Press, 1939.

Crile, Lucinda, *Bibliography on Extension Research*, Extension Service Circular 416, Extension Service, USDA, Washington, 171 Pages, (mimeographed) October 1944.

Crile, Lucinda, *Review of Extension Studies*, 1946–7 and semi-annually since, Extension Service, USDA, Washington: (mimeographed).

Joint Committee Report on Extension Programs, Policies and Goals, USDA, and Association of Land-Grant Colleges and Universities Washington: Government Printing Office, 1948.

Kelsey, Lincoln, D., and Cannon C. Hearne, *Cooperative Extension Work*, Ithaca, N. Y.: Comstock Publishing Company, 1949.

Smith, Clarence B. and Wilson, Meredith C., *The Agricultural Extension System of the United States*, New York: John Wiley & Sons, 1930.

True, Alfred C., *A History of Agricultural Extension Work in the United States*, USDA, Miscellaneous Publication No. 15, Washington: Government Printing Office, 1928.

Chapter 4:

GENERAL FARMERS' ORGANIZATIONS AND COOPERATIVES

While some of the programs of general farmers' organizations and cooperatives are thought to be economic in purpose, others are known to the general public only in terms of their political implications. Each of these organizations, however, attempts to involve the greatest possible number of farm people in an understanding of the economy and society of which these economic and political activities are a necessary part. The effective educational techniques by which farm organizations seek to involve farm people in their programs are: (1) to help or encourage farm people to believe that they have, or can develop valid opinions on and an understanding of, all community, state, national, and international issues concerning the economy and the society of which they are a part; (2) to convince farm people that it is their obligation to discuss all these issues and it is their right to express their opinions publicly; (3) to create or provide opportunities for, and provide assistance in the organized discussion of these issues, and to provide channels for communicating their opinions to all other sectors of the society.

This chapter will attempt to describe and explain each of the major farmers' organizations in as brief and graphic form as possible. The description will be focused upon the organized channels of communication by means of which educational processes operate. The following chapter will describe the educational programs which flow through these channels and the various educational techniques used by the different organizations.

The reader's attention should be challenged by the fact that a conservative estimate shows that a minimum of 3,000,000 different American farm families are members of one or more of the four major farm organizations discussed in this chapter. Tables 1 and 2 give total membership figures per state and the proportion members of the general farm organizations are of the state's farm population. The vast majority of members are proud of their membership and are loyal to the avowed objectives of these organizations. Because of this, ideas which travel through the organized channels of communication of the farm organizations meet a receptivity not normally accorded to other agencies which seek to involve farm people in a consideration of the same issues, ideas, and purposes.

THE GRANGE

The Grange (Patrons of Husbandry) is the oldest of the general farmers' organizations. It was founded in 1867 "to give farmers in the United States opportunities for social intercourse and intellectual advancement." These basic educational purposes were overshadowed during the 1870's by economic and political activities which for a time greatly increased its membership and influence but within a decade threatened its existence.[1] It reached a membership of more than 850,000 in 1875 and then fell to a membership of only a little over 100,000 in the early 1890's. After this debacle, it returned to its original purpose and on that basis has now grown to a membership of more than 858,000. The Grange has a number of economic enterprises or undertakings and still brings its influence to bear on state and national legislation, but is primarily a

[1] E. W. Martin, *History of the Grange Movement*, Philadelphia: National Publishing Company, 1874 and S. J. Buck, *The Granger Movement*, Cambridge: Harvard University Press, 1913.

TABLE 1
Memberships in General Farmers' Organizations, November, 1951

State	Farm Bureau	Grange	Farmers' Union Families	Farmers' Union Total members
Total	1,452,210	857,009	185,104	462,760
Alabama	61,193	—	325	812
Arizona	3,362	—	—	—
Arkansas	49,019	798	10,750	26,875
California	61,279	44,586	—	—
Colorado	7,626	11,788	11,100	27,750
Connecticut	8,648	30,420	—	—
Delaware	760	2,153	—	—
Florida	11,000	—	—	—
Georgia	50,253	—	—	—
Idaho	11,637	12,496	900	2,250
Illinois	183,510	9,731	—	—
Indiana	96,354	5,988	—	—
Iowa	125,022	3,080	1,024	2,560
Kansas	58,008	16,952	9,900	24,750
Kentucky	64,188	—	—	—
Lousiana	10,033	—	—	—
Maine	—	62,489	—	—
Maryland	10,217	3,249	—	—
Massachusetts	5,287	50,624	—	—
Michigan	47,768	28,640	2,100	5,250
Minnesota	61,954	3,576	9,200	23,000
Mississippi	23,084	—	—	—
Missouri	38,989	2,829	330	825
Montana	1,242	1,888	12,300	30,750
Nebraska	7,956	1,426	18,250	45,625
Nevada	1,406	—	—	—
New Hampshire	4,869	33,344	—	—
New Jersey	8,819	20,980	3,100	7,750
New York	82,902	143,143	—	—
New Mexico	6,503	—	325	812
North Carolina	58,025	11,135	—	—
North Dakota	8,752	—	37,800	94,500
Ohio	58,978	147,524	425	1,062
Oklahoma	30,852	2,789	35,600	89,000
Oregon	4,953	30,650	2,100	5,250
Pennsylvania	521	80,688	—	—
Rhode Island	3,259	7,977	—	—
South Carolina	14,693	4,836	—	—
South Dakota	2,776	359	16,500	41,250
Tennessee	40,001	504	475	1,188
Texas	50,000	2,292	1,700	4,250
Utah	6,425	—	650	1,625
Vermont	9,422	19,051	—	—
Virginia	8,762	2,202	550	1,375
Washington	4,681	50,942	1,400	3,500
West Virginia	11,620	941	—	—
Wisconsin	29,578	3,495	8,300	20,750
Wyoming	5,944	1,443	—	—

Table 2
*The Ratio Between Number of Members of General Farm Organizations and Farm Population 15 Years of Age and Older, by State**

State	Total membership	Farm Bureau	Grange	Farmers' Union
Less than 10 percent				
Virginia	2.5	1.8	0.4	0.3
Louisiana	2.8	2.8	—	—
Mississippi	3.4	3.4	—	—
West Virginia	4.6	4.3	0.3	—
South Carolina	4.7	3.5	1.2	—
Texas	5.4	4.8	0.2	0.4
Missouri	6.0	5.5	0.4	0.1
Tennessee	6.2	5.9	0.1	0.2
Arizona	6.8	6.8	—	—
Florida	7.2	7.2	—	—
North Carolina	8.0	6.7	1.3	—
Georgia	8.4	8.4	—	—
New Mexico	9.0	8.0	—	1.0
10 to 19.9 percent				
Kentucky	10.0	10.0	—	—
Alabama	10.3	10.2	—	0.1
Maryland	10.7	8.1	2.6	—
Wisconsin	11.1	6.0	0.9	4.2
Delaware	12.0	3.1	8.9	—
Pennsylvania	13.1	0.1	13.9	—
Michigan	13.9	8.1	4.9	0.9
Nevada	14.4	14.4	—	—
Arkansas	15.1	9.6	0.2	2.3
Utah	15.8	12.6	—	3.2
Minnesota	17.8	12.5	0.7	4.6
Wyoming	19.1	15.4	3.7	—
20 to 29.9 percent				
Nebraska	20.2	2.9	0.5	16.8
Indiana	21.6	20.3	1.3	—
California	23.3	13.5	9.8	—
Idaho	24.5	10.8	11.6	2.1
Iowa	24.6	23.5	0.6	0.5
Oregon	25.2	3.1	18.9	3.2
South Dakota	26.0	1.6	0.2	24.2
Illinois	28.3	26.9	1.4	—
Ohio	29.1	8.3	20.7	0.1
30 to 59.9 percent				
Washington	31.1	2.5	26.8	1.8
Kansas	31.7	18.4	5.4	7.9
Oklahoma	33.3	8.4	0.8	24.1
Colorado	35.9	5.8	9.0	21.1
Montana	36.3	1.3	2.0	33.0
New Jersey	43.7	10.3	24.4	9.0
New York	48.6	17.8	30.8	—
Vermont	52.2	17.7	34.5	—

TABLE 2—*Concluded*

State	Total membership	Farm Bureau	Grange	Farmers' Union
60 percent or over				
North Dakota	62.2	5.3	—	56.9
Maine	73.9	—	73.9	—
Connecticut	81.0	17.9	63.1	—
Massachusetts	86.0	8.1	77.9	—
New Hampshire	111.2	14.2	97.0	—
Rhode Island	143.7	41.7	102.0	—

* Because of the differing ways these organizations count memberships it was decided using farm population as a base would give the truest equation. Relative strengths per state are readily ascertained from this table.

fraternal, educational, and local community type of organization.[2] Figure 1 is presented as a preface to the discussion of how the channels of communication function in terms of adult education.

The hierarchical organization of the Grange is established by the fact that it is a fraternal order with seven degrees. The first four degrees are conferred by Subordinate Granges; the Fifth Degree is conferred by Pomona Granges, the Sixth Degree by the State, and the Seventh Degree by the National Grange. This same hierarchy of relationships provides the organizational machinery by which delegates are elected from Subordinate and Pomona Granges to state conventions and from State Granges to the national convention. It also provides the channels of communication by which each higher level in the organization assists the lower levels by the whole order. Jurisdictions are absolute in so far as fraternal work is concerned; they are completely democratic in so far as educational and other services and activities are concerned. This will be made amply clear in the following descriptions of each type or level of Grange organizations and activities.

The Subordinate Grange.—The Subordinate Granges are the basic units of the Grange organization in every way. They are the only units of the Grange hierarchy of which every Granger is a member. Together with the Pomonas, they are the arenas in which the basic issues of rural life which receive consideration at state and national conventions are first discussed. Subordinate Granges are local community organizations which State and National Granges serve. In addition, each Subordinate Grange is a local community organization in its own right. As such it promotes any program which is considered good for its members or for the community in which it is located. It elects its own officers (which are prescribed by the charter granted by the National Grange) and controls its own affairs in all local matters. The Subordinate Grange receives ideas and assistance in implementing them from its Pomona, State and National

[2] C. W. Gardner, *The Grange, Friend of the Farmer*, Washington: The National Grange, 1949.

Granges, but outside of following the ritualistic requirements of the national fraternal order of which it is automatically a part, it carries on its activities in its own way. It must have the prescribed officers but may appoint any committees and initiate any activities which it deems necessary or desirable.

It is in the so-called "lecture period" of each Subordinate Grange meeting that the chief educational activities are carried on. With the exception of the Master, and many would not make this exception, the Lecturer is the most

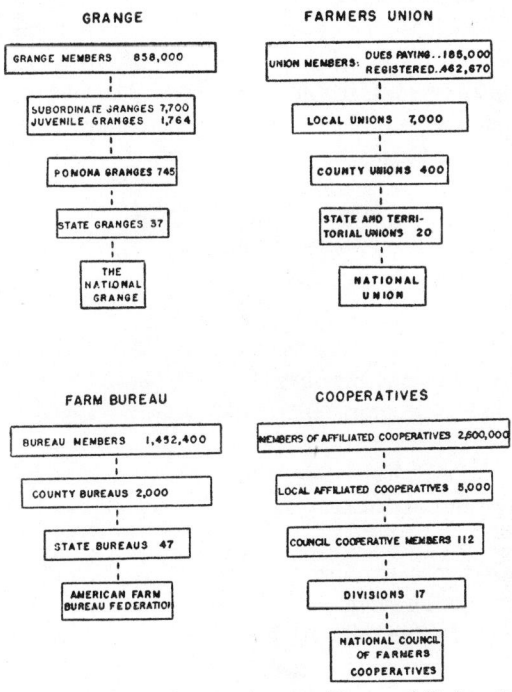

```
           GRANGE                           FARMERS UNION
  ┌──────────────────────┐          ┌──────────────────────────────┐
  │ GRANGE MEMBERS 858,000│          │UNION MEMBERS: DUES PAYING..185,000│
  └──────────┬───────────┘          │               REGISTERED 462,670│
             │                      └──────────────┬───────────────┘
  ┌──────────┴───────────┐                         │
  │SUBORDINATE GRANGES 7,700│          ┌───────────┴────────────┐
  │JUVENILE GRANGES   1,764│            │  LOCAL UNIONS  7,000   │
  └──────────┬───────────┘            └───────────┬────────────┘
             │                                    │
  ┌──────────┴───────────┐            ┌───────────┴────────────┐
  │ POMONA GRANGES 745   │            │  COUNTY UNIONS  400    │
  └──────────┬───────────┘            └───────────┬────────────┘
             │                                    │
  ┌──────────┴───────────┐            ┌───────────┴────────────┐
  │  STATE GRANGES  37   │            │ STATE AND TERRI-        │
  └──────────┬───────────┘            │ TORIAL UNIONS  20       │
             │                        └───────────┬────────────┘
  ┌──────────┴───────────┐                         │
  │        THE           │            ┌───────────┴────────────┐
  │     NATIONAL         │            │       NATIONAL          │
  │      GRANGE          │            │        UNION            │
  └──────────────────────┘            └────────────────────────┘

         FARM BUREAU                          COOPERATIVES
  ┌──────────────────────┐          ┌──────────────────────────────┐
  │BUREAU MEMBERS 1,452,400│          │MEMBERS OF AFFILIATED COOPERATIVES 2,600,000│
  └──────────┬───────────┘          └──────────────┬───────────────┘
             │                                     │
  ┌──────────┴───────────┐          ┌──────────────┴───────────────┐
  │ COUNTY BUREAUS 2,000 │          │LOCAL AFFILIATED COOPERATIVES 5,000│
  └──────────┬───────────┘          └──────────────┬───────────────┘
             │                                     │
  ┌──────────┴───────────┐          ┌──────────────┴───────────────┐
  │  STATE BUREAUS  47   │          │COUNCIL COOPERATIVE MEMBERS 112│
  └──────────┬───────────┘          └──────────────┬───────────────┘
             │                                     │
  ┌──────────┴───────────┐          ┌──────────────┴───────────────┐
  │  AMERICAN FARM       │          │      DIVISIONS  17           │
  │  BUREAU FEDERATION   │          └──────────────┬───────────────┘
  └──────────────────────┘                         │
                                     ┌─────────────┴────────────────┐
                                     │     NATIONAL COUNCIL          │
                                     │       OF FARMERS              │
                                     │      COOPERATIVES             │
                                     └──────────────────────────────┘
```

FIG. 1. Organizational charts for the Grange, Farmers' Union, Farm Bureau, and Cooperatives.

important officer in the Subordinate Grange. Other than the official business which must be transacted, the programs of the lecture period are planned and staged by the Lecturer. These programs are part educational, part entertainment, part inspiration, part recreation.[3] The Lecturer may have assistants or may involve a number of individuals or sub-groups in planning and conducting programs, but is himself or herself the chief educational officer of the Subordinate Grange. Meetings are generally held every two weeks and each meeting is generally dedicated to one theme. Members come prepared to participate in group or panel discussions, essays, talks, or debates on a specific topic. At times, but not usually, an outside speaker is heard. The more universal practice is

[3] *Grange Lecturers Handbook*, Washington: The National Grange, 1948, pp. 6–10.

to utilize members as the participants and the good Lecturer involves, over a year's time, as many different members as possible.

All Juvenile Granges are under the jurisdiction of the Subordinate Granges. Most of them meet at the same time and at the same place, in a separate room, as the Subordinates which sponsor them. Some Juvenile Granges, however, meet at separate times and places, often in schoolhouses. The structure of the Juvenile Grange is the same as that of the subordinate; it has the same prescribed officers, its members pay dues, and it has an impressive ceremony of its own. In every way it is a training place for future Grangers and future citizens. Its membership is restricted to those between the ages of five and fourteen and the children of all persons eligible to membership in the Subordinate Grange are eligible to join the Juvenile Grange. Programs are adapted to this age group. The Subordinate Grange designates one of its members as Patron or Matron of its Juvenile Grange, who in addition to affording general supervision, renders special assistance to the educational officer.

The Pomona Grange.—Only members of Subordinate Granges can be members of Pomona Granges. All Fourth Degree members in good standing in any Subordinate Grange within the jurisdiction of a Pomona Grange are eligible for election to membership in that Pomona Grange. Each must, however, be nominated or approved by two Pomona members of his Subordinate. The jurisdiction of each Pomona Grange is geographic, generally covering a county. It is the duty of each Pomona Grange to assist the Subordinate Granges under its jurisdiction in the social, educational, legislative, and business interests of the Order. Recently the services and assistance have been strengthened and increased, especially the lecture services.

The Pomona Grange is organized exactly like a Subordinate Grange. The prescribed officers are the same and the Lecturer is the same important educational officer as in the Subordinate Grange. He or she, however, has the additional responsibility of rendering all possible assistance to Subordinate Lecturers in the jurisdiction of the Pomona. Representation of Pomonas at State Grange conventions is the same as that of Subordinates. The major differences between Subordinates and Pomonas are that the members of all Pomonas are mature Grangers and their projects are concerned with units larger than local neighborhood or community areas. The Pomona Granges generally meet only once a month while Subordinates meet every two weeks.

The State Grange.—State Granges hold only one full delegate convention a year, but many have additional conferences, institutes, or workshops for Deputies, Lecturers and other responsible Subordinate and Pomona officials. The State Granges are composed of officers and their wives or husbands, all past Masters and their wives, and delegates elected from Subordinate and Pomona Granges.

The prescribed officers of the State Grange are the same as those prescribed for Subordinate and Pomona Granges. The State Lecturer as the chief educational officer, however, functions in quite a different role, namely that of rendering leadership and assistance to Subordinate and Pomona Lecturers and their programs. Some outstanding examples of how this role is played will be presented in the next chapter.

While the official body of the State Grange convention is composed only of voting delegates, many other Subordinate and Pomona officials attend in order to participate in conferences, workshops, or "associations" composed of those who hold similar offices in Subordinate and Pomona Granges. All candidates for the Sixth Degree must be present for part of the convention because only State Granges can confer this Degree. Many other Grangers attend to hear the programs and observe the procedures. Approximately 1,200 were in attendance at the 1951 New York State Convention, and more than 1,000 at the 1951 Ohio State Convention.

At state conventions, resolutions are passed which become the policies of the organization, and broad statements are formulated which reflect attitudes on economic, social, and even political issues. Such statements and resolutions are published in official organs, quite often in separate bulletins or leaflets, and through these instruments and the State Lecturers, travel down the organization's channels of communication to become program materials for Subordinate and Pomona Granges.

The National Grange.—The National Grange held its 85th National Convention in November, 1951. This convention is a delegate body, the voting members being the State Masters and their wives. Like State Grange conventions the National Grange is attended by hundreds, many times by thousands of other Grangers. The conventions are generally in constant working session for nine or ten days, during which time the work of all Grange states and of all officers and standing committees is reviewed. The address of the National Master is heard and considered, and resolutions are passed. Conferences of various state officers are held in which ideas are exchanged and debated. In terms of education and educational processes, the whole field of agriculture, rural life, and public issues is considered by various committees and finally by the delegates. The ideas presented, conclusions reached, and statements formulated travel back down organizational channels to State, Pomona, and Subordinate Granges, where most of them originated.

In addition to the Journal of Proceedings, two major pronouncements, the address of the National Master, and the Resolutions passed by the convention are issued for the consideration of the general public. These might very well be described as the statesmen's pronouncements of the Grange. They deal with foreign policies and all important international issues, with domestic economic issues and policies, with broad agricultural problems and issues, with national welfare and public ethics. All such statements, even the address of the National Master, are winnowed by committees and in open delegate session and finally crystallized by an orderly and democratic process. None of these statements is an edict to subsidiary units of the Grange; the impact and final influence depend solely upon the extent to which they influence the programs and activities of Subordinate and Pomona Granges and influence the opinions, attitudes, and behavior of individuals. The fact, however, that members are loyal to and proud of their membership in the Grange makes them especially receptive to the intent and purposes of all such statements. Thus, they are led to consider many broad issues to which their otherwise busy lives would keep them from giving attention.

THE FARMERS' EDUCATIONAL AND COOPERATIVE UNION

The Farmers' Union was founded in 1902, reached its height in membership around 1913, declined somewhat between then and 1920, and has increased steadily in membership and influence since that time. Until 1913, the Union was almost entirely a southern (Cotton Belt) farmers' organization, although it did by that time have some strength in Kansas and Nebraska in the Middle West and California in the Far West. North Carolina at that time was the Union's greatest center of strength. From 1915 to 1919 North Carolina in the South and Kansas and Nebraska in the Middle West contributed more than fifty percent of all dues paid to the National Union. Since 1920 the center of strength of the Union has been in the Great Plains.[4]

The Union was at first a fraternal order but quite early abandoned all ritual. However, it has never abandoned its original purpose to give prime attention to education and cooperation. The Union's motto is, "To secure equity, establish justice and apply the Golden Rule." Its widely used symbol is a triangle, with "Education," "Cooperation," "Legislation" on the three sides and "Organization" in the center of the triangle.

From the organization chart, Figure 1, the reader can see the normal channels of communication over which ideas flow from local and county unions to the state and national unions, and from the national and state unions down to farmer members. Anyone not acquainted with the strong loyalty of farmer members to the purposes and programs of their general class organizations may not understand the great potential that these educational channels provide. The flow over these channels, through the delegates from local and county unions to state and national conventions, is the process by which farmers' opinions and attitudes get crystallized into carefully formulated organization policies. The flow back down these channels to the local and county unions of these policy and opinion statements and the flow of aids which the national and state offices provide through these channels are the basic educational processes of the organizations.

The channels of communication are less formal than those of the Grange since the procedures are not prescribed as specifically as in a fraternal order.

[4] Carl C. Taylor, et al., *Rural Life in the United States*, New York: Alfred Knopf, 1949, Chapter 29.

Because of this there is less surety in communications, but there is greater opportunity to by-pass organization machinery and communicate directly from national and state levels to local and county organizations.

The Local Union.—The National Union Constitution prescribes that five farm families can petition for a local charter.[5] There were in 1951, 7,000 local unions with a dues-paying membership of 185,000. This figure does not, however, measure the membership strength of the organization because all members of the dues-paying family, fourteen years of age and over, are also members of the Farmers' Union. Family members are specifically recorded and counted in the prorationing of delegates in other official affairs of the organization. As will be seen later, they are all involved in the work of the Union and all served by its program. The total registered membership of the Union is approximately 500,000.

The local union does not have a formal educational officer such as the Lecturer in the Subordinate Grange, but always has a chairman of the educational program, usually one of the elected officers. Quite often a program or "action" committee is appointed to guide and stimulate educational activities. On this action committee is the educational director, the cooperative director, the legislative director, and the regularly elected officers. The amount and effectiveness of the educational activities of the local union depend on this important committee.

The local union meets once a month and attempts to operate as a complete community organization, including in its program of activities not only education, but recreation, entertainment, cooperative business, and community improvement projects. Each local union has a junior division. The educational director is responsible for the junior program and may divide the juniors into two or three groups, each with a sponsor or leader. As will be seen in the following chapter, the educational programs in some junior divisions are exceedingly well planned and carried out. Awards are made for specific attainment, the junior being given the merit title of "Torch Bearer" after completing a prescribed amount of project work. He is also awarded a $1,000 life insurance policy with a year's premium paid at the end of his first year of approved work. Each succeeding year he can earn one-half of the annual premium by completing approved projects.

County Unions.—Any three organized local unions may petition for a county union charter. Once a county union is formed, it becomes a sponsor and stimulator, although not an organic supervisor, of all local unions. The county union also often assists in organizing additional local unions in the county. Because the county union's membership is larger and because it represents a larger geographic area, it can and does sponsor more of the cooperative business enterprises and more county-wide improvement projects. Its program and cooperative directors use and assist their counterparts in the local unions in carrying

---

[5] *Handbook for Farmers Union Locals*, p. 2.

out many union and community projects. There were in 1951, 400 county unions. In North Dakota every county in the state has a county union.

State Unions.—A state union may be formed when there are as many as 5,000 dues-paying members of local or county unions within a state. There were in 1951, 20 state and territorial unions.

The strongest state union is in North Dakota, and its organization and program of activities therefore best illustrate the relations of a state union with local and county unions in one direction, and with the national union in the other direction.

North Dakota has 38,000 members, approximately twenty percent of all the dues-paying Union members of the United States. It has 450, or about $6\frac{1}{2}$ percent of all local unions. In some counties as many as ninety percent of all farmers belong to the Union. The members of the N. Dakota State Union own a great deal of cooperative business property, filling stations, grain elevators and other storage facilities, lumber yards, etc. Since the purpose here is to describe only the educational program of this State Union, only descriptions of those properties in terms of their educational functions are presented. There are two substantial buildings at Jamestown, the State Headquarters, the Central Office and Conference Building, and the Insurance-Radio Building. The State Union also owns a camp near Jamestown.

The Central Office-Conference building has an auditorium, equipped for sound movies which seats 500; a dormitory which accommodates 40 persons; a kitchen and dining room, and a library. Many conferences, usually five days in length, Monday through Friday, use these facilities. Such meetings include member conferences, usually men and women separately, junior conferences, and county and local officers' conferences. These conferences are held to discuss local organization and program techniques, cooperatives and other businesses, but they give much time to discussing the problems of agriculture, problems of other sectors of the national economy, and national and international issues.

Five camp conferences are held each year, generally for youth and/or women. The average attendance per camp conference is 90 and the period, two weeks. These camps are efficiently organized and conducted, with a camp director, a camp manager, a recreational director, camp instructors, camp cooks, camp secretary, dean of boys and dean of girls. These staff members all assist in a group leadership program and the camp instructors direct regularly scheduled class or discussion groups.

The radio director conducts a thirty-minute program from 7:00 to 7:30 A.M. six days a week, the programs consisting of United Press and Northwest News and the "Farm Bulletin." A wide range of topics, from Farmers' Union news and shop talk to United Nations and other world news and issues, are discussed.

The director of the radio program is also editor of the *North Dakota Farmers' Union Action Bulletin*. This bulletin is sent each month to the 3,500 action officials and is primarily designed to aid local and county unions in planning and conducting programs. The official organ of the State Union, *The North Dakota Union Farmer*, is sent to all members twice a month, most of whom also receive the *Grain Terminal Association Union Herald*, a monthly magazine.

The Educational Division of the State Union renders personal service to county and local unions by way of appearing on programs, and almost everyone at headquarters from the two field men and six field women to the state president, participates in this type of service. This division also circulates discussion materials, songs, skits, and reference materials. It has built up a small, carefully selected library of books, bulletins, and clippings from which loans are made free of charge, except postage, to any member of the Union anywhere in the state. These materials together with program outlines and suggestions on content materials carried in the *Action Bulletin* are all designed to help in the educational program of the organization.

The National Union.—The National Farmers' Union is composed of all members of local, county, state and territorial unions. Most members are, of course, members of each type of subsidiary, but need not be, for individual membership is direct. All those members of families who are listed as dues-paying members are also direct members of the National Union. As indicated by the organization chart (Figure 1), there are a number of subdivisions of the National Union—state and territorial unions, county unions, and local unions. State and territorial unions are the first subdivisions below the National Union. As was seen earlier, state unions consist of 5,000 or more dues-paying members. Territorial unions are found in those states or combinations of states which have fewer than 5,000 dues-paying members. Territorial unions are under the direct jurisdiction and are served directly by the National Union. Unlike state unions they do not have the right to regulate their own dues and fees or to regulate the dues and fees of the local unions in their areas. Groups of states may be designated as a state union and are known as a division.

The governing body of the National Farmers' Union is the Board of Directors, composed of all presidents of state unions. The President and First Vice-President are elected by the delegates at the biennial national convention. Other vice-presidents may be appointed, and the Secretary-Treasurer and an Executive Board of five members constitute the Board of Directors. The President and First Vice-President are also full voting members of the Executive Board.

Delegates to the biennial convention are allotted on the basis of one to each 5,000 (or major fraction thereof) voting members in each state union, and one to each territorial union. In addition all members of the Board of Directors, the President and First Vice-President may be delegates. Delegate votes may be divided into fractions and distributed among as many persons as is desired. The National Union pays the expenses of one voting delegate for each 5,000 members. Thus the actual participating body at the convention may be quite large. The number of voting delegates at this time is approximately 80. The

Board of Directors must meet once a year and may meet oftener; the Executive Board must meet quarterly and may meet oftener.

Preceding each national convention, a Resolutions Committee of from seven to nine members, appointed by the President, meets in a session of four or five days to consider the great volume of resolutions submitted by state, county, and local unions, and even by individual members. Any member of the Union may appear before the Resolutions Committee or may speak on the floor of the convention. The convention proper is in session for four days.

The resolutions adopted and the broad policy statements formulated by the national convention deal with everything deemed good for the organization itself, but go far beyond this. They are pronouncements of all kinds on agricultural and rural life issues and on domestic and international issues. Just as they originated and were discussed in state, county, and local unions before they came to the national convention, so do they become program materials for meetings of these subdivisions following the national convention. Delegates in attendance at the convention and the National Union headquarters staff are prime promoters of the educational follow-up of the national convention.

The services of the national headquarters' staff are predominantly educational. These services are implemented by the Farmers' Union offices in Denver and Washington, by the publication of an official house organ, the *National Union Farmer*, which goes monthly to each member family, by a *Weekly Report*, two copies of which go to each local, by an action leaflet mailed to program committees of local and county unions, and by a number of other published program aids. Not only the National Educational Director, but also practically all members of the staff including the legislative representatives in Washington and the President, personally assist all subdivisions of the Union with their educational program. Special institutes, workshops, and camps are conducted, staffed, and subsidized to train state, county, and local union leaders and educational directors. In these institutes and workshops, educational techniques as well as source and content materials are developed. The following chapter will describe some of these contents and techniques of education.

THE AMERICAN FARM BUREAU FEDERATION

The American Farm Bureau Federation was founded in 1919; its thirty-third annual convention was held in December, 1951. It was formed as a federation of a number of State Farm Bureaus which were already in operation. The first of the State Federations was organized in Missouri in 1915. Other State Bureaus organized early were in West Virginia, New York, California, Minnesota, and Vermont. These five, plus seven other states, were invited by the New York State Federation to meet in Ithaca, New York, in February, 1919 to consider the formation of a national federation. This meeting was followed, nine months later, by a meeting in Chicago of twenty-nine states.[6] The American Farm

[6] O. M. Kile, *The Farm Bureau Movement*, New York: The Macmillian Co., 1921, Chapter 9.

Bureau Federation was launched at that meeting, on November 14, 1919. Its membership has increased steadily since that time and at the time of its 33rd convention stood at 1,452,410. Because Farm Bureau membership is always that of a family, it is conservative to estimate that its participants number well over three million farm people.

The following skeleton organizational chart, Figure 1, shows the way in which the American Farm Bureau Federation is built out of local, county, and state Bureaus and the organic relations of each of these levels to all others.

The County Farm Bureaus.—The most universal local unit in Farm Bureau organization is the county Bureau. In many states there are, however, township or community Farm Bureaus, or local Farm Bureau centers. Early in its history, the county Farm Bureau was described as follows: "A county farm bureau is an association of people interested in rural affairs, which has for its object the development in the county of the most profitable and permanent system of agriculture, the establishment of community ideals, and of the well-being, prosperity, and happiness of the rural people, through cooperation with local, state, and national agencies in agriculture and home economics."[7]

This is a broad description of the way a typical Farm Bureau still functions. In many counties there are local Farm Bureau centers below the county units. These, however, are not organic subdivisions of the county Bureaus. Each township or community Farm Bureau makes its own local program, discusses whatever issues and problems it pleases, and conducts any local projects which it deems worthwhile. It is in no way regimented by the county Bureau. County Farm Bureaus are not delegate organizations built up from township or community Farm Bureaus and, although the locals are accorded the privilege of nominating persons for election to the county Farm Bureau Board of Directors, the election of the members of the Board is in the open county convention.

County Farm Bureaus came into existence in many different ways, a number of them having been organized before there were any state federations. They have tended to become more of one type over the years as they have been federated into state organization, but each still has complete autonomy, except in such ways as it agrees with other county Bureaus in the state to perform certain functions. It must charge the dues agreed upon by the body of delegates to the state convention, must collect these prescribed dues and transmit to the state Bureau that share of each member's dues prescribed by the state Bureau's by-laws. Otherwise, it operates autonomously. Its county convention elects delegates to the state federation convention, and prepares, discusses, and submits to that convention any resolutions which it desires to have adopted.

In counties where there are township or other local Farm Bureaus, the county Bureau meets once each month; where there are no locals, it usually meets oftener. The county meetings are composed of all Farm Bureau members in

[7] M. C. Burritt, *The County Agent and the Farm Bureau,* New York: Harcourt Brace and Co., 1922, p. 213.

the county, each with equal privileges. The duties of the county Board of Directors and officers are prescribed by its own by-laws and are elected for whatever terms and by whatever procedures specified in these by-laws. The only thing prescribed by the State Bureau is the number of voting delegates each county Bureau may seat in the state convention.

In six states, laws require Farm Bureaus as sponsoring organizations and in three other states the name "Farm Bureau" is mentioned in laws providing for extension work. In six additional states, laws require that Extension have some sponsoring "association of farmers" and in at least four of these, Farm Bureaus are these associations. These practices, some of them prescribed by state laws, came into existence chiefly during the period of the first World War when the Agricultural Extension Service was being expanded rapidly and a drive was being made to organize farmers for an all-out production of food. In counties where membership is large, and especially where there are township or other local bureaus, farm bureau personnel provides many voluntary project leaders for various educational activities. As will be seen later, in some states, they have paid county workers of their own. In two states, Illinois and Iowa, Farm Bureaus provide approximately 40 and 20 percent respectively of total Agricultural Extension budgets.

State Farm Bureaus.—The state Farm Bureaus are federations of county Farm Bureaus. In the states organized early, the state Bureaus came into existence after a number of counties were already organized, but once state Bureaus were organized, they became the promoters of other county Bureaus. Each state, like each county Farm Bureau, makes its own program and manages its own affairs. Its Board of Directors is elected at the annual convention by delegates from county Bureaus, and it is, therefore, a constitutional link as well as an operative link between county Bureaus and the American Farm Bureau Federation.

Because of the pronounced decentralization of the whole Farm Bureau system of organization, state Farm Bureaus differ greatly in their form of organization and specific activities. Because of limited space, a brief description of only one of the oldest and strongest state Bureaus (Iowa) will be presented here. Iowa, in 1951, had 100 county Bureaus in its 99 counties, with a combined membership of more than 125,000. The membership dues were $10 per family. From these facts it can be seen that there were ample funds to carry out its many activities. Out of each member's dues, collected by county Bureaus, $5 is retained in the county and $5 is sent to the state Bureau. The state Bureau forwards national dues of 75¢ to the American Farm Bureau Federation. It is not the purpose here to describe any of the many business enterprises of this state Federation but to describe only its educational work and policy-making procedures.

Policies are made by the House of Delegates at the annual state convention, one representative being elected at the annual convention from each of the 100 county Farm Bureaus. (One county has two Farm Bureau organizations.) The policies are formed from resolutions submitted from county Bureaus, reviewed, debated, and synthesized by a resolutions committee appointed by the President, and submitted by this committee to the House of Delegates. Any Farm Bureau member in the state may appear before the resolutions committee and may speak on the convention floor, but cannot vote in either body. Once the resolutions are passed, they become the policies of the state organization and become part of the educational program of county Bureaus. The state convention also decides what resolutions it wants to formulate and submit to the American Farm Bureau Federation.

The chief educational services of the Iowa State Bureau are carried on by Organization, Research, and Information Departments. The organization Department, in addition to assisting in membership acquisition, supervising records and accounts and other organization chores, assists 81 county Farm Bureau field men and approximately 15,000 volunteer workers to carry on their promotional and educational programs. The Research Department works on problems and issues, the analysis of which provides information to leaders, members, and employees. It also maintains a reference library. The Information Department edits and distributes *The Iowa Bureau*, the official organ of the state Bureau, and two semi-weeklies, *The Spokesman* and *The World*, which provide news to daily and weekly newspapers in the state. Through the publication of pamphlets and other types of releases, and through films and film strips, the state Bureau provides educational materials for use in county and local bureaus. Because of the close relationship in the counties with Extension Service personnel who are carrying on programs of adult and youth education, these materials are made available to practically all communities in the state.

American Farm Bureau Federation.—The American Farm Bureau is a federation of state Farm Bureaus. Its stated purpose is "to correlate and strengthen the State Farm Bureaus and similar state organizations of the several states in the national Federation; to promote, protect, and represent the business, economic, social and educational interests of the farmers of the nation; and to develop agriculture."[8] Its "members" are State Farm Bureau Federations and State Agricultural Associations, its "associate members" are County Farm Bureaus and even individuals where no county Bureau exists, and its "affiliate members" are national organizations of farm women and farm youth.

The American Farm Bureau Federation is governed by a Board of Directors elected by the voting delegates at the national convention. This Board elects six of its members who, together with the President and First Vice-President, constitute an Executive Committee. The Board of Directors meets quarterly, the Executive Committee on call.

The procedures of the national convention indicate the democratic methods by which policies are made and the opinions and ideas from the large membership are registered. Resolutions, many of which originated in county conventions, are sent to state conventions, and then are sent to the national con-

[8] Kile, *op. cit.*, p. 120.

vention resolutions committee well in advance of the annual meeting. The resolutions committee is in continuous session for four days before the convention meets and also part of the time during the convention. The results of the committee work are submitted on the opening day of the convention, and four days later are taken up one by one for thorough debate. Any delegate may appear before the resolutions committee or debate resolutions on the floor of the convention. The Farm Bureau, therefore, believes that its policies are as nearly democratically derived as is humanly possible. Once adopted by the voting delegates of the convention, the resolutions govern the actions of the Board of Directors, the Executive Committee, and all employees. More important, they become the publicly stated judgments and ideas which then filter back down to all county Bureaus and members of the organization by means of educational programs.

In addition to the educational processes which operate through the organizational machinery thus far described, the American Farm Bureau Federation publishes *The Nation's Agriculture*, a 24-page monthly magazine which goes to all members, and the *Official News Letter*, a 4-page weekly which goes to 30,000 Farm Bureau leaders. In addition to these, pamphlets and circulars, some of the quite substantial bulletins on public issues, are published and widely circulated. Radio programs, participation of officials in all kinds of public meetings, and the staging of conferences, institutes, and workshops are also educational functions of the national organization. Examples of the contents and techniques of these educational activities will be discussed in the following chapter.

NATIONAL COUNCIL OF FARMER COOPERATIVES

The National Council of Farmer Cooperatives is the national and public representative and general policy-making organization for five thousand local, state, and regional farmers' marketing and supplies cooperatives in which 2,600,000 families participate. Membership in the Council itself is composed of 112 state and regional cooperatives, state councils and associates. The National Council was organized in 1929. Its purposes, as described by its Executive Secretary in 1951 are stated as follows:[9] "The National Council seeks to promote effectively the interest of agriculture by: (1) serving as a conference body through which farmers' cooperative associations can solve their mutual problems through the medium of self-help and coordinate their individual principles into an over-all policy; (2) advising the Congress and administrative agencies of government; (3) maintaining and defending the right of farmers to pool their economic resources by organizing and operating their cooperative associations to engage in the marketing of agricultural commodities or purchasing of essential farm supplies; (4) providing the means through which farmer cooperatives can be advised quickly and accurately of current national and international developments which affect the interests of farmers; and (5) pro-

[9] *Official Yearbook of the National Council of Farmer Cooperatives*, Washington, D. C.: The National Council of Farmer Cooperatives, 1951, p. 13.

viding a forum through which farmer cooperatives may develop a better understanding and a stronger bond of friendship."

Figure 1 describes graphically the operational structure of the Council of Farmers' Cooperatives and its member organizations. A local cooperative normally relates itself to the governing body through channels which follow hierarchical lines represented in this organization chart. A local cooperative may, however, have direct contact with the national office and does in fact receive direct assistance from the national office as well as from state councils or regional and state cooperatives. Each cooperative obtains membership in or affiliation with the National Council by submitting to the Council its articles of incorporation and by-laws and its marketing and purchasing agreements. These must meet the requirements of the by-laws of the Council. Each applicant must also satisfactorily answer a questionnaire supplied by the Council. After attaining membership, its participation in the Council, both in financial obligations and in delegate rights and responsibilities, is in accordance with its volume of business. The services it received will be made clear in the discussions of the National Council and state councils.

THE NATIONAL COUNCIL

The National Council consists of the delegates from its member cooperatives. Its governing body is composed of 53 Directors elected from its 17 Divisions, each Division being a state or regional federation of from 2 to 23 cooperative units. The Division nominates candidates to represent them, but election is by the delegates to the national convention. The Board of Directors elects the President, two Vice-Presidents, the Executive Secretary, the Treasurer, and the Executive Committee of the Council. The Executive Committee of 17 is composed of one member from each Division. The National headquarters staff is small, consisting of only the Executive Secretary, the Assistant Secretary, the Attorney, the Secretary of the Farm Products and Supply Division and the Director of Information.

It is at the annual convention that all Council policies are made. Chief items for the agenda come out of the deliberations of standing committees, each of which holds sessions at the time of the annual conference and sometimes additional sessions between conferences. Recommendations are referred to the conference Resolutions Committee, composed of the chairmen of the standing committees and a representative of each of the 17 Divisions. From the Resolutions Committee, they go to the delegate body for discussion and approval. Once approved, the resolutions become the policy of the Council.

The educational work of the Council is its most important function, and while it naturally renders service to the business operation of cooperatives, its function is basically educational and policy-making. The function of the State Councils, of which there are 26, is also basically educational. Their educational work includes holding institutes for in-service training clinics on operational problems, and constant counsel on all functions of member cooperatives. They hold meetings and conferences with county agents, vocational agricultural and veterans' training teachers, and other operators of and specialists in adult education techniques. Recently, special emphasis is being placed on youth education by member cooperatives.

The relations and cooperation of the Council with the American Institute of Cooperation is so close that in educational programs they are almost one. The Institute purpose is to promote research and disseminate information concerning cooperation. This work has particular reference to the economic, social and legal phases of cooperation. The American Institute of Cooperation is the chief educational agency and the National Council of Farmer Cooperatives functions as a national conference and action agency for the farmers' cooperative movement.

More than one-half of some 10,000 farmers' cooperatives in the United States are affiliated with the Council in ways that have been briefly described here. The most consistent channel of communication between farmers' cooperatives is the National Council of Farmer Cooperatives. By means of its annual national conference and committee deliberations, policy statements are formulated out of and on the basis of issues and ideas sent up through its channels of communication with cooperatives all over the country. By word of mouth of those who participate in the conference and by publications, especially the *Annual Proceedings* and *The Blue Book*, these policies are relayed to member cooperativer and individual farmers. By means of *The Washington Situation*, a mimeographed bulletin, *The Legislative Digest*, issued while Congress is in session, news releases, various *Information Pamphlets*, and through radio programs, these policies are given more frequent and wider publicity. The State Councils, working constantly and more intimately with member cooperatives and various other farmer groups and educational agencies, are the grass roots ends of the channels of communication and education.

State Councils.—As was shown in the organization chart, the next typical links below the National Councils are State Councils and regional and state cooperatives; below them local cooperatives. The diversity of types of local cooperatives is so great that no attempt is made here to describe them. The state and regional cooperatives are also quite different one from the other, and furthermore are for the most part engaged chiefly in economic activities. State Councils are more purely educational in purpose. A brief description of one of them (Wisconsin) is presented below.

The Wisconsin State Council of Agricultural Cooperatives was formed in 1926, three years before the National Council was organized. From the beginning it was a council of farm organizations and educational institutions and agencies. From its early days the Wisconsin Council has been concerned with keeping its own membership active in planning proposals for, and means of education. The Wisconsin Council does not act solely as a communication channel between local cooperatives and outside resource agencies but rather that the council itself is a resource agency for its membership.

In 1950, 89 farmers' marketing and supply cooperatives were members of the State Council. They represented more than 500 local farmers' cooperatives with a combined membership of more than 100,000. The services of the State Council to these locals include assistance in all phases of cooperative operation and business efficiency, but its educational programs go far beyond these aims. The State Council's recently stated purposes indicate its intentions. The next chapter will present a few illustrations of activities which implement these intentions. The State Council's objectives with reference to education are concerned with developing understanding between farmer cooperatives, to improve cooperative education, to conduct educational programs with farm youth, to obtain better understanding of cooperatives among business or other non-cooperative groups, and to work with state and federal agencies in the interests of Wisconsin farmers.

A year later the Wisconsin Council stated that it had distributed 28,800 copies of *The News Letter*, a four-page semi-monthly, to its members, 5135 "special releases" to directors and managers, prepared 37 radio releases, and 1338 newspaper releases. It had sponsored 14 Young Farmers' Conferences in cooperation with the State Department of Agriculture and the State College of Agriculture, with a combined attendance of more than 3,000. It also sent two carloads of Wisconsin youth to the Summer Institute of Cooperation at Logan, Utah. These are illustrations of the Council's activities.

The Council has a headquarters staff of only three members, the Executive Secretary, the Assistant Executive Secretary, and the Treasurer. But because these officers and the whole organization tie in so closely with and make such great use of the various levels of institutional education, agencies of adult education, all types of farmers' volunteer organizations, and even labor and business organizations, they are able to accomplish many things which could not be done by a larger staff, and which they would not feel justified in supporting financially out of membership dues.

Some of the regional and state cooperatives maintain full staffs which engage in educational activities similar to those of State Councils but none of them are as purely educational in purpose as are the State Councils.[10]

                Carl C. Taylor
                Division of Farm Population and Rural Life
                Bureau of Agricultural Economics
                Department of Agriculture
                Washington, D. C.
                and
                Wayne C. Rohrer
                Department of Sociology and Anthropology
                Michigan State College
                East Lansing, Michigan

---

[10] Since this and the following chapter are integrated, conclusions and bibliography will appear at the end of the subsequent chapter.

Chapter 5:

ADULT EDUCATIONAL PROGRAMS OR ACTIVITIES OF THE GENERAL FARMERS' ORGANIZATIONS AND COOPERATIVES

In the previous chapter the description of general farm organizations and cooperatives emphasized their objectives and the structural channels of communication by means of which members are involved in organizational activities. This chapter will deal with the content and techniques of adult education which flow through these channels of communication.

Most of the material for this chapter comes from field interviews or mail questionnaires. The authors conferred at length with the national officers and headquarters staffs of the organizations, visited ten state headquarters, and attended one or more local meetings of each general farm organization. Contents of completed post card questionnaires yielded most of the quantitative data presented in this chapter.[1] The authors also studied volumes of published materials provided by the organizations.

SOME GENERAL CONSIDERATIONS

It is impossible to understand and appreciate the great potential for and the actual accomplishment of adult enlightenment on the part of millions of Americans who participate in general farmers' organizations and cooperatives, without understanding the genius of these organizations. Participation in the organization is voluntary. They are not manned by a giant corps of professional employees. They are self-supported, self-manned voluntary associations of persons who attempt to gain specific objectives by means of organized self-help. One of their chief objectives is the development of an understanding of the economy, the culture and world of which the member and his organization are a part. Most of the active members of these organizations seek such understanding. In addition, the active members' loyalty to and sentiment for the objectives of their organizations makes them stalwart supporters and promoters of these objectives and ready listeners to all ideas expressed by them. The fifty or so employees of these organizations who were personally contacted for data, were unanimous in their conviction that adult education is a principal activity of farmers' organizations. Eighty-seven percent of the local leaders of farm organizations responding to the question said their organizations are doing adult education. To obtain information on programs or activities in the three fields of interest respondents were asked to indicate whether or not their organization had carried on programs in these fields in the past year.[2] About three-fourths

[1] The sample county technique has been fully presented in Appendix C.
[2] The three fields of interest are those adult educational programs or activities in the areas of international understanding for peace, understanding and strengthening the economy, and trengthening of democracy. These will be referred to as "the three fields of interest."

of the respondents indicate their local unit of a general farm organization is engaged in this kind of non-vocational adult education. One in six of the cooperatives were carrying on adult education in the three fields. A summary of these findings for the several farm organizations may be found in Figure 1.

The farm organization leaders specified over 200 programs that they considered as falling into the three fields of interest. Of this number, 30 percent were concerned with strengthening the economy, 27 percent with strengthening of democracy, 23 percent with international understanding for peace, and 20

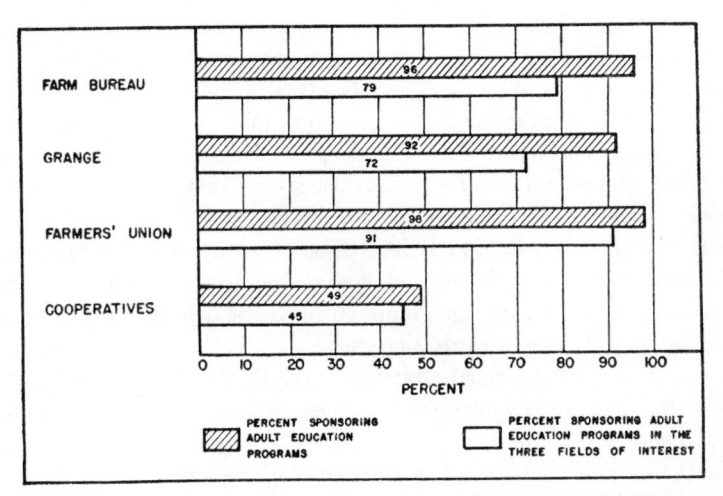

FIG. 1. Percentage of farm organizations and cooperatives reporting sponsorship of adult education programs in general and reporting sponsorship of adult education programs in the three fields of interest in the past EEar.

percent with related programs which could not properly be classified as any one of the three fields of interest.

These organizations' programs in the three fields deal more with economic than with the other concerns. The following are typical designations most often given by respondents: under economics—inflation, government agricultural programs, cooperatives; under democracy—the legislative process, structure of government, and organized discussion programs; under international understanding—study of the United Nations, visits of foreign students, talks by foreign persons or by Americans who have traveled abroad. The "other" category includes 26 specifications of "meetings." It is not known whether respondents meant by the "meetings" designation the form of program wherein such content are presented or if they meant that meetings *per se* are an activity which contributes to understanding and/or strengthening one or more of these fields.

The Audience.—In adult educational programs sponsored by these organizations, 76 percent of the respondents reported that the audience consisted of people living in the open country or in centers of 2,500 people or less. In terms of organizations, 76 percent of the Farm Bureaus, 69 percent of the Granges, 61 percent of the cooperatives, and 98 percent of the Farmers' Unions which responded are located in counties which are more than 50 percent rural. In an analysis of the data, classified by rurality, it was found that rurality is not a factor in determining whether or not an organization sponsors adult educational programs in the three fields of interest.[3] These data on rurality emphasize that no matter how rural a county is: (1) the chances are good there will be a local unit of a farm organization or cooperative present, and (2) this unit will be involved in an adult educational effort in the three fields of interest.

A complete analysis of age and sex structure of the organizations' membership was not attempted either in the field work or in the questionnaire. Therefore, the following statements are based upon judgment and cursory observation. Because the general farm organizations stress family participation in their activities, the audience is not restricted to segmentalized age or sex categories. However, family participation is less emphasized by cooperatives; thus the audience is more likely to be restricted to males. It seems safe to say that in terms of farm operators, the age group, 40–64 years, is best represented among the membership of these organizations.

A judgment regarding social stratification is that farmer members of these organizations are "successful farmers," those who produce a surplus for the market. Therefore, a number of rural people are not reached through these organizations. Some who are not reached are the Negro or white southern share croppers and laborers, the self-sufficient farmers of the Southern Appalachians or Lake States cutover region, and the migrant agricultural workers. Some 12,000 to 20,000 of the people in these areas are organized in the National Farm Labor Union (AFL).

The number of people reached in the adult educational programs of any one local unit of these organizations is not large. Fifty-six percent of the respondents indicate that their unit reaches less than two hundred people in their adult educational work. More than 80 percent of the respondents indicate that the audience is less than one thousand people. For those respondents who reported numbers reached in the best program in the three fields of interest the smaller size groups were more heavily represented than was true in the general adult program. For these programs, 63 percent of all respondents indicated that the audience was made up of fewer than two hundred persons.

In the educational work of these organizations the audience is not limited

[3] Using 1940 census data, rurality was determined by dividing the total county population into total rural population (rural farm plus rural-nonfarm) resulting in the percent rural population is of total population. The percentages responding that their organizations sponsored adult programs in the three fields, by rurality, are: 0–24% rural—74%; 25–49% rural—76%; 50–74% rural—77%; and 75% and over rural—75%.

to the membership. Nor do local units work solely with personnel of the particular farm organization. Other agencies are involved in supplying resource per-

TABLE 1
Numbers and Proportions of Respondents Reporting on Organizations with Which Farm Organizations Worked in Their Adult Educational Programs and Activities

Organizations worked with	Total Number	Total Percent	Farm Bureau Number	Farm Bureau Percent	Grange Number	Grange Percent	Cooperatives Number	Cooperatives Percent	Farmers' Union Number	Farmers' Union Percent
Total responding	909	100	404	100	307	100	78	100	120	100
Colleges and universities	290	32	169	42	68	22	27	35	26	22
Schools	408	45	180	45	153	50	24	31	51	43
Churches and religious organizations	384	42	160	40	163	53	14	18	47	39
Farm organizations	806	89	393	97	252	82	53	68	108	90
Cooperative extension service	658	72	351	87	185	60	44	56	78	65
Federal and/or state government bureaus	243	27	136	34	52	17	16	21	39	33
Elected or appointed government bodies	137	15	80	20	29	9	4	5	24	20
Community councils	207	23	121	30	47	15	8	10	31	26
Inter-agency councils	22	2	15	4	2	1	1	1	4	3
Civic and service organizations	240	26	116	29	82	27	13	17	29	24
Welfare councils	97	11	51	13	32	10	2	3	12	10
Libraries	120	13	31	8	71	23	3	4	15	13
Political parties and/or organizations	94	10	43	11	19	6	2	3	30	25
Professional organizations	53	6	30	7	17	6	2	3	4	3
Labor unions	55	6	12	3	1	0	1	1	41	34
Women's clubs	202	22	97	24	87	28	2	3	16	13
Patriotic and veterans' organizations	78	9	38	9	27	9	3	4	10	8
UNESCO organizations	14	2	6	1	2	1	0	0	6	5
Parents' organizations	163	18	74	18	66	21	3	4	20	17
Fraternal organizations	106	12	25	6	73	24	3	4	5	4
Other organizations	49	5	21	5	8	3	6	8	14	12

sons, materials, or as audiences for farm spokesmen. Without an exception these organizations work most often with farm organizations, followed by the Cooperative Agricultural Extension Service. See Table 1. A large proportion of the choices made by the Farm Bureau respondents are of the two categories mentioned, plus colleges and universities, and schools. Returns from the Grange respondents are more widely diffused, with most of the selections being given to the two categories noted above, followed by churches and schools. Farmers' Union respondents listed farm organizations and Extension Service most frequently, followed by schools, churches, and labor unions. The Cooperatives most frequently mention farm organizations and Extension Service, followed by colleges and universities, and schools.

TECHNIQUES OF ADULT EDUCATION OF THE FARM ORGANIZATIONS AND COOPERATIVES

Participation in Organization Meetings.—The most universal educational process carried out in local meetings of these organizations, is by discussion. The authors estimate that there are more than 30,000 local units of these organizations in rural areas of the United States. More than four-fifths of all respondents reported group discussion as the technique used in their local adult educational programs. See Figure 2. The lecture technique is quite popular but lectures are not highly formalized and do not eliminate discussion. The Grange lecturer, for example, is not so much a lecturer as a program planner and discussion leader. Table 2 shows "public meetings" and "conferences" listed more often than any other forms of programs. Apparently the discussion technique is used in such meetings.

The following are typical illustrations of local meeting techniques.

We attended a Farmers' Union local meeting in the area near Jamestown, North Dakota. The meeting was held on a farm in an area of sparse settlement. The meeting hall, which is in a farm building, is donated by the farm operator to neighborhood groups for meeting purposes. In attendance were a majority of the member families including their children. A local officer read the latest issue of the *North Dakota Farmers' Union Action Bulletin* to the group. Knotty procedural problems of the annual election were handled expeditiously by officers. Members displayed great ability in participating in the election process.

A feature of this meeting were talks given by the Director of Education of the North Dakota Farmers' Union and her husband, based on their recent trip to Israel. The talks, which were rather long and rapidly given, nevertheless held the attention of the members. One talk was historical-descriptive in telling of sites and scenes in the Holy Land, and the other talk related the story of Israeli cooperatives—their problems, successes, and lessons American farmers could learn from the Israeli experiences. Both travelers answered questions in informal situations during the refreshment period. The refreshments were prepared and served by young girls, which was an experience in taking responsibility and also a means by which they are made part of the local unit.

The Louisa County Farm Bureau's annual meeting was held in Wapello, Iowa. Rain, plus a competing Farm Bureau Services meeting, kept attendance low. An open discussion of resolutions framed by the County Resolutions Committee resulted in reversing some recommendations the committee had made.

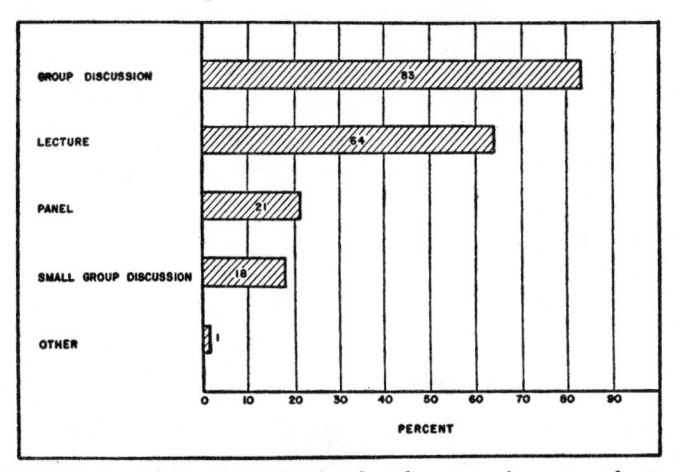

FIG. 2. Proportion of farm organizational and cooperative respondents reporting kind of meeting technique used in their adult educational programs and activities.

TABLE 2
Numbers and Proportions of Respondents Reporting the Form Used in Their Best Adult Educational Program or Activity

Form of program	Total Number	Total Percent	Farm Bureau Number	Farm Bureau Percent	Grange Number	Grange Percent	Cooperatives Number	Cooperatives Percent	Farmers' Union Number	Farmers' Union Percent
Total responding*	673	100	324	100	202	100	32	100	115	100
Conference	207	31	105	32	43	21	6	19	53	46
Workshop	75	11	30	9	20	10	2	6	23	20
Public meeting	567	84	271	84	162	80	27	84	107	93
Demonstration	128	19	59	18	50	25	7	22	12	10
Institute	43	6	21	6	8	4	2	6	12	10
Tour	97	14	54	17	11	5	3	9	29	25
Radio listening group	72	11	32	10	10	5	6	19	24	21

* Percentages do not add to 100 percent due to more than one selection on the part of respondents.

The Executive Secretary of the Iowa Farm Bureau talked about accomplishments of the Louisa County Farm Bureau and the Iowa Farm Bureau.

This case and the previously cited case illustrate a role played by organizational employees in that they frequently speak on local programs. At every county annual meeting an employee of the Iowa Farm Bureau will present information on the state organization, discuss relevant policy questions, and review the achievements of the past year. The Executive Secretary's talk covered these and in addition he gave vocational information relevant to the business of farming.

In the Ohio Farm Bureau there are 1600 Neighborhood Advisory Councils with 16,000 participants meeting each month for a discussion group program. About one-fourth of all members of the Ohio Farm Bureau participate in these discussion groups. Farm Bureau employees do not attend local meetings as discussion leaders or resource persons, but every month local discussion groups are provided a discussion guide by the state organization. The rationale for organizing these groups is that an autonomous local group will best serve the local community, the larger organization, and the nation by initiating local action. Most councils range in size from eight to twelve couples. The theory of organization used is that local people select the members of the group, thus achieving congeniality. Also meeting in members' homes contributes to this atmosphere.[4]

The State Organization.—The second level on the organizational chart is the state organization. In most instances, it is at the state level (regional level for many cooperatives) that local units are interrelated one with another into an established program. Members of local units of the farm organizations or cooperatives pool their resources to maintain state organizations. One function of the state organization is to contribute to local educational programs or activities.

The following are some typical illustrations of some educational programs or activities originated by state organizations.

In 1951 the Lecturer of the Massachusetts State Grange initiated a program in international understanding titled, "Our Friends Around the World." Each Pomona lecturer took a foreign country for study and presented a tableau to each subordinate Grange in the Pomona's "jurisdiction." Thirty-five of the thirty-six Pomona Granges in the state participated so that nearly all 50,000 members of the Massachusetts Grange saw such a program. There was considerable opposition to the program when it was proposed but face to face discussion and persuasion resulted in all but one Pomona lecturer joining the program. The technique used to interest Pomona lecturers was that of meeting in a Lecturers' Conference.

Procedures varied between Pomonas except that all made a flag of the country being studied and all had available a costume which was indigenous to the country. Government, economy, and customs of the country were studied and dis-

---

[4] For a more thorough treatment of the Ohio Farm Bureau's Neighborhood Advisory Council program see: Hutchinson, Carl, "Function of the Small Group in the Ohio Farm Bureau," *Autonomous Groups Bulletin*, Vol. IV, Nos. 2–3.

cussed in Grange meetings. A tableau was presented to the State convention in which costumes and flags of the 35 countries were displayed. Many diplomatic officials attended Grange meetings to speak about their home country. An unintended consequence was in the knowledge gained by many Grange members of the structure of political action in some countries. The state lecturer said one finding was the "ruling group of many countries (Egypt and Iran specifically) do not represent the people. The UN spokesmen do not represent people but represent governments."[5]

Representatives of 120 cooperatives affiliated with the Wisconsin Council of Agriculture Cooperatives met with the Future Farmers of 110 high schools, in a series of nine conferences. The program was a mixture of short talks, panel discussions, and student quizzes. (The whole program was on cooperation and cooperatives.) The youth were told about the history of cooperatives from the founding of the first Wisconsin cheese ring in 1841, through the struggles of the Grange and Wisconsin Society of Equity to present modern cooperatives, local, federated, and national. In terms of the short talk by the Executive Secretary of the State Council, they were told that "cooperatives have succeeded or failed in direct proportion to the need that caused them and their application of sound business principles"; that "successful democracy consists of a loyal, well-informed and participating citizenry."

The Iowa Farm Bureau Federation, an organization with 125,000 member families, has 100 employees, central office and field, all of whom do some work in adult education. None devotes all his effort toward these fields of interest but they are in constant contact with both local and state offices. In addition to personal contact, members are also mobilized for action through direct mail contacts, newspaper articles and radio. In determining policies, group discussion techniques are used at township, county, district, and state levels of the Iowa Farm Bureau.

The North Dakota Farmers' Union is a state organization with 38,000 member families. To obtain participation the state organization sponsors annual Members Conferences of County Union officers. These discussion meetings include sessions on the problems of agriculture, our industrial economy, and international affairs. The small group discussion technique is used in these meetings to increase participation of the 100–150 people present. The most effective educational technique for presenting information "in the three fields is done by face to face discussions. This is done largely by staff people."[6]

Consumers Cooperative Association of Kansas City is a regional organization made up of more than 1400 local cooperatives with 425,000 members. The organization staff includes 14 full-time employees in education and 70 who

---

[5] Personal interview with Mrs. Marion L. Johnson, Massachusetts State Grange Lecturer, Chelmsford, Massachusetts.

[6] Personal interview with R. C. Joyce, Secretary-Treasurer, North Dakota Farmers' Union, Jamestown, North Dakota.

devote part-time to this end. The Educational Section of the 1951 annual convention featured an application of group dynamics. The Educational Section was broken into subject matter groups. Participants in each group meeting were selected by drawing cards, thus insuring that (1) all groups were well attended and (2) all the participants in any one group were not of the "same cloth." The groups were informally structured with group singing as an icebreaker. Reports from these groups became the basis for resolutions on educational activities. By virtue of this technique "people feel the meeting is theirs. This is a step toward a two-way flow of communication."[7]

Following are some of the topics discussed and techniques of procedure used in the Citizen Leader Training School of the New York State Home Bureau Federation: Planning a county Citizenship Program (Testimony); use of State and Federal Taxes for Local Welfare purposes (Talk); how the school may help your community citizenship program (talk and discussion); how are leaders elected to town, village, county boards? (quiz and discussion); what characteristics do we want in our local government leaders? (panel discussion); methods of presenting citizenship information (discussion); town and county officers and their duties (panel); United Nations organization and operation (talks). Local Home Bureau leaders, land-grant college specialists, and government officials contributed content to the different sections.

A three day *Rural Youth Leadership Training Conference* held at Kentucky Dam State Park in 1949 brought together Farm Bureau youth leaders, the Bureau's state youth directors, and in addition staff persons from American Farm Bureau Federation and State and National Extension Services. Considerable time was given to "Farm Bureau Philosophy" and "Farm Bureau Organization," but one period for each of five sessions was given to "Education." In these periods youth were instructed on how to write, how to read effectively, how to carry on effective discussion, and do group thinking. All conceivable "Methods of Education"—talks, discussions, movies, tours, skits, etc.—were given attention toward the end of training leaders in better program methods in all levels of meetings. A summary of the conference was made available to others than Farm Bureau youth leaders. It was, however, forthrightly stated that only participation in such meetings in their own states and locals could reveal the dynamic educational value of these methods of education.

National Meetings.—In meetings of the national organization provincial beliefs are tempered to achieve national policy. This does not preclude disagreements which are numerous, but national policies are agreed to by participating members, and later executed by staff officers and state and local organizations. National meetings are in and of themselves educational. They are the arenas where active members, employees, and leaders can meet to scrutinize past action and plan for the future. Members from different areas meet and exchange ideas

[7] Personal interview with Cecil Crews, Educational Field Director, Consumers Cooperative Association, Kansas City, Missouri.

and directly communicate with one another. Employees and top organization leaders and outside speakers present food for thought to assembled delegate-members. It is at these meetings that policy is made based on resolutions formed by democratic procedures.

The Resolution Process.—In all these volunteer membership organizations, policy is made by the democratic and educational process of resolutions. Each organization lays great stress on this fact. Each has well ordered procedures by which resolutions are presented, debated, and finally approved. At each organizational level committees discuss and carefully frame resolutions dealing with local, state, national, and international issues. In the national conventions resolutions are again debated, refined and adopted. Once approved they become the policies of the organizations. These policy statements then travel back down the organization channels and become materials for program discussion in state and local meetings. Resolutions finally approved are distributed to members, and others, through newspapers, printed pamphlets, and by word of mouth at state and local meetings.

Resolutions become an educational technique in still another way. Inasmuch as formal resolutions cannot cover every issue and variations of issues and because resolutions are the basis for action following their enactment, leaders of these organizations must, in fulfilling their roles, interpret resolutions. Leaders' interpretations of resolutions stimulate members to think and act on matters of interest to the organization. Interpretation of resolutions culminating in action is of educational value.

Extra-organization Involvement.—The four national organizations treated in this report work together in the International Federation of Agricultural Producers. Each organization pays an equal share of the funds to support the IFAP, and each has one-fourth of a vote. This means that differences between the four American organizations must be resolved if the American farmer is to be consistently represented in the international organization. These organizations also serve together on advisory councils in national and international programs of the federal government. Through such involvements organizational beliefs are carried to a wide audience and each organization in time relays experiences and ideas thus gained down to its state and local units.

Institutes.—These organizations sponsor institutes, camps, workshops, and leadership training conferences for their leaders and employees. The Grange lecturers at state and national levels meet to exchange ideas on programs. A Grange workshop in Ohio calls on Grange leaders, State University specialists, and church leaders for information which helps local leaders plan and organize meetings. A Farmers' Union camp has classes on the problems of full employment, civil liberties, and rural health. Speakers are Farmers' Union employees, representatives of organized labor, the Anti-Defamation League, and the Urban League.

The American Farm Bureau Federation Institute is a meeting for "Farm

Bureau people in organization work." Speakers are Farm Bureau employees, land-grant specialists, specialists in sales training, and sales consultants. Farm Bureau philosophy, policy development, public speaking, discussion techniques are some of the subjects treated.

The Dairymen's League sponsors an annual Youth Leadership Institute for its Young Cooperators which is aimed at developing "an understanding of the philosophy of cooperation, also of the objectives, structure, and operation of the Dairymen's League. . . ." Techniques of conducting effective meetings is a course offering.

Aids in Program Planning.—These organizations have developed numerous program aids for assisting local people to carry on educational programs. Program aids contain content materials such as discussion guides on specific issues, or they may be directed toward the mechanics of local group functioning. Handbooks on how to conduct meetings, books of songs, dramatics, or other recreational activities are usually included. Program kits for local units are quite elaborate for the stronger state organizations. The Women's Committee of the Iowa FBF publishes individual booklets on foreign countries for study in local women's groups. Industries, educational systems, government, agricultural organization, language, and much other information is presented in these booklets. Discussion guides of the Ohio Farm Bureau Federation and Midlands Cooperative Wholesale and the Farmers' Union Action leaflets are program aids. Subjects treated in these program aids stimulate analysis of such problems as race prejudice, farm surpluses, the family farm. Embree's *Peoples of the Earth*, and an accompanying workbook is distributed by Farmers' Union for use in programs.

Institutes and training courses have program planning as the core of their interest. The Grange lecture system and the Lecturers' Conference illustrate the value placed on educational program planning in the Grange. Farmers' Union Action Committees and state Educational Directors perform similar roles in their organization. Field men of the larger cooperatives are often responsible for local educational programs. Consumers Cooperative Association of Kansas City, the Grain Terminal Association of St. Paul, and Midlands Cooperative Wholesale have field employees who participate in this way.

Assistance in planning local programs is given by state and national organizations. The report of the Summer Conference of the Iowa Farm Bureau Women states, "program planning is no one-woman job. . . ." In attendance were 96 voting delegates, 94 vice chairmen, and 50 home economists whose discussions "resulted in a program of activities that will be a challenge to women's committees in every township and county. . . ." At this conference women are given materials on FAO's program for expanding food production in under-developed areas, a report on the American Farm Bureau convention, the tax structure of Iowa, inflation, rural leadership, and establishment of health councils. State and national offices have libraries stocked with books of interest to Grange members. The Midland Cooperative Wholesale maintains a library of film strips which are available to any organization in its region. One film from its library was shown to 600 schools during 1951. The educational specialist functions as a resource person in making available to local groups relevant materials which will make programs meaningful for local members.

Program planning is carried on through printed materials distributed by the organization. The Lecturers' Column in the Grange monthly magazine and in the State Grange publications is widely used by lecturers of local Granges. Discussion guides do more than stimulate discussion; they are aids to program planning. Legislative reports contain a wealth of information on which local programs may be based. The Missouri Farmers Association has 1200 local legislative chairmen who regularly receive legislative reports which contribute to their Farm Club programs.

Participation Techniques.—It is a judgment of the authors that one of the most significant developments of techniques of participation are the group discussion programs of the Ohio Farm Bureau and Midlands Cooperative Wholesale which were mentioned above. Farmers' Union philosophy with respect to cooperatives is that "a cooperative is a training ground for democratic participation. Members have a right and a responsibility to attend the cooperative's annual meeting."[8] Training in socio-drama to enhance participation in discussion is given in the American Farm Bureau's National Institute and its National Rural Youth Leadership Training Conference and in the Farmers' Union Institute. The Ohio State Grange Annual Workshop devotes sessions to presentations of role-playing.

At a Juvenile Grange meeting (members between 5 and 14 years of age) the various officers, the Worthy Master, Overseer, Lecturer, Chaplain, etc., 13 of them have taken their stations, gone through the prescribed ritual, probably initiated some new members and completed their formal work. They come to the Lecture hour and stage their own program of recreation and education. A Matron or Patron has trained them for all these parts but most significant in terms of education is that they themselves develop ability to participate. There are in the United States more than 1700 Juvenile Granges.

The rationale for youth activity sponsored by these organizations is to develop in youths ability to participate. A Youth Council program gives youths experience in discussion groups. Youths become members of the Grange or the Farmers' Union at an early age. By youth sharing experiences with older members the young people "grow up" in the organization and become its stalwart supporters.

Tours and Exchanges.—These organizations sponsor domestic tours as a technique of education. The Iowa Farm Bureau sponsored two youth tours in 1951. One to the eastern United States and Canada mixed history and recreation

[8] Personal interview with Glenn Talbott, President, North Dakota Farmers' Union, Jamestown, North Dakota.

with gaining knowledge of farming in regions far removed from Iowa. The other was intra-Iowa tour on which youths visited outstanding farms, agricultural experiment stations, and industrial enterprises.

Farmers' Unions sponsor tours to Washington, D.C. In a week's time tourists are given information on UMT, farm prices, farmer committees in the USDA, valley basin development projects, as they visit Congress and executive departments of the Federal government. The Farmers' Union actively supports the Missouri Valley Authority and in this interest has sponsored tours to the Tennessee Valley development.

Consumers Cooperative Association and the Grain Terminal Association sponsor tours of their facilities. Two thousand members of local federated cooperatives of the Farmers Grain Dealers of Iowa Association visited its facilities during the past year. Local members of this Iowa Association are encouraged to bring clergymen, editors, or county agents as guests.

Foreign tours of Americans, and foreigners' visits to our farm organizations' national and state offices and outstanding cooperatives are important activities in achieving international understanding. The International Federation of Agricultural Producers is a means by which international understanding might be achieved. Tours are part of the program of the triennial conferences of the Associated Country Women of the World.[9] On returning from tours, members of these organizations speak of their experiences before farm groups or other interested groups. Farmers from other countries or student exchangees speak before local farm groups. One in five of the local units reporting had a foreign person on the program during the past year. Larger percentages of Grange and Farmers' Union than Farm Bureau or Cooperative respondents reported having foreign persons appear on their programs.

Legislative Activity as an Educational Technique.—These organizations regard legislative activity as so important that much of their research effort is devoted to matters in which legislative action is paramount. Employees that specialize in legislative activity take stands based on the organization's resolutions. Legislators, members, and the general public are informed of organizational beliefs and objectives through this activity. The structure must reach to the grass roots to effectively mobilize testimonials for or against legislation. Researches and regular legislative reports are channelled to local readers whose function it is to inform members on these issues. When taxation of cooperatives, new agricultural programs, price control legislation, etc., are being considered the farm organizations and cooperatives can arouse members to communicate with appropriate legislators.

Awards as Techniques of Education.—These organizations sponsor programs

---

[9] This organization's membership is 5,600,000 farm and village women of whom one-half are Americans. Its strongest member societies are in the United States, British Commonwealth of Nations, and the countries of northern and western Europe. Mrs. Raymond Sayre, Ackworth, Iowa, is president.

of awards by which organization beliefs are carried to the members and the public through participation of individuals or groups in essay contests, public speaking meets, community improvement projects, etc.

Some achievement programs of the farm organizations are aimed at developing individual ability and an understanding of organizational beliefs. The Farmers' Union Minute Man Project, Farm Bureau's Talk Meets, and a Farmers Grain Dealers of Iowa contest are public speaking meets for youths which give participants such understanding. The subject matter for the 1951 Talk Meets was international affairs. The Grange is interested in contests on the subjects of conservation and safety. The Farmers' Union Writers Project aims at developing writing ability and also to give the participant knowledge of social and economic issues. The best efforts submitted in these activities are publicized within the organization and in some cases, beyond the organization to the public.

The various awards given by the different farm organizations are prizes for accomplishment, but their object is not so much as rewards for accomplishment as incentives to action. The Grange awards for Community Service go to less than 200 subordinate Granges, the prizes ranging from $15,000 for first place in the National Contest to $50 for the last places in state contests. Nevertheless, 1700 Subordinate Granges entered this contest and almost certainly each of them were thereby motivated to greater efforts in behalf of their communities. A few sentences selected from the announcement of awards to be given and promotion of the contest will serve to illustrate both the educational techniques and contents of this program. One paragraph from the National Masters' letter announcing the 1952 awards, said, "America is really a family of communities. Like a chain, our nation can be no stronger than its links. It is therefore imperative that each of us as individuals make our own contributions, which we can most effectively make through our own Grange institution, toward building and supporting the finest sort of which we and our neighbors are capable."

Each Subordinate Grange is urged to "Survey the needs of your community. ... Check not only with your own members, but with other leaders in your community as to the needs and the priority you should give them ... Have a progress report at each Grange meeting ..." Space does not permit the many stories to describe accomplishment which have resulted. Enough has been reported briefly to describe the technique and something of the educational content of the award type of activity.

House Organs.—Each of these organizations has a newspaper which goes to its membership. Many cover a wide range of subjects including international affairs, the economy, and democracy. Generally speaking, publications originated by state and national offices are more general in content. *The Nation's Agriculture* of the American Farm Bureau, *National Grange Monthly*, and the *National Union Farmer* are house organs of the national farm orgizations. In every issue there are stories concerned with the three fields. Many organizations publish monthly or quarterly publications for local board members, field employees, and other persons in agriculture. *The GTA Digest* of the Grain Terminal Association in St. Paul is such a publication. This Digest does not deal solely with technical subjects, but attempts to get people to think broadly on such issues as land reform in Italy, famine in India, etc. The monthly magazine of the Ohio Farm Bureau is an example of a state level originated publication featuring abroad editorial and news policy. In every issue of 1951 there was at least one article in one of the three fields of interest.

The Mass Media.—Radio is used by these organizations. Some use it in the traditional business fashion in that news and market programs are sponsored. Top leaders of these organizations participate in radio discussions, thus informing members and the public of the organization's stand on public issues. Some of these organizations use radio as an educational device. The North Dakota Farmers' Union sponsors a daily half hour program which informs its audience of policy issues, general news, the United Nations, and features in which the Farmers' Union is interested. The Ohio Farm Bureau owns WEFD, a radio station whose coverage is greater than Ohio. Round table discussions between representatives of farmers, businessmen, industry and organized labor participate in some of the weekly discussions of current issues. Once a month WEFD devotes a half hour to airing a recording of a Neighborhood Advisory Council discussion. The Women's Committee of the Iowa Farm Bureau sponsors a weekly radio program over WOI at Iowa State College. Three programs in the summer and early fall of 1951 were devoted to international understanding. The eight-station Rural Radio Network is sponsored by the general and some specialized farm organizations in New York area. Its format includes a daily UN news report and many educational features.

In discussing mass media with employees and leaders of the various organizations they said that motion pictures are widely used in local meetings. Local Granges often have open public meetings when motion pictures are shown. Table 3 demonstrates the importance of this medium in local groups' educational programs. Second to films is the newspaper. The "other" category is dominated by magazines. Although we did not obtain names of newspapers or magazines used, we suggest that organization sponsored media are important in carrying content to local members. Organizations' newspapers or magazines devote much space to local happenings to maintain interest of local members. The urban-centeredness of television, and perhaps cost, is probably responsible for the low mention this medium receives.

Pamphlets in Education.—These organizations distribute through their channels of communication, numerous pamphlets on subjects of interest. An illustration of this technique for helping farm people understand an important but very complex domestic economic problem was a Farm Bureau pamphlet entitled, "Is Your Choice Inflation?" It was written on the level of school children and well illustrated. A few sentences from this pamphlet will illustrate how simply one basic issue was put across. "With inflation you soon find that you have to swap a lot of cheap money for a little of the valuable things you need." "Because of the plentiful flow of money and the smaller trickle of things to buy with it, we are willing and able to pay higher and higher prices, bidding against each other on every item for sale..." "But the ones whose incomes can't change are really left behind in the race." This pamphlet apparently proved to be a more effective educational instrument than a much more profound leaflet on Inflation put out by the same organization. Its distribution by the Ameri-

TABLE 3
Numbers and Proportions of Respondents Reporting on Mass Media Used in Adult Educational Programs and Activities

Mass media used	Total Number	Total Percent	Farm Bureau Number	Farm Bureau Percent	Grange Number	Grange Percent	Cooperatives Number	Cooperatives Percent	Farmers' Union Number	Farmers' Union Percent
Total responding*	677	100	309	100	235	100	34	100	99	100
Radio	191	28	92	30	37	16	17	50	45	45
Television	10	1	6	2	2	1	2	6	0	0
Newspaper	463	68	202	65	147	63	25	74	89	90
Films	511	75	221	72	200	85	15	44	75	76
Other	79	12	44	14	15	6	12	35	8	8

* Percentages do not add to 100 percent due to more than one selection on the part of respondents.

can Farm Bureau reached 100,000 and an additional 30,000 copies were distributed by Safeway Stores.

CONTENTS OF ADULT EDUCATIONAL PROGRAMS OF THE FARMERS' ORGANIZATIONS AND COOPERATIVES

Local Units.—Local units of these organizations discuss and act on issues whose content may be local, state, national, or international in scope. The Louisa County Farm Bureau's resolutions of 1951 covered local school and health programs, UMT, federal taxation, and foreign aid. A discussion group in Ohio talks about costs and administration of local welfare. A discussion group of a middle western cooperative talks pro and con on the UN, Point Four, the Marshall Plan. Women's Committees of the Dairymen's League use in their local programs, UN documents on Political Rights of Women, and the Universal Declaration of Human Rights. A subordinate Grange decides a public dumping ground can be made over into a roadside park. Farm Bureau women in Ohio and Washington meet with wives of urban workers to better understand the problems each has.

Rollins Grange of Lenawee County, Michigan, participated in the National Grange Community Achievement Programs. Lenawee County, Michigan, was selected as a pilot study for a national foundation-sponsored self-survey of health needs and resources. The action was motivated largely through formal organizations. Leaders of the Rollins Grange, which had been active in local civil defense activities as its community achievement project, saw in the self-survey a complementary activity to the civil defense work. This Grange gave impetus to the self-survey by being the first organization in the county to join in and complete its township self-survey. Its participation was publicized in county and nearby city newspapers and is credited with "kicking off" the total effort. Leaders of the Grange wrote and enacted a skit based on their interviewing experiences which also helped to interest other organizations in the self-survey. A further note on this action is contributed by researchers from Michigan State College, who observed the county action. All interviewers who participated in the county self-survey were female except in Rollins township, where men and women interviewed. This is a demonstration of the farm organization's emphasis on participation by family units rather than individual participation.

State Organizations.—The state organizations originate much of the materials which are content in local units' programs. One way state organizations work in education is illustrated by the "Save the Dollar Campaign" spearheaded by the Arkansas Farm Bureau. This state Farm Bureau involved thirty-five business and industrial associations in a statewide fight on inflation. Program kits were distributed to interested groups. These kits included prepared radio scripts, newspaper acticles, advertisements, and cartoons.

The Arkansas Farmers' Union has practiced democracy in local meetings and at state conventions by breaking down bars of racial segregation. Twenty-five percent of its members are Negroes. The state president says, "We never think of members as white or Negro; we think of them as people."[10] Negro and white delegates have attended the last three state conventions and banquets which were held in a first class Little Rock hotel.

The Missouri Farmers' Association has sponsored quite extensive research in rural health on the location in rural areas of medical doctors and other medical personnel. Findings in these researches are used to buttress the organization's campaign for improvement of rural roads since medical doctors are not readily available to rural people if roads are not passable. This organization favors construction of a new State Medical School and Hospital to increase the number of medical personnel available to Missourians. The Missouri Farmers' Asso-

---

[10] Personal interview with Albert Hopkins, President, Arkansas Farmers' Union, Little Rock, Arkansas.

ciation sponsors these medical developments because research findings showed that many Missouri-trained medical personnel practice in nearby states.

National Organizations.—The national organizations originate statements and resolutions which are content for educational programs. Typical statements, some of which are discussed in this section, go down the organization's channels to local units. For each of the four national organizations we have analyzed one document which is directed toward concerns in the three fields.

The American Farm Bureau has put tremendous emphasis on expressing its views on understanding and strengthening our economy. A few excerpts from a pamphlet published by this organization will illustrate content of an economic nature.

Price and wage controls are an ineffective and unworkable approach to the problem of preventing inflation; they are a clumsy and inefficient substitute for the automatic functioning of a free economy. They cannot possibly prevent inflation because they strike at the symptoms of the problem and not at its real causes. As a matter of fact, if a government were to decide to deliberately create an inflation, it would want first to put on price controls so as to conceal from the people, as long as possible, the fact that the value of their money was being destroyed.

If we really want to control inflation, and our national welfare demands that we do control it, we must do the following things:
1. Meet increased demand with increased production wherever possible . . . .
2. Eliminate all non-essential Federal expenditures and institute real efficiency in all Government activities, including defense . . . .
3. Continue to emphasize measures to restrain credit . . . .
4. Encourage increased private saving. This will be much easier to do if we adopt a realistic program to control inflation and thereby reassure our people as to the future value of present savings.
5. Continue to stress the sale of Government bonds to individuals and non-bank investors and take steps to prevent a further drift of non-bank held negotiable bonds to the banking system.
6. Manage the public debt so as to make a maximum contribution to price and economic stability instead of with the objective of keeping interest costs at minimum.
7. Finally, we must pay the bill through higher taxes.

It is an illusion to believe there is any other alternative, or to believe that price controls in any way contribute to the solution of the problem. If the bill is paid by taxes, people will know that they are paying it, and we will have the opportunity to distribute the burden equitably on the basis of ability to pay. At the same time, we can reduce the inflation threat by bringing consumer purchasing power more nearly in line with the available supply of consumer goods.[11]

To illustrate content whose theme is international, excerpts will be quoted from the National Farmers' Union, *Resolution on Building Strength for Peace, Prosperity, and Democracy.*

Farmers' Union believes that the guiding principles of our foreign policy should be the earliest possible attainment of a world brotherhood of prosperous democratic

[11] *Control of Inflation*, May 25, 1951, Statement of AFBF before Senate and House Committees on Banking and Currency, made by Allan B. Kline, President.

nations living at peace with one another under international authority with limited sovereignty.

There are today two major threats to true world brotherhood and peace.

One is the existence in the free world of uncorrected and indefensible evils which provide the seed bed for agitation, uprising, and revolt. The other is the fact that Russian rulers, instead of cooperating to end these conditions under free governments, have revealed imperialistic world aims and a determination to exploit every wrong for her own imperialistic purposes....

It is clear that time to establish freedom and equity must be bought by the creation of military as well as economic strength throughout the free world. For that reason, the Executive Committee endorses the full support which we have given to federal action to build these strengths outside the Iron Curtain.[12]

The National Grange.—The 1950 resolutions of the National Grange are prefaced by these Grange Guide Posts:

1. All prosperity springs from the production of wealth.
2. The compensation of each should be based on what he contributes to the general welfare.
3. The prime purpose of government is to protect its citizens from aggression—both physical and economic.

These themes are consistently carried through the resolutions which are cited:

Inflation:

Inflation robs the thrifty. It decreases purchasing power ruthlessly. To be indifferent to inflation is to be dishonest, but to treat symptoms of inflation and fail to attack the causes is futile and shows a lack of courage. Accumulation of government debt is a major cause of inflation.

The United Nations:

Our major objective in the field of international relations is to prevent aggression and build world peace.... The inability of the U.N. to agree upon all questions of policy and action is not so much a sign of inherent weakness as an indication of democratic structure, whereby the principles of freedom which we pride as the basis of our republic are being enlarged to a world-wide scope.

Communism:

We recognize Soviet-directed Communism as a dangerous threat to security of our nation and the peace of the world, and will support the following program of action:

1. Stimulate in all Subordinate Granges an active study and discussion of the purposes and methods of Communism, and promote programs of destroying its influence by reactivating the principles of our Order, our Republic, and Christianity....

Food and Agriculture Organization:

We believe that F.A.O. should be supported more liberally than heretofore and that it should emphasize extension work in improving the capacity of poorly fed nations to produce more food."[13]

[12] From *Resolution on Building Strength for Peace, Prosperity, and Democracy*, adopted by the Executive Committee of National Farmers' Union, July 27, 1951.

[13] Summary of National Legislative Policies and programs for 1951: The National Grange.

A statement of the Executive Secretary of the National Council of Farmers' Cooperatives is relevant to all three fields of interest of this study.

For five years, the Council has been active in the formation and promotion of agricultural policy designed for what we hoped would be a world at peace. We have advocated an expanding economy in terms of productivity and purchasing power per worker as the basis for a higher standard of living for everybody. We have promoted not only more efficient production of farm products, but also more efficient processing, handling and merchandising all along the line. We have recognized the need for good land management and conservation and for support programs at fair prices in line with current costs and consistent with desired trends and adjustments. We have urged and insisted that farm programs be kept sufficiently flexible to permit sound progress to take place at as rapid a rate as possible. We have advocated that government's prime responsibility with respect to agriculture should be that of: (1) stimulating and aiding basic research and an effective extension educational program; (2) providing incentives for voluntary adjustments in line with over-all objectives; and (3) "taking the shock" temporarily, where necessary, for those persons who are "victims of progress" in the sense that they must be helped to find new productive opportunities. We believe that government always should seek to minimize its "action programs" by encouraging farmers to solve their own problems for themselves on a voluntary basis. Farmer cooperatives are an important tool to this end.

For the most part, the broadening of the economic base within a country will have to be done by the people within such country acting to help themselves. Ideas, ideals and spiritual values are more important than money from outside sources. Any help from the outside, such as aid from the U.S. needs to be directed toward helping people to help themselves. It should never be in the spirit of buying their support.

I can think of no economic tool for self-help which is more potent than cooperatives. The smaller the productive units of an area and the more limited the available capital per person, then the more the need for a device which enables such people to pool their economic resources in a way which still permits each to retain his own personal freedom and autonomy. The cooperative is a natural for this purpose.[14]

SUMMARY

General farmers' organizations and cooperatives must be appraised in terms of what they are, namely, voluntary organizations which prosper only to the extent that they meet the economic, social and civic desires of their adherents. They attempt to meet these desires on all levels—local, state, national and international. Members participate in the organization's activities either because they gain pleasurable experience in self-expression and self-development, or because they gain economic and political objectives through organization.

In the tens of thousands of local meetings, hundreds of thousands of farm men, women and youth who may meet primarily for the first of these objectives, to some extent, become engaged in the discussion of issues which transcend local concerns. In and of themselves such discussions are educational. To the extent that adequate source materials and assistance in discussion techniques

---

[14] Statement of the Executive Secretary in the "Proceedings of the 1951 Annual Meeting of Delegates," National Council of Farmer Cooperatives, Chicago, Illinois, January 8–11, 1951.

are provided, they do intelligently discuss public issues and problems. In the authors' judgment, the upward flow of opinions and ideas, most effectively expressed in the process of resolution making, operates more effectively than does the downward flow of ideas and program aids. State and national officials are often concerned because local meetings do not always utilize the pronouncements and information issuing from national conventions and national offices. Members can be and are reached and influenced only by educational techniques. The educational programs must however, and do, go beyond training members in efficient organizational procedures. They operate to help farm people understand the whole economy and culture in which the organizations operate and which they seek to influence. All of their educational endeavors which are successful, therefore, are of great importance in a democracy.

The constant effort of these organizations is to involve an increasing number of farm people in their programs. The degree of success they have is a measure of their educational contribution. Participation in their activities and loyalty to the organizations themselves are the *sine qua non* of their survival and expansion. The effectiveness of their educational programs and techniques are equally the *sine qua non* of effective membership participation and loyalty. To the extent they can amplify and improve the content and techniques of their educational activities will farm people of the United States, relatively few of whom are effectively reached by other agencies, more thoroughly participate in adult education programs.

>Wayne C. Rohrer
>Department of Sociology and Anthropology
>Michigan State College
>East Lansing, Michigan
>   and
>Carl C. Taylor
>Division of Farm Population and Rural Life
>Bureau of Agricultural Economics
>Department of Agriculture
>Washington, D. C.

BIBLIOGRAPHY

A Selected List

The authors of the chapters on farmers' organizations and cooperatives have a bibliography of over 200 typewritten pages which illustrates the tremendous volume and diversity of literature in the field of general farmers' organizations and cooperatives. There are listed here per organization, only a few of the basic books and samples of types of other published literature.

The Grange

Books

Atkeson, T. C., *Semi-centennial History of the Patrons of Husbandry*, New York: Grange-Judd Company, 1916.

Buck, Solon J., *The Granger Movement; A Study of Agricultural Organization and its Political, Economic and Social Manifestations, 1870–1880,* Cambridge: Harvard University Press, 1913.

Gardner, C. M., *The Grange, Friend of the Farmer, 1867–1947,* Washington, D.C.: The National Grange, 1949.

Kelley, O. H., *Origin and Progress of the Patrons of Husbandry in the United States; A History from 1866 to 1883,* Philadelphia: 1875.

Martin, E. W., *History of the Grange Movement,* Philadelphia: National Publishing Company, 1873.

Publications of the National Grange, 744 Jackson Place N.W., Washington, D. C.

Journal of Proceedings of the Annual Sessions of the National Grange, for years 1874 to 1952.

National Grange Monthly.

THE FARMERS' UNION

Books or articles

Barrett, Charles S., *The Mission, History and Times of the Farmers' Union,* Nashville: Marshall and Bruce Company, 1909.

Brooks, T. J., *Origin, History and Principles of the Farmers' Educational and Cooperative Union of America,* Greenfield, Tennessee: National Union Printing Company, 1908.

Davis, A. C., *The Farmers' Educational and Cooperative Union,* Texarkana, Texas: Texarkana Courier, 1910.

Fisher, C. B., *The Farmers' Union,* Lexington: University of Kentucky, 1920.

Hunt, R. L., *A History of Farmers' Movements in the Southwest,* College Station: Texas A and M College Press, ND.

Knight, H. W., *Grass Roots—The Story of the North Dakota Farmers' Union,* Jamestown: North Dakota Farmers' Union, 1927.

Loomis, C. P., "The Rise and Decline of the North Carolina Farmers' Union," *North Carolina Historical Review,* Vol. III, No. 3, July, 1930.

Taylor, Carl C., et al., *Rural Life in the United States,* New York: Alfred A Knopf, 1949.

Publications of the National Farmers Union, 1555 Sherman Street, Denver, Colorado

Minutes or Proceedings of the National Farmers' Educational and Cooperative Union, published in various forms and at various places, 1907–1950.

The National Union Farmer (house organ).

THE FARM BUREAU

Books and articles

Burritt, Maurice C., *The County Agent and the Farm Bureau,* New York: Harcourt Brace and Company, 1922.

Kile, Orville M., *The Farm Bureau Movement,* New York: The Macmillan Company, 1921.

Hutchinson, Carl, "Function of the Small Group in the Ohio Farm Bureau," *Autonomous Groups Bulletin,* Vol. IV, Nos. 2–3.

Publications of the American Farm Bureau Federation, 38 East Washington Street, Chicago, Illinois

Annual Reports of the American Farm Bureau Federation, 1920–1951.

The Nation's Agriculture (house organ).

Pamphlets

Of, By and For Farmers, The American Farm Bureau Federation, ND.
Who Shall Speak for Farmers, The American Farm Bureau Federation, ND.
You and America's Farm Program, The American Farm Bureau Federation, ND.

NATIONAL COUNCIL OF FARMER COOPERATIVES AND OTHER COOPERATIVE ORGANIZATIONS
Publications of the National Council, 744 Jackson Place N.W., Washington, D.C.
  Blue Book—Annual Official Yearbook of the National Council of Farmer Cooperatives, 1951.
  Proceedings of the 1951 Annual Meeting of Delegates, Chicago, Illinois, January 8–11, 1951.
  The National Council of Farmer Cooperatives—What It Is and How It Functions, ND.
Publications of the Cooperative League of the U.S.A., 343 South Dearborn Street, Chicago, Illinois
  The Cooperative League Yearbook (Annual report).
  Europe's Cooperatives—As We Saw Them, Campbell, et al.
Publications of the Farm Credit Administration, United States Department of Agriculture, Washington 25, D.C.
  LeBeau, O. R., *Educational Practices of Farmer Cooperatives*, January, 1951.
  Abrahamsen, M. A., and Scearce, Jane L., *Handbook of Major Regional Farm Supply Purchasing Cooperatives*, 1948 and 1949, June, 1950.
  Wanstall, Grace R., *Statistics of Farmers' Marketing and Purchasing Cooperatives, 1947–1948*, March, 1950.
Some Publications of State or Regional Cooperative Organizations
  Dairymen's League News, Dairymen's League Cooperative Association, (issued biweekly).
  Midland Cooperator, Midland Cooperative Wholesale, Minneapolis, Minnesota, (weekly house organ).
  Eastern States Cooperator, Eastern States Farmers' Exchange, West Springfield, Massachusetts.
  The Cooperative Consumer, Consumers Cooperative Association, Kansas City, Missouri.
  Farmers' Union Herald, Farmers' Union Grain Terminal Association, St. Paul, Minnesota.
  MFA Cooperator, Missouri Farmers' Association, Columbia, Missouri.
  GLF Week, Grange League Federation, Ithaca, New York.

Chapter 6:

SERVICE, PROFESSIONAL AND OTHER CIVIC CLUBS

Introduction

Community Interest versus Special Interest Association.—The distinguishing feature of a community is that it is not organized for a single purpose. Its organization consists of the interrelations of various institutions and associations which are included in it. Traditionally, most institutions making up the different parts of communities function locally, that is, the area of participation or interaction has been confined to a limited territory, but most modern organizations have grown to the point where they extend beyond the local community. Broader modes of organization tend more or less to parallel the governmental structure composed of towns, townships, counties, states and nation and more recently, inter-nation. The spread of institutions may be said to extend the limits of the community.[1]

[1] William F. Ogburn and Meyer F. Nimkoff, *Sociology*, New York: Houghton Miffln Company, 1940, p. 551.

The increase in the number and variety of man's social activities has come about as a result of the growth of culture. The multiplicity of associations is a phenomenon of modern times, particularly of the last hundred years.[2] Specialization and differentiation are furthered by urbanization, and by the development of transportation and communication. Rural social organization has been greatly influenced by this far reaching expansion of culture.

The distinguishing features of associations are the specific and limited nature of the relations between members. As one writer states:

> We become members by virtue of particular attributes or qualifications, corresponding to the particular object for which it is organized. We profess a faith or cultivate an art or pursue some kind of knowledge or run some kind of business, and find it desirable or advantageous to join with others in so doing. It is thus that practically all associations arise.[3]

A classification of modern associations according to interest is difficult to make since, as MacIver points out, the ostensible interest is not always the determinant one. It is only in the light of considerable study of an association's structure and its activities that the nature of its latent as well as its manifest interests can be understood. It is difficult even to determine the primary interest of associations. Furthermore, the local units of large-scale associations often respond differently in rural and urban environments.

The proliferation of special interest groups in modern society has induced a shift in the individual's interaction pattern from emphasis on the primary type of human relations found in the family and neighborhood group to an increased emphasis on such secondary types as occupational, special interest and large scale organizations. Since so many present day human activites are carried on through secondary type relations it is necessary to recognize them as important channels of education for adults. It is true that rural people are less involved in secondary types of social organization than urban people but the phenomenon is one of degree rather than a difference in essential character.

Another important characteristic of associational life is that the individual may choose, within certain limits, whether or not to affiliate himself with any association. As MacIver writes, "We are born into communities, but we create or are elected into associations."[4]

In reference to the types of organizations to be discussed in this chapter (as distinct from such organizations as the school, the church, government bureaus, etc.) there is an aspect of importance which has not been sufficiently dealt with by empirical investigations, but which needs to be mentioned, at least, here. This aspect is that of the function of these types of voluntary associations as agents of social change.

First of all, the very existence in a rural community of the types of organ-

---

[2] *Ibid.*, p. 561.
[3] R. M. MacIver, *Society*, New York: Farrar and Rinehart, Inc., 1937, p. 252.
[4] *Ibid.*, p. 12.

izations dealt with in this chapter is an *ex post facto* indication of the occurrence of social change. Furthermore, this change can be only in a direction leading away from the traditional ordering of social life in the rural community. Though no *a priori* judgments may be made as to the exact nature of specific changes which have occurred in any particular community it may at least be assumed that they have been (and will continue to be) many and varied. They may for instance (taking an hypothetical example) be in the nature of a direct effect upon a limited segment of the community's social life, as in the case of the displacement of a series of interrelated friendship cliques by the substitution of a formally structured association. And on the other hand, a formal association may, through its lobbying practices, be instrumental in bringing into the community a factory which in its turn is likely to produce far reaching effects upon most of the community.

The existence of many of these formally organized associations in localized communities provides in many cases the necessary formal structure whereby change may be instituted. By gaining the assent of an association, of let us say a Kiwanis club, to a particular plan for changing some aspect of community life the plan is, for many segments of the community, thereby lent an aura of "respectability" and is consequently partially legitimized.

The link between the large-scale association and the local unit is also very important in respect to the process of social change. The national, state, and district offices through their direct communications and through the association's publications serve to furnish stimuli to the local unit. The effectiveness of these stimuli depend on numerous factors, among which are their appropriateness to the local felt-needs of member clubs, and their potentiality for being translated into "action programs" at the local level.

Federative Principle in Organization.—In this chapter it has been assumed that should an educational program be attempted by an organization such as the Fund for Adult Education, the effort would be needlessly cumbersome and proportionally less effective if an attempt were made to reach all locally organized clubs and councils. However, nationally organized associations allow easy and rapid channelizing of communications from a few central points down to local units. Consequently this chapter concerns itself mainly with a selected number of national organizations which have a rather wide distribution of local units and an integrated hierarchy of levels of administration, with a national headquarters which has a continuous working relationship with its various subordinate or federated units.[5]

[5]Under A are listed those organizations with which this chapter will occupy itself. For various reasons beyond the control of the authors, those organizations listed under B were omitted from the study. Reconnaissance study of each of these organizations revealed that they might reasonably be omitted from consideration for the following reasons: (1) little rural emphasis, (2) no local units, and (3) lack of access to national directory.

A 1. American Association of University Women (A.A.U.W.). 2. American Medical Association (County Medical Society). 3. Altrusa International. 4. Chamber of Commerce of the

Rural Coverage of Service, Professional, and Civic Associations.—Variability in the scope of coverage is an important fact when considering the flow of educational materials through large scale associations. The existence of local clubs

TABLE 1
Number and Percentage of Service, Professional and Other Civic Clubs Located in Rural and Urban Areas

Clubs	Total Number	Total Percent	Rural Number	Rural Percent	Urban Number	Urban Percent
Service Clubs (Men)						
Lions	720	100	405	57	315	43
Rotary	370	100	127	34	243	66
Kiwanis	273	100	67	24	206	76
Optimist	51	100	2	4	49	96
Civitan	34	100	12	35	22	65
Service Clubs (Women)						
Altrusa	31	100	2	6	29	94
Quota	15	100	1	7	14	93
P.T.A.*	424	100†	171	40	253	60
G.F.W.C.*	293	100	108	37	185	63
Chamber of Commerce	282	100	56	20	226	80
A.A.U.W.	98	100	2	2	96	98
B.&P.W.*	69	100	7	10	62	90
League of Women Voters	67	100	8	13	59	87
County medical societies	236	100	58	24	178	76
N.A.A.C.P.	94	100	14	15	80	85

* Tabulations for P.T.A., B.&P.W., and G.F.W.C. are based upon returned questionnaires; all other clubs based upon total units in the 263-county sample.

† 23 percent of P.T.A. units not ascertainable as to location. Most of these no doubt would fall in rural areas, which if true, would increase the number of rural units.

United States (C. of C.). 5. Civitan. 6. General Federation of Women's Clubs (G.W.C.). 7. Kiwanis International. 8. League of Women Voters of the United States. 9. Lion International. 10. National Association for the Advancement of Colored People (N.A.A.C.P.). 11. National Federation of Business and Professional Women's Clubs (B.&P.W.). 12. Optimist International. 13. National Congress of Parents and Teachers (P.T.A.). 14. Quota International. 15. Rotary International.

B 1. American Association for the United Nations. 2. American Dental Association. 3. American Legion. 4. American Federation of Soroptimist Clubs. 5. Association of Junior Leagues of America. 6. Child Study Association of America. 7. Council of World Affairs. 8. National Association of Colored Women. 9. National Association of Negro Business and Professional Women. 10. National Congress of Negro Parents and Teachers. 11. National Council of Negro Women. 12. National Council of Women of the United States. 13. National Exchange Clubs. 14. National Recreation Association. 15. Pilot International. 16. Southern Regional Council. 17. United World Federalists. 18. Veterans of Foreign Wars of the United States. 19. Zonta International.

does not, in itself, assure the spread of educational programs, but is, of course, greatly dependent upon the extent to which the local units are actively functioning.

The number of local clubs of each organization included in the national sample to which postcard questionnaires were sent and the number of questionnaires returned by each association are shown in Appendix C. The proportion of all clubs returning card questionnaires varies from 13 percent of all P.T.A's to 49 percent of all B.&P.W. Clubs. The geographic distribution of clubs returning questionnaires closely parallels the geographic distribution of the total National Sample. The sample of selected service, professional and other civic clubs is distributed generally throughout the major type-of-farming areas with relatively greater concentration in the Dairy and Cotton Belts and fewer numbers in the Wheat and Range Livestock areas.

The size of the population center in which a club is located is an important indication of its rural focus and of its closeness to rural people because the rural community is composed of the town service center and those surrounding farm families identifying with it.[6] (See Table 1.) The most rural clubs (that is 33 percent or more located in rural areas) are Lions International, P.T.A., G.F.W.C., Civitan, and Rotary. Those with 75 percent or more urban clubs are Kiwanis, Optimist, Altrusa, Quota, Chambers of Commerce, A.A.U.W., B.&P.W., League of Women Voters, County Medical Societies, and N.A.A.C.P.

CLASSIFIED LUNCHEON SERVICE-CLUBS OF BUSINESS, PROFESSIONAL, AND EXECUTIVE MEN OR WOMEN

What They Are.—Classified luncheon-service clubs are both urban and rural phenomena, but their importance in rural areas in recent years has increased considerably. From a sociological point of view, the growth of luncheon-service clubs may be seen as a correlate of the rapid urbanization of America and the expansion of its economic and social institutions. The luncheon-service club in the United States began with Rotary in Chicago, Illinois, when Paul P. Harris, a young lawyer, experiencing the loneliness of a big city desired to enlarge his circle of acquaintants. In February, 1905, therefore, he met with a few friends to discuss the formation of a club, the purpose of which was to be that of mutual helpfulness. In explaining what it was that brought these men together in the first place, the founder of Rotary is quoted as follows:

> Personal ambition had been largely responsible for the grouping. United they would stand; divided they might fall. And so they helped each other in every way that kindly heart and friendly spirit could suggest.[7]

Thus, in the universal kernel of mutual aid, the businessman sought a meas-

[6] Carl C. Taylor, *et al.*, *Rural Life in the United States*, New York: Alfred A. Knopf, 1950, p. 55.
[7] *Adventure in Service*, Chicago: Rotary International, 1949, p. 15.

ure of security from the highly competitive business of his times and in so doing, gave impetus to a movement which has since encircled the globe. From thirty members in 1905, Rotary has grown to a present membership of 350,000 organized into 7,388 clubs throughout the world. But it is important to note that the "club" of thirty to fifty members still persists, in the majority of cases, as the basic unit of organization. The average size of Rotary Clubs in 1951 was about 42 members. Beyond a certain size, organizers have found that the primary character of the group is lost and with it the spirit of the smaller community which gives the individual the satisfaction of a "feeling of belonging." The dynamics of the luncheon-service club idea rest on the congeniality of small groups and the interpersonal relations that are encouraged within them. That the leaders of the movement have mastered some of the techniques of small-group development is evidenced by the prevailing custom of club members addressing each other by their first names or "nicknames", by the procedure of assigning members to smaller groups or committees to work on community service activities, and by requiring regular attendance of members in luncheon meetings where a congenial and friendly atmosphere prevails.

Business and professional women soon began to organize luncheon-service clubs patterned closely after the men's organizations. By 1921 five women's organizations had taken their places beside the six major men's organizations. Current statistics relating to these eleven classified luncheon-service club organizations are given in Table 2.

Table 2 shows that a total of almost 23,000 classified luncheon-service clubs are presently organized, including more than a million members. Women comprise less than four percent of the membership and their growth has been slower due to the fewer number of business, professional and executive women in smaller centers. In fact, leaders in women's service clubs have operated on the principle that women's classified luncheon-service clubs should not be encouraged in small cities; estimates of the minimum size required for effective functioning varies from 25,000 to 50,000 population. The main reason for such a limitation is a recognition that a minimum population base is necessary in order to support and provide a proper nucleus of personnel for a club. Men's clubs on the other hand, do not suffer as much by such limitations, but, they do tend also to be concentrated in middle size and large cities.

Lions Clubs have had the greatest growth in membership, shifting from third to first place among the service clubs since 1934. Taken as a whole, membership in all classified luncheon-service clubs has increased steadily since the first Rotary was formed in 1905. However, some organizations have had their "ups and downs" due to economic depression or wartime crises. For example, Kiwanis had a membership of approximately 90,000 in 1924, rising to over 103,000 in 1929. But by 1934 Kiwanis membership declined to about 80,000. At the same time, overall membership in service clubs continued to rise, increasing more than a quarter million between 1924 and 1934.

The term "classified luncheon-service clubs of business and professional men or women" serves conveniently as a short operational definition; that is, the mode or organization referred to is a club made up of "representative" business and professional men or women of a city or town who meet regularly at weekly luncheons and who participate in community service activities. The classification principle is not rigidly adhered to in practice although some control on membership is enforced. Compulsory regular attendance attempts to assure sufficient social interaction between members (at meetings at least) so that lines

TABLE 2
Number of Men's and Women's Classified Luncheon-Service Clubs and Number of Members, 1951

Clubs	City and year founded	Number of clubs	Number of members
Total................		22,936	1,158,121
All men's clubs...........		21,464	1,113,621
Lions.................	Dallas, 1917	8,850	430,000
Rotary................	Chicago, 1905	7,388	350,000
Kiwanis...............	Detroit, 1915	3,128	199,621
Exchange..............	Detroit, 1911	1,000*	75,000
Optimist..............	Detroit, 1919	749	45,000
Civitan...............	Birmingham, 1920	349	14,000
All women's clubs........		1,472	44,322
Soroptimist............	Washington, 1921	454	12,000
Altrusa...............	Nashville, 1917	275	9,500
Zonta.................	Buffalo, 1919	214	8,000
Pilot..................	(?) 1921	296	7,500
Quota.................	Buffalo, 1919	233	7,322

* Estimated.
Sources: Official literature, annual directories of organizations for 1951, or *World Almanac*, 1951.

of communication may be opened up and some persistency in human relations may be secured.

Members are chosen ostensibly because they are recognized "leaders" in their business or profession and as such serve to bring to the deliberative aspects of the club's activities the particular points of view and sentiments of their respective vocations. In turn, it is maintained, members carry back to their business and professional colleagues the precepts and principles of the organization. It is not clear that this principle of representative leadership actually works. Although members are recognized "leaders" before they join, they are accorded some measure of leadership status by the fact of membership in a civic club.

National and International Coverage.—The effectiveness of any organization is directly related to its scope of coverage. In promoting educational programs through any existing organization one of the questions to be asked is: "How widespread is the presence of effective units through which educational processes can be channeled?" From the geographic point of view it is important to know just where the organizational units are located so as to appraise the capacity of any large scale association to reach people. Table 3 summarizes the distribution of selected service clubs by regions of the United States. In general, service clubs are found quite generally throughout the United States although densities vary regionally from 2.9 clubs per urban place of 2,500 inhabitants or more in

TABLE 3
Distribution of Nine Selected Service Clubs (Both Men and Women) in the United States by Geographic Regions

Region	Number	Service club density*		
		All clubs	Mens' clubs	Womens' clubs
United States total	17,143	4.0	3.7	.27
New England	838	3.8	3.5	.27
Middle Atlantic	2,352	2.9	2.7	.15
East North Central	3,074	3.6	3.4	.18
West North Central	1,755	4.0	3.8	.21
South Atlantic	2,739	4.8	4.4	.37
East South Central	1,285	4.5	4.2	.30
West South Central	2,121	4.3	4.1	.24
Mountain	975	4.4	3.9	.49

* Number of service clubs divided by number of places with 2,500 inhabitants or more in 1950. National Exchange and Zonta clubs not included because of lack of data.
Source: Summarized from Annual Directories of Service Clubs, 1951.

the Middle Atlantic Region to 5.6 clubs in the Far West. A considerably wider range in service club density prevails by states. New Jersey has the lowest service club density of any state and Maryland the highest. No clear cut evidence of a sectional bias appears in the current data although the North Central, Middle Atlantic and Northeast states in general tend to have fewer service clubs than do states in other parts of the grounty. A general "westward bias" in service club density noted by Marden in 1931 is not evident at the present time.[8]

It is clear from these data that service clubs can no longer be considered as purely urban phenomena since in every state more clubs exist than there are number of places with 2,500 inhabitants or more. Conditions which have fa-

[8] Marden, *op. cit.*, p. 123.

vored the growth of service clubs are the rapidity of urban growth with a generally rising standard of living. However, it is clear that population growth does not wholly account for the spread of this type of association. The change in character of "small town" to "urban," and the rapid flow of urban culture through local lines of communication are also important.[9] The relevance of levels of living to the existence of service clubs can be illustrated by reference to Lions Clubs. Only 31 percent of all Lions Clubs are located in counties with rural levels of living below the U. S. average, whereas 42 percent of the sample counties are below average. This same general tendency occurs in the case of all other associations included in this study.

Groups formed on an international basis face problems in human relations that are not faced by national groups. Although wide latitude of local initiative and control is allowed by the various constitutions of service clubs, international officers and committees are forced to think "internationally" on policies, service activities and publicity. Internationalism imposes restrictions on the scope and specificity of action of the overall organization which cannot be overcome entirely by a large measure of local autonomy which is undoubtedly enjoyed by local clubs. Thus, an international organization which includes clubs from countries with divergent forms of government cannot enunciate policies for or against one particular system of government without offending some member clubs or cutting them off from support in their own country. This may partially account for the wide substantial support that most of these associations have given to the U.N. and its affiliated agencies, for they are in a position to appreciate many of the problems and obstacles facing a world organization. On the other hand, it accounts for the restriction of Exchange Clubs to the United States because of its leaders' conviction "that the principle of democratic government of the organization might be violated by governing the clubs in other countries from outside their borders."[10]

Rotary is the most international of the service clubs having 3,111 foreign clubs located in 85 countries.[11] Lions is second in international scope having 942 clubs in 31 foreign countries. All of Kiwanis' and Civitan's foreign clubs are located in Canada. Optimist's 54 foreign clubs are in Canada, Mexico and Cuba. Among women's service clubs, Zonta is most international in scope having clubs in 10 foreign countries, followed by 6 for Altrusa; 5 for Pilot; 3 for Soroptimist; and 2 for Quota. However, Quota International among the Women's Service Clubs has the largest number of foreign clubs but they are concentrated in Canada and Australia. Lions Clubs are prevalent in small towns

[9] Marden, *Ibid*.
[10] Marden, *op. cit.*, p. 11.
[11] *Annual Directory of Rotary International*, 1951. The total number of clubs and the percentage that are foreign follow: *Men's Service Clubs:* Rotary, 7,357—42%; Lions, 8,694—11%; Optimist, 749—7%; Kiwanis 3,197—5%; Civitan, 349—2%; and Exchange, approximately 1,000—0%; *Women's Service Clubs:* Quota, 233—18%; Zonta, 214—12%; Soroptimist, 464—8%; Altrusa, 287—4%; and Pilot, 296—2%.

as well as cities, whereas other service clubs tend to be concentrated in places above 2,500 population. (See Table 4.) The rapid spread of service clubs into small towns has brought the rural and urban segments of the population closer

TABLE 4

Percentage Distribution of Selected Service, Professional and Civic Clubs in the 263 Counties, by Size of Town Where Located

Names of clubs	Number of clubs	Total	Under 500	500–999	1000–1499	1500–1999	2000–2499	2500–4999	5000–9999	10,000 and over
Men's Service clubs										
Lions	720	100	18	17	9	8	5	14	13	16
Rotary	370	100	4	5	9	8	8	18	22	26
Kiwanis	273	100	9	2	5	4	4	11	27	38
Optimist	51	100	2	—	—	—	2	2	8	86
Civitan	34	100	6	17	3	3	6	15	6	44
Women's service clubs										
Altrusa	31	100	3	3	—	—	—	—	7	87
Quota	15	100	7	—	—	—	—	13	—	80
P. T. A.*†	551	100	2	12	8	5	4	9	9	28
G.F.W.C.*	293	100	10	11	6	5	4	21	21	22
Chamber of Commerce	282	100	3	2	6	7	2	13	28	39
A.A.U.W.	98	100	—	—	—	1	1	14	25	59
B.&P.W.*	69	100	—	—	6	1	3	19	26	45
League of Women Voters	67	100	3	2	3	2	3	6	13	68
County medical societies	236	100	5	5	6	4	4	19	22	35
N.A.A.C.P.	94	100	4	1	7	1	2	11	21	53

* Tabulations for P.T.A., B.&P.W., and G.F.W.C. are based on returned questionnaires rather than upon total number of units in the 263-county sample.

† Owing to the method of distributing questionnaires it was not possible to identify by size of town all of the cards that were returned; consequently the size of place where 23 percent of the P.T.A. units were located was not ascertainable. The authors, however, have reason to believe that this 23 percent was heavily weighted toward the smaller sized population centers.

Source: Size of town taken from *1950 Census of Population*; number of service clubs tabulated from *Annual Directories, 1951.*

together. In smaller places the service club often serves many of the functions of a "general interest" organization in the community. As size of town increases the greater the probability there is that a service club will be present. The one exception to this functional relationship between size of towns and the presence of clubs is found in the case of the Lions Clubs which increase above and below places of 2,500 population. Lions International has apparently spread widely into predominantly rural communities, more so than any of the other service organizations included in this analysis. Consequently its local units are distributed quite equally among rural and urban places.

Recognition of the Adult Education Function.—It is of considerable importance to ascertain the attitude of officers of local clubs relative to the education function of the organization. Do local service, professional, and civic club leaders acknowledge the educational nature of their activities? Replies were sought to the following question: "Does your organization have any educational programs or activities for adults?" A high degree of awareness (at least 74 percent replying "yes") is found among respondents of the League of Women Voters, A.A.U.W., P.T.A., and G.F.W.C. Moderate recognition of the educational function (between 40 and 65 percent replying "yes") is shown by replies from Altrusa, N.A.A.C.P., Rotary, Kiwanis, B.&P.W., Lions, Optimist, and Quota. Low degree of recognition of education (40 percent or less replying positively) is indicated for Civitan, and county medical societies. It should be pointed out in connection with this question that no attempt was made to define adult education for the respondent. Replies therefore are based entirely upon the respondent's own definition of adult education and its application to the programs and activities of his club. It is important to recognize in planning an adult education program for presentation through these particular associations that wide differences of opinion appear as to what constitutes adult education. Club activity itself may or may not be considered an educational venture. Accepting the figures cited at face value, however, it would appear encouraging that over three-fifths of all respondents for service, professional and civic clubs consider their programs and activities as contributing to adult education.

Indication of the extent to which these particular associations reach rural people is found in replies to the question inquiring as to what proportion of the people reached by adult education programs or activities live in rural areas, (rural areas being defined as open-country and places of less than 2,500 population). Sixty-one percent of the P.T.A.'s, 46 percent of G.F.W.C., and 45 percent of all Lions Clubs, reported that "almost all" of those reached by their programs and activities live in open-country or centers of less than 2,500 population. These figures confirm the definitely rural character of P.T.A., G.F.W.C. and Lions International in contrast to the predominantly urban character of Optimist, Quota, Altrusa, A.A.U.W., B.&P.W., N.A.A.C.P. and county medical societies.

Furthermore, analysis of respondents not answering the question on the proportion of the rural audience indicates that clubs not reporting tend to be located in centers of population of 2,500 and over. For example, 82 percent of Kiwanis Clubs and 76 percent of Rotary Clubs not answering the question are located in towns of 2,500 population and over. However, less than half of Lions Clubs respondents not answering the question are located in towns of 2,500 population and over. This tends to confirm the characterization of Lions International as being of a more rural nature than the other service clubs.

Structure of Organization.—The form of organization is at once a clue to its capacity for effective operations as well as its limitations. All service club organizations, with the exception of National Exchange Clubs are reasonably similar in structure so that a general description serves for all.

First, it cannot be emphasized too often that the local club is the key unit of organization upon which the whole organizational structure rests. The territorial limits served by each club are carefully delineated and may include rural territory surrounding a city or town, but must be limited to that from which active membership can be secured and maintained. The limiting aspect of territoriality is thus explicitly recognized.

A conventional number of executive officers presided over by a president are provided for in the administrative structure. A board of directors determines the policies and activities of the club and is in charge of general management. Most activities of the club are usually handled by small standing or special committees. Luncheon or dinner meetings, usually of a specified duration, are held weekly in a designated place within the territorial limits served by the club. In addition, each club is required to hold an annual meeting of members.

Growth necessitated the subdivision of the international associations into districts usually comprising sections of the country smaller than states. The number of subdivisions of each organization varies from 8 districts in Exchange to 292 districts in Rotary. The functioning of the district organizations is educational and promotional. Each district is under the jurisdiction of an administrative office (district governor or vice-president) who is in most cases elected at the annual District Convention, by delegates of the clubs in the district. These District Conventions are held customarily 30 to 60 days prior to the annual International Convention and are designed to foster a closer bond of union among clubs geographically proximate.

The overall administration is handled by the International Office which is composed of Executive Officers and Directors. Usually the Secretary and Treasurer are appointed officials, while the President and Vice-Presidents are elected. Top executive officers and members of the Board of Directors are elected at the International Conventions held each year. It is at these conventions also that the policies of the International are advanced. Each club, irrespective of size of membership, is represented by a designated number of delegates.

A system of standing and special committees is provided at the international level of organization. These overall subject-matter committees help spur and direct local clubs to action along the lines of committees' interests. Thus, a study of these committees shows the points of emphasis in the international program. For example, Kiwanis had international standing committees on the following subjects: Achievement Reports, Agriculture and Conservation, Attendance and Membership, Boys and Girls Work, Inter-Club Relations, Key Clubs, Kiwanis Education and Fellowship, New Club Building—Canada, New Club Building—U.S., Past International Presidents, Programs and Music, Public and Business Affairs—Canada, Public and Business Affairs—U.S., Support of Churches in Their Spiritual Aims, and Underprivileged Child. The following were special committees: Convention Program, Kiwanis History and Resolutions. Such a large set of international committees are not found in all service club structures but Kiwanis may be used to illustrate the possible range of committee functions at the international level. Furthermore, in those service clubs covering broad areas of the world it is customary to set up advisory and extension committees for geographic regions. Thus Rotary has committees for European, North African, and Eastern Mediterranean regions.

The national organization of the Parents and Teachers Association may perhaps best be described by quoting from official literature:

> The individual membership of the local associations in the state branches constitutes the membership of the National Congress of Parents and Teachers, the nation-wide organization through which the parent-teacher movement is promoted. The annual convention is the governing body of the National Congress of Parents and Teachers. (PTA Manual, Chicago, 1944, pp. 3–4.)

The officers of the national P.T.A. are composed of the following:
1. The presidents of each state branch.
2. The chairmen of national standing committees.
3. The president of National Parent-Teachers, Inc.

This ensemble is called the Board of Managers of the National Congress.

The state branches are organized on a very similar basis, and these in turn may be broken down into district organizations within each state, and further into councils. The essential purpose of the district and the council is to provide a structure which may facilitate the integration of programs and activities of the individual units within their respective boundaries.

Finally, the local unit is organized into a system of formal offices and standing committees. The offices usually consist of a president, one or more vice-presidents, a secretary, and a treasurer. An Executive Committee, consisting of the officers, the chairmen of standing committees, and the principal of the school, acts as the governing body of each local unit.

As many as 33 standing committees may be established by a local unit, though those suggested as basic committees for all clubs consist of the following: (1) Congress Publications, (2) Membership, (3) National Parent-Teacher, (4) Procedure and By-Laws, (5) Programs, (6) Founders Day, (7) Publicity, (8) Budget and Finance, (9) Room Representative, (10) Hospitality, (11) Study Groups.

It may be safely stated that a cultural pattern seems to exist in American society around the formal structuring of voluntary association. The elements of this value system which seem to figure most prominently in the determination of the formal structure of associations are exemplified by such concepts as "democratic procedure," "fair play," "delegation of powers," and "organizational efficiency." It would seem that the creation of offices, boards, and committees to which members of voluntary associations are elected (although committees quite often are appointed) has become a *custom*. That is to say, with the formation of a voluntary association an almost automatic structuring will occur in terms of elected offices, delegation of authority, standing committees, etc. Thus, it is found that almost any large-scale, voluntary association (particularly of the types discussed in this chapter) will be structured generally in the same manner as service clubs and P.T.A. It is further noted that as the level of organization approaches that of the primary (face-to-face) group at the local level the formality and rigid lines of authority so characteristic of the national or international levels of organization tend to become more personalized and informal.

Objects of Organization.—Written aims and objects of organizations are signs of the manifest purposes for which the members are organized. Such documentary material often tells little of the actual accomplishments or latent purposes of the organization. However, the repetition of expressions of the aims and purposes in written word and speech gives an ideological rationale for group experiences.[12]

The manifest objectives of practically all service clubs as stated in official literature relate explicitly to (1) improving international understanding among peoples, (2) developing good fellowship among business and professional people, (3) promoting the spirit of community service and (4) raising business and professional standards among members. Two other objects are stated by a few of the service club organizations relating to (1) recognizing the worth of occupational pursuits, and (2) providing a forum for discussion and education.

Although only six of the eleven service clubs specifically mention international relations as a stated object all have at least one aim which includes a concern for international understanding. The range in specificity of purpose in this regard extends from the explicit aim of Rotary which reads:

> The advancement of international understanding, good will, and peace through a world fellowship of business and professional men united in the ideal of service.

to the more poetic and richer symbolism of the Civitan Creed which reads in part as follows:

> My ears hear the cry of children, the prayer of women for peace, the appeal of man for guidance, the call of the race for progress, and the song of the poet for unity.
> ... My hope is for a better world and a better city, through better men and Civitans.

[12] Marden, *op. cit.*, p. 93.

Only two service organizations, Optimist and Civitan, omit any specific mention of a concern for business and professional standards. "Fellowship" and "acquaintanceship" are repeated in the literature of service clubs as a major aim of the organization and along with the aim of "service" are the most generally accepted goals of service clubs. Thus, the service club helps to fill two needs in present day society of which people, particularly in urban areas or areas coming under the urban influence, are acutely aware. First, there is the need for an adequate circle of acquaintances, and second, the need for feeling oneself to be a recognized part of the community.[13] Good citizenship is specifically referred to in the printed aims and objectives of Lions, Optimist, and Soroptimist and, of course, may be implied in many other aims.

Five of the service clubs include in their written aims some statement concerning the worthiness of useful occupations in business and the professions. It would seem as though this may be indicative of some underlying desire and need on the part of businessmen and professionals for recognition as prestige groups in the community. Marden suggests that the service club idea is a means of bringing the status of business men on a par with professional men and accordingly concludes that "the fundamental dichotomy of contemporary society is between business and working class."[14]

Only three of the service clubs, Lions, Exchange and Altrusa, specify education or discussion as one of their primary objectives. On the basis of written aims and objectives it is clear that most service clubs do not think of themselves primarily as educational agencies. One can infer such a function, however, from the methods which are used in the club programs, including talks, discussion, parliamentary procedure, citizen participation in community affairs and related activities.

A sample of service club members belonging to Lions, Rotary, and Kiwanis were asked in 1931 why they joined. Results of this survey showed that the reasons given fell into seven categories ranked in order of importance from high to low as follows: (1) Fellowship or sociability; (2) interest in community service activities; (3) prestige; (4) business advantage; (5) self-expression; (6) cultural development, including educational advantages; and (7) recreation, "fun," or relaxation.[15] This summary of members' opinions adds the elements of "sociability" and community "service," as major functions of service clubs. It is clear that considerable difference exists in the way aims are expressed by the service clubs and by the individual members. The individual member recognizes functions of the service club which are not often reiterated in the literature and official documents of the organization, particularly his opinion as to the prestige value of belonging to a club and a certain amount of business advantage which accrues to membership.

[13] Marden, *op. cit.*, p. 124.
[14] Marden, *op. cit.*, p. 125.
[15] Marden, *op. cit.*, p. 92.

In most cases, each year, the incoming administration elected at the annual convention adopts a series of objectives for the particular year, all based upon the overall objects which do not change. Thus, Kiwanis adopted for 1951 the theme: Freedom Is Not Free, and spelled it out in nine foci for action, namely; (1) upholding the U.N.; (2) cultivating relations between Canada and the U.S.; (3) combatting Communism; (4) promoting economy in government; (5) resisting trends toward socialization; (6) demanding local rights and responsibilities for both management and labor; (7) fostering safety and conservation of resources; (8) expanding services to youth; and (9) strengthening the home, church and school. Although most of the clubs are less specific than Kiwanis, all tend to reduce overall aims to annual working objectives in line with the apparent needs of the times. Service clubs, in varying degrees, are fairly accurate barometers of what representatives of the business, professional, and executive community think are the crucial current issues.

The main emphasis of the P.T.A in terms of its claims for existence center around the child. The influence on the child of the home, school, church, and community in general are each a claimed focus of attention of P.T.A members.

The official objects of the P.T.A are as follows:

To promote the welfare of children and youth in home, school, church, and community.
To raise the standard of home life.
To secure adequate laws for the care and protection of children and youth.
To bring into closer relation the home and the school that parents and teachers may cooperate intelligently in the training of the child.
To develop between educators and the general public such united efforts as will secure for every child, the highest advantages in physical, mental, social, and spiritual education. (*Parent-Teacher Manual*, 1944)

Programs and Activities in the Three Fields of Special Interest.—Almost three-fourths of the Rotary Clubs, one-half of the Kiwanis Clubs and two-fifths of the Lions Clubs report that they carried on programs or activities during the last year in the three fields of special interest to this study, namely, (1) international understanding for peace, (2) strengthening of democracy, (3) understanding and strengthening the economy. The League of Women Voters and A.A.U.W. reported a larger number of clubs carrying on programs in the three fields than did any of the service clubs.

In the case of the P.T.A., 54 percent of the replies indicated that activities or programs in the three fields were being carried on, while the replies from the B.&P.W., and G.F.W.C. indicated a somewhat higher rate of activity. Furthermore, a larger proportion of service clubs' larger centers indicate that they conduct programs in the three fields of special interest than those in small towns. More than 80 percent of Kiwanis' affirmative responses came from the larger centers of population. Almost three-fourths of Rotary's also came from places of 2,500 population and over. Lions, however, follows its previous pattern of being more equally distributed in this respect among rural and urban centers.

The B.&P.W. units reporting that they carried on programs or activities in the three fields of special interest are almost exclusively in non-rural areas. On the other hand, about one-third of the positive replies from the G.F.W.C. and P.T.A. came from places of less than 2,500 population. In fact, almost one-half of positive replies from G.F.W.C. came from places of less than 5,000 population.

More clubs answered the question relating to programs and activities in the three fields of special interest than answered the general question on any adult education program. This would seem to infer that the officials filling out the questionnaire tend to follow the general cultural pattern in American society of thinking of "education" (whether it be for adults or children) as being more or less exclusively formalized pedagogy.

Obviously these three fields are broadly conceived and the respondents were given no instructions to indicate in which of the three fields their programs fall. However, from the brief description of the program or activity, an attempt was made to classify the responses.

The women's service clubs and Rotary gave the greatest emphasis to programs in international understanding for peace. Strengthening of democracy is the theme of two-thirds of all programs and activities of the N.A.A.C.P., The League of Women Voters has the most balanced program among the three fields. Finally, a considerable number of the men's service clubs conducted programs and activities which were not easily classified in the three fields of special interest.

The tabulation of responses from local units of the P.T.A. shows a rather equal division between programs emphasizing international understanding for peace and strengthening of democracy. Little emphasis was apparently placed upon the subject matter field of understanding the economy. In addition it may be stated that a considerable number of those responses falling in the unspecified category referred to direct school-related programs, (such as how best to consolidate a school district, or problems arising around the furnishing of finances for a larger school building).

The G.F.W.C. shows a greater emphasis upon programs and activities in the field of international understanding than in any of the other fields. Almost all of the units reporting activity in this field also reported having had a foreign person on their programs. Foreign students, displaced persons, and exchange teachers were the predominant classes of foreign persons mentioned in this regard.

Size of Audience Reached.—The typical service club listens to forty or more speakers in the course of a year on almost as many subjects. Speeches are considered to be an important adjunct to the weekly luncheons and contribute in varying degrees to the stimulation and understanding of individual members. However, the fact that there are many speakers and a diverse array of subjects 'leads to a false illusion of all-roundedness which, when sifted out, does not prevail."[16] But the potentialities for adult education in service club luncheon meetings is tremendous if intelligently and constructively planned.

Most service clubs and G.F.W.C. present educational programs designed to reach small audiences in contrast to the larger "out-group" audiences of N.A. A.C.P. and League of Women Voters. The luncheon club of 30 to 100 members is the dominant educational group for most service clubs although a considerable number have programs and activities designed for the general population. The general-service function of Lions Clubs is indicated by the relatively large number of clubs that report reaching audiences of over 1,000. In general, the number of persons reached by programs and activities in the three fields of special interest is of the same magnitude as the number reached by general education programs and activities. A relatively large percentage of Men's Service Clubs, P.T.A. and G.F.W.C. reach persons in rural areas with programs and activities in the three fields of special interest. Forty-four percent of Lions Clubs and 61 percent of P.T.A. reporting said that their programs and activities reach "almost all" rural audiences.

The size of the national forum which service clubs provide during any one week of the year can be estimated by a simple count of service clubs in the United States, approximating 20,000 weekly luncheon meetings averaging 50 members with a total participation of perhaps a million members or more.[17] To complete the picture it is necessary to add an estimated 5,000 luncheon meetings held in foreign countries and U.S. territories involving another quarter of a million participants.

The P.T.A. according to the responses indicated on the questionnaires, would seem to reach out to a considerable number of people through its programs and activities. Just over one-half of the replies from P.T.A. indicated that between 100 and 500 persons were reached. The G.F.W.C. and the B.&P.W. were distributed in more or less the same size pattern as the P.T.A., though with slightly fewer large audiences. It is to be noted that few of the local units of any of the associations discussed in this chapter indicate that they have programs or activities which reach mass audiences of more than 500 persons.

From the responses concerning the use of mass media in their programs, it is clear that service clubs rely heavily on movies as a mass medium of communication. Motion pictures are generally presented in conjunction with luncheon meetings primarily for entertainment purposes. Half of the mass media reported by P.T.A. were motion pictures. The emphasis of service and P.T.A. clubs on movies as a technique of adult education is in marked contrast to the League of Women Voters and the N.A.A.C.P. which rely heavily upon radio and newspapers to reach mass audiences. Newspapers, on the other hand, are the second most important mass medium used by the service clubs and P.T.A.

[16] Marden, *op. cit.*, p. 27.
[17] Approximations based on official count of clubs.

The use of television is as yet very restricted in rural areas. Its importance as a means of mass communication is yet to be realized by all these organizations. Such factors as isolation from transmitting stations and a general lack of receivers in rural areas are barriers to more widespread use. Of the 13 clubs reporting the use of television, five were League of Women Voters, and a predominantly urban organization.

For the purposes of generalizing, it is possible to characterize the types of communication upon which educational programs in these organizations are based as ranging on a continuum from predominantly face-to-face and interpersonal sets of relations to indirect and impersonal relations (as exemplified in mass media communication). In the face-to-face group the origin-response ratio approaches one-to-one, whereas in the large group little or no response from the audience is possible. Associated with the face-to-face group is an emphasis on the "in-group," as the primary audience for which programs are designed; while

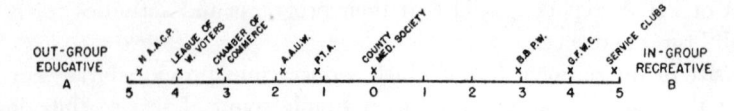

FIG. 1. The schematic arrangement of service, professional and other civic clubs on a continuum ranging from point A, "out-group educative" to point B, "in-group recreative" in communication patterns. Note that NAACP falls nearest point A while the service clubs fall nearest point B.

the designation of an "out-group" orientation seems more characteristic of those organizations such as the League of Women Voters and N.A.A.C.P., consciously attempting to influence non-members. Figure 1 shows the placement of the different organizations on such a continuum. Those to left of center, that is closer to pole A, are characterized as being more oriented towards an "out-group educative" function. Similarly those to the right of center, and approaching pole B, are characterized by an "in-group recreative" function. Frequent and regular dinner or luncheon meetings are one of the most important criteria of face-to-face groups and a crucial index of the primary character of the organization.

The success of the luncheon meeting technique is due in part to the fact that under present community conditions the typical business man or woman lives distant from his daily occupation and consequently is accustomed to eating his midday meal away from home.

Form of the Programs and Activities.—The "public meeting" is the most extensively used form of program in the three fields. The conference method is second in importance as a form of conducting educational programs among service clubs. The N.A.A.C.P. and Chambers of Commerce make widest use of conferences. In contrast, women's civic clubs such as A.A.U.W. and League of

Women Voters make considerable use of workshops rather than conferences. This major difference in educational methods shows up in another way in that women's civic clubs (A.A.U.W. and League of Women Voters in particular) rely on both group discussion and lectures while service clubs use only lectures as the principal technique. Furthermore, considerable numbers of A.A.U.W. and League of Women Voters clubs employ the technique of splitting large groups into small groups for discussion purposes. Apparently, service clubs make little use of this technique for group involvement. The N.A.A.C.P. and Chambers of Commerce emphasize institutes and radio programs in their activities.

Foreign Persons on Programs.—The question was asked: "During the past year, did any foreign person appear on your program?" Response to this question enables one to gauge somewhat the relative degree to which the "inter-

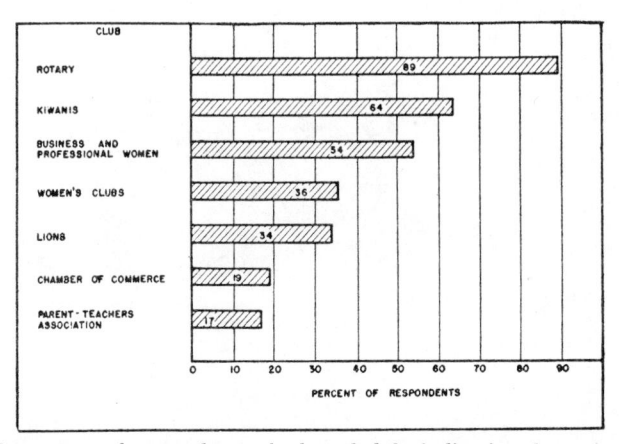

FIG. 2. Percentage of respondents of selected clubs indicating that a foreign person had appeared on their program in the last year.

national mindedness" of organizational policy and publicity has been translated into active programs at the community or local club level. (See Figure 2.) A.A.U.W. reports the largest number of clubs having a foreign person on programs during the past year. Rotary holds first place in this respect, among service clubs, supporting a view received in interviews and from literature that the organization is highly oriented toward a "broader-than-national" outlook. This high rate of affirmative response certainly also serves to give added meaning to the fact that more than 40 percent of Rotary Clubs are located in foreign countries. Only 25 percent of the Lion's Clubs report foreign visitors during the past year. P.T.A., N.A.A.C.P., Chambers of Commerce and county medical societies were low (15 percent or less) in percentage of all clubs on whose programs a foreign visitor was included during the year. Civitan reported none.

Working Relations in the Community.—The community is a web of interpersonal and inter-group relations. In order to trace the pattern of inter-group relations each club respondent was asked to check other organizations which the club works with, or through, in its educational programs and activities. The results of this check list procedure are shown graphically in Figure 3.

The P.T.A., as was to be expected, indicated working most with schools, and in addition with other parent's organizations (most likely with other P.T.A. groups and perhaps with local child study groups). These two general types are mentioned by almost one-half of the local units of P.T.A. which reported. In descending order of frequency of mention are found churches, civic and service

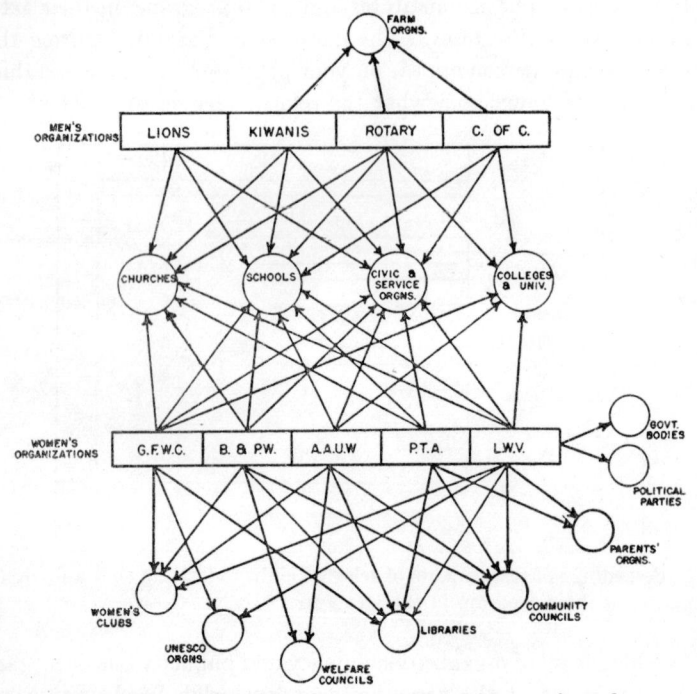

Fig. 3. Diagram showing the organizations with which men's and women's clubs work most frequently in their educational work with adults.

organizations, community councils, and libraries. However, all of these were mentioned by at least 25 percent of the P.T.A. units reporting.

The G.F.W.C. reports most often working with other women's clubs and schools, followed closely by cooperation with civic and service organizations, churches, libraries, and colleges. The B.&P.W. pattern follows quite closely that of the G.F.W.C., although the percentage mentioning each general type is not precisely the same.

It is to be noted that a different patterning of organizational interrelationships prevails among men's organizations than among women's organizations. All associations interact with the schools and with other civic and service type organizations, and most of them work with churches. However, it is exclusively the women's organizations and the P.T.A. (predominantly a women's organization) which work with libraries, welfare councils, women's clubs, UNESCO, community councils, and parents' organizations. The women's associations also out-number the men's three-to-two in cooperation with colleges and universities. On the other hand Kiwanis, Rotary, and the Chamber of Commerce indicate farm organizations as the type worked with by at least twenty-five percent of the local units.

The basic pattern of working relations among specified organizations is not altered materially by replies to the question in the questionnaire: "What specific organizations do you work with, or through, the most?" Thus a tabulation of these responses shows that schools are most important for service clubs, followed by civic and service clubs; elected or appointed government bureaus for the League of Women Voters; colleges and universities for the A.A.U.W.; churches for the N.A.A.C.P.; professional organizations for the county medical societies; schools and parents' organizations for the P.T.A.; women's clubs and schools for the G.F.C.W.; civic and service organizations and schools for the B.&P.W.

SUMMARY

Data presented in this chapter are the result of an attempt to analyze certain selected types of voluntary associations prevalent in contemporary American communities. Certain aspects of these associations are determined by like "*interests*" of the members, while other aspects (structural) are influenced greatly by the prevailing *customs* of the American value-system. Still other aspects (selectivity) are influenced or determined by age, sex, occupation, and social status. In one instance the familial status of parenthood is a selective factor.

Although it is manifestly true that present day American society has as one of its characteristics the proliferation of voluntary associations there needs yet to be done a considerable amount of basic and definitive research in this area. It has been often observed by native-born Americans as well as foreign visitors that Americans in general join various sorts of organizations, and many of them. To what extent these "impressions" validly describe a characteristic of the *whole* society is a question which needs yet to be answered. There is some evidence leading to the hypothesis that the "joining" tendency, so generally thought of as typical of the whole society, is strongly influenced by the social stratification systems of urban and rural social organization. Furthermore, such evidence indicates that a marked rural-urban differential in participation in interest associations does exist.

This analysis of selected service, professional and other civic societies, reveals some significant generalizations which might help guide the efforts of any agency or organization attempting to reach rural people through these channels of organization.

Classified luncheon-service clubs in particular have certain elements necessary for a potentially vast expansion of informal adult education. In the first place, in contrast to mass organizations which rely heavily on mass media, classified luncheon-service clubs function to a large extent through a system of interpersonal relations that are well established over a relatively long period of time. Second, many individual members take a keen interest in the club's activities and feel a personal responsibility for success or failure of any endeavor. The basis for this interest is multifold, having elements of economic self-interest, fellowship, recreation, prestige-gaining as part of the complex of reasons for joining and attending regularly. Third, the morale of the service club is normally high and an excellent *esprit de corps* is frequently present. Fourth, a community action and service program is a recurrent ideological theme. Fifth, the stated ideals, the types of community service activities, and the sorts of subjects discussed at organizational meetings are such that a program of informal adult education dealing with the three fields of special interest fits well into the institutional framework.

The negative aspects of service clubs appear to lie in too vaguely and generally defined programs in the three fields, and in a lack, or inconsistency, of focus on well formulated problems. Innumerable topics may be delivered by lecturers and afterwards discussed by members, but there is little concentration along any particular lines designed to reveal basic relationships. Consequently, the value of these lectures is primarily recreational and too segmented to properly serve as a sustaining system of informal education.

It seems probable, however, that a scheme might be worked out whereby general areas in the three fields of interest could be broadly yet systematically defined. Then a series of focused lectures designed to cover the major points of the defined areas could be gradually introduced into club meetings. This series of lectures should be supplemented by a parallel and complementary series of articles in the organization's own publications. Also pamphlets dealing with timely points of current interest and consistent with the systematized lecture and article series, would add to the effectiveness of the program.

Strong emphasis must however be placed on the point that service clubs are not primarily educational organizations and that care must be taken in trying to introduce such a scheme. Otherwise strong opposition is apt to develop from suspicion that an attempt is being made to turn them into educational institutions.

In conjunction with the systematic lecture, article, and pamphlet series, outlined above there is one more characteristic of the service club which could be utilized in enhancing the meaningfulness of the education program. This characteristic is the theme of action, or service, as the clubs themselves call it. It amounts to a desire, wish, or drive to be *doing* something. This is usually resolved by doing something for the whole local community or segment of it, or for an individual. In order to secure the most significant results, this characteristic of service clubs should be taken into account, and some way of translating the principal meaning of the more informational aspects of the educative process into an action program ought to be made an integral part of the over-all scheme for adult education.

It must be kept in mind that service club members are drawn from a particular segment of the occupational range and consequently do not encompass all gainfully employed persons in the community. There are doctors, public officials, bankers, insurance salesmen, proprietors, and various self-employed businessmen, farmers, lawyers, and other professionals and managers in service clubs. But, significantly, there are no persons with low occupational status such as farm tenants, or hired hands, clerical workers, factory workers, nor in fact wage earners in general. A salient problem to be considered, therefore, is that attitudinal changes among lower status groups are not to be expected. Channels of communication with lower status groups in the community simply are too weak and infrequent. Attitudinal changes will be necessarily restricted to middle and upper-middle social classes.

The importance of informal, non-classroom adult education, as typified by service clubs is stressed in all organizations covered in this chapter and an understanding of the group processes of local units would be of great help to club leaders. Adult education will be made more effective if responsible leaders of clubs have training in appropriate organizing skills and educational methods. Change in attitudes comes about as a result of social situations in which new motivations are offered and which are accompanied by institutional means of reinforcing them. On the one hand, service clubs tend to be guided more closely by prevailing community sentiments in developing their programs, such as helping boys and girls, the sick, the lame, the blind, etc., than do other civic clubs. On the other hand, the N.A.A.C.P. and the League of Women Voters take up causes that may or may not have widespread community approval. Such a comparison of divergent sentiments illustrates the need for diverse kinds of interest groups in building a better community. It may be that service clubs cannot espouse controversial causes and continue to function effectively as congeniality groups. However, some experimentation along such lines (as mitigating tensions in human relations) might be attempted.

There is a generally recognized need for a reliable source from which local clubs can secure materials in regard to many concrete aspects of the three fields of special interest. Such materials should be adapted to the special needs of service, professional, and civic clubs. Professional societies in particular need considerable stimulation and guidance in informing the community generally about their particular competence.

Effective adult education requires that programs begin with interests and felt needs, both individual and social. The service, professional and civic clubs are a broad-gauged national forum for developing an awareness of needs and provide the seedbeds in which local leadership can grow to help meeting recurring problems and satisfying the people's needs.

> T. Wilson Longmore
> Division of Farm Population and Rural Life
> Bureau of Agricultural Economics
> Department of Agriculture
> Washington, D.C.
> and
> Frank C. Nall
> Department of Sociology and Anthropology
> Michigan State College
> East Lansing, Michigan

BIBLIOGRAPHY

Banning, Margaret Culkin, "Shall We Adjourn?" *McCalls*, Vol. LXXIV, June 1947, p. 18.
Handbook of Adult Education in the United States, New York: Institute of Adult Education, Columbia University, 1948.
Hill, Frank Ernest, *Man-made Culture*, New York: American Association for Adult Education, 1938, p. 120.
Jubilee History, National Congress of Parents and Teachers, Chicago 1947.
MacIver, R. M., *Society*, New York: Farrar and Rinehart, 1937.
Marden, Charles Frederick, *Rotary and Its Brothers: An Analysis and Interpretation of the Men's Service Club*, Princeton: Princeton University Press, 1935.
Ogburn, William F. and Nimkoff, Meyer F., *Sociology*, Boston: Houghton Mifflin Company, 1950.
Overstreet, Harry and Bonaro, *Where Children Come First*, Chicago: National Congress of Parents and Teachers, 1949.
Rotary International, *Adventure in Service*, 1949.
Rotary International, *Service is My Business*, 1948.
Taylor, Carl C., *et al.*, *Rural Life in the United States*, New York: Alfred Knopf, 1949.

Chapter 7:

SPECIAL AGENCIES WITHIN THE THE DEPARTMENT OF AGRICULTURE

Introduction

The Department of Agriculture performs many functions among which adult education is one of the most important. When the Department was established it was directed by law to acquire and diffuse information on agricultural subjects in the most general and comprehensive sense. Research is conducted in the following fields: (1) Agricultural and industrial chemistry; (2) the industrial uses of farm products; (3) entomology; (4) soils; (5) agricultural economics; (6) marketing; (7) crop and livestock production; (8) production and manufacture of dairy products; (9) human nutrition; (10) home economics; (11) conservation. Results of the research are extended to farm people as well as the general public through the Cooperative Extension Services and Experiment Stations located in the forty-eight states. The Extension Service coordinates the educational activities of the bureaus of the Department and of the State agricultural colleges.[1]

However, in addition to general education carried on by the Extension Service, described elsewhere in this report, the Department of Agriculture includes a number of administrative agencies designed to carry out special "action" programs which by their nature involve considerable adult education. The most important of these *ad hoc* agencies are: Farmers Home Administration, (FHA), Soil Conservation Service (SCS), Rural Electrification Administration (REA), Production and Marketing Administration (PMA), Farm Credit Administration (FCA), and Forest Service (FS).

FARMERS HOME ADMINISTRATION

Administrative Structure.—The Farmers Home Administration stems historically from the rehabilitation programs of the Resettlement Administration and Farm Security Administration which were set up during the depression years and immediately following. FHA offers credit services to farm families who are unable to borrow from other sources on reasonable rates and terms. Loans are made for operating the farm, for buying family-type farms or enlarging or developing uneconomic farms into family-type units, for building or repairing farm houses and buildings, and in the 17 western states, for water facilities.[2]

The largest number of FHA borrowers have operating loans totaling almost 130,000 in November, 1951. These loans are primarily to finance farming and livestock operations for the current year. About 44,000 loans for buying a farm are currently active, and an additional 10,000 loans are made for building new farm houses. Some farm ownership and farm housing borrowers may also have operating loans. About three percent of all farms in the U.S. are FHA borrowers, varying from 2.3 percent in the Midwest to 4.1 percent in the West. There is a noticeable westward and southward bias in the FHA borrower rates. See Table 1.)

Administration of the FHA programs is centralized in Washington. The Finance Division has field offices in St. Louis, Montgomery, Dallas and Denver. The Federal Office has no personnel designated as functioning in educational capacities. State Directors in 40 State Offices, some serving more than one

[1] *Directory of Organization and Field Activities of the Department of Agriculture, 1950,* Agriculture Handbook No. 12, USDA, Washington, D. C.
[2] Authorized by the Farmers Home Administration Act of 1946, the Bankhead-Jones Farm Tenant Act of 1937, the Housing Act of 1949, and the Water Facilities Act of 1937.

state, are administratively in charge of the FHA program in their respective states. The State Director is responsible to the Administrator, and has the assistance of a State Farmers Home Administration Advisory Committee of nine members.[3]

The Committee System.—FHA supervisors are in charge of 1,619 local county offices, some serving more than one county. They receive applications from farmers, make loans, receive payments, and handle other phases of local program administration. There are 77 women home supervisors each of whom serves more than one county. Each local county office is assisted by an FHA county committee made up of three local persons, at least two of whom are farmers. All loans made through the agency's local offices must first be approved by the FHA county committee.

TABLE 1
Farmers Home Administration Active Operating Loan, Farm Ownership, and Farm Housing Borrowers as of November 30, 1951

Area	Total active borrowers Number	Total active borrowers Percent	Percent of total farms 1951
United States	157,393	100	2.9
East	9,561	6	2.4
Midwest	42,989	27	2.3
South	86,049	55	3.2
West	18,794	12	4.1

Source: Farmers Home Administration Statistical Records.

Functions of State FHA advisory committees are defined as follows:

1. To advise the State Director with respect to adapting broad national Farmers Home Administration policies to local conditions in the respective States, and to submit recommendations that may be helpful in shaping the future program of the Farmers Home Administration.
2. To consider the problems and advise the State Director concerning agricultural, health, credit, and other needs of low-income farm families in the State and to suggest ways for the Farmers Home Administration to meet these needs more effectively.
3. To inform the State Director and the Administrator of the committeemen's reactions, and of the reactions of the public in general, to the Farmers Home Administration program.
4. To assist in coordinating the Farmers Home Administration program with the activities and programs of other agencies operating in the field of agriculture with the State.
5. To advise the State Director concerning farm debt adjustment activities.[4]

---

[3] *Directory of Organization, op. cit.,* p. 67.
[4] Paul V. Maris, *The Land is Mine,* Agriculture Monograph No. 8, November, 1950, FHA-USDA, GPO, Washington, D.C., p. 44.

State committees have exercised in varying degrees and only at particular times the important function of advising with respect to broad national policies and adapting national policies to local situations. As clearly stated in the second function above they were conceived as advisory to the State Director concerning agricultural, health, credit, and other needs of low income farm families and were meant to suggest ways for the FHA to meet these needs more effectively. But at the present time their function is less general than conceptualized in this statement. On the other hand, they have served to curb somewhat the unfavorable developments that had manifested themselves; they have established loan limits and average value of efficient family-type farms; and have participated in tours for the purpose of inspecting farms of borrowers.[5]

State committees are appointed by the Administrator and are composed of nine members representing as many of the major types of agriculture and geographic areas of the State as possible. They may be farm organization representatives, editors of farm or metropolitan publications, or other persons identified with or interested in agriculture.[6] At least four of the nine State committeemen must be persons actually engaged in farming.

The county committees are appointed by the State FHA director and are composed of three individuals residing in the county, at least two of whom shall be farmers residing on a farm and deriving the principal part of their income from farming.[7]

County committees are independent of State Advisory Committees and perform their duties within their respective counties. They work directly with their county FHA supervisors and with applicants for loans and recipients of loans. They review the progress of borrowers annually and advise the FHA on current trends in farm business on which many administrative decisions are based.

Current instructions provide that:

> State directors are responsible for seeing that county committeemen are provided the training needed by them to understand the objectives of the Farmers Home Administration and to understand and perform properly their duties and responsibilities as prescribed in the various operating instructions. Training meetings for county committees will be held annually as soon as practical after the beginning of each fiscal year, and should be scheduled so as to derive the benefits of a concerted effort. The number of persons assembled at any one meeting should not be greater than can participate advantageously in group discussion. In the training program, particular attention will be given to (a) evaluating the qualifications of applicants. (b) interpreting the family-type farm definition in local terms, (c) explaining supervised credit, (d) reviewing borrowers' progress to determine future credit needs, and (e) defining the duties and services of county committeemen as prescribed by law. County supervisors are responsible for keeping county committeemen advised currently of changes in the policies of the Farmers Home Administration which affect their work, and of the status of the program in counties in which they serve.

---

[5] *Ibid.*, p. 45.
[6] *Ibid.*, p. 48.
[7] *Ibid.*, p. 57.

"The national Farmers Home Administration office issues a county committee manual or handbook. It is revised from time to time as laws or policies are changed. It is used somewhat as a text book in committee schools.[8]

Technique of Supervised Loans.—The most significant feature of the lender-borrower relation as worked out in practice by FHA supervisors is the technique of supervised loans. That is, supervisors advise borrowers as well as supply them with needed credit. Together the borrower and the supervisor determine how farm and home management may be improved, make plans for carrying out improvements, and see that the plans are carried out as nearly as possible. If administered wisely and democratically, this supervision becomes an important educational mechanism for farm families.

Eighty-eight percent of 89 Farm Supervisors in the 263 sample counties who returned card questionnaires report that they are carrying on adult education programs and activities. Only 8 of the 89 respondents reported that they did not have educational programs, while 2 did not answer the question. A general awareness on the part of Farm Supervisors of the educational nature of their work is indicated by these figures. In explaining what supervision is, Maris says:

> This brings us to the very heart of the whole matter of arriving at an understanding with an applicant before he receives a loan. He should know just what supervision involves and whether he desires to enter into a supervisory relationship with the Farmers Home Administration.[9]

It is necessary that an understanding be reached between lender and borrower that farming conservation practices will be carried out; sound farm and home plans will be carried out; and complete and accurate record books will be kept. The procedure by which these objectives are accomplished has been well-developed in practice.

A comprehensive farm and home plan is drawn up as the basis for a farm ownership loan. Less detailed plans are required for farm operating loans only. In general terms the planning and supervision of an FHA loan takes the following form:

1. Long-range farm and home plan is developed by the farm family with the aid of the county FHA supervisor, showing cropping system, farm practices, health and sanitation, garden, canning, housing, clothing, surroundings, and education.
2. Annual farm and home plans are developed with the aid of the FHA supervisor covering details with respect to specific undertakings and with respect to the management of financial affairs which it is impractical to incorporate in a long-time plan.
3. The farm family keeps accounts in FHA family record books.
4. The FHA supervisor visits farms of borrowers during the year to confer and advise with farmer about cropping systems, rotations, varieties, fertilizer applications, pest control, livestock management, and the like.
5. County supervisor meets with the borrower for annual checkout, involving an

---

[8] *Ibid.*, p. 68.
[9] *Ibid.*, p. 107.

examination of the borrower's family record book for completeness and accuracy, analyzing the year's business and completing farm and home plans for the coming year.

6. Annual meeting of all borrowers is held to revise and summarize progress during past year, and get suggestions and outlook for year ahead.

Annual Meeting of Borrowers.—FHA makes use of annual meetings of borrowers to educate farm families in better farming and to raise their living standards. It is a technique of group supervision and education.

Carefully worked out illustrative educational materials have evolved out of practice and are described in the "Handbook of Illustrations for Annual Business and Educational Meetings of Farm Ownership Borrowers."[10] The purpose of the annual meetings as specified in this handbook is to compare the efficiency of various systems and methods of farming and home making as revealed by actual analyses of borrowers' records. The meetings are conducted by the discussion method and directed toward group decisions that lead to action by individual families.

The customary procedure is to summarize the individual records of borrowers and present the results in statistical and graphic form, using charts, flannelgrams, demonstrations, short talks and discussion techniques such as agree-disagree questions and small groups. It has been found that an effective way of securing borrower acceptance of farm and home practices is to use kodachrome slides illustrating a specific practice which has been adopted by a borrower in the county. The effect on the group is to stimulate each borrower family to follow one of their peer "leaders."

In addition, records and related data from such sources as experiment stations, the Agricultural Census, Agricultural Conservation Payment records, etc., are presented by the county supervisor to provide some wider basis for comparing the efficiency of various systems, methods, and practices of farming and home making. The borrower thus arrives at group decisions and conclusions with respect to the facts revealed. This leads to individual action resulting in improvement in farming and home making which is based on actual borrower experience and supported by group analysis, discussion and decision.[11]

Small meetings are more desirable than large meetings because attendance is better and interest of families is increased because problems are more similar. Borrowers speak up more readily in smaller group meetings. In fact, experience has shown that there is great value in meeting in borrowers' homes because of the personal touch. Generally speaking, however, annual business and educational meetings are held in churches, school houses, court houses, lodge halls, and other suitable places as well as borrowers' homes. A committee of borrowers often have charge of general arrangements, such as time and place of meeting, entertainment features, dinner, etc. A social hour at lunch time is emphasized and since many borrowers know each other personally they enjoy visiting to-

[10] Farmers Home Administration, U.S.D.A.
[11] Maris, *op. cit.*, p. 238.

gether. Educational and entertaining movies or colored slides are sometimes shown during the social hour.

Approximately 1500 annual borrowers meetings of FHA borrowers are held annually. In 1948 the latest year for which complete records are available, 46 percent of all borrowers invited were represented and 35 percent of the borrowers' wives attended.

Achievement or Progress Day.—In some states it has become a practice for heads of colleges to invite FHA borrowers to an achievement or progress day on the college campus. For example, Georgia honors families who have made outstanding progress in better farming and better living. The 1951 Achievement Day program attracted 246 farmers, 179 wives and 106 children. Total attendance was well over 1,000 people, counting FHA committeemen, supervisors and visitors. Negro acheivement day was held at Fort Valley State College while white borrowers attended at Athens and Tifton, Georgia.

Other state FHA offices which make use of achievement day are Michigan, Iowa, Texas, and Indiana. Land grant colleges of Michigan, Iowa, and Indiana invite FHA families to visit the campuses for programs at which formal recognition is given of outstanding families. In Texas, the achievement day is held in conjunction with the Texas State Fair. Some counties in Michigan hold a Progress Day for the borrowers of a single county.

SOIL CONSERVATION SERVICE

The function of the Soil Conservation Service is to give assistance to farmers and ranchers chiefly through soil conservation districts which the farmers organize and operate under State laws. SCS technicians give assistance in conservation, surveying, planning and application of suitable soil and water conserving practices on individual farms, watersheds, or other areas having common problems. The program is designed to help prevent soil erosion, to preserve natural resources, to control floods, to prevent impairment of reservoirs, to maintain navigability of rivers and harbors, and to protect public health.

The SCS is a centralized organization with top administrative officials in Washington, seven Regional offices, and a State Conservationist in each state. Below the state level there are 2,418 soil conservation districts in the U.S. covering about three-fourths of all farm land. The soil conservation district is the work unit through which technical and educational information is channeled.

All but four of 103 card questionnaires returned by Soil Conservationists in the 263 sample counties replied that they carry on educational programs. This indicates widespread awareness among SCS personnel of their educational functions. Soil conservation districts in cooperation with State Extension Service carry on educational programs through organizations, such as farmers' organizations, community clubs, civic groups, schools, 4-H Clubs, etc. In addition,

SCS conservationists work with individual farm families in developing farm conservation plans. But SCS has found it desirable in order to extend the scope of activities, to use a variety of techniques for getting groups of farmers together. Often the only way to begin is to call together a few farmers on a hand-picked basis, another way is to circulate a petition to secure names of farmers who are willing to meet together to discuss soil conservation. Still another technique is to get farmers who have shown an interest to call in their neighbors. Some groups are organized on a school district basis, others by getting owners or operators of contiguous farms together, and still others on a watershed basis. Many groups are organized after the soil conservationist, or the county agent, selects the people and invites them to attend a meeting.

Many problems have been encountered. Attendance is hard to maintain and often depends upon the "spellbinder" tactics of the person conducting the meeting. Groups called together for one purpose, such as planning conservation activities, do not work well when attempting to function in other ways such as applying farm practices.

Neighbor Group Techniques.—Recently, SCS has initiated a program drawing on its past experience in getting groups of farmers together which relies on the principle of working through natural groups. Natural groups are made up of farmers who associate with one another because of proximity to one another, and who recognize their common needs. The family, neighbor-group, neighborhood, and community are natural groups. These groups come into being by natural processes and develop slowly and endure because they serve continuing needs of the members. This is in contrast to formally organized special interest groups, such as farm organizations, civic clubs, ladies aid societies, school districts, formally organized extension or soil conservation groups and the like.

The natural group approach presumes a working knowledge of rural community organization on the part of the SCS supervisor. A useful technique for developing conservation-minded farmers and ranchers is the identification of "neighbor groups" and their leaders, and then to work with these leaders and followers to speed up acceptance of conservation programs on their farms by improving the leaders' understanding.

The term "neighbor-group" as used by the Soil Conservation Service should not be confused with "neighborhood." Rather a neighbor-group is similar to groups described by rural sociologists as "informal," "friendship," "mutual aid," congeniality or "clique" groups. The neighbor group is a limited number of families, not over 15 or 20, living in close proximity to one another and who are bound together by mutual likes and interests. An enduring and effective type of cooperation among farm people occurs in these farm families who visit, borrow, exchange work, discuss common problems and ideas, and help each other in crises. Within such groups there are always one or two "good neighbors" who are looked upon as being the most willing to help the others in the group. These so-called "neighbor-group leaders" are the members who are most often looked to for advice, and who, if they try something new, are most likely to be copied by their neighbors.

One can frequently observe such neighbor groups at auctions, at the crossroads store, or preceding or following more formal and larger group meetings, or on street corners on Saturday. In such huddles, people discuss things freely and become personally involved in activities of mutual interest. Here ideas are stripped of fancy trappings and are discussed, analysed, and revised. In such groups it has been found that soil conservation becomes a part of the group's way of thinking and believing which profoundly influences every-day discussions and actions.

A definite technique for locating natural groups and leaders was worked out by SCS personnel, and training was given through actual interviews with farmers by persons experienced in those techniques. Briefly, the steps followed are:

1. Consult with several overall district, or county-wide, leaders to secure the names of the most important community leaders.

2. Talk to these community leaders and gather all information possible about neighbor groups and their leaders.

3. Using the names secured in this manner, talk to enough people in each neighbor group to verify the membership of the group and determine as positively as possible who the leader or leaders are.

4. Consult with the leader and check with him as to the membership of the group. Let him decide where borderline cases fit. Likewise, find out from him whom he considers to be the real community leaders.

5. With the leader, determine the group's interest and understanding of soil conservation. Plan with him the course of action to be taken with the group to move them along in soil conservation work.

6. Call on the community and over all leaders to encourage and assist the neighbor group leaders.

Training SCS personnel, on site, in these methods began in early 1947. To date, with but few exceptions, all work unit conservationists and district conservationists have been taught these principles and techniques by on the job training methods. As of January 1951, 32,914 neighbor-groups including 284,025 farmers and ranchers, have been located in the United States by SCS technicians. Of this total, 23,549 neighbor groups have carried on one or more activities in planning and application or maintenance of soil conservation work.

PRODUCTION AND MARKETING ADMINISTRATION

The organization of the Production and Marketing Administration consists of an Office of the Administrator, 9 commodity branches, 12 functional and staff branches, 5 area Management Offices, 2 Area Photographic Laboratories, 9 PMA Commodity Offices located throughout the United States, and state, county and commodity committees.

PMA administers programs relating to: (1) agricultural conservation; (2) production adjustments; (3) price support and stabilization through loans, purchase agreements, purchases and other means; (4) stabilization of sugar production and marketing; (5) international commodity agreements; (6) surplus removal; (7) procurement for supply; (8) foreign purchases; (9) school lunch; (10) marketing agreements and orders; (11) marketing research and standardization; (12) marketing services; (13) marketing regulation; and (14) other production and marketing activities, including assistance to and collaboration with other Departmental Federal and State agencies in administering federal crop insurance, water resources and flood control activities, eradication of foot and mouth disease in Mexico, and foreign economic assistance operations.[12]

Only three of these varied programs relate themselves directly to people in their counties and communities. These three are: (1) the Agricultural Conservation Program designed to preserve and improve soil fertility, promote the economic use and conservation of land, diminish the exploitation and wasteful use of national soil resources and aid in flood control; (2) Production Adjustment Programs through acreage allotments and marketing quotas, whenever supplies are out of line with demand; (3) School Lunch Programs, through which grants-in-aid are made to states, to purchase foods served in the lunches; also the program provides for direct distribution of food to assist them in meeting minimum nutritional requirements.

The ACP and Production Adjustment programs are administered in each county by a PMA committee and in each community by a community committee. The county and community committees are farmers residing in the county of community and are elected by their fellow farmers each year. The School Lunch Program is handled locally by the schools, and PMA has little control of the funds after they have been turned over to the states.

Three farmer-elected county committeemen in each of the Nation's 3,006 agricultural counties and more than 85,000 community committeemen are elected each year and take office January 1 to direct PMA programs. Each county committee consists of a Chairman, Vice-Chairman and one other member. Replies by card questionnaire from county PMA chairmen show that 35 percent do not consider their activities during the year as educational in nature. However, community committeemen usually attempt to contact every farmer in the county in person, at meetings, or by mail to assist him in planning conservation work on his farm in accordance with the needs of his land. Wherever the SCS or other agency works out a conservation plan for a farm, the farmer is encouraged to make full use of it, fitting in ACP assistance on a cooperative basis. Farmer committeemen are paid on a per diem basis for the days officially worked. The average pay for the year 1951 was $372 for county committeemen and $45 for community committeemen.

[12] Directory of Organization, *op. cit.*

During 1951, under the Secretary's consolidation plan, PMA offices and those of other Department agencies have been brought together in nearly half of the 3,006 agricultural counties. As a part of the defense program of the federal government, PMA has established Mobilization Committees at the national, state and county levels. These Committees include representation from Federal and state agencies working among farm people. They carry out programs such as scrap metal drives, increased food production, and information programs. In some cases they serve as sources of farmer information on conditions and requirements in rural areas.

RURAL ELECTRIFICATION ADMINISTRATION

The primary functions of the Rural Electrification Administration are to administer loans (1) for rural electrification facilities and (2) for extension and improvement of rural telephone service. Loans are made to persons now providing or who may provide telephone service in rural areas and to cooperative, non-profit, limited dividend or mutual associations. There are 1,077 borrowers (1951).

The REA provides advisory assistance to borrowers in connection with the financing and construction of rural electric and rural telephone systems. It has no field offices, with the exception of a small liaison office in Spokane, Washington. However, there are 10 regional supervisors with offices in Washington, D.C.

The basic local unit is the member-controlled REA cooperative. On June 30, 1951 REA had loaned almost 2.5 billion dollars to rural electrification borrowers, energizing approximately 1,150,000 miles of line serving more than 3.5 million rural customers, 78 percent of these customers being farmers.[13] Estimates show that slightly more than half of all farmers who are receiving central station electric service are served by REA lines.[14] The average borrowers' system consists of about 1,100 miles of line, connecting more than 3,400 consumers. To do this the system has borrowed an average of over 2¼ million dollars.

One of the major phases of REA's job is to provide guidance to borrowers in establishing efficient system management, operation and maintenance programs and power use activities. Member education is implicit throughout as REA organization moves from the peak construction period to the long-time management and operating function. For many REA consumers of electric power the operating organization is no different than any other privately owned business. The cooperative nature of the REA organization is little understood and consequently may be easily undermined by those who would like to take the systems

---

[13] "Accomplishments of REA and the Job Ahead," address by E. C. Weitrell, Program Analyst, Rural Electrification Administration Field Conference, Salt Lake City, Utah, June 25–29, 1951.
[14] Ibid.

away from the consumers. Some lack of understanding is attributable no doubt to the fact that borrowers' systems have been operating an average of less than 6 years. Recognition of this problem was acknowledged at the first Conference on Electrification Advisor Programs, held in Washington, D.C., December 4–7, 1950. Discussants at these sessions commented upon the "indifference by the members instead of loyal participation, misunderstanding and griping instead of cooperation with management, unwise decisions instead of intelligent action."[15] Many cooperative members are unaware that the co-op belongs to them and as a consequence a considerable number of individuals feel a lack of responsibility for it.[16] Some cooperatives are threatened with "sell-outs" to private power companies because members are not informed or active in the cooperative organization.

Some of the large REA cooperatives employ an "electrification advisor" (designated also as an agricultural engineer and home economist). The "electrification advisor" devotes himself to member education, power use problems and community relations work. Some of the small cooperatives have no volunteer committees of members to carry on activities designed to promote the most efficient use of co-op power, to familiarize members with the REA story and the principles of cooperation, and to secure community understanding and acceptance of the co-op. The annual meeting of members is generally regarded as the most important single opportunity to inform and educate members. Some co-ops have conducted annual meetings which are outstanding community events not only to members but many others outside the membership.

Board meetings can be educational, but their influence on the membership is limited unless steps are taken continuously to inform the general membership of problems and issues facing the board.

FARM CREDIT ADMINISTRATION

The Farm Credit Administration was created by executive order effective May 27, 1933, which provided for consolidating within one organization the powers and functions of all Federal agencies dealing primarily with agricultural credit.

The Washington office supervises and coordinates activities and makes examinations of all the institutions comprising the farm credit system. The United States is divided into twelve Farm Credit districts, in each of which are four major credit units located together in a headquarters city. One of these major credit units is called a Production Credit Corporation that supervises and partially capitalizes local cooperatives known as Production Credit Associations which make operating loans to farmers and stockmen.[17]

Approximately 500 Production Credit Associations are located at convenient

---

[15] "The Educational Job Ahead," PA-165, REA, USDA, p. 6.
[16] *Ibid.*, p. 6.
[17] The other credit units are: Federal Land Bank, Bank for Cooperatives, and Federal Intermediate Credit Bank. No analysis will be attempted of these agencies here.

points. The associations serve on the average of six counties with approximately 1,000 members per association. Total membership in Production Credit Associations in 1951 was roughly 470,000 with a total loan volume of 1.3 billion dollars.

The membership elects the Board of Directors at the annual meeting, each Director serving staggered three-year terms. The Board hires a Secretary-Treasurer who is the paid manager of the Association. The Board selects two of its members who with the manager make up the committee which acts on all loan applications. Loans are made for production purposes and are strictly business-type loans based upon such factors as: (1) the man's character; (2) his financial position and progress; (3) the repayment capacity of the farm enterprise; (4) the purpose of the loan; and (5) the collateral. The Associations are cooperative forms of organization although at the present time only about half of them have repaid all the capital stock held on behalf of the Government by their respective Production Credit Corporations.

Education of members has been recognized by the Corporations as an important adjunct of the production loan program. However, personnel devoting full time to educational work has been cut sharply in recent years. Activities related more or less to the educational function continue and in fact the administrative officers are aware of an increasing demand from Associations for servicing programs of education for members. Educational meetings are encouraged but no blue print is suggested. Table 2 summarizes some of the activities which are considered as educational by administrative personnel.

One of the principles of cooperatives is member participation in the affairs of the organization. The Annual Meeting of Stockholders is the most important institution for bringing about member involvement in the affairs of the Association. Although news letters and personal contacts are used extensively to inform the membership, they cannot completely satisfy the requirement of cooperative organizations that owner-members be able to speak up and be heard. More is involved than the dissemination of factual information. Annual meetings provide the necessary setting within which a certain amount of group consciousness and understanding can grow. Because of this fact management of many Associations makes considerable effort to get a high proportion of membership to the annual meetings. The Associations concentrate upon developing a better understanding of the economy and reasons for farmer credit devices such as the Production Credit loans.

The following statement taken from one of the production credit news-letters illustrates some of the thinking of production credit leaders:

> The continuing necessity of getting the full support and active help of the stockholders in such matters as raising capital, adjusting interest rates, and in maintaining sound loan policies is gradually convincing the directors and management that the annual meeting is a wonderful opportunity to promote whatever the association needs. Some have not caught on to this as well as others, but it becomes more convincing

every year that no board and secretary-treasurer can do the whole job. Members must raise the capital, members must support the necessary charges on loans, and they must support sound loan policies. Their willingness to do these things depends almost entirely on their understanding of what it is all about. Eighteen years of ex-

TABLE 2

Selected Membership and Public Relations Activities Carried on by All Production Credit Associations in the U.S. During 12-Month Period Ending June 30, 1951

	Number
Associations at end of period...................................	500
Membership and Public Relations Program.......................	
Associations which followed some type of planned membership activity program reasonably close during the period.........	253
County Membership Committees	
PCA's having committees that met 2 or more times during period	146
Membership committee meetings held during period..........	1,257
Members on membership committees.......................	6,245
Personal Contacts	
Associations having some reminder system for contacting good nonborrowing, former, and prospective members while in the immediate vicinity on regular field work....................	324
Associations contacting, personally or by mail, most of their satisfactory nonborrowing and former members twice during period	349
Use of the Mail	
Associations issuing a mid-year report during the period........	383
Associations distributing 2 or more issues of membership newsletter during the period....................................	281
Associations writing a welcome letter to all new members and enclosing some appropriate circular during the period........	255
Educational Work on Short-Term Farm Credit	
Associations that discussed short-term farm credit before at least 2 Vo-Ag, 4-H, or other youth groups during the period......	221
Associations that discussed short-term farm credit before at least 2 veterans' groups during the period.......................	243
Associations that discussed short-term farm credit before at least 1 Vo-Ag adult night class during the period................	124

perience have clearly demonstrated that the great majority of the members will do whatever it takes when the directors and management do their part and treat them as they deserve to be treated as the owners and users of the association.[18]

In commenting on attendance at annual meetings in this same article the writer noted that there was a gradual build-up in attendance for the state of

[18] *Production Credit News*, Vol. 11, No. 4, Dec. 1951. Houston, Texas, p. 1.

Texas from 29 percent in 1936 to 52 percent in 1941. Then with the war and difficulties of travel during that period, attendance went down to 24 percent by 1943 and was steady until 1946. Attendance has since increased steadily to 41 percent in 1951. This is indicative of the trend generally in the United States for attendance at annual meetings.

Attendance records of the series of annual meetings held from July 1950 through July 1951 throughout the United States shows that 68,858 stockholders, or 22 percent of all stockholders attended annual meetings during the 1950-51 series of meetings. This figure compares with an average of 28 percent attendance for the years 1939-42 indicating that attendance at annual meetings is still below that of prewar. Only 4 percent of stockholders without current loans attended in 1950-51 revealing a much lower participation on the part of those not currently borrowing from the Associations. Attendance at annual meetings is not uniform over the country; actually there appears to be a "westward bias" in as much as the Plains and Pacific Coast States have membership participation considerably above the national average.

Awareness of the need for education in regard to farmer production credit has led to the production of a new moving picture on farmer credit. Cost of producing this film was financed by voluntary contributions from the various Associations. It will be presented to members and nonmembers alike.

The Federal Farm Loan Act required the formation of national farm loan associations as the local cooperative units for the Federal land bank system. Approximately 1,200 national farm loan associations are serving the United States and Puerto Rico. Each association is a separately chartered organization of member-borrowers under its own by-laws. The main purpose of the national farm loan associations is to afford farmers an opportunity to make applications for Federal land bank loans. Each association has a loan committee of three or more members designated by the board of directors.

Annual meetings are held at which directors are elected and other formal decisions are reached. At these meetings reports are made on the business affairs of the organization. These annual meetings constitute the most important single activity directed toward stimulating member interest and participation in the affairs of the association. Annual meetings vary in effectiveness from "outstanding" to simple compliance with the by-laws.

Most of the land banks have developed booklets containing helpful material and suggestions for association use in conducting annual meetings. Borrowing heavily from the ideas and suggestions which have proven successful in the various land bank districts, the Federal office has prepared a circular entitled "Planning Effective NFLA Annual Meetings," for distribution to local associations.

In addition to the formal assistance to production credit associations and national farm loan associations, the Farm Credit Administration provides educational materials to farmers' cooperatives in general. In 1939, the Cooperative Research and Service Division was established in the federal office. The staff of this division engages in research studies and advises with officials and directors of farmers' cooperatives in practically all states. In addition, members of the staff discuss problems confronting particular groups at annual meetings of cooperative associations.

A series of circulars entitled "You and Your Co-op" was begun in 1939. These educational circulars, written from the point of view of the member of a cooperative association marketing a specific commodity, or offering a particular service, are used by teachers of vocational agriculture, 4-H Club leaders, and by officials and members of cooperative associations.

It is generally agreed that research in membership relations and education was neglected during the World War II period. Since the war, staff members have participated in cooperative "clinics" at which organization and operation problems are discussed by directors, managers, auditors and attorneys of cooperatives.

Under the Research and Marketing Act of 1946, funds were allotted to research on problems of membership relations and the education of students and young farmers in cooperative principles, in addition to problems of financing, processing and distribution. The professional staff of the Cooperative Research and Service Division consisted of some 50 employees in 1952.

It is a policy of the Division to carry on research studies cooperatively with state agricultural colleges, experiment stations, and other institutions and agencies serving agriculture. In this way, and by frequent conferences, the staff has had an influence on the research and educational work conducted in the states. In this connection, mention should also be made of cooperation with the American Institute of Cooperation[19] in studies of membership relations and education. The Division helps to direct the training and observation of foreign visitors, especially officials of government and farmers' cooperatives, in the United States under technical assistance programs.

Theoretically, each cooperative association has a great potential for adult education wherein the "learning-by-doing" principle may be given full play. Annual meetings, committee meetings and discussion groups constitute important teaching devices if effectively handled. In the main, however, educational activities of farmer cooperatives are directed toward the building and maintaining of good relations with members and the public. A study of 237

---

[19] The American Institute of Cooperation is a national organization sponsored by farmer cooperatives and other farm organizations, and by leaders from the Land Grant Colleges. Its staff works primarily with cooperative leaders, research, educational, and extension workers, state cooperative counsels, and the press.

Throughout the year it works closely with the Land Grant colleges, departments of education, and other institutions and agencies in sponsoring workshops and training schools for cooperative directors, managers, and employees, extension workers, college teachers, and research workers. Likewise, it sponsors workshops for teachers of vocational agriculture, veteran-on-farm trainers, and the leaders of farm youth programs.

leading farmer cooperatives in the United States shows that only about one-tenth of the titles of staff members having responsibility for educational work were designated as strictly "educational" employees.[20] The job of getting educational work done has been approached in a variety of ways. The manager takes the major responsibility for educational work in about half the associations reporting. Furthermore LeBeau's study shows that almost half of the staff members who have the major responsibility for educational work spend less than 20 percent of their time on this work.

When managers were given an opportunity to check 12 devices useful in educating members, replies indicated that they gave about equal importance to annual meetings and personal contacts. The importance of interpersonal relations as a means of educating members is given added emphasis by these replies. Ranking next were monthly publications, local discussion groups, circular letters, and periodical reports. Of lesser importance were radio programs, all family programs, cooperative projects with Future Farmers of America and 4-H Clubs, and educational exhibits.[21]

Patrons of Southern States Cooperative were asked to appraise specified educational devices. They put personal contacts second only to the periodic publication or house organ in importance, while the local annual meeting was relegated to seventh place.[22]

To develop more understanding of cooperative farm business by members of 4-H Clubs and young men and women's groups, the Farm Credit Administration and Extension Service have developed a series of circulars devoted to suggested demonstrations, illustrated lectures and dramatizations.[23]

Illustrative of joint efforts of cooperatives are the state, district, and local cooperative councils which keep a close tab on legislation affecting farmers who belong to cooperatives. Tours, exhibits and contests are other ways in which cooperatives work together. But periodical interagency meetings and discussions offer the best opportunities to present common educational programs.[24]

Of interest to membership of farmer cooperatives is the Farm Credit Administration's monthly publication, "News for Farmer Cooperatives." This publication contains timely and well-written articles of an educational nature and includes accounts of significant programs and activities of farmers cooperatives throughout the United States.

[20] Oscar R. LeBeau, *Educational Practices of Farmer Cooperatives*, Misc. Report 140 Washington: U.S. Department of Agriculture, FCA, January 1951, p. 2.
[21] *Ibid.*, p. 5.
[22] Oscar R. LeBeau and John H. Heckman, *Patrons Appraise Cooperative Relations*, Circular C-140, Washington: USDA, FCA, May 1951, p. 9.
[23] Farmer Cooperation An American Way:
    Section A—4-H Dramatizations (C. F. Christian).
    Section B—4-H Illustrated talks (C. F. Christian).
    Section C—4-H Demonstrations (J. H. Heckman).
    Section D—YMW Illustrated Talk (J.H. Heckman).
[24] *Educational Practices of Farmer Cooperatives, op. cit.*, p. 48–9.

Outlines and subject matter references for five teaching units were developed at three workshops attended by supervisors, teacher trainers, and teachers of vocational agriculture; supervisors and instructors of veterans; representatives of state colleges and cooperatives; and representatives of the American Institute of Cooperation and of the Farm Credit Association.[25] This guide is based on the principle that a well-rounded program of instruction in vocational agriculture includes training in the economic and social aspects of agriculture as well as in production, farm mechanics, and farm family living.

The Cooperative Research and Service Division has compiled a list of farmers' cooperative periodicals, including house organs and news letters. This list includes 150 associations engaged in cooperative marketing or purchasing that are publishing their own periodicals or have selected established periodicals as official publications.[26]

A considerable number of motion picture films on cooperation are available from the Farm Credit Administration and cooperatives. Many are available on a free loan basis to responsible organizations.[27]

In summary, it is clear that the Cooperative Research and Service-Division does much of its educational work indirectly through the publications issued presenting research findings. However, it has prepared special publications from time to time of a purely educational nature and has cooperated extensively with land grant colleges, the Extension Service, the Office of Education, and other educational organizations to bring farmers essential information on how to use cooperatives effectively.

FOREST SERVICE

The Forest Service is charged with responsibility for promoting the conservation of the nation's forest lands. It cooperates with states and private owners in programs for the protection and proper management of forest lands. It conducts research in 12 experiment stations, and makes results available to individuals, industries, and public and private agencies generally. The bulk (76 percent) of the commercial forest land is in private ownership and consequently special emphasis is being given to cooperative programs to encourage sound management of private forest lands. The Federal Government, most of the states, and many counties and private owners are cooperating on protecting the forests from fire.

In 1950, some 220 technically trained foresters gave on-the-ground assistance to small-woodland owners. These specialists, generally known as the farm foresters, work with farmers, local agricultural technicians, small-sawmill ope-

[25] John H. Heckman, *Guide for Teaching Farmer Cooperation*, Circ. E-34, Washington: USDA, Farm Credit Administration, May 1950.
[26] Pauline T. Gartside, *Farmers' Cooperative Periodicals*, Washington: Farm Credit Administration, USDA, Misc. Report No. 5, Revised October, 1945.
[27] *Motion Picture Films Available on Cooperation*, Misc. Report 144, Washington: Farm Credit Administration, USDA, Revised January 1952.

rators, and others to help solve forest-management problems. About 1,000 counties are included in the areas now served; some foresters cover 3 to 5 counties.[28] One of the most important educational programs facing the Forest Service is in relation to the owners of these small forest properties. They are generally in the poorest condition.[29] On the other hand they are the most accessible and potentially the most productive forest lands in the country. They require on-the-ground technical assistance. In 1950, 68 extension foresters in the cooperating states developed extension programs and carried them out through the county agricultural agents in cooperation with other state and federal agencies. Two extension foresters are employed by the Federal Extension Service to assist the states, giving special attention to subject matter, extension methods, and cooperative procedures.

ORGANIZATIONAL STRUCTURE

The federal administrative office is located in Washington, D.C. with 10 regional offices scattered throughout the country. Each of the 150 national forests has a has a forest supervisor under whom the Forest Rangers operate. The Forest Ranger is considered to be one of the most coveted positions in the organization and carries with it considerable responsibility and decision-making opportunities of a specific and practical nature. Many decisions of Forest Rangers are necessarily made "on the ground" and this contributes to a fairly decentralized administrative structure, keeping in mind, however, the relatively narrow area of decision making within which the typical ranger is forced to operate. His main concern is protection of the forest resource and he can make any decision which contributes to that end. There are roughly 700 to 800 ranger districts, many of them having assistant rangers. The function of the farm forester has already been pointed out. His role at the present time is a relatively minor one although it is growing in importance.

The National Forest Advisory Council is constituted to advise on matters of broad, general policy relating to national-forest administration. In a few cases, local National Forest Advisory Councils have been set up to advise the forest supervisor in his supervision of the national forests. These are the only laity dominated groups in the Forest Service administrative structure.

Wherever personnel of the Forest Service make their permanent home, it is customary for them to take an active part in the community and to that extent they can be said to be cooperating with civic organizations, churches, schools, etc. However, there are no organized programs and activities at the local level.

The Forest Service relies heavily on mass media such as movies, television, textbook materials and national advertising. A good illustration of the latter is the widespread awareness of the animal character "Smoky Bear." This character

[28] *1950 Report of the Chief of the Forest Service*, U.S.D.A. Superintendent of Documents, GPO, p. 16.
[29] *Ibid.*, p. 16.

has been built up through mass advertising contracted for through the Advertising Council, a private organization.

FEDERAL AGENCIES AND THEIR RELATION TO ADULT EDUCATION

Card questionnaires were sent to FHA supervisors, SCS conservationists and PMA county chairmen. For various reasons, it was impractical to sample REA, FCA, and Forest Service county personnel. The agency representatives were requested to indicate the number of persons reached by their programs and activities. A summary of the replies indicates that the SCS reached a larger and more general population than does FHA. That is, FHA supervisors report an average of 340 people per county supervisor as compared with an average of 3,000 persons per Soil Conservation District. PMA, on the basis of replies from county chairmen, reach audiences of over 500 people in 39 percent of the counties.

Almost all of the people reached by FHA and PMA programs and activities live in open country or places of less than 2,500 population while only 54 percent of the SCS educational audience lives in rural areas. The more general nature of soil conservation subject matter is indicated by these comparative figures.

When FHA and SCS supervisors were asked by card questionnaire whether any of their educational programs or activities were related to the three fields of particular concern in this study, namely, international understanding for peace, strengthening of democracy, and understanding and strengthening of the economy, 54 percent of the FHA supervisors, 50 percent of the SCS conservationists, and 37 percent of PMA committeemen answer affirmatively.

These figures indicate considerable lack of awareness as to how the respondents' particular program contributes to education in the three fields. It is clear that almost half of FHA and SCS field representatives and two-thirds of the PMA respondents do not recognize the contribution of their technical or supervisory work in the three fields of special interest. It is estimated that SCS reaches about 1,000 persons per district with programs and activities in the three fields and 92 percent of this audience lives in rural areas. About half of the PMA respondents report audiences of 500 persons or more per county. FHA on the other hand has a smaller clientele as indicated previously.

The form of the best FHA, SCS, and PMA programs and activities in the three fields were reported. FHA and PMA made most extensive use of public meetings of borrower families and conferences, while SCS supervisors reported most widespread use of tours. In addition, SCS personnel relied heavily on public meetings and demonstrations and PMA on conferences. FHA made considerable use of personal contact in conferences of borrowers.

The procedures used by administrative agencies are important factors contributing to effective programs and activities. Educational procedures of FHA and SCS are quite similar in at least three respects, both place considerable emphasis on group discussion techniques and make little use of either panels or large groups split into small discussion groups. See Figure 1. They differ markedly in that SCS places much more reliance on the lecture method than does FHA, the latter stressing individual family discussion. These facts point to the more supervisory and intensive approach of FHA personnel in contrast to the traditional lecture methods of SCS. PMA relies heavily also on group discussion techniques but makes more use of "large groups split into small groups."

Cooperation with Other Organizations.—Most agencies that operate locally are impelled from time to time to cooperate with each other, and with other organizations, because they all serve the same people and the "community" forces some cooperative relations from time to time. Particularly is this true of such

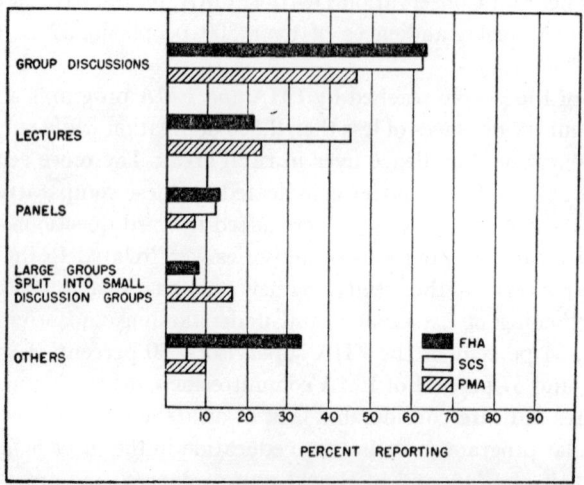

Fig. 1. Proportion of FHA, PMA, and SCS respondents indicating the procedures used most frequently in adult education activities.

ad hoc agencies as FHA, SCS, and PMA which are concerned mainly with a specific educational emphasis such as credit, soil conservation or agricultural price programs, but whose programs must be generally understood by all people in the community.

It is significant therefore that more than three-fourths of all SCS district conservationists reported that they work with farmers' organizations, the Extension Service, schools and other governmental bureaus. (See Table 3.) Almost two-thirds work with civic and service clubs in the community at some time during the year. Other important cooperative relations of SCS personnel were with colleges and universities and churches. Of lesser importance overall are cooperative relations with inter-agency councils, community councils, women's clubs, professional organizations, patriotic and veterans organizations, and parents organizations. Little or no cooperation is reported with welfare councils, libraries, political parties, labor organizations, UNESCO organizations, and fraternal organizations.

Communication Media Used.—A comparison of mass media employed in educational programs and activities reveals that SCS and PMA tend to rely more upon mass media than FHA. Thirty percent of FHA respondents report no mass media used. However, the data show conclusively that FHA supervisors make considerable use of group meetings of borrowers; almost a third

TABLE 3

Organizations That SCS, FHA, and PMA Work With, or Through, in Educational Programs or Activities for Adults

Organizations	FHA Number	FHA Percent	SCS Number	SCS Per cent	PMA Number	PMA Per cent
Total number of questionnaires returned..	89	100	103	100	57	100
Farmers' organizations................	64	72	89	86	41	72
Agricultural Extension Service...........	76	85	88	85	33	58
Schools............................	28	32	80	78	11	19
Federal and/or state gov't. bureaus......	73	82	79	77	19	33
Civic and service organizations..........	24	27	66	64	7	12
Colleges and universities................	38	43	15	15	6	11
Churches and religious organizations......	16	18	51	50	13	23
Elected or appointed gov't. bodies.......	13	15	46	45	14	25
Inter-agency councils...................	27	30	23	22	5	9
Women's clubs.......................	3	3	20	19	4	7
Professional organizations...............	11	12	19	18	0	—
Patriotic and veterans organizations......	27	30	14	14	3	5
Parents organizations..................	2	2	12	12	2	4
Fraternal organizations.................	3	3	6	6	3	5
Libraries............................	4	5	6	6	1	2
Welfare councils......................	12	14	3	3	1	2
Political parties and/or organizations.....	0	—	0	—	0	—
Labor unions.........................	1	1	0	—	0	—
UNESCO organizations................	0	—	0	—	0	—
Community councils...................	0	—	0	—	2	4
Others..............................	0	—	21	20	9	16

Note: Each respondent may check more than one organization.

of all report the use of group meetings even though it was not one of the specified check items. FHA and PMA make relatively less use of motion pictures than does SCS. PMA uses circular letters to a greater extent than either FHA or SCS.

With the current emphasis on international understanding and the development of extensive exchange programs sponsored by the Federal Government it is of considerable significance to know how many county FHA supervisors have made use of foreign visitors on borrower programs, what use SCS districts have made of foreign visitors and whether PMA has had foreign visitors on their programs. Only about 8 percent of FHA supervisors, and 5 percent of SCS conservationists and PMA committee chairmen report having foreign persons on their programs. These data show that little emphasis is put on arranging for foreign visitors to visit or address FHA and SCS audiences.

SUMMARY

The educational objectives of government agencies tend to be subordinated to more specific functions for which the agency has been organized. Farmers Home Administration, Farm Credit Administration, and Rural Electrification Administration are primarily credit agencies for farmers and are concerned only incidentally with broader educational objectives. Soil Conservation Service and Forest Service are concerned mainly with conservation objectives and to a lesser extent with general education. Production and Marketing Administration concentrates on matters of agricultural policy, crop control, and prices. As a consequence of this specificity of function which characterizes Federal agencies, personnel of these agencies tend to view their roles more narrowly than the educator with the result that the greatest educational potential is not achieved.

These government programs provide an extensive laboratory for "learning by doing" and each of the programs has developed its peculiar institutional arrangements. Within each institution are present all the elements necessary to facilitate the educational process, i.e. purpose, norms, personnel in role and status positions, materials to work with, and a localized unit. But the limiting factor in many instances is the breadth of vision of the supervisory personnel. Some are undoubtedly aware of the educational potential inherent in the agency situation but many are not.

To be most effective and to extend the scope of coverage of any government agency's program it becomes necessary to work closely with such community organizations as civic and service clubs, youth organizations, women's clubs, farmers' organizations, churches, schools, business associations, labor groups, legislators, state and federal agencies, newspapers, radio stations and others. The channels of communication in American society are so numerous that no one channel can be relied upon entirely to do the job. Also the procedures that may be used are numerous and include meetings of all kinds (i.e. board, annual, called, etc.) demonstrations, lectures, booklets, newsletters, committees, in-service training sessions, posters, charts, exhibits, slides, movies, newspapers, radio programs, contests, tours, personal visits, and others. Most agencies are under some compulsion to use most, if not all, of the procedures to administer, supervise and educate their clienteles.

More important perhaps, than either cooperative relations or procedures, is the way in which decision-making is made in the bureaucratic structure and how much use is made of democratic processes. It is clear that the federal agencies analyzed in this chapter arrange for farmer participation in the program in varying amounts. Thus Production and Marketing Administration has farmer committees in the states, counties, and even in local communities whereas the Forest Service has only a limited number of advisory councils to assist the supervisors of the national forests. The extent to which farmers control or help direct other Federal agencies varies somewhat between these two poles of exemplifying farmer participation.

No doubt the character of an agency's program has much influence on the relative amount of farmer control. In general, the wider based the program is, that is the more divergent groups it serves, the greater need for local and farmer control. However, the amount of local and federal control is one of degree, as all agencies studied have both controls in varying proportions.

       T. Wilson Longmore
       Division of Farm Population and Rural Life
       Bureau of Agricultural Economics
       Department of Agriculture
       Washington, D.C.

BIBLIOGRAPHY

Butz, Earl L., *The Production Credit System for Farmers*, Washington: The Brookings Institution, 1944.

Funderburk, R. S., *History of Conservation Education in the United States*, Nashville, Tenn.: George Peabody College for Teachers, 1948.

Gaer, Joseph, *Men and Trees*, New York: Harcourt, Brace and Co., 1939.

Loomis, Charles P. and Beegle, J. Allan, *Rural Social Systems*, New York: Prentice-Hall, Inc., 1950.

Maris, Paul V., *The Land Is Mine*, Washington: Agriculture Monograph No. 8, FHA, U. S. Dept. of Agriculture, 1950.

Yearbook of Agriculture, *Soils and Men*, Washington: Government Printing Office, 1938.

Yearbook of Agriculture, *Trees*, Washington: Government Printing Office, 1949.

Part Two

Chapter 8:

PUBLIC LIBRARIES

Introduction

History.—Since the first tax-supported library maintained to serve all the citizens of a community was opened in 1803,[1] the public library has contributed to the education of adults. At the beginning of the 20th century, county libraries, planned to serve rural as well as urban people, were established in Maryland, Ohio, Oregon, and California.[2] A "book-wagon" to serve people in outlying districts was first used in Washington County, Maryland, in 1905.[3]

In 1924, the American Library Association appointed a Commission on Adult Education, and in 1926 made the Commission a permanent body, called the Board on the Library and Adult Education.[4] This Board, now called the Adult Education Board, is still an active part of the Association.[5] Eight hundred members of the Association belong to the Adult Education Section.

During the past 25 years, library interest in adult education has grown. The principal activity of the public library in the field has been to provide materials to individuals who wish to read to increase their knowledge. The Readers Advisor has been added to the staffs of many libraries in order to help readers select materials which will give them information in subject fields of their own choice. Libraries have supplied materials to groups for use in programs, and where personnel has been available, have counselled groups in program planning and presentation. Forums, discussions, and lectures have been organized by libraries and held in library buildings. With the development of the 16 mm. film, libraries have provided films for groups, and held film showings and forums for the public.[6] However, librarians themselves have not been satisfied with their accomplishments and are sharply aware of the lack of development of the library's potential in adult education.[7]

Organization.—Local public libraries are autonomous units, supported by government funds and usually under the direction of a board appointed by the appropriating body or bodies. The chief functions of the board are to set policy, employ an administrative staff, and to serve as interpreters of the library to the community, and of the community to the staff. Although the board is re-

---

[1] Arthur E. Bostwick, *American Public Library*, New York: Appleton, 1926, 4th ed., p. 5.
[2] *Ibid.*, pp. 189–92.
[3] *Ibid.*, p. 129.
[4] *Ibid.*, p. 374.
[5] "Committees and Boards, 1951–52," *American Library Association Bulletin*, Vol. 45, No. 11, December 1951, p. 379.
[6] Robert D. Leigh, *The Public Library in the United States: The General Report of the Public Library Inquiry*, New York: Columbia University Press, 1950, pp. 103–108.
[7] Wayne W. Shirley, "What Happened to Our Adult Education Hopes," *Library Journal*, Vol. 72, November, 1947, pp. 1503–1507.

sponsible for setting policy in relation to the adult education activities of the library, in actual practice as revealed by interviews in this study, the librarian frequently determines the policy and the program, and convinces the board of its desirability.

For the purpose of this study, three types of library organizations are considered. The first group includes county and regional libraries.[8] These libraries are organized to serve a county, two or more counties, or a region.[9] Such a library has a headquarters staff, and may have branches, stations, or units in other parts of the area served. In addition, it usually has one or more bookmobiles to extend service into those parts of the area not otherwise served. In some instances, the bookmobile provides the only service outside of the headquarters.

Of significance to the adult education activities of such libraries is the fact that stations are simply deposits of books in retail stores, gas stations, or other public places, with only the proprietor to distribute the books to readers. Branches, unless they are very large, are often staffed by local people, paid on a part-time basis, and without library or other academic training.

Bookmobiles are usually staffed by professionally trained librarians. However, the short stay of the bookmobile in each community limits the function of the librarian to brief individual reader guidance. Many bookmobile librarians do some reference work, but very few are able to perform any adult education services. For the most part, the headquarters staff directs or conducts any adult education activities which are carried on.

The second group of libraries considered in this study are the state agencies.[10] Although these vary markedly in structure and function, they are all supported by state funds, have policy making boards, and perform certain functions in regard to the extension of library service to all of the people in the state. The adult education activities of some state agencies are limited to the same state department (reference or circulation) which fills requests from individuals or groups for specific books, or materials on given subjects. In other agencies, collections are sent to organizations for use in their program work.

In the larger state agencies, the adult education work is done by the extension division. The field workers in this division work directly with local libraries, and with state and local organizations, agencies, and governmental units. In some smaller state agencies the administrative staff does as much field work as time permits.

Village and city public libraries constitute the third group considered in this

---

[8] Helen Ridgway, *County and Regional Libraries: The United States, Its Territories and Canada* (a selected list), Chicago: American Library Association, 1949, Revised. Includes county and regional libraries with a minimum annual income of $5,000 or 10 cents per capita, whichever is larger. In addition to the above libraries, less well supported libraries on the American Library Association official addressograph list were included in this study.

[9] Leigh, *op. cit.*, pp. 61–63.

[10] Leigh, *op. cit.*, p. 69.

study. Since it was obviously impossible to contact every village or city library in the United States, the list is limited to three public libraries in the villages and cities of 263 sample counties.[11] Among these are libraries in communities of 200 people (Waco, Nebraska) up to the Denver Public Library with an area of service including over 300,000 people.[12] These libraries have in common the function of providing the public with educational materials. They vary in every other way,[13] and no attempt has been made to chart the structure of their boards, the source of their income, or the size and function of their staffs. Except in the large city libraries, the adult education activities reported by the village and smaller city libraries are the joint responsibility of the one or more staff members in addition to their other duties.

DISTRIBUTION OF LIBRARIES

Seven hundred thirty-five counties out of the 3,069 counties in the United States have county-wide library service. Four hundred eighty-eight counties have no library service of any kind.[14] Of the 263 sample counties considered in this study, 104 have county-wide service.

The number of counties served by county or regional libraries varies according to the type of farming area. Sixty-two percent of the counties of the western specialty-crop area in the sample have county-wide service, whereas only 6 percent of the counties in the wheat areas have such service. See Table 1.

The percent of rurality among the sample counties is in direct relation to the lack of county-wide library service. Thirty-six percent of those counties in which half or more of the population lives in rural areas have county-wide service. Fifty-two percent of those counties in which less than half of the population live in rural areas have such service, as shown in Table 1.

Half of the sample counties which fall between 1 and 49 in rural level-of-living index (national average = 100) have county-wide library service. Fifty percent of the sample counties with a level of living index of 50–99 have county-wide library service. Thirty-one percent of the counties with a level-of-living index of 100–149 have such service. See Table 1.

From the distribution of counties having county-wide library service according to their level-of-living, it would seem that the living standard of a county is relatively unimportant in the process of establishing such service. The determining factor thus far appears to be the degree of urbanization of a county, with the more rural counties less likely to have established county-wide service.

Village libraries have closer contacts with people from rural areas than the large city libraries are likely to have. However, of necessity they cannot provide

[11] For explanation of sample counties, see Chapter 1 and Appendix C.
[12] *American Library Directory, 1948*, New York: R. R. Bowker Co., 1948.
[13] Leigh, *op. cit.*, pp. 53–56.
[14] "Free Public Library," *Wilson Library Bulletin*, Vol. 26, No. 2, October 1951, pp. 188–189.

bookmobile or other extension services to reach people beyond the village limits. Small units of service such as these have been proved to be uneconomical and unable to provide adequate service.[15] Therefore, even in the New York region

TABLE 1
Sample Counties with County-Wide Library Service by Type of Farming Area, Rurality, and Level of Living

Type of farming, rurality, and level of living	Counties in sample	Counties with county-wide library service	Counties in sample with county wide library service
Type of Farming			
	Number	Number	Percent
Total	263	103	38
Western specialty-crop areas	13	8	62
Cotton belt	62	32	52
Residual areas	37	19	51
General and self-sufficing areas	45	20	44
Range-livestock areas	19	7	37
Dairy areas	31	9	29
Corn belt	40	7	18
Wheat areas	16	1	6
Rurality			
Total	263	103	37
24% and less	12	7	58
25%–49%	36	18	50
50%–74%	98	34	35
75% and over	117	44	38
Level of Living			
Total	263	103	38
1–49	6	3	50
50–99	106	53	50
100–149	150	47	31
150 and above	1	0	0

where of five counties, one has four libraries, one 7, one 11, one 13, and one 20, all rural people will not have convenient access to adequate library service until the smaller units are united into a county or regional agency. A study of the role of the library in community adult education programs in New York state indicates that inadequacies in service are especially apparent in villages and rural areas. Rural people have access only to state library services in many

[15] Leigh, *op. cit.*, p. 153.

instances. The small community library service is often limited to the circulation of books of a more or less popular nature.[16]

Of the 30 million people in the United States without library service, 26 million live on farms and in small villages.[17] These people have no general public supply of books, pamphlets, maps, periodicals, films, and other materials from which to borrow. The organizations in the communities without libraries have no public source of materials for the subject matter or conduct of their activities. Except for certain agencies, such as the Cooperative Extension Service, which provide material in the fields of their special objectives, no source of stimulation nor supply of information exists except commercial mass media. Some rural people are within reach of a village or city library. Even the more adequate of these do not extend their service beyond the limits of their area of support, (unless they are units or headquarters for county-wide service). Many of them fall far below the minimum in population served and amount of support necessary for adequate library service.

ACTIVITIES IN THE EDUCATION OF ADULTS

Two questionnaires, one concerning their overall adult education activities, and the other concerning their use of books and films were mailed to the 1,383 libraries considered in the study.[18] Fourteen percent of the first mailing of these questionnaires was returned. On a sample second mailing of the same materials, 39 percent was returned.

General Adult Education Activities.—One hundred two of the 238 libraries reporting indicate that they have some educational activities for adults. See Figure 1. Sixty-six percent of the county and regional libraries report activities. Forty-four percent of the village and city libraries indicate that they conduct programs or activities, but the number of responses from this group is very small.

Only 53 of the libraries reporting programs indicate the proportion of adults reached last year who live in open-country or centers of less than 2,500 people. Eighty-three percent of this number report that half or more of the participants in their activities live in rural areas. Only 13 percent report that almost none of the people reached are from rural areas. No city or village library reports that more than one-fourth of the people reached are from rural areas.

Reporting on mass media used in their programs and activities, librarians checked the list on the following page:

[16] Katherine O'Brien, *The Role of the Public Library in Community Adult Education Programs*, Albany, New York: The University of the State of New York, The State Education Department, 1947, p. 3. (Mimeographed.)

[17] "Free Public Library Service," *op. cit.*, p. 188.

[18] Ridgway, *op. cit.*, and note following *American Library Directory, 1948, op. cit.* For an explanation of sample procedures, see the details in Appendix C.

Mass media	Times checked
Radio	22
Television	2
Newspapers	37
Motion Pictures	20
Other	31

Interviews indicate that radio is used for regular book review or reference questions and answers, spot announcements on books or library activities, or interviews with staff by radio personnel concerning books or activities. The newspapers are used for general publicity feature articles on services, and annotated book lists or columns of comments on books. Motion pictures are those which the library lends to groups, or shows to groups, in the library or

HAVE YOU CONDUCTED EDUCATIONAL PROGRAMS FOR ADULTS? YES - 102 / NO AND NO ANSWER - 136

IF YES, DID ANY PROGRAM INCLUDE THE THREE FIELDS OF INTEREST? YES - 60 / NO AND NO ANSWER - 43

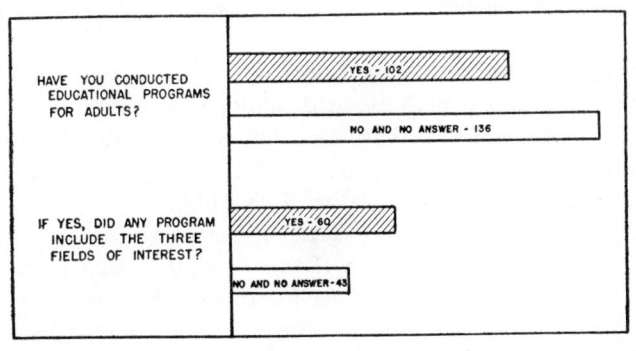

FIG. 1. Percentage of librarians reporting that they conduct educational programs for adults the proportion reporting that such programs were in the three fields of interest.

at outside group meetings. Other mass media mentioned most often were books, speakers, group meetings, phonograph records, exhibits, and book reviews.

In order to determine what kinds of agencies, organizations, and governmental bodies libraries serve, a list of 21 such groups was printed on the questionnaire. The librarian was asked, "What other organizations do you work with or through in your educational work with adults? Check as many as apply." Women's clubs, schools, parents' organizations, and churches and church organizations, in that order, are checked most often by the librarians reporting.

The organizations checked least often are UNESCO organizations, political parties and/or organizations, and labor unions. Probably few of these groups have units in less urban communities. Among the better supported county and regional libraries, 20 percent report work with elected or appointed government bodies, but only 5 percent of the less well supported county and regional libraries and of city and village libraries report work with such bodies.

Asked to name the three organizations through and with which they work most, the librarians most frequently name schools. However, from the evidence of interviews and comments on the questionnaires, many librarians report on their service to school children, rather than on cooperation with school adult education programs. Other organizations named most frequently are Women's Clubs, Parent Teacher Associations, Cooperative Extension Service (specific references are invariably to Home Demonstration Clubs) and churches and church organizations, in that order. There is no significant number of other organizations named.

In general, the findings on library educational activities for adults from rural areas indicate that over half of the libraries reporting have programs or activities in these fields, and that they use a variety of mass media channels in these activities. They cooperate with a number of organizations in their work, principally with women's clubs, parents' organizations, and churches and church organizations.

Programs or Activities in the Three Fields.—Of the 102 libraries reporting some information on educational activities with adults, 60 answer "yes" to the question: "Was any program or activity for adults that included 1) international understanding for peace, 2) strengthening of democracy, or 3) understanding and strengthening of the economy, carried on within or by your organization during the past year?" Of these 60, 20 report that of the people reached, half or more were from "rural areas," 15 of them indicating that almost all were rural people. Six report that about one-fourth were from rural areas, and 9 report that almost none were from such areas. Twenty-five libraries do not give information on this question.

The number of people reached by the best programs in the three fields of the libraries reporting range from 20 to 15,000. The libraries reporting the numbers above 1,000 are describing radio programs, book distribution, or service to organizations holding series of forums. Less than half of the libraries reporting are able to estimate the number of people reached.

Checking a list of forms of activity, librarians indicate that their activities most frequently take the form of public meetings. Other forms checked are conferences, radio listening groups, workshops, demonstrations, institutes and tours, in that order. To the check list, librarians add the following forms: book displays, film forums, reading programs, promotion of books, art exhibits, club meetings, book collections, service to individuals, and "read and discuss" forums.

Librarians indicate, through a check list, that group discussion is the procedure used most frequently, with lectures and panels following, in that order. Other procedures listed are film showings, films and talks, films followed by discussion, talks and slides, talks with question periods, program planning, previews and conferences with group leaders, general discussion, exhibits, book collections, bookmobile service, and service to individuals.

Fifty-eight percent of the libraries reporting activities in educational work with adults report work in the three fields of primary interest. The greatest number of programs in these fields take the form of public meetings, at which discussion and lectures are the most frequently used procedures. The variety of forms and procedures reported in addition to those on the check lists seem to indicate, however, that libraries do not follow any prescribed pattern in their adult education activities.

Those libraries reporting programs in the three fields were asked to fill out a form giving a detailed description of their best program. The libraries reporting the details most frequently choose one in which they cooperate with other organizations. A feature of each of these programs is the exhibit of materials or the preparation of a book list.

In Licking County, (Newark, Ohio), the librarian met with the Rural Church Fellowship, made up of five churches, for discussion of the individual's part in strengthening democracy. The meeting, in which lectures and discussion were used, was open to the public. The librarian reported that the book collection exhibited was the most effective part of the program. Seventy-five people participated.

Kent County Library, (Grand Rapids, Michigan), cooperated with the Rural Urban Council, composed of eight organizations, in sponsoring a local government workshop under the direction of the Continuing Education Division, Michigan State College. The all-day meeting was open to the public. About half of the 300 people present were from rural areas. Panels and group discussions were used, with the split-group technique reported as most effective.

In Louisiana, the Calcasieu Parish Library cooperated in a Louisiana social welfare conference on government in home, school, community, and church. This was a public meeting at which lectures and group discussions were used, with the latter reported as most effective. About one-fourth of the 60 participants were from rural areas.

Fontana Regional Library, (Bryson City, North Carolina), Morris County Library, (Morristown, New Jersey), and Dunklin County Library, (Kennet, Missouri), all report cooperation with the local branch of the Association of American University Women in programs in the three fields. Weston (Ohio) Public Library reports work with a Young People's Forum, and Ashland (Pennsylvania) Public Library reports cooperation with a local dinner club on a lecture series.

Two of the larger county libraries report cooperation with large public forums as their best programs. Kern County Library, (Bakersfield, California), prepared a reading list for each Open Forum held by the Bakersfield Adult Evening High School and distributed it at the meeting. Typical topics have been *Venezuela Venture*, and *Algeria*. The books and pamphlets on each list were displayed at the library and announced by radio and newspaper. The materials were frequently requested as a result of this activity. About one-fourth of the people who attended the Forums were from rural areas, but the announcements of the materials available reached a much wider audience.

Cuyahoga County Library (Cleveland, Ohio), prepared a fact sheet and book list for each discussion on world affairs which is co-sponsored by the library and the Council on World Affairs. Almost all of those participating were from the urban area, however.

Somerset County Library, (Somerville, New Jersey), Atlantic County Library, (Mays Landing, New Jersey), Rossford Public Library, (Ohio), Cairo County Library, (Grady, Georgia), and others report that they prepare book lists and exhibits for various topics in the three fields. Book lists received varied from simple mimeographed sheets to printed folders. The most frequently used topic was "The American Heritage in a Time of Crisis," the theme of the American Library Association for its 75th anniversary year.

Making films available to groups in the community is reported as their best activity in the political, social, and economic fields by five local libraries— Yakima Valley Regional Library (Washington), Umatilla County Library (Oregon), Jefferson City and Cole County Library (Missouri), Fort Atkinson Public Library (Wisconsin), and Ballinger County Library (Missouri).

Ector County Library (Odessa, Texas), Haywood County Library (Waynesville, North Carolina), and Cass County Library (Cassopolis, Michigan) report book reviews or talks in the three fields of primary interest as their best programs.

Reading programs for Home Demonstration Clubs are reported as their best program by the Randolph Public Library (Ashville, North Carolina), Hunds County Library (Raymond, Mississippi), and Deadwood Public Library (South Dakota). In each case, this is part of a state or county-wide activity. Reading lists for the club members' personal reading, collections of the books in local libraries or branches and, in some cases, the granting of a certificate to each member who read a certain number of books are the principal elements of the programs.

Tyrrell County Library (Columbia, North Carolina), and Flint River Regional Library (Griffin, Georgia), report special observances of United Nations Week. Almost none of the forty people present at the club meeting in the Flint River region, at which the librarian presented a panel on the United Nations, was from a rural area. All the thirty-five people in Tyrrell County who attended the special meeting for United Nations Week conducted by the library were from rural areas. A lecture followed by group discussion comprised the program.

Great Books programs are reported by four libraries, but no participation by rural people is reported.

The Mississippi County Library (Osceola, Arkansas), held a monthly half-day workshop for Negro teachers and community leaders. The County Negro Teachers Association, the School Community Association, the County Supervisor of Schools, a local author, the mayor and a state library consultant worked with the librarian in planning the program. Teachers, local farm people, and young people have taken part. The purpose was to establish group feeling, to aid appreciation of life in the county, to train leaders, and to teach them the use of materials. Individual reports and group discussion were the procedures used. The program has been successful in acquainting the participants with community resources and in helping them to feel free to use the library. There is evidence that those who participate encourage other people in the community to use the library. The principal difficulty in carrying out the work is to find enough material of high interest and low reading level according to the librarians' report.

Although all the libraries contacted in this study were asked for certain information on their over-all educational programs or activities for adults and for details of their best program or activity in the political, social, or economic fields, it was impossible to secure a complete picture of the total programs for adults offered by the reporting libraries serving rural people. However, in visits to selected libraries,[19] such a picture was obtained. The Door-Kewaunee Regional Library, (Sturgeon Bay, Wisconsin) is of unusual interest.

Door-Kewaunee Regional Library, established in November, 1950, is the first demonstration library established under the Wisconsin Library Law of 1949.[20] The State granted $28,500 for the first year's operation. Door County contributed $15,000 and Kewaunee County contributed $13,500 on a per capita basis of $1.50. The contract between the counties and the state specifies that the adult and children's programs shall share in the budget equally.

The basic adult service at Door-Kewaunee is through unit library and bookmobile distribution of materials. In addition, a community services program has been an integral part of the library's service. The basic planning is done by the staff, state library consultants, board members, and the People's Library Council. This body was originally appointed by the Board of Supervisors, and nominated the candidates for the Regional Library Board. Any citizen may now belong to the Council.

[19] The following libraries were visited:
    Wisconsin—Door-Kewaunee Regional Library, Sturgeon Bay.
    California—San Bernardino County Free Library, San Bernardino; Los Angeles County Public Library, Los Angeles; Kern County Free Library, Bakersfield; Fresno County Free Library, Fresno; California State Library, Sacramento.
    Oregon—Oregon State Library, Salem.
    New York—Erie County Public Library, Buffalo; New York State Library, New York.
    Tennessee—Lawson McGhee Public Library, Knoxville.
    Louisiana—Louisiana State Library, Baton Rouge; Iberville Parish Library, Placquemine; East Baton Rouge Parish Library, East Baton Rouge.
    Missouri—Missouri State Library, Jefferson City and Cole County Library, Jefferson City.

[20] "Report from the Demonstration," *Wisconsin Library Bulletin*, Vol. 47, No. 2, Wisconsin Library Commission, March 1951, pp. 39–48.

A survey of the community by members of the Council resulted in a list of community organizations and groups, and of meeting places, projectors, public address systems, and other facilities. Staff and Council interviewed many citizens to determine what community needs could be served by the library.

Staff members indicated interest in group activities and were invited to meetings. Occasionally, they were invited to bring exhibits of materials. Repeated visits are made in an effort to understand the purposes and plans of the organizations and to prepare helpful exhibits.

A definite program service was established offering library help to organizations in (1) setting up programs, (2) analyzing weaknesses in programs or organizations, (3) preparing effective publicity, (4) securing materials on any subject, arranged and planned for group study and discussion, (5) arranging for speakers and assisting in the choice of films. Mimeographed folders explaining the service were widely distributed to organizations in the region.

An Institute for Leaders and Program Planners was sponsored by the Library and conducted by the University of Wisconsin Extension Division. The Institute was a two hour, non-credit course. The $4.00 fee was paid in many cases by the organization sending a representative. Five weekly sessions were held, on what it takes to be a leader, how to plan a program, technique of discussion leadership, how to use films effectively, and essentials of parliamentary procedure. Of the thirty-two people taking part, half were from rural areas. Three-fourths of the group were men. Farmers, a priest, industrial workers, housewives, teachers, and others attended.

In cooperation with the Kewaunee County Home Agent and the Kewaunee County Agricultural Agent, Gardening Institutes were held in three locations in the region in the spring. Programs on vegetable growing, pest control, and home freezing were presented. Exhibits of gardening tools and supplies from local merchants, of pamphlets and bulletins from the Kewaunee Extension Office, and of garden books from the library were featured.

Bi-weekly preview film sessions were held in three places in the region over a period of four months in cooperation with the Bureau of Visual Instruction, University of Wisconsin. This was an informational service for organization representatives to help them in critical appraisal of the films they were to select for their meetings.

The establishment of a film circuit by the State Library Commission in cooperation with the State Bureau of Visual Instruction provided Door-Kewaunee Library with an opportunity to secure ten films each month. These are loaned to organizations for a service fee of $1.50. The Library offers to supplement the film showing with an exhibit, discussion leadership, or a speaker.

In the future, Door-Kewaunee plans to offer a film program for the in-service training of retail business personnel, and a Great Men and Great Issue film discussion series. An evaluation study of the effects of the community services program on the adults of the community is planned.

The Door-Kewaunee program is significant for several reasons. The emphasis on service to adults was part of the policy of the library from the beginning. The staff has had leadership and assistance from a trained and experienced state library commission staff that was able to give an unusual amount of time to Door-Kewaunee because of the demonstration nature of the project. One of the important contributions of the state staff was the implementation of the use of state departments and the University by the regional library and other local libraries in the state. The involvement of the citizens of the community was inherent in the policy on which the library was founded.

Door-Kewaunee Regional Library is not typical of libraries serving rural areas. It demonstrates, however, that a planned program of distribution of significant materials to adults, and of services to groups in a community can be carried out successfully by a regional library serving a largely rural population.

Two of the large, well supported county libraries of California conduct special adult education activities. For the past three years, Fresno County Free Library in California has held an annual Library Week celebration. Although the primary purpose of the event is the strengthening of public relations, the week provides many educational opportunities for adults as well as stimulation to use library resources in many fields of interest.

Fresno County Free Library serves an area of over 274,000 population. About 173,000 of these people live in rural areas. The per capita budget in 1950–51 was $1.11. The Reader's Adviser and the Extension Department under the direction of the assistant librarian are responsible for adult education activities, and all divisions provide services for adults. The entire staff works, through committee organization, on Library Week.

The theme of Library Week in February, 1951, was "Doorways to Opportunity for Fun and Profit." In addition to the extensive headquarters activities in providing radio programs, governmental proclamations, newspaper stories, organization contacts, reading lists, and programs, each of the thirty-eight branch libraries which chose to participate had an exhibit and open-house with various other activities. Some of the topics chosen by the branch library assistants were:

California the Golden	Del Roy Branch
Cotton	Tranquility Branch
Korea	North Fresno Branch
March of Democracy	Selma Branch
United Nations	San Joaquin Branch
World Affairs	Eaton Branch

At Fowler Branch, the American Legion Auxiliary cooperated with the branch library in providing a display of current books on Americanization.

The county librarian chose the activity at Monmouth Branch Library as an example of community participation in the strictly rural area of the county.

The program was planned by a committee of fourteen local residents and library users who also carried out details. Exhibits were planned and an evening meeting was scheduled. The exhibits were arranged on tables—one for each topic chosen. Books, magazines, pamphlets, and book lists were included. On the special evening, each table was attended by a library patron who through the use of library materials had developed an interest in the subject represented. Two hundred fifty people attended and many of them discussed library resources with the patrons in charge.

A formal program of library films, *Help Yourself* and *It's Your Library*, brief comments by headquarters personnel, and music were presented. The evening ended with a social hour and refreshments served by the women of the community.

Although no formal attempt at evaluation has been made at Fresno County Free Library, the staff feels that ample evidence exists to justify the annual observance of Library Week. Letters have been received from many people in the community commenting on their new knowledge of library resources, circulation has increased, and community interest has been greater each succeeding year.

The theme for 1952 will be based on the theme of the American Library Association for its 75th anniversary year, "The American Heritage in a Time of Crisis." Library Week provides an opportunity to acquaint the public with all of the resources of the library and to stimulate interest in materials which are not in great demand until such interest is awakened.

Kern County Free Library (Bakersfield, California), among its other activities, makes extensive use of reading lists. This large county library, serving 135,000 people with a budget of nearly $400,000, has a staff artist who designs unusually attractive bookmarks and brochures. In most of the lists, fiction and non-fiction, new books and old, are included. Japan, China, and the Near East have been among the subjects of short lists. Extensively annotated lists have been made on labor, on the White House, and on a quotation from Eleanor Roosevelt, "Wind is rising throughout the world of free men everywhere, and they will not be kept in bondage."

Lists are made and distributed on special occasions. Oil Progress Week was one such occasion. At the public ceremony celebrating the completion of the Central Valley Project when water first came to Kern County, the library distributed a folder listing historical highlights in the development of the Project and statistical material on the installations. The *Forty-Niners* was the title of a list prepared for the California Centennial Celebration.

A *Documents Bulletin* is distributed regularly through Kern County branch libraries and to direct mailing lists. Occasionally, the *Bulletin* lists state and national documents on a variety of subjects but frequently material on one topic is listed in an issue. Some of the topics have been: "The A-Bomb and Civilian Defense," "Korea" (which included a brief description of the terrain), "Central Valley Project," "Minerals, Mines and Mining," and "Conservation."

The *Public Administration Bulletin* is distributed regularly to Kern County officials and to officials of incorporated towns in the county. It lists books, pamphlets, and magazine articles on government, finance, zoning, recreation, and other matters of concern to public officials.

Brief bibliographies on the subject of the regularly held Bakersfield Evening High School Open Forum are prepared and distributed. The staff of Kern County believes that much of the effectiveness of a list is in its distribution. For that reason, they place lists on home repair in paint and hardware stores and lists on marriage and child development in doctors' offices. No formal evaluation of the effectiveness of the lists is made, but the staff reports that many people come to the Library to request books which they have found on the lists.

Books, Pamphlets, and Films.—On a separate questionnaire enclosed with the first, librarians were asked to list the books, pamphlets and films in the three areas of primary interest most used by rural patrons during the past year. One hundred seventy-one libraries returned the questionnaires without listing any titles. They gave as reasons the fact that they have no records to indicate the use of such books by rural people, or that there is no demand in their communities for such materials. However, 236 different titles were reported. Fifty-one of the better supported county and regional libraries report 224 titles, 3 of the less well supported county and regional libraries report 19 titles, and 13 of the municipal libraries from the sample counties report 67 titles. Certain titles are reported by all three groups.

Although the numbers are too small to be significant, the fact that certain titles are reported by more than one library is of interest. Nine libraries report *Partners: The United Nations and Youth* by Eleanor Roosevelt and Helen Ferris; and six libraries report *East of Home* by Santha Rama Rau, *War or Peace* by John Dulles, *How the United Nations Works*, by Tom Galt, and *This I Do Believe*, by David Lilienthal.

Five titles by Winston Churchill are reported, four by John Gunther, three by Stuart Chase, and three by Barbara Ward. Sixteen authors were represented by two titles each. Five United Nations publications are listed, including two published by UNESCO. Twenty-eight pamphlets are reported, including such inclusive titles as Public Affairs pamphlets, U.S. State Department publications, and United Nations pamphlets.

The titles reported indicate good standard book selection. The books are important ones, reviewed as such by responsible reviewers.[21] In addition, they would probably pass tests for readability based on human interest and clarity of presentation. However, many adults of limited education are unable to read books like this with ease and understanding. See Table 2.

Films can meet the needs of people who are not ready to read the kind of

---

[21] *Book Review Digest*, New York: H. D. Wilson Company, 1945 to date.

TABLE 2

Book and Pamphlet Titles Reported by Three or More Libraries

Book or pamphlet title	Total	Reported by better supported county and regional libraries	Reported by less well supported county and regional libraries	Reported by municipal libraries in sample counties
Roosevelt, Eleanor and Ferris, Helen *Partners: Youth and the United Nations*.	9	8	—	1
Dulles, John *War or Peace*.	6	4	1	1
Lilienthal, David *This I Do Believe*.	6	5	1	—
Rau, Rama Santha *East of Home*.	6	5	—	1
Galt, Tom *How the United Nations Works*.	6	6	—	—
Churchill, Winston *Hinge of Fate*.	5	5	—	—
Eisenhower, Dwight *Crusade in Europe*.	5	4	—	1
Higgins, Marguerite *War in Europe*.	5	2	—	3
Johnson, Gerald *Incredible Tale*.	5	4	—	1
United Nations Pamphlets.	5	3	—	2
Bradley, Omar *Soldiers Story*.	4	2	—	2
Bush, Vannevar *Modern Arms and Free Men*.	4	2	1	1
DeToledano, Ralph *Seeds of Treason*.	4	3	—	1
Fisher, Lois *You and the United Nations*.	4	4	—	—
Kefauver, Estes *Crime in America*.	4	2	—	2
McCune, George *Korea Today*.	4	2	—	2
Ward, Barbara *Policy for the West*.	4	2	1	1
Arne, Sigrid *United Nations Primer*.	3	2	—	1
Blanchard, Paul *American Freedom and Catholic Power*.	3	3	—	—
Blanchard, Paul *Communism, Democracy and Catholicism*.	3	3	—	—
Bowan, Catherine Drinker *John Adams and the American Revolution*.	3	3	—	—

Book or pamphlet title	Total	Reported by better supported county and regional libraries	Reported by less well supported county and regional libraries	Reported by municipal libraries in sample counties
Churchill, Winston				
Gathering Storm	3	3	—	—
Grand Alliance	3	3	—	—
Their Finest Hour	3	3	—	—
Hoffman, Paul				
Peace Can Be Won	3	3	—	—
Michener, James				
Return to Paradise	3	3	—	—
Payne, Robert				
Mao-tse-tung	3	2	—	1

books listed by the librarians, but evidently few libraries serving rural people are able to provide them. Fifty-nine films are listed by 18 libraries. Of these film titles, six are reported by more than one library. Some of the film titles reported more than once are the following: Brotherhood of Man, (4 mentions); Boundary Lines, (3 mentions); Man in the 20th Century, (2 mentions); Does it Matter What You Think? (2 mentions); Hymn of Nations, (2 mentions); Of Human Rights, (2 mentions).

Librarians were asked to indicate whether the titles listed had been circulated, reviewed by the librarian, or used as material for group discussion. Of the 319 listed titles of books and pamphlets, including duplications, all but 17 are reported as having been circulated. Fifty-eight are reported as having been reviewed for groups by the librarian and 119 as having been used as material for group discussion.

Of the 68 listed film titles, including duplications, 37 are reported as having been circulated, 50 as having been shown to groups, and 31 as having been used as material for group discussion.

According to these reports, printed material is used primarily by the individual, but can be and is put to group use by librarians. The film is used chiefly for groups (circulation of a film is most often for group use) and is also used by the librarian to stimulate interest and group discussion.

The State Agency.—The role of the state agency in library adult education is principally to supplement the resources of local libraries, and to provide direct materials service to people in areas unserved by local libraries. Some state agencies provide guidance and leadership for local libraries in adult education. They cooperate with organizations at the state level in program planning and in distribution of information on library resources to local units and individual members.

Twenty-two of the forty-eight state library agencies responded to requests for information concerning their activities in adult education. North Carolina,

Virginia, South Dakota, West Virginia, Oregon, Illinois, and Louisiana reported reading programs. The first four work entirely with Home Demonstration Divisions of the State Agricultural Extension Service and extend the program to the members of the Home Demonstration groups. All of these except West Virginia award certificates of accomplishment to members reading a certain number of the books listed, or substitutes suggested by librarians.

The Oregon, Illinois, and Louisiana State Libraries extend their reading programs to any interested individuals in the state. Illinois reports that 32 percent of the 106 people receiving certificates in 1950–51 were from Home Bureau groups (the names of the divisions of the Agricultural Extension Service vary from state to state). Fifty-four percent were people who had been stimulated by the publicity program and 14 percent were from state prisons. In 1950–51 there were 593 new enrollees in the program. Louisiana grants a certificate, but the staff feels that the program has served its purpose and should be discontinued or modified. Oregon does not give a certificate but prepares lists on any subject at the request of the individual. A percentage of those served are from the Oregon State Prison.

All of the state libraries conducting reading programs list some subjects in the social, political, and economic fields. Among these are the family, citizenship and tolerance, American life, labor relations, leadership, the world tomorrow, and conservation. Ohio reports work in progress with the Ohio Home Economics Association, Farm Bureau, and Grange to develop and conduct a rural reading and discussion program built around the American Heritage theme.

New York State Library and Oregon State Library have both conducted book review training sessions for Home Demonstration group leaders on a state and county basis. The procedure consists of a talk on the principles of book reviewing and demonstration reviews. Both libraries furnish mimeographed material on reviewing. The participants in these sessions are group leaders who return to their groups and teach what they have learned. South Dakota Free Library Commission, with the aid of local librarians, gives reading demonstrations at Home Demonstration leadership meetings at the district and county level.

In the fulfillment of their function to encourage the establishment of local libraries, state agency personnel organize, conduct, or participate in meetings of local people interested in library service. Missouri State Library encourages the establishment of community councils for the purpose of developing county or regional library service. In New York State, where an extensive library development program is under way, the state agency staff meets with trustees of established libraries to help them with the problems of establishing larger units of service.

The education of trustees in the duties, problems, and potentialities of their positions, which are assumed voluntarily, is a function to a greater or less degree undertaken by many state agencies. Michigan, from 1946 to 1949, had a trustee consultant on the State Library staff under a three year foundation grant. The members of the extension staff now hold meetings of trustees and librarians on an area basis, with the objective of education in their responsibliities and in library purposes and philosophy. The annual one week vocational workshops for untrained library personnel held in Michigan include a day and a half session for trustees. In Wisconsin, an annual institute on public library management is held in cooperation with the Bureau of Government of the University of Wisconsin. Trustees are an important group among the participants. Regional laboratory workshops, of which twelve were held under the auspices of the Wisconsin State Library Commission for the purpose of studying community aspects in relation to library activities, also included trustees.

State agency personnel frequently participate in state-wide meetings of various organizations. They sometimes display exhibits, take part in the program, or represent the library point of view in discussion. New York State Library has tried a follow-up program which has proved successful. The State Extension worker who attended an Institute on Community Leadership sponsored by the New York Citizens Council wrote to each person who had attended, suggesting that he visit his local library for materials to supplement the information he had obtained at the meeting. Lists of the names of the participants at the Institute from their area were sent to local librarians with suggestions concerning the type of materials which might be requested. Letters from both participants and librarians indicated that they appreciated the service. A list of suggested readings was distributed at the Institute and the books, as a unit, made available to any group requesting them from the State Library.

State library agencies, like all other types of libraries, indicate an interest in films. Many, however, report that they circulate films concerning libraries only. Louisiana reports a collection of eighty-eight general interest films available to libraries, groups, or responsible individuals. Illinois lends projectors to responsible groups. Louisiana and Illinois have prepared lists of films available to libraries and groups from agencies, organizations, and commercial sources throughout each state.

Ohio, Wisconsin, and Missouri report film circuits originating from the state agency. In Ohio, two circuits include libraries serving rural areas. The films are purchased by the State Library. In Wisconsin, the films are secured from the State Bureau of Visual Instruction on a service fee basis. The one circuit now in operation includes metropolitan and rural areas. In Missouri, where the circuit includes 23 county and regional libraries and four municipal libraries, the basic collection was purchased with a foundation grant. In all cases, the libraries on the circuit contribute an annual fee for purchase or rental, replacement, and service.

The state agencies maintaining film circuits prefer this method of distribution to that of maintaining only a collection for loan on request, although such a collection is desirable to supplement the circuit films and to serve groups without local library service. Libraries on a circuit know in advance what group of films will be available to them in a given period. They are able to hold film previews for organization leaders, or to send an annotated list of films to organizations in the community. Groups are stimulated to use films. Types of films in which groups may have evinced no previous interest are called to their attention. As the use of film increases, the local librarians have opportunities to work with groups in film forum techniques and the use of supplementary materials. Librarians who are part of a circuit take an active interest in film selection and have opportunities to preview a variety of films. The State Library Extension worker knows what films will be used in a community and is able to offer more specific help to the librarian in their use.

Some state libraries have attempted state-wide programs of special education. The Louisiana State Library reported a state-wide program in adult education in 1951. Disturbed by public indifference to the responsibilities of citizenship, the State Librarian suggested a citizenship campaign to parish librarians who adopted the project in August, 1950. The overall planning was done by the State Library Staff. Local librarians conducted the program in their own communities and lay leaders, encouraged and helped by the State Library staff, organized activities in those areas without local library service. Twenty-five state-wide organizations pledged their support.

Registration, intelligent voting, respect for and participation in civic affairs were the aspects of citizenship underlined in the program. The slogan was "Be a Full Time Citizen;" the symbol—a ballot box.

A citizenship kit containing book and film lists, posters and car stickers, program and exhibit suggestions, radio and newspaper material, the American Heritage Foundations' "Good Citizen" pamphlet, and the League of Women Voters, quiz on citizenship was sent to 250 local committees and other community leaders. The State Library secured radio and newspaper publicity and governmental proclamations and had a 35 mm. trailer made for local use. Other state departments cooperated in various ways.

The peak of the campaign was reached in March, when communities blossomed with displays and publicity, and schools and clubs held citizenship programs. The campaign will be continued in various ways throughout the year.

Evaluation of the campaign was not possible but a definite increase in requests for films, books, and other materials on citizenship subjects occurred, and librarians and lay people all over the state expressed enthusiastic approval and a conviction that the campaign had called to the attention of a large number of people their responsibilities as citizens. Four parish libraries reported in this study on activities in the citizenship campaign as their best programs.

New York State Library cooperated in a state-wide Freedom Train project sponsored by the State Society of Newspaper Editors and New York State Publishers' Association during 1949. Modelled after the National Freedom Train idea, the six-car train carried an exhibit of New York documents. At each stop, the local library was responsible for its own publicity and activities—in connection with the aroused interest in the state's heritage.

The state agency, while maintaining firmly its purpose of serving libraries, and individuals in unserved areas, has in many cases widened its range to include services to groups, with the purpose of stimulating the use of materials on topics of vital importance in the present scene. Perhaps the state agency's most important adult education function is a vocational one, not within the scope of this study. To the extent that state agencies can stimulate the interest of local librarians in adult education, and train them in the skills necessary—to that extent will libraries be likely to realize their potential in the field.

OBSTACLES TO MORE EFFECTIVE LIBRARY SERVICE

No education of adults through libraries is available to the people living in areas without library service. Without question the chief obstacle to the development of the existing library's potential in the field of adult education is the lack of adequate support. Librarians returning the questionnaires wrote notes of explanation which show the picture graphically. Some representative quotations follow:

"This county library is so under-supported and understaffed that we make no effort to work seriously with adults." (County library in Pennsylvania.)

"We have serious lacks in appropriation space, staff—cannot do adult education planning." (County library in Michigan.)

"I wish I could tell you of the many, many things we are doing for adult education for I am sold on the idea, but with our present staff, and funds our activities have to be limited." (Regional library in Georgia.)

"Since 1946 the per capita support for library service in the rural area has been raised from 23 cents to 75 cents. Since this is a combined city and county system, and the financing at the city level is more adequate, we have been able to inaugurate the beginnings of an adult education program in the urban areas. We hope in time to extend this into the rural areas." (City-county library system in California.)

These comments are substantiated by library statistics. The annual per capita income for libraries in 63 cents, in contrast to the per capita expenditure of $33.69 for elementary and secondary schools.[22] The state with the lowest per capita expenditure is Florida, with 12 cents. Massachusetts, spending $1.56 per capita, has the highest library income.[23]

In many county and regional libraries, the greater percentage of time and money is spent for school service. The librarians wrote:

"We have no adult program here—local funds are not available for anything but the most limited service, and most of that goes to the public schools." (County library in North Carolina.)

[22] "Free Public Library", *op. cit.*, p. 188.
[23] *Ibid.*, p. 189.

"Our work is 85 percent or more with school children." (City library giving county service in Ohio.)

"... Ninety-five percent of our time and books go to work with schools." (County library in Pennsylvania.)

School people have often taken the leadership in the establishment of the county or regional library, and this fact probably has contributed to the emphasis on service to schools. Since in many cases more than half of the service from the bookmobile or branches is given to children in addition to the service given to them in school,[24] little time or money is left for services to adults.

The lack of staff members trained and experienced in work with adults is closely related to the lack of adequate support. However, if there were money enough to create positions in the field of adult services, enough people with training could not be found to fill the posts.[25]

The attitudes of board members and members of appropriating bodies is occasionally given as a reason for not developing an adult education program. Some of the people who control library policies object to any program which must be advertised, on the ground that it stirs up an artificial public demand for more services. Others respond emotionally only to appeals for funds for services to children. Occasionally the fear of inviting criticism from the appropriating body limits the efforts of the library in work with labor unions or minority groups. However, these attitudes seem to be held seldom, and to be rarely effective in hindering the work of the library.

Some librarians report that the people of their communities are not interested in such subjects as international understanding, democracy, or the economic system. They give as proof the facts that books in these fields are rarely borrowed, that audience participation is poor at film discussions, that organization leaders reject programs in these fields as being dull. These reports are offset, however, by the enthusiastic reports of librarians who have found the people in their communities responsive to their efforts in these fields. The variables in this area are too many to permit a conclusion. The vitality of the library's total work, the personalities of the librarians and community leaders, the effectiveness of the techniques employed, the educational level of the community in relation to the reading level of the materials supplied, and many other factors would have to be weighed.

The historical concept of the library as a storehouse of materials distributed only on demand is another obstacle to the development of adult education activities. Collections have been built around the expressed needs and wishes

---

[24] Leigh, *op. cit.*, p. 99.

[25] In 1948, there were 3 times as many library school students as in 1926, but at the University of Chicago Library Conference it was said " . . . but still the profession and the schools are calling for more and better-qualified personnel to fill the ever-present vacancies in library staffs." Bernard Berelson, Editor, *Education for Librarianship*, papers presented at the Library Conference, University of Chicago, August 16-21, 1948.

of the people of the community. Books and materials in fields of significance, but not as yet greatly in demand, have been purchased sparingly or not at all. Such books often have been shelved with the rest of the collection and given no special publicity or attention. Individuals and groups (such as professional or political organizations) which might have an interest in such materials, frequently have not been contacted unless they voluntarily approach the library.

No doubt there are librarians who are satisfied to maintain their service on this basis. Many others would change the pattern if they could. However, the lack of support prevents their doing more than to meet the expressed wishes of their borrowers. If the library is to be supported at all, it must circulate books, and a limited book budget precludes the purchase of books which will be used rarely. It takes staff hours, unshackled by desk schedules, to introduce such books to those who may be interested in them, or to awaken the interest of other people in such vital subject fields.

A librarian in a small city library in Kansas reports: "This education is needed, but I am a lone worker with neither the time or the know-how." From a Washington state county library the librarian writes: "This is a new library in a fast growing county, and we can't keep up with the book demand so far. We hope to expand in the future." A Tennessee regional librarian describes her work in detail. Her letter might be duplicated by county and regional librarians all over the country. She writes:

> Although we fully realize the vital importance of broadening and deepening the understanding of rural people in the fields covered by the survey, we have not been able to operate a formal program for that purpose because of lack of personnel.
> During the past year our region consisted of eight counties and included eight county libraries and 90 deposit stations which were served by the regional bookmobile. Six of the county libraries had a staff of one untrained person. My duty as regional librarian was to assist the county libraries, providing advice, assistance, and supplementing materials, and to drive the bookmobile over the eight counties visiting the community deposit stations. I had one clerical assistant who did all the typing, record keeping and book processing in the regional office.
> You can easily see that it has been impossible to conduct any formal program of adult education. However, I have made contacts with local organizations and have supplied material for their use. Also, in my personal contacts in the small communities I have emphasized the importance of reading on these subjects (democracy, international understanding, the economy) and always leave books dealing with them.
> I am sorry we are not able to make a more encouraging report. Even though we have not been able to set up any educational program, we are making educational materials readily available through a large number of outlets.

SUMMARY

The potential for the education of adults through libraries serving rural areas is largely undeveloped. Two-thirds of the rural areas have no library service.

Existing libraries lack financial support to provide an adequate library program. The more rural the county, the less likely it is to have service.

Libraries conducting adult education activities cooperate with many other organizations, with schools, women's clubs, parents organizations, and churches and church organizations, the most frequently reported. Libraries report a variety of kinds of activity from public meetings to displays of books, with no discernible universal approach evident.

Those libraries reporting on materials in the three fields used in rural areas indicate the employment of acceptable standards of book, pamphlet, and film selection, and the use of all kinds of material with groups. The small number of libraries able to report on the use of such books and especially on the use of films, indicates a lack of significant materials in many collections.

State agencies report a variety of efforts to stimulate adult education. Direct loan service to individuals and libraries is the predominant activity. Staff participation in state level group meetings is considered important. Of greatest significance is the effort of the state agency to train local librarians in adult education skills, and to stimulate local programs.

The greatest need is for education of the public to awareness of the value of library service to a community. Since people who do not have adequate service cannot be expected to appreciate its value, it seems evident that all organizations concerned with educational objectives must join forces with national and state library agencies and organizations for the establishment of nation wide library service, improvement of existing libraries, and development of the objectives of adult education in the library program.

Development of a national recruiting program for librarianship to provide trained people on the local level who can make effective use of state level assistance is another need. Three avenues of approach suggest themselves:

1. Mass media—radio, television, magazines and newspapers.

2. School personnel—particularly vocational guidance counselors.

3. Rural organizations—conducting programs to inform their members of a public service of use to them, and of an attractive vocational choice for young people who wish to live in rural areas and perform public service.

Committees of the American Library Association and State associations have long carried on a recruiting program. In order to match the efforts of other recruiting groups such as the nursing organizations, it would seem necessary to expand the program in the following ways:

1. Secure the services of professional advertisers.

2. Provide for the publication of additional and more attractive printed materials than are now available.

3. Commission the preparation of films and recordings with public appeal.

4. Provide program guides, speakers, panel members, consultants, and factual materials for groups wishing to participate.

Ruth Warncke, Librarian
Kent County Library
Grand Rapids, Michigan

BIBLIOGRAPHY

A Selected List

American Library Association, Adult Education Board, "Adult Education Policy for Librarians," *ALA Bulletin*, Vol. 38, No. 10, November, 1944, pp. 451–452.

Berelson, Bernard, *The Library's Public; a Report of the Public Library Inquiry*, New York: Columbia University Press, 1949.

Berelson, Bernard, editor, *Education for Librarianship; Papers Presented at the Library Conference, University of Chicago, August 16–21, 1948*, Chicago: American Library Association, 1949.

Bingham, Harold, "The State Library Agency," *ALA Bulletin*, Vol. 38, No. 11, December 1, 1944, pp. 478–479.

Bostwick, Arthur E., *The American Public Library*, New York: Appleton, 1926, 4th ed.

Carnovsky, Leon, "Library Service to Rural Communities," in Floyd Reeves, *Education for Rural America*, Chicago: University of Chicago Press, 1945, pp. 143–154.

Chancellor, John, and others, *Helping the Reader toward Self-education*, Chicago: American Library Association, 1938.

Chancellor, John, editor, *Helping Adults to Learn; the Library in Action*, Chicago: American Library Association, 1939.

Humble, Marian, *Rural America Reads; a Study of Rural Library Service*, New York: American Association for Adult Education, 1938.

Joeckel, Carleton B., and Winslow, Amy, *A National Plan for Public Library Service; Prepared for the Committee on Postwar Planning of the American Library Association*, Chicago: American Library Association, 1948.

Johnson, Alvin, *The Public Library—a Peoples' University*, New York: American Association for Adult Education, 1938.

Kotinsky, Ruth, *Adult Education Councils*, New York: American Association for Adult Education, 1946.

Leigh, Robert D., *The Public Library Inquiry in the United States, the General Report of the Public Library Inquiry*, New York: Columbia University Press, 1950.

"Libraries Get Adult Education Role; Official Summary of a Survey of New York State's Resources for Adult Education in Public Libraries," *Library Journal*, Vol. 72, No. 11, November 1, 1947, pp. 1517–1522.

O'Brien, Katherine, *Role of the Public Library in Community Adult Education Programs*, Albany: University of the State of New York and the New York State Education Department, 1947. (Mimeographed.)

Ogden, Jess and Jean, "Libraries Attack Community Problems," *Library Journal*, Vol. 72, No. 1, January 1, 1947, pp. 33–35.

McDonald, Gerald Doan, *Educational Motion Pictures and Libraries*, Chicago: American Library Association, 1942.

Merrill, Julia Wright, *Regional and District Libraries*, Chicago: American Library Association 1942.

Prospecting for Library Patrons; a Series of Papers Sponsored Jointly by the American Library Association, Adult Education Section, Public Libraries Division, and the Adult Education Board, Chicago: American Library Association Division of Public Libraries, 1950.

Public Library Statistics, 1944–45, Federal Security Agency, Office of Education Bulletin, No. 12, Washington: United States Government Printing Office, 1947.

Rothrock, Mary U., *"Library Service to the Rural Community,"* in Leon Carnovsky, and Lowell Martin, editors, *Library in the Community,* Chicago: University of Chicago Press, 1944.

Schenk, Gretchen Knief, "Trends in County Library Service," *ALA Bulletin,* Vol. 41, No. 6, June, 1947, pp. 6–11.

Shirley, Wayne, "What Happened to Our Adult Education Hopes?" *Library Journal,* Vol. 72, No. 11, November, 1947, pp. 1503–1507.

"The Free Public Library," *Wilson Library Bulletin,* Vol. 26, No. 2, October, 1951, pp. 188–189.

Wilson, Louis R., *The Geography of Reading; a Study of the Distribution and Status of Libraries in the United States,* Chicago: American Library Association and the University of Chicago Press, 1932.

Chapter 9:

ADULT EDUCATION IN THE RURAL CHURCH

Introduction

Several studies have indicated that the most frequent type of participation by farmers in community organizations is in church activities.[1] One study, based on a national sample of rural population, indicated nearly 70 percent participation by heads of farm families in church affairs.[2] In this study it was found that no other community organization, including school activities, farmers organizations and lodges, had as much as 25 percent participation.

By virtue of the scope of its social and community contacts, it is obvious that the church has a tremendous potential outreach for the education of adults in rural areas. Loomis and Beegle have observed that professional "persons interested in changing the attitudes and habits of rural people cannot afford to ignore the church as a possible channel of communication through which the people may be reached."[3] The Soil Conservation Service, for example, has appealed to rural church people through the sentiment of the stewardship of land. However, in an institution which has defined its role principally in religious terms the question can be asked as to the activities of the church in reference to political, economic and social needs of the rural community.

That the church is giving increasing attention to these secular though related concerns, is evidenced by the activities of many religious organizations at the

[1] D. E. Lindstrom, *American Rural Life,* New York: the Ronald Press, 1948, p. 194; E. A. Schuler and R. R. Swiger, *Trends in Farm Family Levels and Standards of Living,* Washington: BAE, USDA, 1947, p. 21; and W. A. Anderson, *Some Participation Principles,* Ithaca: Cornell Extension Bulletin 731, 1947.

[2] Schuler and Swiger, *Ibid.*, p. 21.

[3] Charles P. Loomis and J. Allan Beegle, *Rural Social Systems,* New York: Prentice-Hall, Inc., 1950, p. 454.

national, state, denominational, diocesan and local levels. These movements have as their aim the education of adults along lines of social, political and economic activities of peculiar concern to farmers.

This chapter will describe and assess the organized efforts to strengthen rural life through the medium of the church and related organizations. Not only will the programs of national and state religious rural life organizations be described but an attempt will be made to describe some of the adult education activities of the rural church at the community or local level. The latter task is somewhat more difficult than the former in that descriptive materials are not available as in the case of national, state, and denominational organizations.

To secure information about local church activities in adult education we used questionnaire sampling. Information about the national, state, and denominational groups was secured from interviews with several of the leaders of these groups and from a careful scrutiny of the voluminous literature available from these organizations.

We will look at national adult education programs in rural areas of Catholic, Protestant and Jewish groups and then note the kinds of implementation these programs have received at state and community levels. These national organizations will be discussed in the order of their formation.

The first of these was the Jewish Agricultural Society which received its first charter from the State of New York in 1900.[4] It did not function as a completely separate organization until 1907. It was well financed and functioned as an agency to help Jewish people settle on farm land with the result that today Jews are represented in every branch of farming.[5] The society *has a broader purpose* than that of rural settlement. Educational activities dealing with local, national and international concern are sponsored by the Jewish Agricultural Society among Jewish rural people.

The National Catholic Rural Life Conference grew out of the first meeting of the American Country Life Conference held in 1919. The aims and thinking of the conference have been stated in a Manifesto,[6] which gives major emphasis to the welfare of the family on the farm and educating these families to certain moral, social, economic and political activities. The Conference sponsors a periodical, *Land and Home*, and holds local, state and national conferences for the improvement of rural life.

The major Protestant activity in bringing together rural church workers into a national organization is the Committee on Town and Country of the National Council of Churches of Christ in America. The first Convocation of this group was held in Columbus, Ohio in 1945. Annual meetings are held and some Catholic rural leaders attend as well as the Protestant leaders. The conference con-

---

[4] Gabriel Davidson, *Our Jewish Farmers*, New York: L. B. Fischer, 1943.
[5] *Ibid.*, Chapter VI.
[6] *Manifesto on Rural Life*, National Rural Life Conference, Milwaukee: The Bruce Publishing Co., 1939.

cern themselves with such matters as rural reconstruction, farm tenure, farm laborers and share croppers, the church and community agencies, the rural church and the seminaries, rural church extension, the relationship of the rural church to international problems, the agricultural colleges and the rural church, financing the rural church and rural religious education.[7]

Another agency of considerable importance at the national level is The Rural Christian Fellowship which grew out of the Agricultural Missions Foundation. It publishes a regular series of pamphlets dealing with the rural church and rural affairs and has stimulated the organization of numerous state and denominational fellowships dedicated to the education of adults in rural areas along economic, political and sociological lines.

Although closely related to national rural life organizations, separate mention should be made of the denominations and state councils of churches having town and country departments or sub-committee units with other titles which are devoted to rural adult education activities. Many of these receive their impetus or plans of organization and procedure from the previously mentioned national organizations. For example, the Methodist church is developing a nationwide rural church program which gives emphasis to the need for social security in the rural family. Similar efforts on behalf of the church in rural areas are being put forth by the Church of the Brethren, the Lutherans, the Presbyterians, the Baptists and other denominational groups in rural areas.

Numerous state councils of churches have important programs aimed at strengthening rural life through its sponsorship of adult education programs in local churches. One such example is the Rural Life Committee of the Iowa Inter-Church Council. Working in close cooperation with Iowa State College the committee sponsors rural pastors' institutes, pastors' county soil conservation meetings, merit awards to rural churches making significant community contributions, rural leadership programs, study and discussion groups dealing with problems peculiar to rural life.

At the academic level there have been several significant developments. Conferences are being held between theological seminaries and colleges of agriculture. Recognizing the need in the ministry for men trained in rural life, representatives of the seminaries and colleges of agriculture met in 1939 to develop cooperative projects. One of the results was the creation of a curriculum in the colleges of agriculture for a pre-theological major which included courses in rural sociology and economics. Many of these colleges of agriculture sponsor rural pastors schools and various kinds of rural life-in-service training.

Religious bodies in the United States vary considerably in their rurality as shown in Figure 1. This figure indicates the percentage of rural membership in

[7] For more detail see *The Rural Church in These Moving Times*, New York: A Report of the National Convocation of the Church in Town and Country, Committee on Town and Country, Home Missions Council, The National Council of Churches of Christ in America, 1947.

several selected Protestant, Catholic and Jewish religious groups. Protestant groups have a much larger proportion of rural membership than do Catholic and Jewish groups which are predominantly urban. With Catholics showing only 19 percent rural membership and Jews less than one percent rural membership, it is significant that educational efforts of these two groups among adults is to encourage them to move to the farm while Protestant rural life educational activity is directed more to the development of educational activities designed to provide a basis for understanding the significance of the rural way of life.

The Farm Foundation has cooperated closely with the Town and Country Committee of the National Council of Churches of Christ in America in holding a series of regional church-land tenure conferences. The foundation has also

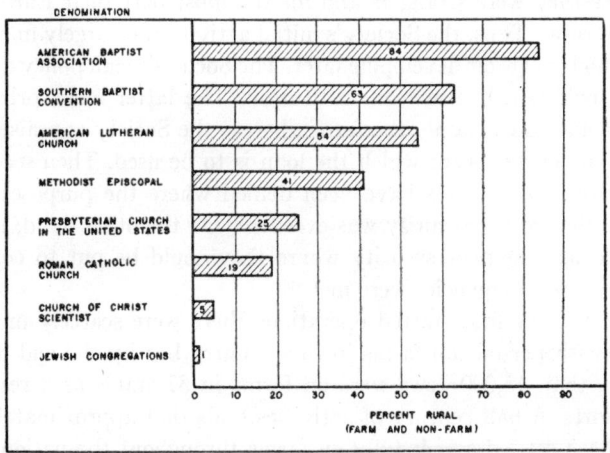

FIG. 1. The rural strength of selected American religious groups (*A Survey of Catholic weakness*, 1948.)

been vitally interested in the family farm and has sponsored a series of Institutes to which rural church and lay leaders have been invited.

THE JEWISH AGRICULTURAL SOCIETY[8]

History and Origin.—The Jewish Agricultural Society was founded in 1900 for the purpose of promoting farming and educating for the rural way of life among Jews. The society maintains itself from the substantial philanthropies of Baron Maurice de Hirsch whose successful railroad and financial ventures placed him in the front rank of Europe's financiers and industrialists.[9] The Jewish Agricultural Society of America functions as an affiliate of the Baron de Hirsch Foundation.

[8] Grateful acknowledgement is made here for the assistance given to the writer by Samson Liph, Mid-west Director of the Jewish Agricultural Society, 130 North Wells Street, Chicago, Illinois. The interview took place in Chicago, August, 1951.

[9] For more detail on this point see Samuel Joseph, *History of the Baron de Hirsch Fund*, The Jewish Publication Society, 1935, Ch. I, The Creation of the Baron de Hirsch Fund, and Ch. IV, The Jewish Agricultural Society.

Early in the history of the Jewish Agricultural Society an allied organization known as the Industrial Removal Office was created by the officers of the society. This was for the purpose of breaking up the ghettos and removing Jewish people to smaller communities. Through this agency over 100,000 Jews were removed from the large eastern cities, particularly New York City.

The formal separation of the Industrial Removal Office and the Jewish Agricultural Society took place in 1907 which meant that the latter was free to use its resources exclusively for agricultural work and educational activities in rural areas.[10]

When the society was founded and for many succeeding years, *farm* credit was woefully inadequate. This difficulty was more acutely felt by American Jews because they were strangers and for the most part their European heritage was not rural. Thus, the Society's initial activity was largely financial with the educational programs developing later. The Society's loan policy differs from that of the traditional farm loan institution. The latter looks principally to security and appraises mainly the farm whereas the Society appraised first the farmer and the purposes for which the loan is to be used. Then secondly, the security is appraised. Loans have been denied where the purposes appeared unwise even though the security was excellent. On the other hand, loans have been granted against poor security where they could be put to constructive activity or where emergencies were met.[11]

When the Society first started operations there were scarcely more than a thousand Jewish persons on farms in this country but by the end of the first decade more than 15,000 Jews were on farms in 37 states as a result of the Society's efforts. A half century of activities finds that approximately 150,000 Jews have been settled successfully on farms throughout the nation.[12]

Objectives of the Organization.—The following objectives of the organization are all allied to the basic purpose of the society which is to encourage and advance farming among Jews in the United States

1. The Society advises urban dwellers who are interested in taking up farming as a livelihood and provides expert counsel in the selection of the farm and in the financing of it. The Society maintains a Department of Farm Settlement for these purposes.

2. The society will not only give advice on purchase negotiations but will also make loans where conditions warrant it. These loans are based not strictly on tangible security but also on human factors such as faith in the ability of the borrower to make good. A Farm Loan Department is maintained for this type of work. The Society has made loans aggregating over $12,000,000 since its inception.

[10] Davidson, *op cit.*, p. 22.
[11] *The Jewish Agricultural Society, Inc.*, Report of the Managing Director for the Period 1900–1949, p. 10.
[12] Interview with Mr. Liph. See footnote 8.

3. The Society sponsors various kinds of educational activities among the adult Jewish farmers. This is designed to bring agricultural information to the Jewish farmers by travelling Jewish agricultural specialists. In addition to instruction by its own staff members the Society also uses the personnel and facilities of the state agricultural college in the area.

The meetings involve not only specifically agricultural topics but also discussions on subjects coming within the scope of the three major areas of interest to the Fund for Adult Education established by the Ford Foundation.[13] It was reported to the writer by Mr. Samson Liph, manager of the Chicago office of the Jewish Agricultural Society,[14] that discussion of these topics was important in that farming so integrated into the economic, political and social organization that effective farming requires these broader understandings.

To fulfill these educational objectives the Society maintains a Department of Agricultural Education and Extension which also publishes an agricultural magazine, *The Jewish Farmer*.

4. Relating to the general objective of making the farmer more effective in his task are additional departments which carry on work to promote higher standards of sanitation on farm premises; to assist in the formulation of farm management plans; to assist in the purchase of farm equipment and supplies; to assist in the placement of farm workers.

Organizational Structure.—The governing body of the Jewish Agricultural Society is the Board of Directors, consisting of 15 prominent American Jews. The board is elected by the membership of the Jewish Agricultural Society. The Society is composed of 35 American Jews and is a self-perpetuating body. New members are added on the basis of recommendation and vote by existing members. Basic policy decisions are made by the directors with action implementation by a staff of professional workers.

Staff positions include the following: Managing Director,[15] Manager, Assistant Manager in Charge of Farm Settlement and Farm Loan, Two Settlement Specialists, Settlement Clerk, Director of Public Relations, Director of Agricultural Extension, Editor—The Jewish Farmer, Associate Editor, Extension and Settlement Specialists, Two Extension Specialists, Manager of Mid-west Office,[16] Manager of Western States Office,[17] Cashier, Administrative Clerk, Two Consultants.

The Adult Education Program.—As the Society grew it became increasingly necessary to supplement the financial activities of the organization with various kinds of educational endeavors. The Society maintains an extension department

---

[13] 1. International Understanding for Peace; 2. Strengthening of Democracy; 3. Understanding and Strengthening of the Economy.
[14] Interview with Mr. Liph. See footnote 8.
[15] 386 Fourth Avenue, New York 16, New York.
[16] 130 North Wells Street, Chicago 6, Illinois.
[17] 208 South Spring Street, Los Angeles 12, California.

for its educational activities which center largely around agricultural problems and technical advice related to the operation of the farm.

The major kind of activity by the extension department is in personal visitation to farms by the extension specialists. The Society's yearly report for 1950 indicated the type of activity as follows: The staff of the department made 4,038 farm visits, held 3,000 office consultations, conducted 93 farm meetings with an estimated attendance of 7,000 and sent out 12,000 letters of information and service.[18]

As indicated previously in the staff assignment it is obvious that the Jewish Agricultural Society devotes a considerable portion of the staff's time and energy to educational effort and direct personal contact with rural Jews. While the work in adult education is not structured in terms of the three major areas of concern to the Fund for Adult Education,[19] it is clear that the Jewish Agricultural Society makes definite contributions along these lines.

Since there have been no studies of the adult education program of the Jewish Agricultural Society it is rather difficult to give precise definition to the many activities as they relate to the three Ford fields of interest. On the basis of interviews with leaders of the Society and an examination of the literature of the organization, it is clear that the major emphasis is in strengthening economic foundations. The Society gives continual instruction in agricultural techniques, farm finance and the role of the farm in the total economy. This is done by personal visits of extension specialists, meetings, discussion groups and extensive distribution of the Society publication, *The Jewish Farmer*. Work of the Society in providing purchasing service, the development of cooporatives and credit unions and its employment division would also come in the category of strengthening economic foundations.

As to strengthening democracy and international relations, the educational approach of the Society would be less direct than in the case of economic foundation. Certainly the Society's emphasis on and assistance in the development of the family type farm is making a contribution to the American way of life, the farmer's sense of dignity and freedom essential to democratic processes. The Society's work with refugees from Nazi countries and displaced persons has been quite extensive and thousands of them have taken advantage of the Society's facilities to get established in this country.

In meetings sponsored by the Society, speakers frequently are brought in from the state colleges and universities who do not limit their discussions to strictly agricultural concerns. Topics relating to democracy and international relations are discussed at these meetings in addition to the usual agricultural topics.

[18] The Jewish Agricultural Society, Inc., Report of the Managing Director, 1950, p. 18.
[19] International Understanding for Peace, Strengthening of Democracy, and Understanding and Strengthening of the Economy.

Procedures.—The chief educational instrument, according to Gabriel Davidson, is the individual visit.[20] Instruction is carried direct to the man on the farm by travelling teachers who are picked for teaching ability, temperamental fitness and their Jewish background. This itinerant instruction antedated by several years the systematic agricultural county agent work made possible by federal statute in 1914.

These teachers go from farm to farm and assist the farmer in the solution of his problems. They do more than impart technical knowledge. They establish a close rapport with the individual farmer and assist him in the solution of numerous problems not strictly within the agricultural sphere. He is invited to social functions, weddings, bar mitzvays, and addresses Chanukah and Purim parties.

The Society's visitation facility is regarded as the most important single procedure in getting the results the organization hopes to achieve.[21] Other procedures are: conducting night adult education classes in Chicago, New York and Los Angeles, maintenance of bureaus for consultation by correspondence, holding regional conferences, local meetings, displaying exhibits, showing movies and arranging a variety of eductational demonstrations.

Ecological Factors.—The approximately 150,000 Jews who are living on farms in the United States are found in practically every state. The largest numbers are found in the northeast, particularly in New Jersey, New York and Connecticut, and in the mid-west, particularly in the South Haven and Benton Harbor areas of Michigan. There also is a considerable concentration in California. Other states of considerable activity in the east are Rhode Island, Massachusetts, Vermont, Maine and Pennsylvania; and in the mid-west, Ohio, Wisconsin and Indiana.

As the number of Jewish families established on farms increased, there gradually evolved fair sized Jewish farming communities. The Society had deliberately sought to settle Jewish farmers in fair proximity to each other "in order to promote adjustment to the American milieu while preserving cultural and religious Jewish identity."[22] This enabled the Jews to maintain synagogues and religious schools and yet become part and parcel of the general farming community.

It will be noted that many of the Jewish farm communities are located fairly close to large metropolitan centers. This may be due in part to previous urban backgrounds with which there are friendship and kinship ties but more likely to be based on the exceptional marketing opportunities provided by proximity to a city. Mention also is made of the fact that such locations provide opportunity for outside earnings, a factor of considerable importance in times of

---

[20] Report of the Managing Director For the Period 1900–1949, *op. cit.*, p. 15.
[21] *Ibid.*
[22] *Ibid.*, p. 13.

economic stress.[23] Very important too is the factor of greater accessibility of the services of the Jewish agricultural society.

Nature of Audience.—In regard to age composition a sociological study involving a sample of 300 Jewish farmers of 17 states showed that 60 percent of the farmers were under 50 and only 10 percent over 60 years of age.[24] The modal group was in the 40 to 50 years of age category and constituted 38 percent. This study showed that 81 percent had been in the country 20 years or more, while only a fraction of one percent had been here less than 10 years.[25] Only four percent were natives.

From this study it is evident that the bulk of present-day Jewish farmers are foreign-born who came here early in life. Eighty-three percent were citizens and three percent declarants.

Occupational backgrounds indicate that the Jewish farmer in the main is middle class. A large diversity of occupations is represented in the recrutitment: skilled trades and labor, white collar occupations, business and manufacturing and the professions. The needle and fur trades made up the largest single occupational category. Seven percent had attended farm schools or agricultural colleges here or abroad. It is obvious that the American Jewish farmer is not indigeneous to the soil but simply the immigrant urban Jew transplanted to the American farm. Since World War II this situation has changed somewhat in that the majority of Jews served by the Society in this period have been displaced persons from Europe with a rural background.

When the survey was made, general farming predominated, (33 percent); poultry farming was next with 32 percent. Then came dairying, 18 percent; followed by truck farming, 10 percent. Dairying has become increasingly popular with Jewish farmers and likely is predominant today. Close to half the farmers surveyed had supplemental sources of income. Higher than average farm living standards are experienced by the Jewish farmers. The survey showed, for example, that 66 percent of the farms had sanitary plumbing; 88 percent electricity; 52 percent central furnace heat. This might be accounted for by the fact that Jews had become accustomed to these conveniences in the city.

Evaluation.—Since there has been very little done in the way of evaluational studies of the Jewish Agricultural Society it will be necessary to rely on statements of leaders within the Society, comments about the organization by non-Jewish agricultural and rural life leaders and the literature available on the movement.

The fact that there are about 150,000 Jews living on farms as contrasted to a few hundred a half century ago when the Society started is in itself testimony to the effectiveness of the guiding organization. The survey, previously

[23] Report of the Managing Director, 1950, *op. cit.*, p. 11.
[24] Davidson, *op. cit.*, p. 162.
[25] *Ibid.*

referred to, indicated that these farmers are satisfied with their life on the farm. Ninety percent indicated that they would rather be on the farm than in the city.[26] These same farmers were almost unanimous in saying that they were getting along well with their non-Jewish neighbors. Over 90 percent described their relationship as good and nine percent as simply fair.[27] Data pertaining to farm children showed that 37 percent of those over 18 remained on the farm.

The Jewish farmers have been successful in virtually every type of agricultural enterprise: dairying, poultry raising, truck farming, floriculture, or charding, viticulture, cattle raising, tobacco, grain, cotton, sugar beets.

Tenant farming is extremely rare among Jewish farmers. The Society has given every possible aid to enable the Jew to own his own farm. Historically, land ownership has been denied to the Jew and apparently he wants a spot he can call his own.

Dean W. I. Myers of the New York State College of Agriculture and formerly governor of federal land banks, makes the following summary evaluation of the Jewish Agricultural Society:

In essence the Jewish Agricultural Society has supplemented and intensified the work of the Extension Service, not as a competitive force, but in cooperation with the extension service. We are grateful to the Society, and to Dr. Davidson who has contributed so generously to its progress, for the sound foundations they have given to so many farm families, for the good practices they have promoted, and for the wise counsel they have offered.[28]

In summary it is clear that there are many thousands of Jewish families conducting successful farming enterprises, with accompanying personal satisfactions, who otherwise would be adding to the difficulties associated with high urban concentration.

Recommendations.—1. While the Society is expanding its public relations activities, it would seem wise to step these up even further. For an organization with the scope and record of successful operations such as the Jewish Agricultural Society, there should be a much greater awareness on the part of the American public than now seems to be the case. There is some evidence that the Jewish layman needs more information about the activities of the organization.

2. Closely related to the above point is the suggestion that a more intensified effort should be made to acquaint American Jewry with the activities of the Society. While no claim is made by the writer for scientific validity on this point, an informal check made by the writer among his Jewish friends indicated that they had very little knowledge of the activities of the Society. The recommendation at this point would be for synagogues and Hillel organizations

---

[26] Davidson, *op. cit.*, p. 164.
[27] *Ibid.*, p. 165.
[28] I. W. Myers, "Farm Service—A Constant Goal," *The Jewish Forum*, Vol. XXX, No. 6, June 1947, p. 141.

to observe a Jewish Agricultural Sabbath or to set aside a day or a week for study of the problems of Jewish agriculture. The Rabbinnical Council of America has approved such a plan but there is need for more extensive observance than now seems to be the case.

3. Work of the Jewish Agricultural Society could be better appraised and future plans for the Society could be made with greater assurance if there were more fundamental human relations research. Particularly in the evaluation of the program could strengths be noted and weaknesses spotted and thus more effective programming and planning could be made. To be more specific, the writer recommends a survey-study in which Jewish farmers of United States indicate both the kinds of Jewish Agricultural Society activities which have been of greatest benefit as well as additional areas of greatest need. The suggestion is made at this point that research assistance could be secured from the state colleges and universities and/or from Jewish research agencies such as the American Jewish Committee.

4. While the central interests of this study of international understanding, strengthening of democracy and understanding and strengthening of the economy are dealt with partly by implication and partly by direct action and instruction, it would seem that the work of the Society would be strengthened by more adult education programs dealing directly with these topics. It might be argued that there are other Jewish agencies better equipped to sponsor educational programs of this nature. However, the Jewish Agricultural Society is the direct contact agency with the farmer and is in a unique position to administer the educational program which would likely involve the utilization of facilities of other Jewish organizations.

5. While the record of the Jewish Agricultural Society is outstanding in terms of settling urban Jews on the land in successful farming operations the recommendation can be made for expanded operations. In order to maintain a balanced population more urban Jews need to go to the land. This would involve, also, a better distribution of rural Jews into good farming land in addition to the areas in which they are now settled.

THE NATIONAL CATHOLIC RURAL LIFE CONFERENCE

In the United States, Catholics are overwhelmingly an urban people. This together with the demographic fact that urban people are not reproducing themselves sufficiently to maintain population provides the circumstances from which was developed the National Catholic Rural Life Conference. Catholic literature has given serious attention to population studies[29] with special note being made of the impact of declining urban population on Catholic religious and social structure.

[29] For example see the approximately 50 pages of population statistics, graphs and tables in L. G. Ligutti, *A Survey of Catholic Weakness*, Des Moines: The National Catholic Welfare Conference, 1948.

The Catholics call attention to the fact that Protestant urban and rural population is balanced whereas among Catholics it is not. Only eight percent of Catholics live on the land as full time farmers and one Catholic spokesman indicates that Catholics can at least aspire to the national percentage, which is sixteen and seven-tenths percent.[30] From the Catholic point of view a serious consequence of urbanism is that Catholic families, too, follow the declining birth rate.[31] It was this series of conditions that indicated the need in the Church for a rural life movement which, at present, is epitomized in the National Catholic Rural Life Conference and whose origin we will now trace.

History and Origin.—The formation of the National Catholic Rural Life Conference was not the beginning of rural life education in the Church; it was simply the pooling of the efforts of many rural life leaders in the Church into one national movement.

After many years of unorganized rural life activity, Father Edwin Vincent O'Hara appeared on the scene and provided the leadership which gave national integration of the rural life movement under a single banner. In 1919 Father O'Hara was asked by the National Catholic Education Association to prepare a paper on Catholic rural education. On accepting the invitation, he spent a year in gathering data on the basis of interviews and a careful questionnaire study. This provided the substance for his lecture which stated the nature of the rural problem, its religious implications and some suggestions for the solution.[32]

He conceived the idea of founding a national headquarters for the direction of a program for rural welfare. In 1920 Father O'Hara was appointed by Bishop Peter Muldoon of Rockford, Illinois to head a new section of the National Catholic Welfare Conference to be known as the Rural Life Bureau. Father O'Hara became very active in The American Country Life Association and decided to hold a national Catholic rural meeting in connection with the Association meeting in St. Louis in 1923. Here was born the National Catholic Rural Life Conference, the start of the crusade.

The leadership was selected, the campaign outlined and the organizational structure tentatively defined. It should be pointed out that in the early years, the Conference was in no sense an action group but as the name implied a discussion group only. It had no existence outside the convention and the officers functioned merely as planning agents for the next meeting. This, however, was of extreme importance to give the movement a philosophy, a working plan, an organizational structure. The years of careful and sound planning did much to insure the permanency of the organization as an action agency.

Objectives.—The National Catholic Rural Life Conference is just what the

---

[30] Personal interview with Monsignor L. G. Ligutti, August, 1951.
[31] Raymond P. Witte, Twenty-five Years of Crusading—*A History of the National Catholic Conference*, Des Moines: The National Catholic Rural Life Conference, 1948, p. 2.
[32] The complete speech and report of the research project is reproduced in Witte, *Ibid.*, pp. 46–57.

name implies, a conference, a discussion group, an educational agency. One of the executives of the organization has defined it as:

> ... an organization of bishops, priests and lay persons dedicated to the economic, social and spiritual interests of American farmers. It functions as an educational and propaganda agency within the Church for the application of the principles of Catholic philosophy to the sphere of agriculture.[33]

At Des Moines in 1929 the delegates to the Conference decided to formulate a set of objectives as they had expanded and developed during the six years of the Conference's existence which we summarize as follows:
1. The general objective is rural life ... with proper unity and proportion for its different factors.
2. Physical life: Health, rural medical care.
3. Economic life: Credit unions, cooperatives, land ownership.
4. Family Life: The heart of the rural life problem.
5. Religious Life.
6. Training for Life: Leadership training, adult education.
7. Community Life: Relating parish welfare to community welfare.
8. Relations to wider life: of church and state.[34]

The achievement of the above objectives has continued to be the goal of the Conference. Msgr. Ligutti has seen the necessity of preparing a more compact statement of the aims of the Conference which could have wide circulation in a small folder and be understood by everyone. The folder amplifies the four points listed below with a paragraph under each point. The title is: Four Working Aims of the National Catholic Rural Life Conference:
1. To care for underprivileged Catholics now on the land.
2. To keep on the land Catholics now on the land.
3. To settle more Catholics on the land.
4. To convert non-Catholics on the land.

Organizational Structure.—The Conference is organized on a Diocesan basis. The Bishop of the Diocese appoints a rural life director and cooperates in the establishment of a rural life bureau. The director specializes in the field of rural life and becomes thoroughly familiar with the work of government rural agencies as well as Catholic. The rural life bureau studies ways and means of furthering and developing rural life in the Diocese.

There are 130 Dioceses in the United States but not all of them have rural life directors. At the present time there are 85 Diocesan rural life directors in the United States.[35] The Conference gives instruction to the Directors who in turn channel materials, techniques and ideas back to the various rural pastors in the Diocese.

[33] *Ibid.*, p. 143.
[34] *Ibid.*, pp. 83–87.
[35] Personal interview with Msgr. Ligutti.

The Diocesan rural life directors hold an annual meeting in connection with the annual Conference meeting. They elect their own officers, including a chairman, and make recommendations and receive recommendations from the Board of Directors of the Conference. The officers submit a yearly report of Diocesan activities to the Board of Directors and formulate plans for each year's activities to the Board of Directors of the Conference.

Under the leadership of Msgr. Ligutti the scope of the work expanded to such an extent that Regional Directorships were established to coordinate the rural life activities in ten districts designated by the board. The name of their position came to be designated as Regional Coordinators. Their function was to communicate with Diocesan directors, to arrange for meetings, to coordinate the movements of speaker corps from school to school and to plan various details of programs. Those men appointed to these positions are able to specialize in the needs of their areas and tend to relieve the office of many details emanating from the regions.

The administrative direction of the movement is in the hands of a full time executive director, Msgr. Ligutti, who has several lay assistants who have responsibilities for publicity publications. The national headquarters are at Des Moines, Iowa.[36] Msgr. Ligutti spends most of his time travelling in the interests of the Conference and averages only about 50 days a year at the National office.

Finances.—Financial support for the work of the Conference comes from a variety of sources. Private individuals have donated money, some gifts running as high as $10,000. The Diocesan directors have been urged to pledge annual amounts of about $100 per year. The archbishops and bishops have been urged to pledge money annually to the conference. Much of the revenue is obtained from membership dues of members of the National Catholic Rural Life Conference, who are supporters of the movement.

The Adult Education Program.—The adult education program of the National Catholic Rural Life Conference relates primarily to those activities which will promote a balance between Catholic rural and urban populations. This involves propaganda to help urban people see the advantages of the rural way of life and involves both propaganda, education and action in taking care of those people in the Church already on the land.

The Conference adult education program is contained in an important book entitled *Manifesto on Rural Life*. Prominent Catholic social thinkers and religious leaders drafted a series of statements discussed, criticized and approved by the executive board of the Conference. The Manifesto voices the belief of the conference in an intensive educational program and that it "should be adapted to the special needs of the farming group and should be grounded on the Christian philosophy of life."[37]

[36] The address is 3801 Grand Avenue.
[37] *Manifesto on Rural Life, op. cit.*, p. 192.

Content of the Program.—The Manifesto states the position of the Conference on sixteen phases of rural life which we will describe briefly. In terms of the three central themes of interest of this study, it appears that topics dealing with strengthening the economy have the greatest emphasis. This is indicated by the topics listed in the Manifesto and also in questionnaire returns from Diocesan rural life directors. Thirteen out of 20 questionnaires returned indicated that Strengthening the Economy was given the most prominence. Democracy and Peace were mentioned seven times each.

The sixteen points of the Manifesto, which constitute the position of the Conference and is the basis for the programming of its educational work, are as follows:

1. The rural Catholic family.
2. Farm ownership and land tenancy.
3. Rural settlement.
4. Catholic rural education.
5. Rural Catholic youth.
6. Catholic culture in rural society.
7. Rural community.
8. The rural pastorate.
9. Rural church expansion.
10. Rural church health.
11. Rural social charity.
12. The farm laborer.
13. Farmer cooperatives.
14. Rural credit.
15. Agriculture in the economic organism.
16. Rural taxation.[38]

While we have little data on the proportional emphasis given each of these topics in the hundreds of parishes engaging in adult education practice we do know that topics relating to the strengthening of the rural economy are allotted the principal considerations.

Procedures Used.—A large variety of techniques with many and varied locality adaptations are much in evidence in various parishes and dioceses brought to the attention of this study, through the use of interviews, examination of literature and questionnaire data. Also cooperative activities with a large variety of organizations are in evidence in the presentation and preparation of Conference programs. Thirty-six of the 70 Diocesan rural life directors responded to a questionnaire seeking data on Conference programs.

In response to the question "what other organizations do you work with in

[38] *Manifesto on Rural Life,* op. cit., Part I, Chapters 1–16. Part I, which we have summarized briefly states the policies and principles of the rural life program. Part II is an extensive annotation of bibliographic materials relating to the chapters in Part I. For detailed description of each of the above phases of the Church's educational program see Part I of the *Manifesto.*

your educational work with adults," Diocesan rural life directors most frequently mentioned "churches and religious organizations." Schools ranked next in frequency of mention, followed by "Federal and/or State Government Bureaus" and the Cooperative Extension Service. The details of this tabulation may be found in a subsequent table. (See Table 3.)

In regard to cooperation with non-Catholic churches the Catholic rural life movement has been characterized from the beginning by close and cordial relations with the rural leaders of other religious groups. The same policy is being continued by the present leadership and consequently there is a continuous exchange of guest speakers and the development of a united front for a return to basic rural philosophy and action.

Responses of the Diocesan rural life leaders concerning the best procedures used in rural life programs as well as the form of the best program in the three fields of interest are interesting.

Of the procedures checked by the respondents, lectures were used most frequently. Group discussions, panels, large groups split into small discussion groups, and study groups followed, in order of frequency used. When queried concerning the form of their best program in the three fields of interest, the Diocesan rural life directors most frequently indicated it to be a public meeting. Conferences and institutes were also mentioned frequently. Workshops, radio listening groups, demonstrations on tours were mentioned rarely as the form of their best program.

Mass Media.—As a technique of communication and vehicle of propaganda the Conference is resorting increasingly to several of the mass media. In the questionnaire survey it was found that newspapers, motion pictures, and radio, in the order named, were the most commonly used of the mass media.

The Conference maintains a public relations department and feeds material to the Catholic and public press. The Conference distributes a monthly press release, known as The Catholic Rural Life Page to over 100 newspapers throughout the country. In addition the Conference prepares pamphlets and printed reports of conference proceedings.[39] Another type of booklet in the form of guides or manuals for Catholic farmers is prepared and distributed by the Conference.[40] Rev. Daniel F. Dunn, executive secretary of the Conference, publishes a monthly report, "Feet in the Furrow" for the Diocesan directors. The members of the conference receive a monthly newsletter.

Several books dealing with rural life and problems of agriculture from the Catholic point of view have been written by members of the Conference.[41]

---

[39] For example, see *Proceedings of the Twelfth Annual Convention*, 1934; *Catholic Rural Life Objectives*, (Several volumes, each dealing with papers presented at the annual Conference meeting).

[40] *The Manual of Catholic Action Farmers*, 1941; *Leaders Bulletin for Catholic Action Farmers*.

[41] Urban Baer, *Farmers of Tomorrow;* Ligutti and John C. Rawe, *Rural Roads to Security;* Thomas E. Howard, *Agricultural Handbook for Rural Pastors and Laymen; Manifesto on Rural Life*, *op cit.*

Another type of publication the Conference is proud of is a book of rural life songs.[42] This is based on the desire of the Conference to restore to rural life its own distinctive culture.[43]

A number of Diocesan directors of rural life have used local radio stations and smaller networks in the dissemination of information relative to the objectives of the Conference. The work of the Conference has also been publicized over *The National Farm and Home Hour*. This program has made its facilities available to the Conference at its national conventions.

Study Clubs.—The Conference has been active in fostering study clubs among their rural parishioners. In 1943 the Conference began the preparation of study club materials for the seminaries. By 1946 there were 40 seminaries using the study club materials. The Conference has indicated that this is the only method short of furnishing faculty members, open to the Conference, for imbuing the future priests of the United States with an understanding and appreciation for rural work.

Rural Life Schools and Institutes.—From the very beginning the Conference realized that since most Churches are urban and few seminaries include any rural training in their curricula, the Conference would have to function as the principal educational medium to counteract the urban emphasis. Leaders in the Conference and Catholic rural life movement speak regularly at the various Catholic seminaries trying to interest the students in rural life. However, it was soon realized that more was needed than a few formal talks.

The educational committee of the Conference was appointed to develop courses in rural sociology. Out of this developed the rural life schools and institutes. The first rural life school was a twelve day course in rural leadership for Diocesan directors and young priests at St. Johns University in Minnesota in 1938. In situations where such ambitious programs were not practical, rural life institutes of one or two days duration were held. Outstanding authorities in Catholic rural life and in rural sociology were used as faculty members and speakers at these meetings.

This technique expanded very rapidly and by the summer of 1945 the program was expanded to include 55 institutes and 27 schools of rural life. In that summer they enrolled 1,700 priests, 9,600 sisters, 9,900 lay people and 775 seminarians. The schools and institutes were conducted in 35 different Dioceses and 20 different states.[44] Since difficulties are involved in keeping priests away from their parishes over the week end, none of the schools now last longer than five days.

Farmers Retreats.—Laymen's retreats are not new among Catholics. However, the farmers' retreat, aimed at acquainting the man in the field with Catholic rural philosophy is a new concept. The retreats are under the Diocesan

[42] National Catholic Rural Life Conference, *Catholic Rural Life Songs*, 1942.
[43] Witte, *op. cit.*, pp. 174–175.
[44] Witte, *op. cit.*, p. 201.

director of rural life who appoints and cooperates with the host churches in the Diocese. The retreats are attended by farmers and rural women who give attention to problems of the rural family, the stewardship of the land and other aspects of rural society.

Religious Vacation Schools and Correspondence Courses.—Since there are many thousands of rural parishes without schools, the Conference for many years sponsored summer vacation schools for supplementing the work of the Sunday school in giving religious instruction. From a humble beginning of only three such schools in 1921 there are now more than 8,000 with an enrollment of over 700,000.[45] In 1935 the Conference formally transferred this function to the Confraternity of Christian Doctrine, whose function is the teaching of religion.

In teaching religion to rural Catholics, the religious vacation school is not a complete answer. It does not reach Catholic families living 40 or 50 miles from a Catholic center. Consequently the Conference developed a correspondence course of study to reach these remote Catholics. Many centers have been established at seminaries and convents for administering these courses and correcting the papers of the students. In time the correspondence course activities were transferred to the Confraternity of Christian Doctrine along with the direction of the vacation schools.

Nature of Audience.—There is little data on the age and sex composition of the audience reached by the Conference. We do know that the rural Catholic is more native to American than the urban Catholic. There were a variety of social forces to induce the Catholic immigrant to locate in a city. One force is economic in nature. The wave of immigration coincided with the growth of manufacturing in the United States and endless opportunities for work were given to the immigrants. Many of these were poverty stricken and did not have the resources nor the contacts by which they could acquire a farm. In addition there were many friends and relatives already established in the city and it was easier to locate in a settlement or area in which there was general familiarity with existing cultural patterns.

Ecological Considerations.—As seen in Table 1 the states with the greatest frequency of rural Catholic churches are New York and Pennsylvania in the east and Wisconsin, Minnesota, Illinois and Indiana of the midwest and north-central areas. Except for Texas, there is a very small rural representation of the Catholic Church in the south. Georgia, for example, has only nine Catholic churches out of 6,941 rural churches.

Percentage-wise the story is somewhat different. The states with the highest percentages of their rural churches in the Catholic category are in New Mexico, which has more than 75 percent, and in order, Arizona, Montana, Nevada, California, and Colorado.

Evaluation.—Evaluation of the work of the Conference is very informal and

---

[45] Witte, *op. cit.*, p. 186.

TABLE 1
*Catholic Rural Churches by States**

State	Number of Catholic churches in open country	Number of Catholic churches in towns under 2500	Total number of Catholic rural churches	Number of rural churches, all faiths	Catholic percentage
Alabama	30	28	58	5,692	.72
Arizona	33	84	117	278	42.44
Arkansas	5	43	48	3,346	1.43
California	30	298	328	1,287	25.48
Colorado	23	140	163	681	23.93
Connecticut	6	94	100	692	14.45
Delaware	3	19	22	260	8.46
Florida	6	39	45	2,186	2.05
Idaho	5	55	60	541	11.09
Georgia	1	8	9	6,941	.12
Illinois	39	390	429	4,063	10.55
Indiana	37	142	179	3,549	5.04
Iowa	72	352	424	3,109	13.64
Kansas	56	218	274	2,283	11.73
Kentucky	26	61	87	3,659	3.74
Louisiana	103	222	325	2,346	13.85
Maine	7	108	115	934	12.31
Maryland	24	86	110	1,579	6.96
Massachusetts	9	163	172	909	19.58
Michigan	59	309	368	2,617	14.06
Minnesota	103	425	528	3,219	16.40
Mississippi	16	32	48	4,742	1.01
Missouri	53	233	286	3,792	7.56
Montana	27	230	257	661	38.88
Nebraska	39	267	306	1,931	15.84
Nevada	2	27	29	80	36.25
New Hampshire	2	67	69	471	14.64
New Jersey	23	151	174	1,161	14.98
New Mexico	186	272	458	608	75.32
New York	74	624	698	3,978	17.69
North Carolina	4	37	41	5,751	.71
North Dakota	42	266	308	1,780	17.33
Ohio	46	251	297	4,409	6.73
Oklahoma	4	65	69	2,274	3.03
Oregon	6	109	115	684	16.81
Pennsylvania	78	489	567	6,517	8.70
Rhode Island	2	30	32	169	18.93
South Carolina	5	33	38	2,980	1.27
South Dakota	47	262	309	1,532	20.03
Tennessee	6	13	19	4,103	.46
Texas	110	326	436	6,729	6.47
Utah	3	11	14	374	3.74
Vermont	5	102	107	538	19.88

State	Number of Catholic churches in open country	Number of Catholic churches in towns under 2500	Total number† of Catholic rural churches	Number of rural churches, all faiths	Catholic percentage
Virginia	6	41	47	4,510	1.04
Washington	18	143	161	955	16.85
West Virginia	10	68	78	2,799	2.80
Wisconsin	186	455	641	2,911	22.01
Wyoming	2	48	50	236	21.14
Total	1,679	7,936	9,615	116,826	8.26‡

* Data compiled from series of tables in *A Survey of Catholic Weakness, op. cit.*, pp. 12–61.
† Includes figures for churches with and without resident pastor.
‡ Average.

subjective. The leaders believe that the aims are being realized[46] and that the substantial list of successful projects started as a result of Conference propaganda are adequate testimony of the effectiveness of the organization.[47]

Dean Raymond Witte of St. Mary's University who spent three years studying, gathering materials and interviewing leaders of the Conference believes that one phase of the work has been completed successfully but a major task lies ahead:

The future is bright for the Conference, but its full effulgence is a long way off. Remarkable success has been achieved in imbuing Church leaders with rural philosophy, but to translate that philosophy into every day living for the laity is the task of generations. Two centuries of industrialism and their resultant urbanization, have made men forget that cult, culture and cultivation all come from the same root. It will take other centuries to restore that fundamental conception to the prestige it deserves. To reshape the minds of men to such an extent that they will cooperate with the restoration of rural life as a foundation of civilization and the natural habitat of the family, will take not one but many generations of campaigning on the part of yet unborn Crusaders. The members of the National Catholic Rural Life Conference are satisfied that they have started the first concerted action toward that goal, trained leaders to carry it on, and furnished the equipment necessary for the struggle. Their few victories are a foretaste of the future.[48]

While there has been an enthusiastic response to the activities of the Conference there also have been difficulties. Many urban priests have a vested interest in the expensive religious buildings, churches, schools and facilities and are something less than enthusiastic about a movement which would tend to reduce support for those facilities.

Msgr. Ligutti believes that apathy, indifference and carelessness are also

[46] Personal interview with Msgr. Ligutti.
[47] The major projects and activities are described in a previous section of this chapter.
[48] Witte, *op. cit.*, p. 227.

rather important obstacles to the achievement of the goals of the Conference.[49] The dangers for the Church in the intensive urbanization in which it finds itself did not receive the attention warranted, according to Msgr. Ligutti. However, great strides have been made by the Conference in calling this to the attention of both Church officialdom and the laity.

Recommendations.—1. It is as obvious to an observer from outside the Church as it is to writers such as Dean Witte in the Church that much more attention in the future must be given to the task of translating the ideals and philosophy of the Conference into social action among the laity of the Church. Thanks to the efforts of the Conference the Church leaders are well acquainted with the movement or crusade. The task now is to get hundreds of workable programs in operation in the every day living activities of the people.

2. This would imply, too, the necessity of doing more than acquainting the leadership with the philosophy of the movement, but also acquainting the leaders with group action techniques. Mere lectures sometimes are very inadequate techniques for social action.

3. More adequate appraisal of the program could be given if more research was concerned with fundamental human relations. Particularly in the evaluation of the program could the strengths and weaknesses of Conference activity be assessed.

4. It would seem that the Conference might give more attention to problems of democracy and international relations in its educational programs. The questionnaires sent to the Diocesan directors of rural life indicated that much more emphasis was being given to economic matters.

5. Without question there is a substantial reservoir of untapped leadership among the laity. We would recommend the recruitment of lay leadership to work cooperatively with the rural pastor in the development of a rural life program.

6. Without question a high proportion of the thousands of foreign students in the United States are of the Catholic faith. Many of these will return to village society. The Church might well consider the advisability of arranging opportunities for these students to spend their vacations in rural communities, thus becoming acquainted with country churches and farm families. So many foreign students see only the urban aspects of American society and the rural visitation would correct this and also, in a small way, aid international understanding for both the rural community and the foreign student.

RURAL ADULT EDUCATION ACTIVITIES AMONG THE PROTESTANTS

Rural life education and related adult education activities in rural areas are not dominated as much by a single organization among the Protestants as is the

[49] Personal interview with Msgr. Ligutti.

case of the Jewish and Catholic religious groups. There are several groups devoted to rural life education among the Protestants on a national basis[50] and in addition there are rural life commissions and committees among many of the denominations[51] and the state councils of churches.[52]

In contrast to Catholic churches and Jewish synagogues which are dominantly urban, the Protestant churches of the United States are largely located in rural areas. The rural parishes, however, can claim only 31 percent of the total Protestant church membership reported in America. This means that there are many small churches, some of which are inadequately financed and without adequate leadership. While census data on rural churches are inadequate because of incomplete reporting, Dr. Benson Y. Landis, of the Department of Research of the National Council of Churches, reports that present data does indicate high probability "that over two-thirds of all local parishes are found in rural territory, and that they have somewhat more than one-third of the church members.[53]

Space will not permit detailed examination of all of these organizations. Consequently we will devote the space mainly to the rural life organization with the largest scope and having the widest representation of denominations. This is the Town and Country Committee of the Home Missions Council of North America which is one of the major agencies united with the National Council of Churches in the United States of America.

The National Council of Churches came into being in 1950 and united 12 interdenominational agencies.[54] It links together 29 national denominations, with 143,959 local congregations and 32,000,000 members in a genuine effort to bring into focus a unified and coordinated Protestant action program.[55] Consequently, as a part of this larger organization the Department of the Town

[50] The Town and Country Committee of the Home Missions Council; The Rural Christian Fellowship; Conference between Theological Seminaries and Colleges of Agriculture.

[51] Church of the Brethren rural life improvement program; Presbyterian farm settlement program; Congregational-Christian rural training center; Methodist Rural Christian Fellowship; National Lutheran Council (rural life work); similar efforts in rural life by Baptists, United Brethren and others.

[52] Most of the state councils of churches have departments of Town and Country, Rural Life or Rural Research committees. See *Yearbook of American Churches*, 1951 edition, The Department of Publication of the National Council of the Churches of Christ in United States of America, pp. 118–162.

[53] Benson Y. Landis, "Why a Protestant Town and Country Church Movement?" in *Religious Education in Rural America: A Symposium*, p. 67.

[54] Federal Council of the Churches of Christ in America; Foreign Missions Conference of North America; Home Missions Council of North America; International Council of Religious education; Missionary Education Movement of the United States and Canada; National Protestant Council of Higher Education; United Council of Church Women; United Stewardship Council; Church World Service, Inc.; Interseminary Committee; Protestant Film Commission; Protestant Radio Commission.

[55] Yearbook of American Churches, 1951 edition, *op. cit.*, p. 1.

and Country Church has access to its widespread facilities and lines of communication which would be difficult for an independent organization to secure.[56]

History of the Department of Town and Country Church.—The original Town and Country Committee of the Home Missions Council was organized in 1921. In 1931 it was made a joint committee with the Federal Council of Churches and in 1943 with the International Council of Religious Education. From this inter-council committee developed the Department of Town and Country in 1950 at the time in which the National Council of Churches was constituted.

Regular yearly convocations were started by the Committee on Town and Country in 1943. Prior to that there had been two such national conferences in 1916 and 1936. Because of the importance of a strong rural life program to the rural church it was decided to hold regular annual meetings and to make plans for implementing the ideas and plans of the committee into definite action programs.

Objectives of the Organization.—The Town and Country Department made a report to the National meeting of the Home Missions Council in 1950 at Columbus, Ohio which stated the "commitments" of the organization.[57] The educational program of the Town and Country Department is oriented around these objectives. As will be noted in the statement of these objectives, topics relating to the three major areas of interest of this study are included.

I. Services to the Rural Community.
   1. Providing a comprehensive gospel.
   2. Intergrating community activities.
   3. Eliminating discrimination.
   4. Developing a world concept.
   5. Building security.
   6. Promoting land settlement.
   7. Establishing rural people in trade, business and professions.
   8. Developing a concern for farm labor.
   9. Promoting balanced family and community life.
   10. Servicing marginal people.
   11. Opposing disintegrating forces.
   12. Spiritualising rural culture.
II. Services to the Rural Church.
   1. Building a strong church.
   2. Promoting church unity.
III. The Rural Minister.
   1. Recruitment and training.

[56] The writer wishes to acknowledge the assistance given him in gathering information on Protestant rural life activities by Dr. Rockwell C. Smith, professor of rural sociology at Garrett Biblical Institute, Evanston, Illinois, in interview of August, 1951.

[57] *For a Christian World*, booklet published by the Home Missions Council of North America, 297 Fourth Avenue, New York City, 1950, pp. 100–105. Booklet gives detail on each of the phases of the educational program listed herein.

    2. In-service training.
    3. Travel and study.
    4. Salary, pension, mileage and other expenses.
    5. Recognition.
IV. Rural-Urban Relations.
    1. Urban orientation.
    2. Educating urban churches in rural problems.
    3. To challenge the urban section of the church to support an adequate rural ministry program.

Organizational Structure.—The Committee on Town and Country is administered by the Home Missions Council, which in turn is a division of the National Churches of Christ in the U.S.A. The Division of Home Missions is the agency in which the home missions boards of 22 denominations are united for various kinds of cooperative religious and educational activities in United States. The Division meets annually in assembly. Between the annual sessions an Executive Board, comprised of the officers of the division, the chairmen of the standing committees, departments and commissions and not more than 45 members at large elected by the Assembly from its own membership, serves as the responsible body for the division.[58]

The Committee on Town and Country, although administratively under the Home Missions Council, has members appointed by the Federal Council and the International Council.[59] The Committee on Town and Country thus is a representative agency of the councils which renders special services on behalf of rural Protestant churches.

Content of Adult Education Program.—In general the content of the adult education program includes the topics listed in the statement of objectives. Through close cooperation with denominational town and country committees and the denominational rural life programs the ideas are given action implementation at the local level.

At the annual convocations sponsored by the Town and Country Department the program is almost entirely contained in the work of 20 commissions which report the result of their discussion to the Convocation.[60] The areas of the commission reports are as follows:
    1. The church and agricultural reconstruction.
    2. The rural church and land tenure.
    3. The church and the farm laborer and the sharecropper.
    4. The church and rural community agencies.
    5. Church cooperation in the rural community.

---

[58] *Yearbook of American Churches, op. cit.,* p. 9.
[59] "Committee on Town and Country Church, The Report for 1950," in *Town and Country Church,* January, 1951, No. 67, p. 5.
[60] *The Rural Church in These Moving Times,* Committee on Town and Country, 1947, pp. 66–119. This booklet gives considerable detail on each of the phases of the program listed herein.

6. The Theological seminary and the church.
7. Colleges of agriculture and the rural church.
8. The rural pastor as counselor.
9. Evangelism and church extension.
10. The Christian family and rural life.
11. The rural church and agricultural missions.
12. The rural church and minority groups.
13. Financing the church in town and country.
14. Worship in the rural church.
15. Urban-rural relations.
16. The place of women in the rural church.
17. The task of the town and village church.
18. Inter-relations of city and rural churches.
19. Instructors in colleges and seminaries for the rural ministry.
20. Denominational regional directors of rural work.

In-Service Training.—Throughout the entire history of the Committee, in-service training programs have been sponsored and given strong emphasis. These consist of credit and non-credit schools and institutes devoted to country life training for ministers and other religious workers. The main purposes are:

1. To help ministers become acquainted with tested methods of town and country work.

2. To assist them in securing an understanding of the trends and problems of modern country life.

3. To develop fellowship among ministers in town and country.

4. To increase contacts of ministers with agricultural leaders.[61]

The following training centers were sponsored by the Committee in 1951:
1. Schools in which graduate credit is obtainable.
    a. Interdenominational School for Rural Leaders. Garrett Biblical Institute, Evanston, Illinois.
    b. Oberlin Graduate School for Rural Leaders, Oberlin, Ohio.
    c. Institute for Town and Country Ministers, Westminster Theological Seminary, Westminster, Md.
    d. Town and Country Institute, Emory University, Ga.
2. Schools and Institutes for Ten Days or Over.
    a. Training School for Rural Ministers, Rural Church Center, Green Lake, Wisc.
    b. Cornell Town and Country Summer School, Cornell University, Ithaca, N.Y.
    c. Rural Leadership School, Michigan State College, East Lansing, Mich.
    d. Summer School of Christian Education, Faribault, Minn.

[61] "In-Service Training for the Minister in Town and Country—1951," *Town and Country Church*, No. 70, April, 1951, p. 16.

3. Schools and Institutes of One Week or Less.
   a. Town and Country Church Conference, Kansas State College, Manhattan.
   b. Rural Life Conference for Vermont Pastors, University of Vermont, Burlington.
   c. Rural Pastors' Short Course, University of Illinois, Champaign.
   d. Rural Leadership Institute, University of Kentucky, Lexington.
   e. Knowles Institute for Town and Country Ministers, New Jersey College of Agriculture, New Brunswick.
   f. Texas Town and Country Church School, A & M College, College Station, Texas.
   g. Conference for Town and Country Pastors, Pennsylvania State College, State College.
   h. Rural Ministers' Summer School, Virginia Polytechnic Institute, Blacksburg.
   i. Town and Country Leadership Institute, Oregon State College, Corvallis.
   j. Ministers' Short Course, College of Agriculture, Fargo, N.D.

Most of those in-service training centers are held in the summer months. Publicity to these meetings is given by the Town and Country Department of the Home Missions Council, by the denominational rural life agencies, by the rural life departments of the State councils of churches and by the sponsoring university, college or seminary. Thousands of rural ministers take advantage of the training opportunity.

The National Convocation.—Since 1943 the Committee has sponsored a Nation-Convocation on the Church in Town and Country held in different parts of the United States from year to year, promoting a large regional attendance from the local area and the nation. Most of those attending are ministers in rural parishes. Also in attendance are college and seminary professors of rural life and governmental officials. Occasionally Roman Catholic and Jewish rural life people are in attendance. There are always numerous commissions and sub-committees reporting on various phases of town and country church work related to the objectives of the organization.

Methods of Implementation.—Plans are also made at the convocations to implement the decisions made at the national level in order to have effective action at the local church level. The procedure may vary some but in general the procedure involves:[62]

1. Adoption of the report by the Home Missions Council.
2. Each denominational board is requested to notify its state conference or synodical executive of such action urging that each ecclesiastical unit adopt the principles.

[62] "Churching the Rural Church Cooperatively," Department of Town and Country Church, 1950, (Leaflet).

3. The Home Missions Council being notified of denominational approval then notifies the state councils of churches.
4. Both the state conference or synodical organization and the state council of churches are urged to carry on a program of education for the local churches about these principles.
5. The Committee on Town and Country is encouraged to:
   a. Approach all seminaries of these principles in reference to the education of ministers.
   b. Approach all program committees planning in-service training curriculum to include material relative to these principles.
   c. Approach the program committee of the Association of Council Secretaries, seeking a place on this program at the earliest possible date.

Publishing Town and Country Church.—The Committee publishes a monthly periodical, *Town and Country Church* which is addressed mainly, but not entirely, to the rural minister and contains articles on methods of rural church work, rural life education, reports of rural sociological research, reviews of governmental reports of interest to the farmer, reviews of books and pamphlets. It does not devote space to technical agricultural problems but is concerned with the analysis, understanding and enrichment of the rural way of life and ways in which the church can contribute to that goal.

Dr. Benson Y. Landis, is the managing editor, Rev. Don Pielstick is secretary and Ruth B. Robinson, assistant editor. The board of editors consists of the rural life directors of ten major denominations and Dr. Claude Snyder, chairman of the Committee on Town and Country. The subscription price is $1.00 per year, which is less than the cost of printing and distribution. Grants from cooperating home mission boards to the committees have provided the additional funds.

Research and Surveys.—The Committee maintains a department of research under the direction of Dr. Benson Y. Landis. Assistance is given to groups desiring research or surveys and the committee itself sponsors rural church and community research which will be helpful to pastors and other rural leaders.

Rural Church Conferences.—The Committee conducts regional institutes and conferences and assists county councils of churches and local ministerial associations in conducting local conferences relating to rural life objectives.

Cooperation with the International Council of Religious Education.—The Committee cooperates closely with this group in rural adult educational work in the development of study, demonstration, field service and printed materials.

Promotion of Special Rural Observances.—The Committee promotes the observance of Rural Life Sunday to be held on Rogation Sunday, the fifth Sunday after Easter. For the past eleven years it has called for a wide observance of harvest festivals in the churches.

Contacts with Organizations.—The Committee maintains informal contacts with the Department of Agriculture, farm organizations, colleges of agriculture, cooperatives and social agencies. Pertinent information thus secured is made available to the rural minister through the various channels of the organization.

Obstacles to the Achievement of Goals.—It appears that inertia in denominationalism is one of the important handicaps in the effective realization of goals. Simply because in the past many churches could not see further than the immediate denominational requirements they found it difficult to enter wholeheartedly in a movement with national and international concerns which crosses denominational lines.

With so many small churches in rural areas the problem of inadequate budget has been a hindrance. Some of the rural life leaders feel that there should be a repository for rural literature. This would greatly facilitate research efforts and studies of rural life and problems. Denominational centers may have such repositories in reference to their own denominations but there is a need for a central library and repository where rural documents, books and general specialized rural literature could be kept.

THE LOCAL CHURCH AND RURAL ADULT EDUCATION

In an attempt to gather information about rural adult education activities at the local church level it was decided to study churches in 263 sample counties. A questionnaire was prepared and mailed to pastors of Methodist, Lutheran and Baptist churches in selected towns of these sample counties.[63]

A total of 175 out of 543 ministers, or approximately 32 percent, responded to the questionnaire after two mailings. Of the 175 responding, there were 164 or 94 percent, indicating that their churches had adult education activities. The churches in the sample were village and town churches in communities in the sample counties with a population range of 1,000 to 6,000.

Of the 94 percent indicating that they had adult education activities there were some churches which had programs of rather substantial coverage. Eight percent of the respondents indicated programs reaching from 400 to 1,000 different people while six percent indicated programs reaching from 1,000 to 10,000 people in a single year. The precise breakdown of this category may be seen in Table 2.

Most of the people reached by these programs live in the open country or in centers of less than 2,500 people. Thirty-four percent of the respondents indicated that almost all of the people reached by the adult education programs resided in rural areas. Detail as to percentages and numbers is given in Table 2. Loomis and Beegle cite studies showing an increasing membership from the open country in village churches. In 1936 there were 40 percent of the members of village churches from the open country.[64]

---

[63] We were handicapped by not having a mailing list of the pastors by name. Consequently the letters were addressed to The Pastor of the Methodist Church, Pastor of the Lutheran Church, The Pastor of the Baptist Church.

[64] Loomis and Beegle, *op. cit.*, p. 435.

Mass Media.—Almost all of the churches used one or more of the media of mass communication in their adult education programs. Only 11 percent indicated no use of the media. Of the mass media used, 45 percent indicated the use of movies; 36 percent indicated newspapers; 17 percent radio; and one percent indicated television and other media.

Cooperative Educational Activity with Other Organizations.— Table 3 gives clear indication that the church at the local level is cooperating with a consider-

TABLE 2
Number of People Reached by Church Adult Education Programs and Proportions Living in Rural Areas

Number reached and proportion rural	Number of churches reporting	Percent
Number Reached		
Total.	175	100
Under 100.	37	21
100–199.	40	24
200–299.	23	13
300–399.	13	7
400–599.	11	6
600–1,000.	4	2
1,000 and over.	10	6
N.A.	37	21
Proportion in Rural Areas		
Total.	175	100
None.	25	14
One-fourth.	32	18
One-half.	23	13
Three-fourths.	13	8
All.	59	34
N.A.	23	13

able variety of organizations in their adult education work. In this effort a local church works most frequently with other churches, 82 percent of the respondents so reporting. Nearly half of the ministers in the questionnaire indicated that they worked closely with the local schools in their adult education program. Next in order of frequency were civic and service clubs, colleges and universities, parents' organizations, women's clubs, farm organizations and libraries.

Adult Education in the Three Areas of Interest.—The questionnaire returns showed that 131 churches in the sample or 75 percent of the total indicated that the church engaged in educational activities in the three areas of interest, namely, International Understanding for Peace; Strengthening of Democracy;

and Understanding and Strengthening of the Economy. Forty-five percent of the churches indicated use of foreign persons in their adult education program of the past year.

Seventy-two percent of the ministers described the best program in the three areas in an open-end question and answer. About half of the respondents indi-

TABLE 3
Number and Percentage of Organizations With Which the Church Works in Adult Education Programs

	Total mentions		Protestant ministers	Diocesan rural life leaders
	Number*	Percent	Number	Number
Churches and religious organizations.........	169	95	143	26
Schools.......................................	95	53	80	15
Civic and service organizations..............	74	42	65	9
Colleges and universities....................	71	40	59	12
Parent's organizations.......................	66	37	57	9
Women's clubs...............................	56	31	47	9
Libraries....................................	51	29	42	9
Farm organizations..........................	47	26	45	2
Community councils.........................	46	26	41	5
Fraternal organizations......................	46	26	34	12
Cooperative Extension Service...............	32	18	19	13
Patriotic and veterans organizations.........	21	12	18	3
Professional organizations...................	19	11	19	0
Federal and/or state government bureaus....	15	8	0	15
Elected or appointed government bodies.....	13	7	5	8
Inter-Agency councils.......................	10	6	7	3
Political parties and organizations...........	9	5	8	1
Welfare councils.............................	8	4	0	8
UNESCO organizations.....................	7	4	6	1
Labor unions................................	4	2	2	2
Others.......................................	12	7	8	4

* A total of 178 ministers and Diocesan rural life leaders responded to this question.

cated that the international relations program was the best program with subjects relating to democracy in second place with 18 percent. Subjects relating to the strengthening of the economy was given least attention among the three.

It will be noted at this point that this order of emphasis is almost exactly reverse that of the Catholic and Jewish rural life organizations. In these two organizations there was by far the greatest emphasis placed on economic activity and action and the least on international relations. The emphasis on economic concerns would be expected for the Catholic and Jewish rural life organizations since a central task is to educate for and attract urban people to the land which involves the purchase of property. With so many Protestants already on the land the Protestant rural life organizations do not need to stress economic factors as much as the other two organizations.

Form of Best Program.—The ministers in this sample were asked to indicate the form of their best program in the three areas of interest. Public meetings with 41 percent and conferences with 21 percent were the most frequently

TABLE 4

Number and Percentage of the Form of Best Program and the Procedures Used in the Three Fields of Interest

Form of program and procedures used	Number of mentions	Percent
Form of Program		
Total mentions	223	100
Public meeting	92	41
Conference	47	21
Workshop	22	10
Institute	21	9
Demonstration	15	7
Radio listening groups	8	4
Tour	4	2
Other	14	6
Procedures Used		
Total mentions	246	100
Lectures	106	43
Group discussion	84	34
Large groups split into small discussion groups	23	9
Panels	19	8
Other	14	6

mentioned categories of response to this question. Further detail is given in Table 4.

Procedures Used.—Table 4 shows the most commonly used procedures in the presentation of programs in the three Ford areas. Lectures with 43 percent and group discussions with 34 percent were the most common procedures. Additional detail is shown in the table.

Limitations of time and the lack of a mailing list with ministers names in the sample counties caused our local church sample to be rather small, nevertheless it does provide partial evidence that there is rather vigorous activity in the areas of interest at the local church level.

The Church as an Agency of Communication.—Although information about the precise nature of inter-agency communication in the American community is inadequate, we have leads from this study in reference to the extent of cooperation and the frequency of contact between various community organizations and the church. For those interested in social action at the community level it is most important to know the techniques of communication between agencies, the relative power and prestige of these agencies and the procedures used by the agencies for the implementation of action.

First of all, we must provide knowledge as to the location of the interaction, i.e. what agencies interact with other agencies? The staff engaged in this study attempted to contribute to such by systematically asking: "What other organizations do you work with, or through, in your educational work with adults?"

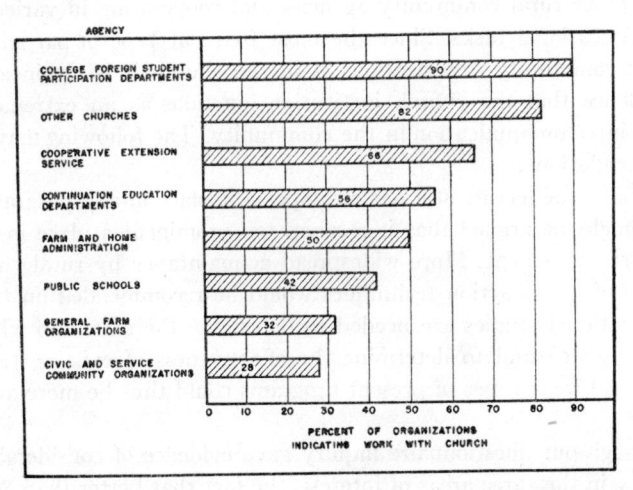

FIG. 2. The church and inter-agency communication.

In analyzing the responses to this question in the various segments of the study, it was found that the church occupies a focal position as a cooperating and contact agency in rural community adult education programs. Most of the other community agencies studied showed that more than half of those reporting had working relationships with the church. Nearly every organization in the community mentions the church as one of the agencies of most frequent contact. Of the following agencies 50 percent or more of the organizations responding to the questionnaire reported cooperation with the church in adult education programs: high schools, county agents, the Grange, the Farmers Home Administration, continuation education centers in colleges and universities and other churches. The details are given in Figure 2.

Varying somewhat by size of institution, an average of 90 percent of all colleges and universities reported foreign student participation in church programs. Rural weekly newspapers reported in this study that churches were given more space than any other community organization. These same newspapers also reported that the church, with greatest frequency, had prepared articles for publication in the papers in the three fields of interest.

In another of the media of communication, radio stations reaching a predominantly rural audience reported that of all community organizations, the church had the highest percentage of usage and participation in radio programs. The church was also found to have the highest percentage of usage and participation in stations with less than 50 percent rural audience.

SUMMARY

Thus we see that the church is a highly interacting agency having much contact with other rural community agencies and cooperating in varied ways in common educational tasks. Since the most frequent type of participation by farmers in community organizations is in the church it is significant to discover evidence that the church institution functions as an extremely active agency of intercommunication in the community. The following may be listed as recommendations:

1. Although the lecture still has an important place in any program of education it might be argued that it receives too prominent a place in the town and country movement. More widespread acquaintance by rural church and lay leaders of group action techniques would be recommended on this point.

2. Evaluational studies are needed to determine the extent to which goals are being realized and to determine the effectiveness of existing techniques. Strengths and weaknesses of present programs could thus be more adequately assessed.

3. Although our questionnaire inquiry gave evidence of considerable vigorous activity in the three areas of interest, the fact that better than 80 percent of the churches did not return the cards indicates that there is considerable apathy at the local level. More attention, therefore, should be given to the task of translating the ideals and philosophy of the town and country convocation into social action at the local church level.

4. The questionnaire study indicated the least amount of effort and action in the area of Understanding and Strengthening the Economy at the local church level. Our recommendation would be for more emphasis in programming in this particular area.

5. There is considerable evidence that the rural ministry is less well trained than the urban ministry. This means that the rural pastor not only is less adequate in the field of theology but has not had the advantage of rural life education in the Protestant seminary. This, then, would necessitate a more intensified in-service training for the pastor of the rural parish.

6. There needs to be a more wide-spread recruitment of lay leadership for assistance in the rural life programs with ministerial and lay leadership working cooperatively in the common task.

7. Closely related to the above recommendation is the suggestion that ministers need the broadest kind of educational background in order that they may give leadership in the three areas of interest. While many seminaries have departments of rural sociology or rural life, the need is for expansion of these departments in all seminaries which send ministers out to rural parishes.

Orden C. Smucker
Department of Social Science
Department of Sociology and Anthropology
Michigan State College
East Lansing, Michigan

BIBLIOGRAPHY

JEWISH RURAL LIFE ACTIVITY

Gabriel Davidson, *Our Jewish Farmers*, New York: L. B. Fischer, 1943.
Samuel Joseph, *History of the Baron de Hirsch Fund*, Jewish Publication Society, 1935.
The Jewish Agricultural Society, Inc., Report of the Managing Director for the Period 1900-1949. (booklet).
The Jewish Agricultural Society, Inc., Report of the Managing Director—1950. (booklet).
The Jewish Farmer, monthly periodical of The Jewish Agricultural Society.

CATHOLIC RURAL LIFE ACTIVITY

Land and Home, monthly periodical of the National Catholic Rural Life Conference.
L. G. Ligutti, *A Survey of Catholic Weakness*, Des Moines: The National Catholic Welfare Conference.
L. G. Ligutti and John C. Rawe, *Rural Roads to Security*, Milwaukee: The Bruce Publishing Co., 1940.
Manifesto on Rural Life, National Catholic Rural Life Conference. Milwaukee: Bruce Publishing Co., 1939.
Proceedings of the Annual Conferences. National Catholic Rural Life Conference.
Raymond P. Witte, *Twenty-Five Years of Crusading—A History of the National Catholic Rural Life Conference*, Des Moines: The National Catholic Rural Life Conference, 1948.

PROTESTANT RURAL LIFE ACTIVITY

For a Christian World, New York: Home Missions Council of North America, 1950.
Benson Y. Landis, "Why a Protestant Town and Country Movement?" in Pamphlet, *Religious Education in Rural America*.
David E. Lindstrom, *Rural Life and the Church*, Champaign: The Garrard Press, 1946.
Mark Rich, *Rural Prospect*, New York: Friendship Press, 1950.
Rural Church in These Moving Times, The, New York: Committee on Town and Country Church, 1947.
Urgent Tasks of the Church in Town and Country, New York: Committee on Town and Country Church, 1945.
Yearbook of American Churches—1951 edition, New York: The Department of Publication of the National Council of the Churches of Christ in United States of America.

Chapter 10:

CONTINUATION EDUCATION IN COLLEGES AND UNIVERSITIES

History and Origin

Continuation education, as it is generally recognized in the United States, began in England in the latter part of the 18th century.[1] Motivated by religious interests, early efforts in the field were restricted to the teaching of elementary subjects in order to increase interest among the general public to read and interpret the Bible. From this austere beginning, content gradually evolved to include social, scientific, and historical subjects. These were seldom adapted to the needs and wishes of their audiences. From England the movement spread to the United States but it was not until 1890 that some of the larger schools, including Johns Hopkins, the University of Chicago, and the University of Wisconsin, had scheduled permanent programs in the field.[2] By the turn of the 20th century the movement had become fairly well dispersed throughout the United States.

Popular acceptance of the movement came slowly in the majority of states. The first real demands were provided at the end of the First World War with the return of the soldiers, many of whom were anxious to regain some of the educational ground supposedly lost while in service. Momentum gained from this development was never lost. Continuation education had come to be accepted as "... worthy of public notice."[3]

With the onset of the economic depression of the early thirties, predictions for the future of the movement were pessimistic but contrary to expectations courses and enrollments continued to increase throughout the thirties and forties. Leaders of the movement offered it as a means to employment, as an effective way to educate all the people and to carry knowledge to the "grass roots" of the electorate. Junior colleges, as well as the larger colleges and universities, added hundreds of courses to their curricula. In 1936–37 only about 15

---

[1] Continuation Education, as the term is used, here refers to non-agricultural extension education offered by colleges and universities.

[2] For a general history of the early development of Continuation Education see: M. E. Sadler, *Continuation Schools in England and Elsewhere*, Manchester, England: Manchester University Press, 1908; also, Clarence Arthur Perry, *Wider Use of the School Plant*, New York: Wm. F. Fell Company, 1910, and George B. Zehmer, "The Development of University Extension Services in the United States," *Proceedings of the Institute for Administrative Officers of Higher Institutions*, 1945, (XVII), University of Chicago Press, 1946; also, Kermit C. King, *The Historical Development of University Extension at the University of California*, A Ph.D. Dissertation, 1947.

[3] See Morse Adams Cartwright, *Ten Years of Adult Education*, New York: The Macmillan Company, 1935, pp. 8–10 for concise history of adult education in the United States.

percent of the total junior college enrollment consisted of special or extension students. By 1943–44 the percentage had increased to about 66 percent of the total enrollment.[4]

The second World War, and particularly its termination, brought tremendous demands on colleges and universities throughout the United States. In order to meet the challenge, most schools, and especially those located in the larger urban centers, began rapid expansions of evening and other extension courses. The number of students enrolled in evening classes for many colleges far exceeded those attending during the day. It has been estimated that by 1948 evening courses in American colleges and universities located in urban areas regularly enrolled more than 500,000 students or one-fifth of the nation's total registrations in institutions of higher learning.[5]

Changes in Objectives of Continuation Education.—A cursory survey of the historical literature on continuation education reveals wide and sometimes abrupt shifts in its purposes and objectives during the past 50 years. Some of these were associated with changes in the direction of the general adult education movement. Many early educators, and strong supporters of education, saw in continuation education a means for alleviating numerous social evils thought to inhere in widespread public and worker illiteracy.[6] With an aim to correct this situation, colleges and universities initiated numerous programs planned at the lower levels of difficulty in order to "reach the greatest number of adults." There was little thought or desire to fit a type of education to the actual need of those involved. Courses in reading and writing were the first to be introduced followed by offerings in mathematics, foreign languages, history and science. Possibilities inherent in vocational education were unrecognized or ignored. Courses launched at the higher levels of difficulty were "campus courses developed to meet the needs of adolescents."[7]

In the latter part of the 19th century the object of continuation education at some of the more progressive schools began to shift from the social to the individual. Such schools introduced a combination type of reaching and apprenticeship purporting to increase worker efficiency and on-the-job earning power. This era witnessed the introduction of the Cooperative Agricultural Extension Service for farm families, a type of adult education and service designed to increase the quantity and quality of agricultural and livestock production.

[4] Walter Crosby Eells, "The Community's College," *Adult Education Journal*, Vol. 4, No. 1, January, 1945.
[5] Jean Mosier, "Problems and Policies of the University Evening College," *Adult Education Bulletin*, Vol. XIII, No. 5, 1948.
[6] Mary Ewen Palmer, "Stages of Development in Adult Education," *Adult Education Bulletin*, Vol. 11, No. 5, June, 1947.
[7] President's Commission on Higher Education, *Higher Education for American Democracy*, Vol. 1, Washington, December, 1947, p. 96. See also Sadler and Perry, *op. cit.*, and Mary L. Ely, (Editor), *Handbook of Adult Education in the United States*, Washington: Institute of Adult Education, 1948, pp. 214–224.

With the beginning of the 20th century, continuation education, in many institutions, suddenly broke away from classical moorings of formalized courses and packaged learning to become centers of service for individuals and groups desirous of meeting more effectively a set of rapidly changing social, economic, and political conditions. Many went far beyond the "practical" and "vocational" although these elements still remained the base upon which more inclusive programs were built. Some of the more concrete objectives of the new programs, as stated by the President's Commission on Higher Education, were to "... help round out the education provided by elementary and secondary schools and by other types of institutions; advance the individual in essential knowledge and skills; provide facilities for self-expression and appreciation in these areas; disseminate information regarding recent developments in fields such as government, economics, the physical and natural sciences; provide opportunities for discussion, at the adult level, of issues vital to national life and international relations; and give to both the older and younger generations a more adequate basis for understanding their mutual problems."[8] Such education, the Commission continued, "rightly conceived and promoted" would "help to bring order into the spiritual chaos of today and to create a democracy with enhanced material, moral and intellectual strength."

Some of the colleges have extended their facilities to alleviate problem situations such as those often precipitated by urbanization and migration to metropolitan areas. The San Jose (California) Evening Junior College is currently extending its evening educational program to include instruction assumed to aid recent arrivals in the area to become an integral part of the local environment. In planning its curriculum this institution recognizes that "there is a basic human need for friendliness, for warm contacts, that are increasingly hard to find in large metropolitan areas. That is why there is a trend toward fellowship in smaller living centers. Adult (and continuation) education has a vital part in that trend..."[9] Education, based upon such broad principles as these, might more accurately be called community, rather than higher education.

THE AUDIENCE OF CONTINUATION EDUCATION

Evaluations available on continuation education programs seldom give more than minor attention to the audiences being reached. Other than occupational interests, previous training and interest, little is known of the vast group of persons annually reached through a multitude of conferences, lectures, correspondence, and short courses planned and directed by a majority of the colleges and universities of the United States. Data from a recent study of the program of the University of California provides a limited estimate of what this universe may be. From information secured through questionnaires completed by 6,500

[8] *Op. cit.*, p. 59.
[9] San Jose Public Schools, *Adult Education*, (Leaflet), 1951–52.

adults enrolled in the southern area of the university's program, the author found that:
1. About twice as many males as females were enrolled.
2. Over 60 percent of the reporting students were 35 years of age or less.
3. About half held bachelor's or higher degrees.
4. A large percent were in the higher income brackets.
5. The largest number of students reported University Extension class schedules, pamphlets, and leaflets as their first source of information about the classes they were taking.
6. Eighty-two percent of the reporting students indicated that they would work toward a degree if it were possible to meet all the requirements in Extension.[10]

EXTENT AND AREAS OF CONCENTRATION OF CONTINUATION EDUCATION

Data secured in this study[11] show that a majority of the colleges and universities in the United States are now offering various types of education programs in addition to cooperative extension education conducted by the land-grant colleges. These programs assume a multitude of forms, ranging from intensive, and relatively brief, study and conference courses, on and off campus, to extensive work by correspondence that is available to interested persons throughout most of the year. Only 32 percent of the 986 colleges and universities supplying the information reported no programs in continuation education for the current academic year. Sixty-eight percent of this number reported continuation education programs.

It is sometimes assumed that continuation education is largely a function of the larger institutions, an assumption that is not borne out by this study. While size of audience reached seems to be closely associated with size of institution, the smaller colleges, and especially the so-called community colleges, are directing their efforts more and more to the surrounding adult populations.

Fifty-three percent of the 552 colleges and universities reporting on numbers reached indicated their audience to be less than 1000 persons. Only 9 percent indicated their audience to be 10,000 persons or more.

Despite variations that obtain between the different sizes and types of institutions continuation education is directed at urban more than at rural people. The special nature of the work conducted by the Cooperative Agricultural Extension Service, appears to have played an important role in channeling continuation education into the larger towns and cities.

Of 537 institutions reporting, more than one-third (36 percent) admitted

[10] Lawrence K. McLaughlin, *Student Population in University of California Extension Classes*, A Ph.D. Dissertation, (UCLA), 1951.
[11] See details in Appendix C.

that almost none of their continuation programs involving adults lived in centers of less than 2,500 population. See Figure 1.

When the data were arranged to show the relationship between size of programs and the percent of people reached, it was found that the smaller programs were more likely to involve the rural population. Of all institutions reaching 10,000 persons or more, however, 11 percent reported that *almost all* their audiences were rural. This may be explained in part by the fact that many of the large institutions are land-grant colleges or a combination of university and land-grant college.

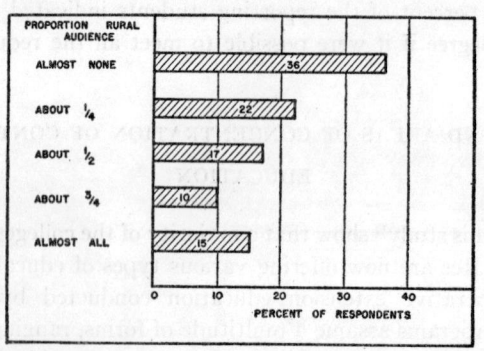

FIG. 1 Percentage of colleges and universities reporting the proportion of their adult education audience that is rural.

REGIONAL ASPECTS OF PROGRAMS AND FACILITIES

The geographic distribution of continuation education programs covers the entire United States with major concentration in the areas of high population density. (See Table 1.) Among individual states, New York and California rank highest, a situation that is due in large part, to the active programs of many of their community and evening colleges.

Use of the Mass Media.—The importance of the mass media in continuation education is evident in the questionnaire data. Most of the larger institutions use all available mass media, with the exception of television, at some time or other. The use of the newspaper was reported more often than was the use of any other medium. Of the 530 institutions having programs, more than half (51 percent) mentioned using this medium frequently. Its use was reported most often in the West and least often in the Northeast.

Although the use of radio in continuation education programs was reported less frequently than the newspaper, the manner in which it was used varied even more. A number of colleges are using the radio as a means for disseminating information to "listening groups" which "listen" and then discuss the materials in terms of their local or some hypothetical situation. Here again, the West led in the use of this medium with the densely populated Northeast last. The use of radio in continuation education does not seem to limit the use of other media. In fact, the reverse of this seems more likely to be true.

Of the 530 colleges and universities reporting, 39 mentioned the use of television in their programs of continuation education. Fifteen of the 39 institutions reporting the use of television were in the South. This is surprising in view of the known concentration of television sets in the Northeast.

The use of the various mass media seems more closely associated with size of institution than with region. The larger institutions make more frequent use

TABLE 1
Regional Distribution* of Colleges and Universities With Continuation Education Programs or Activities

Regions	Number	Percent
Total	654	100
Northeast	142	22
South	190	29
North Central	217	33
West	105	16

* The Regional distribution of states used in the following sections of this report is:
Northeast: Maine, New Hampshire, Vermont, Massachusetts, Connecticut, Rhode Island, New Jersey, New York, Pennsylvania.
South: Delaware, Maryland, West Virginia, Kentucky, Tennessee, Virginia, North Carolina, Arkansas, South Carolina, Georgia, Florida, Alabama, Mississippi, Louisiana, Oklahoma, Texas, Washington, D. C.
North Central: Ohio, Indiana, Illinois, Michigan, Wisconsin, Nebraska, Minnesota, Iowa, Missouri, North Dakota, South Dakota, Kansas.
West: Montana, Wyoming, Colorado, New Mexico, Idaho, Utah, Arizona, Nevada, Washington, Oregon, California.

of all the mass media than do the smaller institutions. In the case of television, 6 percent of the institutions having enrollments under 1000 reported its use. On the other hand, 16 percent of the institutions having enrollments of 10,000 or more make use of television.

Organizations With Which Colleges and Universities Work.—Data of the study show that continuation education programs are often conducted in cooperation with numerous types of local, state, and national organizations. Programs are frequently developed in response to requests of particular groups and aimed at satisfying specified needs. At the local levels, this cooperation involves schools, community councils and various civic clubs and services. At the state and national levels, labor unions, farm organizations and UNESCO are involved. The responsibility of the college or university varies from one place to another and from one time to another, with a general tendency to place increasing responsibility upon the cooperating organization.

The involvement of local organization in continuation education applies to programs at the smaller colleges and universities as well as to the larger ones. The junior colleges, and especially the junior community colleges, frequently depend heavily upon local organizational support in introducing and maintaining their programs. Leaders and instructors are recruited from the immediate area. The result is a degree of autonomy and independence impossible for the larger institutions to achieve.

Critics of this development maintain that this situation is creating a division of labor between the larger and the smaller institutions, not always conducive to overall accomplishment and efficiency. One of the more common complaints arising from the situation is the tendency for the smaller colleges to depend on local resource persons for leadership which might more effectively be drawn from the larger campuses. The result has been, in some cases, to force the larger college and university programs to concentrate in the cities and metropolitan areas where their major divisions most often are located. This situation has become a source of potential difficulty in a few states and may easily be duplicated in other regions where the community college idea is now developing.

Responses of the 582 colleges and universities to specific questions about cooperation with other organizations indicate that continuation education leaders usually consider cooperative educational arrangements with local organizations highly desirable and are continuously striving to increase the number and variety of organizations participating. The incidence of involvement for any particular organization, however, varies from one place to another. One of the closest working relationships observed was that between colleges and universities and the public schools. From available evidence it appears safe to assume that half or more of the continuation education programs at any single site in some manner involves the public school system.

A large portion of all colleges and universities reported cooperating with churches and religious organizations, and only a slightly lower percent with civic and service organizations. Rotary, Lions, and Kiwanis Clubs were mentioned regularly and frequently, as were parent teachers organizations, womens' clubs, and professional and labor organizations.

As the data in Table 2 show, many of the organizations with which the colleges and universities cooperate are autonomous, or at most have relatively little geographic spread. Among these were the Community Councils, Welfare Councils, and certain civic organizations which operated for limited periods and for specific purposes.

Participation of most organizations in programs of continuation education varied markedly from one region to another. Farm organizations were mentioned in each region but most frequently in the West. In fact colleges and universities in the West indicate a level of cooperation with other organizations not evident elsewhere, a phenomenon that leads one to assume that this, in part, may be the result of the community college movement in California, and its efforts to bring a service type of education to local adults. Proof or negation of this assumption would be welcome information to those states now planning or otherwise engaged in promoting the community college movement.

TABLE 2
Percent of Colleges and Universities Reporting Working With Certain Organizations, by Region

Organization	Total	Northeast	South	North Central	West
	Percent	*Percent*	*Percent*	*Percent*	*Percent*
Colleges and universities	55	57	47	59	62
Schools	63	57	58	65	79
Churches	57	49	55	68	50
Farm organizations	29	14	32	28	45
Cooperative Agricultural Extension Service	20	10	23	16	33
Goverment bureaus	27	19	29	23	42
Elected or appointed government bodies	15	12	12	14	27
Community councils	29	29	27	30	32
Inter-agency councils	10	11	5	12	12
Civic-service organizations	56	52	53	55	72
Welfare councils	20	22	16	21	24
Libraries	39	41	34	41	40
Political parties and/or organizations	4	2	3	4	8
Professional organizations	42	43	35	42	56
Labor unions	20	16	10	25	34
Women's clubs	43	36	39	47	50
Patriotic and veterans' organizations	17	8	15	19	30
UNESCO organizations	12	7	5	14	26
Parents' organizations	41	30	37	43	60
Fraternal organizations	11	11	7	13	14
Other	15	21	9	15	18
Number responding	582*	114	177	191	97

* The total includes 3 responses from Colleges and Universities outside territorial United States.

Continuation Education and Rurality.—Although continuation education, as it has developed in numerous institutions, has often been considered as a means for bringing the urban population some of the service offered rural people through the Cooperative Extension Service, its scope is now being extended to include rural as well as urban people. As a result of the high degree of urbanity in the Northeast one would expect that colleges and universities in that region would reach relatively few rural people, an expectation that is substantiated by the questionnaire data. More than half of all institutions in the region reporting the information claimed that *almost none* of their programs involved rural adults. By contrast, this percentage was less than 28 in the more rural South. Furthermore, less than 10 percent of the institutions in the Northeast reported that *almost all* of their continuation education programs involved rural people as compared with approximately 24 percent in the South.

The question concerning the frequency of appearance of rural people in the audiences of "best" continuation education programs, as related to size of institution, yielded interesting results. The much greater concern of the larger institutions for the urban population is evident. Fifty percent of the colleges and universities with enrollments of 10,000 and over report that their "best" program contained *almost no* rural people. Of those which did reach rural people most were land-grant colleges which, by legislation and precedent, have always emphasized services to rural people. For the smallest institutions, 17 percent claimed that *almost all* persons reached through their "best" programs were rural persons, i.e., live in the open country or outside centers of 2,500 persons or more.

PROGRAMS IN THE THREE FIELDS[12]

Evidence that continuation education programs of colleges and universities throughout the nation are becoming increasingly interested in problems of human relations is made explicit by the data supplied by them. Nearly three-fourths (73 percent indicated that they were sponsoring programs in the three fields of interest; twenty-seven percent said they were not. Schools and Colleges in the West and North Central states report more activity in the three fields than do those in the South or Northeast. Most of the larger institutions claim to be offering currently, educational materials, in one or more of the three fields of interest. The forms such efforts assume vary from one region to another and from one type of institution to another. Colleges and universities located in, or approximate to, the major ports of entry, somewhat by necessity give training in democracy and international understanding. Others, with less obvious incentive, promote innumerable workshops, institutes, and conferences in the field of government, citizenship and lectures about other countries and peoples. A few have made such activities a part of their regular curricula. For example, Michigan State College has a program called "Adventures in World Understanding." It involves the visiting of foreign students in small communities. The San Jose Evening Colleges' "Intercultural Division" which was originally designed to speed up the assimilation of local minority groups, has now become a center for the study of various peoples and cultures. A majority of the participants at present are adults who wish to further their understanding of peoples and cultures in other parts of the world. The areas of subject matter

[12] International understanding for peace, understanding and strengthening of the economy, and strengthening of democracy.

include each of the continents and the more numerically important minority groups within the United States.

Letters from officials and faculty, along with catalogues and other literature from colleges and universities, indicate that many institutions with no offerings directly in the three fields are engaged in programs or activities having tangential bearing upon one or more of them. A letter from the Director of Extension at the University of Texas, for example, states that "we feel that several of our services are strengthening democracy, and that they are also doing something in the fields of understanding of the economy." Reference here is to courses, conferences, and lectures sponsored by the university divisions of government and economics.

Evidence of latent interest in the three fields was frequently revealed in the margins or on notes attached to the questionnaires which were mailed to colleges and universities. An example of this interest is a letter from an official at Abraham Baldwin Agricultural College to the effect that "Your letter (questionnaire) has caused us to think that we have perhaps spent too much time on the economic phase of adult life and a faculty committee has been appointed to make plans for offering some courses in the first two fields . . . ," i.e., the strengthening of democracy and international understanding for peace.

A section of the questionnaire mailed to colleges and universities requested information about the *best* programs currently conducted in one or more of the three fields. About three-fourths of the completed forms indicated a *best* program and included a brief description of it. Some of these programs were directly within one or more of the three fields and others were marginal. The more common were government workshops, training for leadership, institutes of local and state governments, and United Nations study groups.

Some of these programs were quite large, particularly in the North Central states and in the far West. Almost 73 percent of the programs, however, reached less than 1,000 persons. Nearly 10 percent, however, reached 5,000 persons or more. Limited audiences were more common among the smaller institutions which depend heavily upon direct and personal contacts with the local people in both the initiation and operation of their programs.

An effort was made to determine the extent to which the *best* programs of colleges and universities were reaching rural people. The results, show that these programs, although available to many rural people, are reaching those living in cities and towns. One-third of all colleges and universities reported their audiences to contain almost no rural persons. Only one-fourth indicated that rural persons accounted for three-fourths or more of their audiences for their *best* programs.

The interest of the various types of colleges and universities in reaching rural people varies from one place to another and from one situation to another. Numerous continuation education directors admitted giving only minor attention to the rural population. The most common explanations for such statements were based upon difficulties inherent in reaching such a dispersed group. Directors of some of the smaller colleges explain that education for rural adults is provided elsewhere. The State College of Washington, for example, reported that its continuation education program (Community College Service) "is not conducting education in these (3 fields) areas in small towns and rural situations. Considerable emphasis is given to all three of the subject matter fields in our Spokane Center operations, but here again it is in a decidedly urban setting." Continuing, he explained that "the Agricultural Extension Service in the State of Washington is doing some work of the type concerning which you inquire." Other colleges and universities, however, are devoting major attention to the small towns and rural villages. The University of Wisconsin, Michigan State College, the University of Georgia, the Unified State System of Higher Education in Oregon, and others, have programs that are reaching an ever increasing proportion of the rural population. Others are planning new programs in one or more of the fields and expanding their old ones. The Pennsylvania State College Extension Office writes that "President Eisenhower last Spring appointed a committee to investigate all possible avenues for the development of a broad program of education in the field of international understanding, both on campus and off campus."

Correspondence Courses.—Although correspondence courses still dominate the curricula of continuation education, other, and less formalized, offerings are receiving more attention. There seems to be general and intense effort in most institutions to offer more conferences, public meetings, workshops and institutes. This is apparent in Figure 2, which shows the more common *forms* the *best* programs take. Although colleges and universities in each region reported a variety of forms in their best programs, the more frequent included workshops, conferences, and meetings.

Educational procedures utilized in "best" programs vary but little among the various regions in the United States. As shown in Figure 2, lecturing was listed as the most common procedure even though educators repeatedly expressed confidence in the greater effectiveness of group discussions and panels. The Dean of the School of Education in a southern college writes ". . . our better work is being done through various discussion groups and workshops"; the director of university extension in a large, midwestern university thinks that "the small discussion group provides the only tried and effective method for combining a maximum of class attendance with subject matter progress." The conviction seems general among leaders in continuation education that discussions and panels involving small groups provide opportunities for developing class interest and facilitating learning not found in large groups and formal lectures.

There is an observable, if somewhat irregular, relationship between the use of the discussion method and the size of institution in "best" programs in continuation education. Although all sizes of colleges and universities seem to be equally convinced of the advantages of the small group discussion procedure, the larger institutions are using it more frequently. This is not to say that a smaller proportion of the larger institutions are using the lecture method in their programs but that they are making greater proportionate use of others.

Approximately 215 of the colleges and universities reported procedures used most often for programs in the three fields of interest. The results indicate

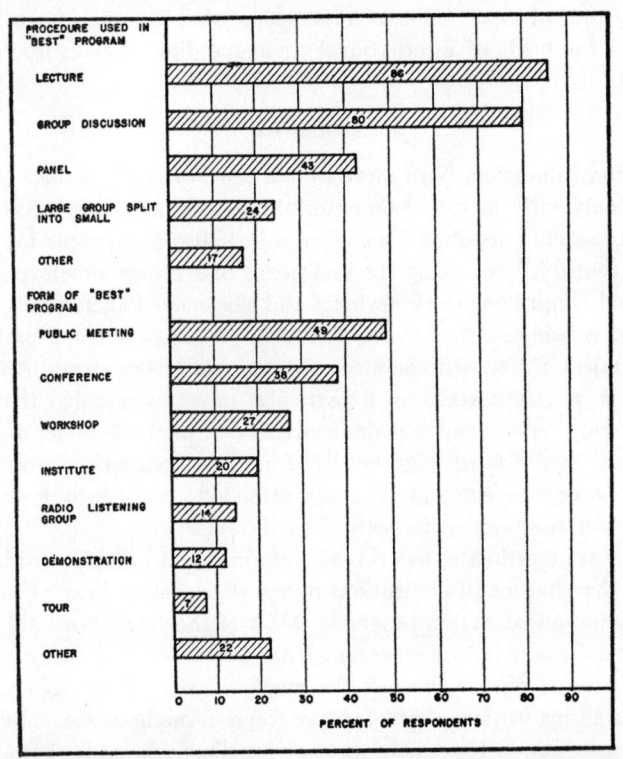

FIG. 2. Percentage of colleges and universities reporting the form and procedure used in their "best" programs.

clearly the emphasis all sizes of institutions are placing on the discussion method. Even the smallest colleges are using the discussion more often than the lecture method for work in these fields, even though use of the method is more pronounced among the larger schools.

Size of Center and Programs in the Three Fields.—It is generally assumed that continuation education has developed more extensively in the larger cities and especially in those which contain one or more of the major colleges and universities. Information gathered in this study show this to be the case throughout the United States. In case of the big urban centers and especially in New York City and Los Angeles, the coexistence of population concentrations and one or more large institutions has facilitated the development of a range of adult education programs and activities hardly possible under other circumstances.

Data available in this study indicate that programs and activities in the three fields are more common and varied in the large, metropolitan centers than elsewhere. Interest in such programs appears to be developing in the smaller cities and towns, however, and local college and university facilities are expanding to meet them. Until recently, these programs have been directed rather specifically toward local problems in democracy but are now increasingly looking toward the fields of international understanding, democracy, and world economics.

SUMMARY

Continuation Education, born more than a century ago and for a long period concerned only with the extension of formalized campus courses, has somewhat suddenly broadened its objectives to include "educating people for life in the twentieth century," "carrying the knowledge of a college or university to the people," and "improving the knowledge and efficiency of all adults."

Just who is being reached through current programs of continuation education is a subject of frequent comment but one that has received little objective examination. A recent study of a particular program revealed that students enrolled were: predominantly male, concentrated in the younger age brackets (20–35), possessed a fairly high level of formalized education, were mostly in the higher income levels, and generally attended classes in order to improve their economic positions or increase their incomes.

A conservative estimate, based upon information available in this study, is that more than half of all institutions of higher education in the United States have continuation education programs. Most of these programs are limited to credit courses conducted by correspondence but other than credit courses are increasingly being offered through the media of panels, discussions, and conferences. In all institutions contacted, the trend in methods seemed to be away from the formalized lecture to the more personalized approach possible through small group and informal instruction.

Most programs of continuation education are designed, at present, for urban people although progress is being made in some areas to reach more rural adults. The development of this type of education in rural areas has been slow because of (1) the wide dispersion of farm and small village residents, and (2) the general assumption that the work of the Cooperation Agricultural Extension Service meets the educational needs of farm adults.

A majority of the colleges and universities with departments of continuation education are currently conducting programs in one or more of the three fields of interest, i.e., international understanding for peace, strengthening of democracy, and understanding and strengthening of the economy. Regionally, these programs are somewhat concentrated in the West. Among all regions, they are found most frequently in the larger institutions, a few of which are now offering several courses in one or more of the three fields.

Continuation education work in the three fields is mostly conducted through conferences, workshops, and public meetings. These are often administered in cooperation with the public schools and with such local organizations as the Rotary, Lions, or Kiwanis Clubs.

The lecture is still the most widely distributed method of presenting educational materials, but group discussions are used more often. The percentage of all institutions reporting the use of the discussion as an educational method was somewhat higher for the larger institutions, although the smaller schools were not far behind. Almost 80 percent of the smallest schools (with enrollments of less than 1,000) reported making use of the discussion method, and many of them seemed confident that it offered educational advantages over the lecture.

Despite recent emphasis in continuation education upon such media as radio, motion pictures, and television, the newspaper is still the most important for distributing subject matter and for relaying information about program and activity offerings. Television, although widely used by the larger institutions is by no means monopolized by them. Six percent of all colleges and universities with enrollments of less than 1,000 reported the use of television in one or more of their programs. Such institutions, by and large, were located in the urban centers or adjacent to them.

There is evidence of some association between the size of center in which the colleges and universities are located and the extent, and nature, of educational programs in the three fields. By and large, educational developments in the three fields have received more attention in areas characterized by large and diverse populations.

Olen E. Leonard
Department of Sociology and Anthropology
Michigan State College
East Lansing, Michigan
and
Sheldon G. Lowry
Department of Sociology and Anthropology
Michigan State College
East Lansing, Michigan

BIBLIOGRAPHY

A Selected List

Cartwright, Morse Adams, *Ten Years of Adult Education*, New York: The Macmillan Company, 1935.

Eells, Walter Crosby, "The Community's College," *Adult Education Journal*, Volume IV, Number 1, 1945.

Ely, Mary L., editor, *Handbook of Adult Education in the United States*, Institute of Adult Education, 1948.

King, Kermit C., *The Historical Development of University Extension at the University of California,* UCLA, Ph.D. Dissertation, 1947.
McLaughlin, Laurence K., *Student Population in University of California Extension Classes,* UCLA, Ph.D. Dissertation, 1951.
Mosier, Jean, "Problems and Policies of the University Evening College," *Adult Education Bulletin,* Vol. XIII, No. 5, 1948.
Palmer, Mary Ewen, "Stages of Development in Adult Education," *Adult Education Bulletin,* Vol. XI, No. 5, 1947.
Perry, Clarence Arthur, *Wider Use of the School Plant,* New York: William F. Fell Company, 1910.
President's Commission on Higher Education, *Higher Education for American Democracy,* Washington, 1947.
Sadler, M. E., *Continuation Schools in England and Elsewhere,* Manchester: Manchester University Press, 1908.
Zehmer, George B., "The Development of University Extension Services in the United States," *Proceedings of the Institute for Administrative Officers of Higher Institutions, 1945,* Chicago: University of Chicago Press, 1946.

Chapter 11:
INTERNATIONAL EXCHANGE OF PERSONS
General and Historical

Study and travel in lands other than one's own is a practice that has its origin deep in the history of mankind. Folk tales of early Greece abound with accounts of persons who journeyed about the Eastern Mediterranean area studying and observing that which aroused their curiosity, freeing themselves from the fetters of superstition and convention and establishing themselves as perhaps the greatest humanists of all times. Athens, beginning with the leadership of Pericles (460–429 B.C.) and lasting more than a hundred years following his death, became widely recognized as the center of learning, not only attracting numerous scholars from other parts of the world, but also dispensing many chosen to teach selected groups or individuals for domestic or foreign court service.

Study in foreign lands was of little quantitative importance, however, until just prior to the Renaissance when groups of students and teachers began a practice of clustering in the larger capitals of Europe, sometimes forming relatively permanent associations out of which seem to have grown the modern university.[1] Some of these groupings became permanent and more widely known

[1] Charles Homer Haskins, *The Rise of Universities,* New York: H. Holt and Company, 1923. Also, a very precise account of the historical development of student exchanges is contained in an unpublished memorandum to the Social Science Research Council, 230 Park Avenue, New York, by Guy Metraux. The privilege of reading the memorandum during the preparation of this report is hereby gratefully acknowledged.

by the end of the sixteenth century, especially those in Spain, France, Germany and England.

The needs and objectives of both students and professors who have sought foreign study seem to have varied from time to time and from place to place. Until the advent of the printing press (fifteenth century) books were extremely scarce and expensive; hence the universities or other seats of learning which had most of the important works in one or more fields attracted students and professors who otherwise would not have had access to them. With the development and widespread use of the printed page the foreign university became functionally less important even though, in many instances, its appeal to foreign students and professors seems to have increased, especially in the latter part of the 18th century and throughout most of the 19th and early 20th centuries.

Although the dissemination of knowledge remained the manifest justification for foreign travel and study, numerous regards were introduced later that tended to lure the venturesome student to study in other cultures and among other peoples. The movement, and the cycle of its transition, seem to have been remarkably similar in most of the western world. Consequently, it may be worthwhile to trace its development in a few of the major countries of Europe in order to better understand the movement in the United States.

FRANCE

France was among the first of the European nations to officially recognize the importance of an international exchange of persons but until perhaps the middle of the 18th century, study and travel in a foreign country was considered a private matter of little concern to those not directly involved. Where students should go, and what they should study was considered of no consequence to the government, since the study contributed only to the knowledge of certain fortunate and economically privileged groups. In France, as well as in England, at least, foreign travel and study was for "infirmity of body, imbecility of mind, and inevitable necessity," the latter including "felons on the way to the Colonies" and "young gentlemen transported by the (sic) cruelty of parents and guardians, and travelling under the direction of governors recommended by Oxford, Aberdeen and Glasgow."[2] Until this time little thought had been given to the use of foreign study for other purposes such as its influence upon the content of formal courses in the student's own country or its role in improving local social, economic, or political life. Beginning in the latter part of the 18th century, France began to establish various educational centers in other parts of the world and to adapt her domestic schools and universities in order to attract a greater number of foreign students to her shores. The influence of this policy, especially in the Near and Far East, soon became obvious not only to France but to her European neighbors. The success of this eastern venture

[2] Institute of International Education, *News Bulletin*, Vol. 26, No. 8, May 1951, p. 20.

encouraged France to extend her cooperative educational efforts to other parts of the Western world.

Programs of education developed by France for the Eastern and Western worlds were quite different in aim and content. Whereas school programs in the East had revolved around and grown out of such services as nursing, medicine, hospitals, elementary schools, etc., those for the West were designed more for "French citizens living in Europe and in Latin America whose children should be given a real French education."[3] Early in the twentieth century France had established schools in most of the European as well as the American republics and annually entertained hundreds of students and visitors in her universities. In part, as the result of this, French, more than any other language, became the common means of communication between countries speaking different tongues. So universal did French become in many of the countries that French speaking professors were imported to the major universities where they could lecture to the students without need of an interpreter.

The First World War interrupted the international program of interchange of persons in France, but as soon as it was over she again turned to this medium as a means for rebuilding her foreign relations. In 1919 a member of the French Parliament reminded his colleagues that "Of all our products for exportation, the finest product and that best fitted to make French genius known, admired, and loved, is French thought."[4]

Between the two major wars France organized an extensive program of cultural cooperation with other nations, a large portion of which was directed at education and schools. Plans embodied both government and private efforts, and the public soon became convinced that they were giving results. The number of students, scholars and technicians coming to take courses and improve their knowledge in various fields increased while greater importance was given to the French language in the programs of other countries. By 1936 France had established a large number of institutions abroad with several hundred professors attached to governments, and courses in French were offered in most of the larger cities of the world.[5]

With the cessation of hostilities in Europe following the Second World War, France again initiated efforts to further her interests abroad which had lagged during the war and during the Nazi occupation. Again major effort was undertaken by the government through activities stretching over widely separated parts of the globe. Funds were made available for fellowships to study in London, Moscow, Ottawa and New York. An early phase of the program involved the sending of 20 advanced French students to other countries—students who were envisioned as representatives of French thought. Their stay abroad, it was

[3] Ruth Emily McMurry and Muna Lee, *The Cultural Approach—Another in International Relations*, Chapel Hill: The University of North Carolina Press, 1947, p. 11.
[4] *Ibid.*, pp. 15–16.
[5] *Ibid.*, pp. 18–27.

reasoned, would do something to advertise French culture and would enable them to return to France with valuable scientific and technical knowledge for "there were fields in which France had much to learn of civilizations which had developed more rapidly than the French in the use of scientific and industrial techniques for the benefit of social progress."[6]

GERMANY

The origin of the interchange of persons movement in Germany is somewhat unique when compared with that in other major nations in Europe. When the migrations from Germany were so marked in the middle and later part of the 19th century there seems to have been a general tendency for the migrants to establish their own schools and churches and in this way retain many elements of their homeland culture. At the end of the Franco-Prussian War, when Germany began her vigorous attempt to unify her people, she soon became intensely aware of the vast potential inherent in the unification of not only the people who were within her national boundaries, but also those who had moved to foreign lands. With the realization of this important factor there came a strong movement to increase the number of schools among such people, not only as a means of strengthening German culture in these communities, but as a strong support for other interests. In the beginning the movement was supported through private sources, tuition and fees, but by 1875 a substantial subsidy was coming from the German government.

Although the intensive educational program of Germany was interrupted during the period of the First World War, it was resumed almost immediately thereafter. It was reasoned that the resurrection of German power in the world must depend upon the unification of the German people throughout the world. Such a vision could not be limited to education, interpreted in a narrow sense. It involved social and political elements as well. In 1921 a member of the German Reichstag reminded members of that body that:

The German universities are especially sought by the students coming from the oppressed peoples and from the newly constituted states, who, as is natural, feel at ease with us because they know that we understand the sufferings that they have undergone, and because on the other hand, they understand that we can and want to give them the best of German knowledge and ability.... The more we encourage cultural and spiritual advancement in these new lands, the more opportunities will be opened to us to establish flourishing economic undertakings there and to carry on commerce. We will win friends, who as products of our economy, of our techniques, of our industry, will gladly purchase from us ... above all, we must not open merely the doors of our university to these students.... The students coming from these young nations must be introduced to German society, to German cultural life, through personal contact with German families, German scholars ...[7]

---

[6] *Ibid.*, p. 36.
[7] *Ibid.*, p. 50.

The government of the Weimar Republic granted funds for the exchange of persons, especially students at the Universities, although the major effort was directed at German community schools in foreign lands. Prior to the First World War, and especially in the latter part of the nineteenth century, a strong tendency had developed throughout the world that some study in a German university was essential to a well rounded program of education, a tendency that involved practically all disciplines. Some of this prestige was regained during the Weimar Republic, but not to the extent that many Germans desired. A prominent German, speaking on foreign policy in 1929, expressed concern over the diminishing number of foreign students attending local universities. He reasoned that such students "... bring returns to later generation in Germany. Why have so many people been drawn to us? Because they have spent some time here; because they have assimilated the German spirit; because this has become a part of their souls; and because they have developed a liking for our country..."[8]

Under the National Socialist party, the foreign educational program established earlier was strengthened rather than modified. Foreign students and technicians continued to be welcome in the universities, but major emphasis was devoted to "any German living abroad." German professors were sent to numerous foreign communities and students from these communities were encouraged to come to the homeland for advanced study and training. Boys and girls of the Republic were sent on guided tours not only throughout the limits of their own countries but to countries near the German frontiers. At the same time groups of young people from other nations were welcomed to travel within Germany. And it was officially stressed that such exchanges of young groups were for the purpose of "mutual understanding" rather than for political motives. The success of this movement is partially measurable, perhaps, in the relative ease with which some of the neighboring countries were occupied when the militant expansion of the Nazis began.

GREAT BRITAIN

Despite the reluctance of Great Britain to recognize officially any paramount benefits to the nation in an exchange of persons and knowledge, the prestige and academic offerings of British schools and scholars must be ranked with the more important in Europe at an early date. Some of this, of course, came about through the needs of the British colonies, such as those in America, which depended in substantial part upon British universities to supply advanced training in the fields of law, medicine and other sciences.

Although the government of Britain remained relatively aloof from any ideas recognizing the exchange of persons and knowledge as an ethical means for furthering its general interest, this was not all true of certain individuals and groups among the island's population. Before the end of the 19th century,

[8] *Ibid.*, p. 57.

foreign trade people and official representatives of the government abroad had begun to realize the harm that was ensuing to British interest through her failure to follow the policy of other countries of Europe in the use of various media of educational propaganda.

An important element in the development of official British interest in educational propaganda was the work of Cecil J. Rhodes who, soon after the beginning of the 20th century, established the famous Rhodes Scholarships for students from the Empire and the United States to do advanced academic work in the various colleges of Oxford. Although originally conceived by Mr. Rhodes as an instrument for uniting the English speaking areas of the world, his final will stated that the purpose of the scholarships was nothing more specific than that they should contribute to international understanding and good will.[9]

Although the British developed an eminently successful program of educational propaganda during the First World War, this failed to continue past the cessation of hostilities. Despite evidence of the success of the Italian, German, and French campaigns of "foreign enlightenment," Britain still refused to follow their footsteps. It was not until 1934 that the British government appropriated any money for this purpose and then only a small sum to establish a Council for the purpose of carrying on a program on "national interpretatation."[10]

The major aims of the Council were: (a) to increase the knowledge of British life and thought abroad, (b) to promote a general program of intellectual exchange with other nations, (c) to promote the study of English in foreign schools, and (d) to permit students and various types of technical and scientific persons to study in the Empire. But until the beginning of the Second World War it seems that the British government remained reluctant to consider the work of the Council as going beyond the original aim of furthering its own knowledge, and that of other peoples, and increasing the amount of mutual understanding and good will among them.

The outbreak of the Second World War interrupted the plans of the British Council for cultural exchange with other nations, but by no means stopped it. Parliament now became convinced of the need of continuing this type of work, even though some functions might overlap the work of the wartime information service. Limitations growing out of the war restrictions prevented major effort in the field of interchange, but a few professors continued to go to foreign universities and the Council continued to import a few graduate, and even undergraduate students, to study various phases of education and industrial training. The annual report of the Council for 1944–45 showed that most of its peacetime activities were continuing, especially in Latin America, a few of the European countries, and parts of the strategic Middle East. Even though most of the

[9] Frank Aydelotte, *The American Rhodes Scholarships: A Review of the First Forty Years*, Princeton: Princeton University Press, 1946.
[10] McMurry and Lee, *op. cit.*, pp. 138–139.

effort and funds of the Council were devoted to the teaching of English, by 1945 one hundred sixty-one students had been brought to Great Britain under Council fellowships while some thirty-seven professors had been sent abroad by the Council to do teaching in major educational institutions.[11]

At the end of the war the budget of the Council was reduced somewhat from the peak obtained in 1944-45, but its work remained highly regarded. Seemingly as a result of the victory of the Allies, world interest in the life and literature of Britain increased and a special effort was made by the Council to supply the demand for publications and pamphlets about the life and customs of the people. This, in turn, seems to have brought a much larger number of students and visitors to the United Kingdom who came to see, observe, and study. In response to this situation the Council increased the number of graduate fellowships offered in 1945-46 to more than 400, most of which were awarded. This number, plus those fellowships made possible through individual and other sources, filled the universities to overflowing.

Instructions from Parliament to the Council at the beginning of the fiscal year 1947 limited the work of the Council to long time educational work, in contrast to purely and immediate information services, and extended its charter for five years, subject to a renewal at that time. The functions of the Council were specifically limited to schools, professors, university students, youth groups and educational organizations of various sorts. This, of course, gave the Council greater latitude in working with other groups including numerous assortments of technicians and specialists. By this time, Britain was completely sold on the value of an exchange program to promote national interests as well as to increase international understanding and good will.

THE UNITED STATES

The United States was relatively slow to recognize the importance of an international exchange of persons. In the later part of the 19th century numerous American scholars were attending European, and especially German, universities but few came the other way. At the beginning of the 20th century, American universities were attracting a few European scholars, but prior to the First World War the number of Americans attending European universities was much greater than the number of Europeans attending American universities. The contribution of the United States to the winning of that war, however, raised the estimate of American culture in the eyes of the Europeans, a part of which was quickly reflected in the interest of Europeans in attending American universities and colleges. Partially as a means of courting American goodwill and understanding, special efforts were made by Britain, Germany and France not only to send additional students to the United States but to attract American scholars into their own university halls.[12]

[11] McMurry and Lee, *op. cit.*, pp. 148-163.
[12] Stephen Duggan, *A Professor at Large*, New York: The Macmillan Company, 1943, pp. 48-50.

The first recognition of the United States government of the importance of the international exchange of students came in the first decade of the 20th century. Under the encouragement of such persons as Elihu Root, Nicholas Murray Butler, and others, Theodore Roosevelt, then President of the United States, promoted the allotment of a portion of the Chinese Boxer Indemnity Fund to the financing of Chinese students to the United States. This program did much to awaken the various universities to the possibilities of encouraging foreign students to come to the United States, and established a pattern that was followed very closely in years following the First World War, by government and various private organizations.[13]

A survey of the literature of this period fails to reveal much evidence that this interest in the international exchange of students was motivated by other than a desire to afford foreign students an opportunity to pursue academic studies in their own specialties. Apparently there was some thinking in terms of a "meeting of minds" derived, perhaps, from the objectives of the League of Nations, but there seems to have been little thought in America, as it had developed in Germany and France, concerning the possibilities of cultivating an exchange of students and scholars as a means for furthering political and economic ends. Students were expected to "measure up" in terms of "scholarship, adjustability and knowledge of the foreign language."

Seemingly the first important organized attempt to further international understanding and good will between the United States and other nations was initiated in 1919 when the Carnegie Endowment granted funds for promoting good will between the United States and other countries. This effort was headed by Stephen Duggan, who first envisioned the work as the collection and dissemination of factual knowledge about various nations and peoples, and was labeled the Institute of International Education. After a brief existence as an information gathering and disseminating organization, it became, and remains, the major agency for servicing universities and other institutions interested in facilitating foreign exchanges, and individual students interested in studying in a foreign land. At the present time this organization is administering more than 3,000 scholarships involving persons from almost every country on the globe and representing everything from "Americans abroad under private grants" to "Finns here on funds available by Congressional action on the Finnish war debt."[14]

The first official step of the United States to promote the international exchange of persons took place in Buenos Aires in 1936 with the meeting of the Buenos Aires Cultural Convention. At this meeting the assembled delegates of the American states passed a resolution favoring the multilateral exchange of both students and teachers. In 1938 the United States Congress gave life to

[13] George A. Finch, "Remission of the Chinese Indemnity," *American Historical Review*, Volume XXXII, 1926, pp. 64–68.

[14] Institute of International Education, *31st Annual Report*, New York: Institute of International Education, 1950, p. 7.

the resolution by creating an Interdepartmental Committee on Scientific and Cultural Cooperation authorizing departments of the Federal Government to grant various types of fellowships to citizens of the American Republics to study and train in countries of their choice. These fellowships were of five general types:

1. Exchange of Students. This was a two-way program limited to mature, graduate students. Selection of candidates was made on the basis of scholarship and general character to be determined by special selection committees established in each of the countries. These grants were to be made on a cooperative basis with the Federal Government cooperating with the individual, his government, or a private agency to make the study possible.

2. Exchange of Professors. Terms for this type of grant required an invitation by a specific institution desiring the services of the professor. In this case the government acted as a catalytic agent in making the visit possible. These grants were usually for a period of one year with short extensions possible upon request from the university or other institution at which the professor served.

3. Visiting Specialists. These were not teaching grants, but aids to specialists in a certain field who desired to visit specific projects or agencies in the United States.

4. Visiting Technical Experts. This was a larger aspect of the program enabling specialists such as engineers, agronomists, and horticulturists, to remain for indefinite periods in countries desiring technical assistance in specific fields of development, such as education, agriculture, and health.

5. In-service Trainees. These were grants given to qualified men and women for periods of in-service training in the United States, generally in the Federal Departments. Persons selected under this type of grant usually worked alongside employees of the United States Government for a year or longer, after which they were expected to return and serve in their own Federal Services for periods of a year or longer. Many of these grantees were expected to return and eventually replace visiting American technicians in special kinds of work. Types of financial assistance to such persons varied from total support from the United States Government, to part and no support, depending somewhat upon the number of requests and upon the resources of the countries from which the trainees came.[15]

Under the stimulus of governmental sponsorship of the international exchange of persons and the efforts of such organizations as the Institute of International Education to encourage colleges, universities and a wide variety of private organizations to provide scholarships and other financial means to encourage the entrance of foreign students into the United States, the movement, beginning in the late '30's, grew by leaps and bounds. By the academic year 1946–47 it was estimated that more than 14,000 foreign students were studying in the

[15] For a more complete description of these grants, see Institute of International Education, *News Bulletin*, Vol. 24, No. 4, January 1949, article by Oliver J. Caldwell.

United States, about 13 percent of whom were receiving aid from either governmental or private sources and 87 percent were supporting themselves. By the following year the number had increased to more than 17,000 with 5,129 from Asia, 3,923 from Latin America and 3,910 from Europe. There were more from Canada than from any other single country (3,163), with China in second (2,370), and India in third place (1,006).[16] Predictions were that this number would decline in 1948 and 1949, but such decreases failed to materialize. By the early part of the 1950–51 school year, the number of foreign students studying in the United States had increased to a new high of more than 29,000 persons from 121 countries and areas of the world. Although the larger colleges and universities were accommodating the bulk of these persons at least some were studying in each of the 48 states, plus Alaska, the Canal Zone, Hawaii and Puerto Rico. The distribution of foreign students by states is shown in Figure 1.

Despite the number of persons coming to the United States the migration was by no means a "one-way street." Although no exact figures are available, the Institute of International Education estimates that in 1950–51 more than 20,000 American students were either attending year-round or summer courses in various parts of the world.[17] The total of more than 50,000 exchanges between the United States and other countries certainly should provide a real test of the merits supposedly inherent in such a program.

The distribution of these students by country has shifted slightly within the past five years, although less than one might assume on the basis of international events during this time. In 1950–51 the Western Hemisphere still led the list with more than 10,000 (Canada was still in the lead for any single country with 4,498) while Europe had risen to second place with 7,157. Asia and the Near East were not far behind with 6,598.[18]

Despite increased financial aid by the United States Government to foreign students in 1950–51, such students represented only slightly more than 5 percent of the total or 1,610. More than 34 percent of all students on which there was information were completely self-supporting.[19]

In 1950–51, 1,435, or approximately 80 percent of all institutions of higher education in the United States, reported one or more foreign students enrolled. More than one-third of these were enrolled in 25 of the larger colleges and universities. The ten fields of major numerical importance were Engineering, Liberal Arts, Social Sciences, Medical Sciences, Physical Sciences, Business Administration, Religion, Education, Agriculture, and Fine Arts, although almost all branches of learning were represented.

Changing Objectives of the Program.—The increased numerical importance of

---

[16] Institute of International Education, *News Bulletin*, Vol. 23, Nos. 2 and 5. For a brief history of the Institute and its functions see Institute of International Education, *First Annual Report, 1920*.
[17] Institute of International Education, *Education for One World*, New York: 1951.
[18] *Ibid.*
[19] *Ibid.*

the exchange of persons between the United States and other nations has been accompanied by a general recognition of its diverse values by the public as well as by state and local officials. Such recognition is reflected in the changing concept of the program's role. Until the First World War there seems to have been little consideration in the United States of the international exchange of persons as more than a means for implementing and improving the educational level of students. As a result of this philosophy, only the best of the students were encouraged—chosen on the basis of examinations designed to test training and ability.

Perhaps as a result of observing the operations of the German and French Foreign Offices in the 1930's, many public officials in the United States became

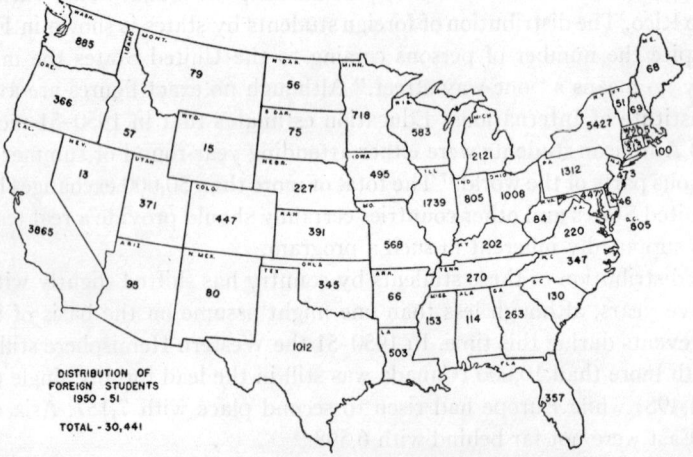

FIG. 1. Distribution of foreign students by state, 1950-51.

interested in the international exchange of persons as a means for furthering economic interests. Some were intrigued by the German idea that people buy not only on the basis of the quality of products "but whether or not they like us."

It was not until the end of the Second World War that the United States began to recognize the international exchange of persons as an effective means for implementing foreign policy. Such a purpose was explicitly stated in a report of the United States Advisory Commission on Educational Exchange to Congress in April 1951, when it urged that more extensive exchanges of students, government officials, labor groups, and youth and professional leaders in all fields, be granted in order "to strengthen resistence to Communism in countries immediately threatened with infiltration or aggression" and "to weaken the forces of Communism and diminish its power in areas now under the domination of the U.S.S.R."[20] Also, it was envisioned that the interchange of persons

[20] *New York Times* (Sunday), April 15, 1951, Section 1, p. 20.

would be an effective counter-attack for propaganda inimical to the political interests of the United States, since judgment of the students and other persons would rest upon "full knowledge of all facts in the case."[21]

Another, and recent, motivation for the exchange of persons program springs from the assumption that a mere equitable distribution of the world's technical and scientific knowledge will reduce inter-national tensions and thus lessen possibilities for armed conflict. This thinking was incorporated in the provisions of the Buenos Aires Convention in 1936 and in the federal legislation that implemented it in 1938.

The broadening of objectives supporting the international exchange of persons has, of necessity, resulted in a change of emphasis upon the type of person thought desirable for exchange. There is evidence that in many colleges and universities much less attention is given currently to scholarship and more to such factors as: position of the person in his home country, political ideology, possibilities for exercising influence in his home country, etc. Regarding a recent visit of Japanese young people to this country, an official of the Institute of International Education, cooperating with the State Department in planning a program for these people, expressed the opinion that "unless these young minds can truly grasp the philosophy of individual freedom there is little hope for the years ahead. They are brought here to do graduate work in their field and to learn how that particular branch of knowledge fits into the fabric of American society. They have been told repeatedly that while the importance of advanced work in their field is appreciated, it is secondary to their learning about our country."[22]

Under the above assumption it is obvious that many persons, other than students and scholars, can qualify for training and study. One might even assume that there are those who would no longer give major attention to scholarship since "when we bring together the workers of different countries we can attain the widest possible base of international understanding because their work and experience reach down to the tap roots . . ." and "One of America's big chances to help raise living standards throughout the world is to bring foreign skilled workers here for limited periods of on-the-job training. . . ."[23]

The tendency on the part of sponsoring agencies, including those of government, to emphasize the importance of understanding American life (including some of its technical and scientific aspects) has been particularly apparent during the past few years. In 1950, the U.S. Advisory Commission on Educational Exchange concluded that "perhaps the most important phase of orientation and education for the foreign student is the understanding of American life,"

[21] U. S. Advisory Commission on Educational Exchange, *Two Way Street*, Department of State Publication 3893, 1950, p. 1.
[22] George Hall, "Welcoming the Japanese Students," *News Bulletin*, Institute of International Education, Vol. 26, No. 1, October 1951.
[23] U. S. Department of State, *Building Roads to Peace*, Department Publication No. 3738, Information and Cultural Series 11, February 1950, pp. 5–27.

and to assure that this occurred, recommended that students be given greater opportunity to "spend time with families, in formal and informal organizations."[24]

This new emphasis has obviously posed some real problems for colleges and universities in terms of scholarship standards, recognition of credited preparation and proper and adequate facilities to carry out new roles such training requires. A few students of the problem have pointed out certain dangers in the new policy, provided it is not carefully controlled. Robert S. Schwantee, writing in *School and Society*, warns that the new emphasis in exchange " . . . is largely an act of faith; its ultimate results lie too far in the future for accurate evaluation," and I. L. Kandel in the same journal concludes that "There is one aspect of the whole problem of student exchange which deserves more attention than it has received. In discussing the exchange of students and the contribution that it can make to promoting international understanding and good will, there is too widespread a tendency to assume that this desirable end can be achieved merely by the fact that students go to countries other than their own. It is assumed that mere presence in a foreign atmosphere will enable the student to absorb a real understanding of the culture of a foreign country"[25] Certainly there is reason for some meaningful evaluation of the results of such programs if current levels of expenditure for the work can be justifiably maintained.

CURRENT PROGRAMS IN THE UNITED STATES

In-Service Training.—One of the more significant provisions of the legislation of 1938 creating facilities for the exchange of persons within the Western Hemisphere was that of granting fellowships for a selected number of persons from the Latin American countries to spend various periods in the United States studying and practicing their selected professions. Most of the grants provided for supervised work in the various governmental departments, supplemented, when necessary, by study in selected colleges and universities. The recipients of these grants were generally referred to as in-service trainees.

More recent legislation has provided additional funds for the in-service trainee programs, notably Public Law 402 (80th Congress), the Economic Cooperation Administration, and such special acts as provided for a large number of persons from Japan and Germany, and the still more recent Point-4 legislation which is now getting into motion. In each instance the trainee grants were aimed at more mature persons who generally had completed their professional training and held key positions within their own governments. Selections were made on the basis of training and experience although some elasticity in the selections were allowed to provide for differential training facilities that exist between the vari-

[24] *Two Way Street, op. cit.,* p. 20.
[25] Robert S. Schwantee, "Results of Study Abroad: Japanese Students in America" and I. L. Kandel, "Foreign Students and American Culture," *School and Society*, December 9, 1950 and April 5, 1951.

ous Latin American countries. Ten Federal Government agencies were participating in the trainee program in 1946–47, eighteen in 1948, and the list grew steadily through 1949, 1950 and 1951. At the present time almost all Federal agencies have one or more trainees studying with them at some time during the year.[26] See Table 1.

Since the beginning of the In-Service Trainee Program constant effort has been made by participating agencies to standardize procedures as much as possible, while recognizing certain limitations that are imposed on the wide range of work in which the trainees are engaged. A brief description of the program in the United States Department of Agriculture will serve to show the general pattern under which training in each of the agencies is conducted.

Grants to the trainees are made through the Office of Foreign Agricultural Relations, the International Branch of the Department of Agriculture, through recommendations of agricultural specialists assigned to foreign countries, the Ministries of Agriculture in the countries, and representatives of the United States Embassies who give them final clearance. Awards are made on the basis of the applicant's competence and training and the particular needs of his country. The majority of the grants are to government employees or to those engaged in some type of strategic work.

Once the trainee arrives in the United States he is generally met by a representative of the Committee on Friendly Relations with Foreign Students and aided, as necessary, in any problems of transportation, visas, or other formalities involving entrance into the country. He is expected to report directly upon his arrival in Washington to a designated official of the Office of Foreign Agricultural Relations, who is responsible for arranging his program of work and study.

If it is found that the trainee is deficient in the English language he is assigned to a local Orientation Center where he may, without financial obligation on his part, study intensely, written and spoken English for a month or more. If it is determined that the trainee has obtained a working mastery of English he is injected into the organizational machinery of the Department, where he becomes acquainted with those technicians in the Department engaged in work closely aligned with his interest. Concurrently with this introduction to the Department, a scheduled itinerary is arranged that upon leaving Washington, will allow him to go immediately to his work either in a field laboratory of the Department or to a land-grant college where both work and study is arranged. While at the college or laboratory he is under the guidance of specialists in his

---

[26] U. S. Department of State, *Cooperation in the Americas*, Department of State Publication 2971, January 1948, p. 57. Also U. S. Advisory Commission on Educational Exchange, *Trading Ideas with the World*, Department of State publication 3551, October 1949, p. 37.

Note: There are many types of exchanges of persons currently conducted by both private and governmental sources which are not included here, such as: specialists, officials, etc. Because of the variety of these programs and the dearth of information about them, it seems desirable to omit them from this analysis.

TABLE 1

Number of In-Service Trainees Participating in Programs of the Federal Government, During the Month of June, 1951, by Servicing Agency, and by Type of Grant

Agency and/or bureau	A	B	C	Total
Total	715	141	208	1064
Executive Office of the President				
Bureau of the Budget	15	3	2	20
Department of Agriculture				
Office Foreign Agricultural Relations	372	18	26	416
Department of Commerce				
Office of Business Economics	1	—	1	2
Bureau of the Census	6	1	2	9
Civil Aeronautics	2	4	23	29
Coast and Geodetic Surveys	1	2	3	6
Maritime Administration	49	—	—	49
Bureau of Public Roads	3	—	45	48
Bureau of Standards	1	—	3	4
Weather Bureau	1	14	2	17
Federal Communications Commission	8	3	—	11
Federal Security Agency				
Office of Education	77	—	—	77
Public Health	66	38	6	110
Vital Statistics	7	9	3	19
Social Security Administration	30	3	—	33
Office of Vocational Rehabilitation	12	3	—	15
Housing and Home Finance Agency	—	1	—	1
Institute of Inter-American Affairs	2	—	50	52
Department of Interior				
Fish and Wildlife	2	—	1	3
Geological Survey	6	2	2	10
Indian Affairs	—	1	—	1
Bureau of Mines	1	1	—	2
Bureau of Reclamation	8	14	—	22
Office of Territories	13	1	—	14
Department of Labor				
Bureau of Apprenticeship	1	—	37	38
Employment Sec.	—	4	—	4
International Labor Affairs	9	9	—	18
Labor Standards	1	—	—	1
Bureau of Labor Statistics	10	4	2	16
Women's Bureau	11	—	—	11
Wilson Teachers College Orientation Center	—	6	—	6

Under Type of Grant: *a*—Financed by United States Government; *b*—Financed by Trainee's Government; *c*—Financed jointly by Untied States and Trainee's Governments.

The above figures do not include 105 persons serviced who were not considered as part of the grant program of in-service trainees.

Source: Department of State, Division of Exchange of Persons, unpublished data.

subject matter field. Independence in work and study is the goal for all in-service trainee work and is gradually increased as the trainee can fit into and contribute to the projects to which he is assigned.

If the trainee is interested in the work of the Cooperative Agricultural Extension Service, part of his time includes travel with county agricultural agents who provide opportunities for visits and conversation with farmers and farm families, thus enabling them to learn of rural and rural-family life in the United States. If he is interested in a more restricted field such as agricultural chemistry or soils, his opportunities for meeting farm people are much less. In instances such as these many colleges are now providing tours and programs which encourage contacts with rural life. This latter phase of the trainees' experience has received increased emphasis recently with general public recognition of the opportunities the trainee program offers as a means of acquainting the grantees with American life and culture and thereby increasing international understanding and good will.

A recent adaptation of a program of trainee exchanges is the International Farm Youth Exchange, a project initiated by the Cooperative Agricultural Extension Service in 1948. This program undertook to exchange young farmers between the United States and other countries of the world with about as many going from the United States as entering it. It seems to have had rather generous support during its brief existence, not only from various branches of the Federal Government, but from a number of private organizations which approve of it as a method for improving international relations.

Perhaps the more significant aspect of the IFYE program, as it is commonly called, is the manner in which it has enlisted support at various levels, from the nation's capitol to many of the more isolated rural counties of the United States. This it has done through a campaign conducted by the 4-H Club Foundation and the Cooperative Extension Service. That the campaign has had some measure of success is evident in the rather generous financial backing that has been obtained for it plus such additional gestures as a willingness on the part of rural people to house these young farmers and in many cases to pay them a small wage.

An analysis of the IFYE objectives indicate that it is, to a large extent, a synthesis of many elements of earlier types of international exchange programs conducted in the United States with certain new features and modifications of old ones. In 1951 its aims were to:

(a) Relieve international tensions, and thus increase likelihood of peace, through greater understanding promoted by the program.

(b) Influence those "who will have a great deal to say about the kind of world in which we live," and especially the areas currently manifesting the greatest political unrest.

(c) Improve technical knowledge of farm people in undeveloped areas of the world and thus reduce tensions and increase possibilities for lasting peace.

(d) Offer the American people an opportunity to know life as it exists in other cultures....

In selecting candidates for the IFYE program, considerable responsibility has been placed upon the smaller units of organized community life, both here and abroad. In the United States, candidates for other countries are nominated at the county level, although final selections are made by the national IFYE Committee in Washington. Some of the factors considered of major importance in the selections include: (a) influence of candidate in his home community, (b) interest in organized activities, (c) language proficiency, (d) age, and (e) personality characteristics. The guiding plan for nominations of candidates for 1951 contained no reference to scholarship or scholastic records. Prime consideration seems to have been given to those interested in and occupying positions facilitating the spreading of news about their foreign experiences through speeches, articles, radio appearances, etc.[27]

Although various studies have been made in recent years of selected aspects of the several trainee programs participated in by the United States, these studies have been fragmentary rather than systematic attempts to evaluate the total results of such exchanges in all their social and political implications. In 1948, Loomis and Schuler published the results of a study of acculturation of Latin-American trainees in the United States, based on tests administered upon arrival and departure of the trainees.[28] Some of the more significant findings of this study were to the effect that attitudes of the trainees were not as much changed by a year's stay in the United States as might have been expected. It was shown that many of the attitudes of the trainees did not change during their stay in the United States, while a smaller number of their attitudes, which would generally be considered as unfavorable toward the United States, became more nearly confirmed.

A recent evaluation of a student and trainee program concerns the attitude changes of more than 300 German youths during their stay of almost a year in the United States. As in the first study, the evaluation consisted of a battery of tests administered just prior to their entrance into this country and again upon their departure. The group was divided by age, training, and experience into: leaders, university students, and secondary or high school students.[29]

[27] Most of the information on the International Farm Youth Exchange program has been taken from mimeographed notices numbered 1152 and 1156, of the Cooperative Extension Service and from various reports of the IFYE Committee to the National 4-H Club Foundation of America. The emphasis in this program upon cultural understanding and appreciation is succinctly expressed in the guiding plans of the IFYE program, Extension leaflet number 1156, to the effect that "If, on parting, both the family and the delegate find it difficult to say goodby, then the visit will have been in the true spirit of the project."

[28] Charles P. Loomis and Edgar A. Schuler, "Acculturation of Foreign Students in the United States," *Applied Anthropology*, Vol. 7, Number 2, Spring, 1948.

[29] Robert T. Bower, Berta McKennie, and Burton Winegrad, *An Analysis of Attitude Change Among German Exchangees*, Philadelphia: Institute for Research in Human Relations, (Mimeographed), 1951. For a case history of one of the German students in the United States,

It was evident that the students were conscious of the political implications of the exchange. The average percentage for the three groups varied from 47–73 in considering the main purpose of the program as a means of promoting international understanding and peace rather than to increase skills and technical knowledge. The percentage considering the former as the *main purpose* of the program decreased during the year's stay, although more than half of the total left with this attitude unchanged.

The study shows that many of the basic objectives of the exchange program were achieved, especially in the field of appreciation for American culture, even though certain experiences, such as discrimination against minority groups, etc. impressed them unfavorably. Changes in attitudes occurring during the year were much more pronounced among the secondary than among the university students and leaders, although the latter were not so extreme in their earlier attitudes and were perhaps better informed. To the extent that this is true, it may call attention to the possibility of giving more emphasis to exchanges at the younger age levels. If knowledge, and especially appreciation, of American culture is a major objective, perhaps the younger groups of foreign students and trainees are the ones to concentrate upon.

Another significant finding of this report is the value of personal contacts in influencing foreign students. Although each group of exchangees reported use, while here, of various types of mass media, and especially magazines and journals, personal contacts with Americans were regarded as the most effective means of influencing their attitudes and opinions. If this finding is generally valid, personal contacts deserve more emphasis in exchange programs, despite greater costs when used extensively.

CURRENT PROGAMS IN THE UNITED STATES

Foreign Students.—Despite recent increases in the number of foreign specialists, technicians, and trainees who are now coming to the United States each year, the total is yet small when compared with the number of conventional foreign students who annually attend U.S. colleges and universities. Even with the increase of exchangees promised under the President's Point-Four program, the total will be but a small fraction of those who annually come to the United States on their own means and resources.

Sponsored fellowship and scholarship programs, however, have exerted an influence on the exchange of persons movement in the United States far in excess of their magnitude. Such programs, in large part, have determined the amount of interest in the movement at any given time, and have provided immediate objectives for the movement from time to time.

Even the foreign student who sponsors his own study in the United States can, and to some extent does, expect certain facilities and services which are

---

see U. S. Department of State, *Preparations for Tomorrow*, Department of State Publication 4138, European and British Commonwealth Series 20, April 1951.

continuously being augmented. Numerous private services are now in operation to increase the probability that the student's introduction to American life will not be adversely conditioned. Any student who now plans to study in the United States may expect:

(a) Preparation in the English language at negligible cost.

(b) Literature and information from the United States government and from colleges and universities enabling him to select the institution which offers facilities meeting his academic and everyday needs.

(c) A reception upon arrival in the United States by organizations such as the Committee on Friendly Relations Among Foreign Students to help with problems of entry, lodging and transportation.

(d) Possibility of aid, if needed, from any of seventy major private and voluntary organizations supporting interchange of persons programs.

(e) Possibility of attending language and cultural orientation centers such as the Wilson Teachers College in Washington, D.C. (Courses there are free to those visiting the United States on a government grant, but are available to others upon payment of a small fee.)

(f) In the larger schools, special persons, foreign student advisers, counselors, etc., have been appointed to advise with the foreign students on any special problems such as visas, immigration papers, and financial problems. Many of the larger schools have International Houses, or similar facilities, which provide opportunities for the foreign student to associate and live with Americans of his own sex and age.

(g) Advice from the Institute of International Education in New York, or at any of its branch offices, concerning special problems which they might have.

(h) Help in securing opportunities for friendly and informal contact with one or more American communities. This is a more recent aspect of the international exchange of persons program and one that has received wide acceptance and support from numerous civic groups in the United States. In New York City alone, some 20 or more organizations carry on a program of hospitality to foreign students, an important part of which encourages visits of these students into American homes. So great has this program become that these organizations recently have organized themselves into the Greater New York Council for Foreign Students, in order to avoid duplication of effort and insure maximum use of their resources.[29a]

The Foreign Student in American College and Universities as a Means for Increasing International Understanding and Good Will.—To the extent that foreign students can effectively promote international understanding and good will between nations, the approximately 30,000 who are now studying in colleges

---

[29a] U.S. Department of State, *Building Roads to Peace*, Department Publication 3738, February, 1950. See also, United States Advisory Commission on Educational Exchange, *Two Way Street, op. cit.*, and William C. Johnstone, Jr., "Point-4 and the Colleges," *Institute of International Education News Bulletin*, Vol. 25, No. 8, May, 1950.

and universities in the United States provide a unique opportunity to contribute to such a goal. This is especially true if one considers the fact that this number is spread over the 48 states and represents almost every nation and territory of the globe.[30]

The foreign student population in the United States is widely dispersed geographically as well as throughout wide varieties and sizes of institutions. The often quoted fallacy that foreign students attend only the larger institutions is manifest in the finding of this study that 63 percent of all colleges with enrollments less than 1,000 had one or more foreign students enrolled in the 1951–52 year. It is true, however, a larger proportion of the larger institutions reported having foreign students. The percentages, by size of institution, are as follows: Enrollment under 1000—63 percent; enrollment 1,000–1,999—7 percent; enrollment 2,000–4,999—96 percent; 5,000–9,999—97 percent; and 10,000 and over—96 percent.

Such a figure not only suggests the influence of private and religious organizations in inducing foreign students to attend the smaller institutions but a conviction on the part of many students, a point frequently advanced by officials and teachers in the smaller institutions, that the smaller schools have certain advantages over the larger ones, especially for the younger and less academically advanced persons.

The results of this study, however, dispel any doubt that foreign students are concentrated in the larger institutions. Even though 423 of the 674 institutions with total student enrollments of less than 1,000 reported one or more foreign students for the 1951–52 academic year, 74 percent of this number reported less than 10 while less than 2 percent reported as many as 50. One-fourth of all institutions having enrollments of 10,000 or more reported 500 or more foreign students. Such distributions clearly illustrate the major role of the larger schools in foreign student education.

Historical evidence has been given for recent shifts in emphasis in foreign student programs from purely academic objectives to broader ones aimed at increased knowledge of American life and contributing to international understanding and good will. A tabulation of the results of the study questionnaire supports this in substantial fashion. Part of the evidence is in the large number of contacts that seemingly are provided now between foreign students and various members of local, state and national organizations. Manifestation of local group interest in foreign student participation in their programs, such as these, argue for the contention that deep convictions regarding the worth of foreign student exchange programs are beginning to penetrate deeply into the consciousness of the American people. Data in Table 2 indicate that most col-

---

[30] See Institute of International Education, *Education for One World, op. cit.*, and The Committee on Friendly Relations Among Foreign Students, *The Unofficial Ambassador*. New York (291 Broadway), 1951 for detailed information on foreign student number and distribution in the United States.

leges and universities are devoting major organized efforts to increase the number and quality of contacts between citizens and foreign students.

Activities on Campus.—Information available from this study indicates that a large portion of American colleges and universities are encouraging their foreign students to participate in campus activities designed to increase the understanding of faculty and students of other cultures and peoples. Methods, of course, vary from one institution to another but it seems that a large percentage of all institutions consider lectures, intergroup panels, discussions, rooming with American students, teas, parties, etc. as the more important means available for furthering understanding between their foreign and local students. Interna-

TABLE 2

Percentage of Colleges and Universities Encouraging Foreign Students to Participate in Specified Campus Activities as a Means for Increasing the Knowledge of Local Students and Faculty About Other People by Total Enrollment of Institutions Reporting, 1951–52

Size of institution	Number of institutions reporting*	Deliver lectures	Room with American students	Folk dances	Parties, teas, etc.	Intergroup discussions, meetings, etc.	International house affairs	Other activities	No special treatment awarded foreign students
		Percent	Percent	Percent	Percent	Percent	Percent	Percent	Percent
Under 1,000	423	57	88	34	64	80	4	21	11
1,000–1,999	108	67	98	35	71	87	10	38	4
2,000–4,999	83	82	92	22	87	99	12	29	6
5,000–9,999	35	77	94	46	80	100	17	54	3
10,000–over	24	88	92	79	100	100	46	33	4

* Includes only institutions reporting one or more foreign students. Percentages do not total 100 since choices may include more than one item.

tional house affairs are generally thought to facilitate contacts between foreign and domestic students but the international houses are found only on the campuses that can support them.

The smaller colleges and universities frequently report no special treatment awarded foreign students. Sometimes this situation is defended on the premise that the predominance of personal relations among students of the smaller schools make it unnecessary to furnish foreign students special attention. At other times it is cited as a weakness, the result of inadequate funds necessary to attend to the problem in a deserving manner.

In consideration of the fact that many colleges and universities in the United States now have had many years of experience in managing foreign student orientation and campus programs, an effort was made to determine the consensus of those responsible for such programs as to the relative effectiveness of some of the more commonly used programs and activities. The results of this question are summarized in Table 3.

One of the more obvious aspects of this table is the relatively minor importance foreign student advisors give to such items as: international house affairs, parties, banquets, dances, festivals and formal lectures, even though the latter appears often in the activity list of Table 4. Results here, supplemented by numerous conversations with foreign student advisors and other officials in the colleges and universities, indicate a much greater value assigned to rooming with American students and participation in intergroup discussions, meetings,

TABLE 3

Percentage of Colleges and Universities Reporting Types of Foreign Student Activities Considered Most Effective in Increasing Knowledge of Local Students and Faculty About Other People, by Type of Activity and by Size of Institution Reporting, 1951–52

Size of institution	Number of institutions reporting*	Where foreign students: Deliver lectures	Where foreign students: Room with American students	Folk, or costume dances or festivals	Parties, teas, banquets, etc.	Intergroup discussions, meetings, etc.	International house affairs	Other activities
		Percent	Percent	Percent	Percent	Percent	Percent	Percent
Under 1,000	423	12	30	3	6	33	1	6
1,000–1,999	108	13	28	3	12	46	2	9
2,000–4,999*	83	19	35	1	17	39	5	8
5,000–9,999	35	14	37	6	17	57	11	26
10,000–over	24	21	33	4	17	67	4	17

* Includes only institutions reporting one or more foreign students. Percentages based on total of institutions reporting one or more foreign students.

etc. Opinion in this matter may have been influenced by certain opinions of the students themselves as shown in recent reports and articles.[31]

Off-Campus Activities.—Another manifestation of the interest on the part of college and university officials in foreign students, as a means for increasing international understanding and good will is found in the increased tendency to provide additional opportunities for U.S. citizens to become acquainted with foreign students in various types of situations. Encouraging foreign students to deliver lectures was reported frequently, both by large and small institutions. The percentage encouraging this activity ranged from 64 percent for institutions having enrollments under 1000 to 92 percent for those having enrollments of 10,000 or more. The larger institutions were more likely to encourage foreign

[31] Louise H. Carpenter, "Adventures in World Understanding" *The Record*, Department of State, Vol. VII, No. 4, 1951.

students to visit in American homes, to room with American students, and to room in American homes than the smaller institutions. Such differences, of course, may be largely a function of size of foreign student enrollment although one may suspect that a substantial part of it is due to differences in ideas that obtain between officials of the larger and of the smaller institutions. But whatever its cause, the larger institutions are doing a great deal more, in an organized fashion to introduce foreign students to U.S. citizens.

During the past few years private and public attempts have been made to motivate both foreign and domestic students to understand each other better. Opinions were sought concerning the techniques through which foreign students might best inform American citizens about their peoples. While there was no consensus in the responses, there was a marked tendency for the smaller institutions to suggest lectures, while the larger institutions preferred visits in homes. Rooming with American students, rooming in American homes and inter-group discussions were frequently mentioned by all institutions.

Although various sorts of information, including correspondence and conversation with numerous college and university officials, revealed major criticism of the foreign student lecture method, evidence from the questionnaires shows that between one-fourth and one-third of all institutions reporting one or more foreign students still use it as one of their more important instruments for bringing foreign students and U.S. citizens together. Many students of international exchange of persons programs will be encouraged to see that no grouping of institutions now places more than minor emphasis upon such activities as parties, teas, dances, and banquets.

Acquainting Foreign Students With American Life.—An increasing realization of the limitations inherent in a campus environment has produced new effort on the part of college and university officials to increase opportunities foreign students now have to study, and learn first-hand, various aspects of current American life and culture. The extent to which this interest is being translated into action is suggested in the questionnaire data from the colleges and universities.

Perhaps one of the more significant aspects of this data is the relatively high incidence of planned foreign student visits to local communities for a day or more. Although the manner in which these community visits are conducted vary from one institution to another, comments from colleges and universities reveal that many are planned and conducted jointly by college and university personnel and members of the local community.

More than one-third of the smaller institutions and more than four-fifths of the larger reported special courses in English for foreign students, and from one-tenth to less than one-third offered special courses in other than English for foreign students. It affords an interesting speculation as to whether these relatively low percentages reflect only an awakening interest in such media for increasing the knowledge of foreign students about American culture or whether it is merely a lack of conviction that such courses are effective in foreign student orientation.

With the exception of such activities as rooming with U.S. students, participating in panels, discussions, and visits to communities for one or more days, there seem to be little agreement between officials of the various sizes of institutions, as to the relative merits of activities designed to acquaint foreign students with U.S. life and culture. Relatively small percentages of colleges and universities indicate preference for such activities as: visiting local farms and visits to local businesses, even though many institutions, both large and small,

TABLE 4
Percentage of Colleges and Universities Reporting Foreign Student Participation in Programs of Specified Organizations, by Size of Institution Reporting, 1951–52

Size of institution	Number of institutions	Schools	Churches and religious organizations	Farm organizations*	Libraries	Civic and service organizations†	Womens' clubs‡	Parent teachers organizations
		Percent	Percent	Percent	Percent	Percent	Percent	Percent
Under 1,000	423	45	81	11	18	45	34	11
1,000–1,999	108	57	88	9	18	61	45	27
2,000–4,999	83	70	98	20	22	72	60	29
5,000–9,999	35	57	100	37	20	74	66	17
10,000–over	24	75	96	29	25	87	67	42

* Includes Farm Bureau, Grange, FFA, 4-H, Farmers Union, FHA, New Farmers of America, etc.

† Includes Rotary, Lions, Kiwanis, Chamber of Commerce, YMCA, AAUW, YWCA, others.

‡ Includes AAUW, Federated Clubs, League of Women Voters, YWCA, Womens' Church organizations, Business and Professional Associations, others.

are utilizing these means widely in their attempts to introduce the students to American life and culture.

Areas of Contact With American Life.—As indicated earlier, a wide range of local, state, and national organizations are now sponsoring programs involving the participation, either as actor or audience, of foreign students. Numerous colleges and universities throughout the United States have welcomed this new interest in the foreign student movement and have been active in increasing it. Its status, at the moment, is suggested in the data of Table 4.

Almost all institutions reported their foreign students participating in church or other religious organizational programs.[32] Of those institutions with 5,000–

[32] Although the questionnaire was designed to include other than purely religious services it seems that the very high incidence of reporting participation here indicates that some institutions completing the questionnaire included such services in their answers. There was no means for checking the size of this error.

9,999 enrollments, all reported that their foreign students participated in some sort of church program during the year.

Table 4 supports the assumption that the public schools are providing programs or situations in which foreign students can take active part. Three-fourths of the larger institutions reported the participation of their foreign students in public school programs. These seem to have included panels, discussions and, more commonly, lectures given by foreign students to school groups.

Civic and service organizations appear to be providing more opportunities for contacts with foreign students. Eighty-seven percent of the larger institutions reported that the foreign students take part in one or more of these programs. Such organizations as the Rotary, Lions, and Kiwanis Clubs were mentioned most often. These three organizations appear to be particularly active around the smaller colleges and universities so often situated in towns and small cities.

The smaller institutions lead the larger ones by comfortable margins, doubtlessly a phenomenon that is due, in part, to the much greater accessibility of students on the smaller institutions to rural areas. For institutions with enrollments of less than 1,000 students, 23 percent claimed that all or almost all of their foreign students spent time off campus in rural areas, while none of the institutions with enrollments of 5,000 and over made such a claim. To the extent that rural life is an effective source of knowledge of American life and culture, this is clearly a field that could well receive a great deal more attention.

SUMMARY

The international exchange of persons is an old rather than a recent development, with roots deep in the history of mankind. Practiced extensively by the Greeks and Romans in ancient days, it became, in the middle ages, the primary carrier of learning and knowledge from nation to nation and from people to people. With the appearance of the printing press, the exchange of persons lost some of its importance in the traffic of knowledge and learning but gained new status shortly thereafter with the development of centers of learning in Europe that attracted scholars over widely dispersed areas. These scholars were interested, not only in acquiring knowledge inaccessible to them elsewhere, but in acquiring prestige that study in a foreign land gave.

The 19th century witnessed an awakening of public interest in the international exchange of students and mature scholars as a means for furthering national economic and political interest in some of the larger countries of Europe. France, during the latter part of the century, established hundreds of language and cultural schools abroad, especially in the Near and Far East, while Germany initiated efforts to increase "spiritual and cultural unity" among the various German communities of the world. These developments, though carefully watched by other western powers, gained but little momentum in other countries until the beginning of the 20th century.

The United States was relatively slow to sponsor foreign student exchanges even though status gained in winning the First World War tended to increase the number of European students studying in American colleges and universities. With the outbreak of the Second World War, however, both official and public interest in the international exchange of persons suddenly began to expand rapidly. Almost overnight the Federal Government began sponsoring a wide range of foreign students, trainees, technicians and officials to come to the United States for study, observation and conference. Numerous private organizations and industries began offering fellowships, scholarships, and apprenticeships while all types and sizes of colleges and universities began to encourage foreign student enrollments. Under the stimulus of the Institute of International Education, and other organizations, fellowships, tuition and other scholarships were substantially increased. The larger colleges and universities began to establish a wide range of facilities for foreign students, including advisors and counselors whose duties included everything from providing an introduction to life on the campus, to securing employment for the needy and deserving. The numerical result of this effort was an increase in foreign student enrollment in American colleges and universities that reached approximately 30,000 in 1950–51.

With the general acceptance in the United States of the broader objectives of an exchange program, colleges and universities have undertaken an additional responsibility—that of encouraging foreign students to return to their home countries with a greater knowledge of American life and culture. Not only have activities been encouraged that would likely bring about closer relations between foreign and domestic students on campus, but many institutions have placed substantial emphasis on acquainting the students with off-campus life, especially as obtained in local organizations and in American homes. Numerous organizations working closely with colleges and universities on the problem sprang up to guide relationships between foreign students and American citizens. These organizations have become particularly active in the larger cities.

Many colleges and universities in the United States are experimenting with new methods and techniques for furthering the mutual understanding of foreign students and American citizens. Although the older methods such as rooming with American students, rooming and visiting in American homes, etc. are still being used extensively, many institutions are placing greater emphasis upon informal meetings and discussions of subjects of mutual interest. In more summary form, trends in most colleges and universities are away from methods and practices that encourage people to think of the foreign student as something of a novelty, effective for mild sorts of entertainment as speaker and lecturer, rather than as guests who are here seeking common answers to common problems through an exchange of knowledge and ideas and mutual understanding. Although effectiveness of the new methods have not yet been tested thoroughly they are, at least, showing that they may be a powerful potential for alleviating world tension and conflicts.

Olen Leonard
Department of Sociology and Anthropology
Michigan State College
East Lansing, Michigan
and
Sheldon G. Lowry
Department of Sociology and Anthropology
Michigan State College
East Lansing, Michigan

BIBLIOGRAPHY

A SELECTED LIST

Aydelotte, Frank, *The American Rhodes Scholarships: A Review of the First Forty Years*, Princeton: Princeton University Press, 1946.

Bower, Robert T., McKensie, Berta, and Winograd, Burton, *An Analysis of Attitude Change Among German Exchangees*, Philadelphia: Institute for Research in Human Relations, (mimeographed), 1951.

Duggan, Stephen, *A Professor at Large*, New York: The Macmillan Company, 1943, pp. 48–50.

Finch, George A., "Remission of the Chinese Indemnity," *American Historical Review*, Volume XXXII, 1926, pp. 64–68.

Haskins, Charles Homer, *The Rise of Universities*, New York: H. Holt and Company, 1923.

Institute of International Education, *News Bulletin*, Published monthly from October through June.

Institute of International Education, *Annual Reports*.

Institute of International Education, *Education for One World*, New York, 1951.

Loomis, Charles P. and Schuler, Edgar A., "Acculturation of Foreign Students in the United States," *Applied Anthropology*, Vol. 7, Number 2, (Spring), 1948.

McMurry, Ruth Emily and Lee, Muna, *The Cultural Approach*, Chapel Hill: The University of North Carolina Press, 1947, p. 11.

U. S. State Department, *The Record*, Volumes I–VII; Also State Department Publications 3738, 3551, and 2971.

U. S. Advisory Commission on Educational Exchange, *Two Way Street*, Department of State Publication 3893, 1950.

Chapter 12:

RURAL LOCAL GOVERNMENT AND POLITICS AND ADULT EDUCATION

Introduction

The organization and operation of local government in the United States has been the subject of both praise and criticism throughout our history. It has sometimes been hailed as the essence and bulwark of democracy, and likewise condemned as an archaic, graft-ridden obstacle to social progress. There are probably valid arguments for both points of view, depending upon the type and location of the units examined, and who is doing the examining. In the existing emotional attachments to particular concepts, as well as the wide variety of functional units, there are few examples of sociological research which provide base-lines for scientific analysis.

In the present instance, we are concerned with the cross-contacts between rural local government on the one hand, and adult education objectives and activities on the other. It need hardly be added that these contacts are numerous and complex, even though they focus upon only one portion of the political structure. This confused situation is highlighted by its comparison with the operation of Soil Conservation Service and other agencies described in Chapter 7. In the latter, contacts between government and education are relatively well-channelized and highly cultivated. But with regard to the area of every-day community politics, as will be treated here, such contacts are elusive and ill-defined.

Given the paucity of available recent data which can be used to determine the structure-operational patterns of local government, it seems essential that some systematic procedure be evolved to sharpen the picture of inter-relations between local governmental organizations and other functional elements in the society.

With this objective in mind, the following discussion of rural government is an attempt to use a field study,[1] performed in one state, namely Michigan, to test certain popular contentions about local government which have already been mentioned above. In other words, what is the real status of that government as seen through the eyes of some of its major participants?

It is obvious that this one study cannot be used to generalize for the nation as a whole. Further investigations carried out in several geographic and cultural regions will be needed before over-all assessments are made. It is only as a preliminary effort in the direction of providing a useful body of research findings

[1] For procedural details, see Appendix C.

that materials from this study are offered. In order to keep the discussion to manageable proportions, most of the data utilized here will refer to county-township government, which, in many cases, is an interlocking system. No organization larger than the county will receive attention. Although substantial space will be devoted to local rural government, *per se*, its connections with adult education will be emphasized wherever applicable. Nevertheless, the reader must remain aware that however fruitful these contacts are, or may later become, they are largely uncharted at the moment. The principal aim of this chapter is to report on the beginnings of the analytical task.

UNITS AND AREAS OF RURAL LOCAL GOVERNMENT

Over-All View.—Recognizing the preceding limitations, it might be helpful to first present some factual background material as a setting for the inter-play of rural politics and adult education.

According to the Bureau of the Census, there are approximately 155,000 units of government in the United States.[2] By far the majority of these units of government are located in rural areas, and are either counties, towns, townships, school districts, or various special districts. Counties are the major and inclusive subdivisions of the state area for general state and local purposes. They are normally vigorous and important units of government outside New England. In New England, the town is the principal segment of local government as well as being the unit which the state depends upon for local execution of state programs. The rest of the northeast quarter of the country is also divided into towns, or townships, which are subdivisions of the county in rural areas. Their functions, however, are inclined to be fewer than those in New England. The remainder of the United States does not have any units equivalent to the New England or the midwestern township. However, in almost all states there are large numbers of school districts and other special purpose districts such as those established for irrigation, flood control, fire control, soil conservation, and grazing. All told there are 3,050 counties in the United States, nearly 19,000 towns or townships, over 100,000 school districts and over 8,000 other special purpose districts, while there are only a little over 16,000 municipalities. Of course, some school districts, special districts, and counties are to be found in urban areas too.

County Government.—The counties then, are the principal units of rural local government for most of the country. They do not perform all local government services, however. Except in a few scattered states, they do not have much control over education, this being the province of special school districts. Also several agricultural functions of local government have been vested in special districts. But the counties find the midwestern township to be a rather weak competitor for performing local government functions. While it is not yet

[2] *Governmental Units in the United States*, Washington: Bureau of the Census, 1942, p. 1.

widespread in most midwest areas, there is evidence that the township is not vigorous.

In the study of Michigan township supervisors, cited previously, it was found that these officials were often far from enthusiastic over conditions in their communities. Of the 74 supervisors rating, constituent interest in town and and country problems responses were: sustained high interest—30; sporadic interest in certain specific issues—14; neither high nor low interest—4; and low interest—31. In commenting upon the reasons for low or sporadic interest, 14 supervisors said people won't attend public meetings, 12 suggested that people won't participate until something goes wrong, 10 said that people don't understand town or county problems, and seven said that people aren't interested enough to vote.

Perhaps such findings are but a reflection of American political apathy in general;[3] yet they are apparently a cause for concern among the officials themselves. It was also found that the supervisors often felt that local government was losing its power generally, and that one of the most important problems was to preserve, and even regain, certain town functions which were being lost to the counties and states.[4] More will be said of this problem later in the chapter.

County government varies in formal legal status and in the functions it performs from county to county and from state to state. In a few instances, county governments utilize a rather complete set of powers, performing almost all functions of government. The more common situation is to find counties which are stripped of one or more functions as a result of the existence of school districts, special districts, towns and townships, or a state government which performs functions normally delegated to counties. Finally, there are counties which have very few functions to perform because of the multiplicity of other governmental units, and the centralization of power in the hands of the state.

Of significance for adult education, besides the legal powers of county government, is the variation in area of these units. In general, they are smallest in the south, largest in the west, and of medium size in the midwest and east. It is convenient to think of 3,050 units of county government as blanketing the rural part of the United States. In some respects it is more accurate to picture 3,050 county seats, often the foci of trade-center communities described in Chapter 1, with some localities hundreds of miles from these centers where many adult education programs would normally be carried out. The extremes in county size can be found by comparing San Bernadino county in California, which is the largest county in the United States in area with 20,131 square miles, with some of the very tiny counties in Virginia which have only one square mile each.

[3] Many observers, particularly foreign analysts, have found this condition striking in a nation which idealizes political liberty. See Gunnar Myrdahl, *An American Dilemma*, New York: Harper and Brothers, 1944, Chapter 33; Geoffrey Gorer, *The American People*, New York: W. W. Norton and Company, 1949, Chapter 9; and Harold L. Laski, *The American Democracy*, The Viking Press, 1948, Chapters 1–4.

[4] Particularly the functions of road maintenance, welfare, and utility improvements.

There is a high negative correlation between the area of a county and its population density. Thus at one extreme there are several hundred counties in mountainous, semi-arid, or forested regions, with large area, sparse population (two persons per square mile and many even less), and usually but little wealth. At the other extreme are several hundred highly urban, industrial, and commercial counties with small area, large population, and great concentration of wealth. Between these extremes lie the great majority of counties, largely agricultural but with some urban population, whose population, area, and wealth generally are medium to small.

As a result of these differences in area, population, and formal legal structure, the adult education programs that are possible or desirable in any one county might be quite different from those that are possible or desirable in any other.

INTERNAL STRUCTURE OF COUNTY GOVERNMENT

County Boards and Commissions.—There is in almost all counties what might be called the county governing body.[5] It has dozens of different names in different states—most commonly it is called Board of Commissioners, Board of Supervisors, County Court, Commissioner's Court, Fiscal Court, Board of Commissioners of Road and Revenue, and Police Jury. It is difficult to designate a group of functions as those characteristically belonging to county governing bodies because of the many variations from state to state. Over 90 percent of the county bodies levy taxes, appropriate money, and issue bonds. They usually exercise the corporate or quasicorporate powers of the county, award contracts, manage county property, pass upon claims, manage county buildings, and exercise general control, however limited, over county affairs. In the non-fiscal affairs of counties, the governing body frequently does not have control over all policies. Special boards and commissions—such as health boards or road commissions—and separately elected officials—such as sheriffs and treasurers—are frequently outside the range of its effective control.

County governing bodies differ in the methods of election of their members. About two-thirds of the governing bodies are made up of three to seven members, elected by the county voters at large, or by districts; in these instances governing body members have general responsibility for a number of administrative details as well as a part of county policy. In New York, Wisconsin, northern Illinois, and Michigan the dominant system is to have boards of township supervisors serve as county governing bodies. Members of these boards represent townships and cities in the county, and in addition to being administrative and legislative officials of the county, they are township, or in some cases city officials, as well. In the south, generally, the county governing body is composed of one or more judges or justices of the peace. County governing body members are usually elected by districts or townships. They are

[5] On this subject generally see Edward W. Weidner, *The American County—Patchwork of Boards*, New York: National Municipal League, 1946.

elected at large in less than a quarter of the cases. Their terms are usually from two to four years, but some are elected for six, others even for eight year terms. Table 1 presents some membership data on these county bodies.

The tenuous legal control exercised by county governing boards over county administration and policy making in most instances is well illustrated by the special-function boards and commissions found in almost all states. County special-function boards and commissions are plural-membered bodies empowered to perform a specific function, such as the governing of hospitals or airports, agriculture, election administration, finance, health, highways, li-

TABLE 1
Number of Members of County Governing Bodies by Type of Governing Body, 1945

Governing body	Number of counties	Total number of members	Average number of members per county	Number of members per 10,000 inhabitants
Total.......................	3,050	21,080	6.9	1.8
Board of commissioners or supervisors.........................	2,012	7,993	4.0	1.0
Board composed of town supervisors........................	297	7,616	25.6	5.1
Judges and commissioners.........	350	1,666	4.8	1.8
Judges and justices of the peace....	193	3,300	17.1	8.0
Single judge.....................	86	86	1.0	2.5
Plural-member court..............	75	359	4.8	.7
Single nonjudical officer...........	32	32	1.0	.5
Nonjudicial ex-officio body........	4	21	5.3	.6
Executive and town supervisors....	1	7	7.0	.2

Source: U.S. Department of Commerce, Bureau of the Census, *County Boards and Commissions*, 1947, Table 3.

braries, penal administration, personnel, planning, recreation, schools, and welfare. In some instances, these special-function boards are accountable to the county governing bodies, being appointed by them or having their budgets controlled by them. In other instances, they are fairly independent, especially when they are elected by the voters, and in these instances they constitute virtually independent special units of government.

The reason for the establishment of special boards in most counties, whether by mandatory provision of state law or by optional decision of county groups, is often a distrust of the central county governing body. Furthermore, the special interests that form behind each function of county government desire the maximum independence for their favorite agency. For example, health people want special health boards, welfare people, special welfare boards, etc. It is also argued that a system in which many boards and commissions operate enlarges the participation in government by the electorate and, therefore, is very democratic.

Many special-function boards and commissions would be much more interested in sponsoring adult education programs than would regular county governing bodies. Their personnel is of a more professional and less partisan political nature and they tend to be more inclined to experiment than the average county government body. At present, there are no data to indicate exactly how many special-function boards and commissions exist in each county. There are some data on how many are authorized and how many exist for particular functions, such as health and welfare.

County Administrative Organization.—The most notable aspect of county administrative organization is its relative headlessness.[6] There tends to be no single head, such as is found in cities with mayors or managers, or in states with governors. The idea of a full-fledged executive has been foreign to county government, for the most part, at least until recent years.

County administrative organization has been influenced greatly by the nineteenth century movement toward the direct election of each of the main administrative officials. In Table 2, the officers most frequently directly elected are listed, and it is notable that nearly all of these officials hold offices established in the nineteenth century. The newer departments, those that have been established in the last fifty years, tend to be filled with appointees of the county governing body, or some other county or state agency. It is probable that the independently elected county officers would be less willing to participate in many adult education programs than most appointive ones. Here again, the factor of lack of special training and professionalization plays an important role.

There have been a number of county departments in the last fifty years whose heads are usually appointed. These include departments of health, welfare, agricultural extension, and others.

Lately, there has been a trend toward vesting some general administrative power in one of the county officials. This trend has developed for the most part because of the many functions that have devolved upon the counties. The most frequent pattern that has developed has been a delegation of general power in the clerk of the general governing body. This official is usually called the county clerk or the county auditor. Sometimes the chairman of the county governing body, or frequently in the South the county judge, has taken over this responsibility. In only a few instances have positions for full-fledged elective executives or appointive managers been established. There are not more than thirty or forty of these counties and the number is growing slowly.

The amorphous quality of county administration has its counterpart on the community level as well. The fact, in Michigan at least, that supervisors are

---

[6] On county executives see Edward W. Weidner, "A Review of the Controversy over County Executives," *Public Administration Review*, Vol. 18, 1948.

TABLE 2

Elective County Administrative Officers, 1946

Office	Number of states in which found
Assessor	28
Attorney or solicitor	36
Auditor or comptroller	16
County clerk	25
Clerk of court	33
Collector or commissioner of taxes	8
Coroner	30
Public administrator	5
Recorder	12
Registrar of deeds	13
Registrar of probate	3
Registrar of wills	3
Sheriff	47
Superintendent of schools	26
Surveyor or engineer	31
Treasurer	37
Constable (as a county office)	27

Source: U.S. Department of Commerce, Bureau of the Census, *Elective Offices of the State and County Governments*, 1946, Table 2.

both town *and* county officials fosters a feeling of divided loyalty in their own minds, and since they are town-elected, their preferences tend to veer in that direction. Apropos of their conception of their job, the Michigan supervisors

TABLE 3

Supervisors' Conception of Their Main Duties as Revealed by a Probing Study of 74 Township Supervisors in Michigan, 1952

Category	Number of times mentioned*
Assessment of property	47
Road and bridge maintenance	24
Taxation problems	25†
County and township committees	19
Health and welfare	12
Represent community wherever necessary	11
Drainage problems	7
Public school affairs	4
Attend to county business	4
Zoning	3
Building and construction	3
Listen to complaints	2
Keep people satisfied	2
No main duties	10

* Respondents were free to name as many categories as they wished.
† Five supervisors believed their job was to keep taxes down.

interviewed showed a considerable lack of certainty as to what they were supposed to do, even though their duties are rather specifically defined by law.[7]

It is significant that the category mentioned most—namely assessment of property—accounted for only 54 percent of the respondents. For other categories, there is even less agreement among the supervisors and some are badly misinformed as to their duties. Twelve percent of the sample stated that they had *no* main duties; 5 percent that their duty was to keep taxes down.

These findings indicate that many supervisors were either unaware of the formal requirements of their office, or that they have minimized, either purposefully or by traditional neglect, certain functions which fall within their province. It is also possible that various disused functions have been relinquished, either legally or informally, to other governmental agencies. An obvious conclusion from the data in Table 3 is that education for the job is lacking on a broad scale, and apparently the public is not holding its local administrators strictly accountable for their activities. It is probably safe to say that the voters as a group are grossly less informed about their governmental machinery than the supervisors, and are little inclined to question how the officials spend their time.

HUMAN RELATIONSHIPS IN COUNTY GOVERNMENT

Power-Formal and Informal.—Something has already been said, in connection with the discussion of units and areas of local government and the internal structure of county government, about the formal power relationships in the county areas. Counties usually do not have extensive powers which can be exercised in any way they see fit. They are severely restricted by a lack of home rule and by numerous state legislative and administrative regulations. At the community level, the powers of rural government are further dispersed in three ways: (1) by the existence of special units of government, (2) by the existence of special-function boards and commissions, (3) by the existence of numerous directly elected administrative officials. The net result is that there are few county governing bodies which hold power equivalent to city councils, and there are few county executives who hold power equivalent to mayors or city managers.

The informal power relationships present quite a different picture. In the South, for example, the county judge is frequently an extremely important official because of his central position in politics in the county.[8] Therefore, out of the confusion of divided authority there may arise a strong and powerful

---

[7] The duties of supervisor, according to the Michigan *Township Officers' Guide*, include: (a) acting as agent for legal township business, (b) acting as assessor of the township, (c) attending all township meetings, (d) reporting periodically to the township board (made up of town judges, clerk, and treasurer), (e) keeping required books and official papers, (f) care and maintenance of township property, (g) represent town on county board of supervisors.

[8] See, for example, Karl Bosworth, *Black Belt County*, University of Alabama, 1941; and *Tennessee Valley County*, University of Alabama, 1941.

leader. This phenomenon is not confined to the South but is spread over the country as a whole. Lacking a sufficient number of case studies, it is impossible to say how many counties have such powerful central figures, but probably the number is substantial.

In field research, it is an arduous and ticklish process to uncover the personal and group relationships which influence decision-making, although their presence is felt everywhere. Political office holders are likely to be wary of revealing or admitting to outside investigators such specialized commitments as they may have.

The preliminary study of Michigan supervisors attempted to penetrate this recalcitrance by inquiring as to the persons and organizations the supervisors sought for advice for the conduct of their offices. The statements of the respondents were compared by occupation, education, age, and length of service to see if there were marked differences. Although this study deals with a small sample in only one state, it is presented to indicate the nature of a type of research we believe to be essential. It is found that consultation by supervisors whose occupation was farming with other individuals[9] was proportionately the same, except that farmer supervisors consulted farm organization leaders much more often than did the non-farmers.

With respect to education (grammar school, high school, and college), it was found that supervisors with less education depended more on the advice of attorneys than did the high school or college groups. This was in line with expectations. Otherwise, education did not appear to determine who was consulted. It should be remembered, however, that the smallness of the sample may influence such findings.

When length of service,[10] is considered, it seemed that newer supervisors, quite understandably, sought the advice of other or retired supervisors more consistently than did those with longer tenure. Those with intermediate lengths of service relied more heavily on informal contacts, especially with farm and business leaders, in seeking advice. This group also relied a great deal upon the city council and township boards. In summary, it was found that certain categories of supervisors, in addition to operating through regular formal channels, did make use of considerable informal assitance in guiding their thoughts and actions. More systematic investigation throughout the country will be necessary before we know the exact meaning of these results.

There is an aspect of these informal power relationships which has some importance for adult education programs. In county government as well as the city, state, and national governments, there are sacred precincts which are inviolate. That is to say, there will frequently be one or more agencies of county government that are relatively untouchable by the county governing body or the county political leader because of community feeling developed

[9] They were designated as "neighbors," "key leaders," and "anybody who might help."
[10] 1–5 years; 6–15 years; and over 15 years.

over many years. The units which hold this position vary widely with the individual counties concerned. Education is so regarded occasionally, libraries and welfare institutions at other times, and indeed almost any function of government might be the subject of such community veneration. Adult education programs for those agencies would probably be difficult to administer through a central group outside the community.

Characteristics of County Officials.—There is a loose but discernible pattern of characteristics which fit most county government officials. For example, the majority of the members of county governing bodies are farmers by occupation, a lesser number are business and professional people, and a few are retired. Other occupational groups are seldom represented in large numbers. About half of the governing body members have failed to go beyond the eighth grade, and usually less than a fifth have ever attended college. They are almost all men, and are mostly over fifty years of age. They usually have been residents of the county for a long time, and are frequently re-elected.[11]

In marked contrast to these characteristics are those of some of the non-elective administrative officials and members of some of the county special-function boards and commissions. For example, welfare executives are often college people, frequently with a special training in social work. Sometimes they have been resident in the county a very short time and they almost never have held any political party office. Most of them are fairly young, under forty-five years of age at least. Welfare board members also are in contrast to members of county governing bodies. Their education has usually been much more extensive. They are not as often farmers or businessmen. Many of them are women, and as a whole, they are younger.

Determination of Agricultural Policy—An Illustration of Power Relations.—The human relationships that come into play in determining the policies that local governments follow may be highlighted by reference to a study of county agricultural politics. County agricultural policy is not wholly a matter for the county governing body, county agriculture committee, or the county agent to determine. All levels of government, all types of public officials, and many different kinds of private groups are used as instruments to influence agricultural policy. This is a primary explanation of the reluctance of certain New Deal and Fair Deal agencies to work through state and local extension services (the state

---

[11] These statements and those that follow are taken from data of a five-state area (Minnesota, Iowa, Wisconsin, North Dakota, South Dakota) which will be published as a part of the reports of Research in Intergovernmental Relations, University of Minnesota. The findings of the preliminary Michigan study corroborate this picture, except that the supervisors tended to have a higher educational level than that found in the University of Minnesota research. In the Michigan sample, slightly more than two-thirds of the respondents had at least some high school, and nearly one-fourth attended college, although few graduated. Also the educational level of the non-farmer supervisors was considerably higher than that of the farmer supervisors.

Cooperative Extension Service and the county agricultural agent).[12] These services have been controlled by the Farm Bureau in many instances, and the Farm Bureau was often opposed to a new agency's program. In some areas, for example, the Farm Security Administration of the 1930's and the Soil Conservation Service of today desire to have their own direct contacts with farmers, including many farmers who are not members of the Farm Bureau. They may also wish to avoid entangling contacts with certain Farm Bureau leaders. Although extension workers frequently deny it, opponents of the Farm Bureau claim that the entire extension program, especially at the county level, is run by the Farm Bureau with its special interests and points of view. There is little doubt that some county agents have been obliged by the local Farm Bureau to work directly for the private activities of the Farm Bureau or lose their jobs as county agricultural agents. However, practically all states have now legally separated extension personnel from direct private control and subsidy.

The position of the Farm Bureau and other groups, relative to the agricultural extension system, has important implications for such appealing phrases as the "grass-roots" approach. In a study of the Tennessee Valley Authority's grass-roots approach in the field of agriculture, it was found that many national policy objectives were abandoned or altered by TVA because of the nature of existing agricultural leadership on state and county levels.[13] TVA established a policy of grass-roots operation in carrying out its agricultural programs— that is, a policy of working with and through existing state and local agencies whenever possible. This meant that TVA would work chiefly through the state extension services and the county agents. The Farm Bureau was very influential in extension work in the Valley, and state and local agricultural personnel were, in general, rather conservatively oriented in such matters as soil conservation and rural rehabilitation. The result was that the TVA found itself thwarting some of the stated objectives of other New Deal agencies, as well as its own, by its determination to establish a grass-roots pattern of contacts with farmers. Whether decision-making was actually decentralized and democratized in such a grass-roots approach is open to doubt, since the farmers at the county level frequently take their cues in farm policy from the *national* farm group to which they belong. The Farm Security Administration and the Soil Conservation Service were two organizations which came in conflict with TVA on policy issues. In the 1940's, the Farm Bureau came to the point of openly opposing the Agricultural Adjustment Administration, (now the Production Marketing Administration) which it had helped create in 1933, and demanded that AAA

---

[12] These paragraphs are taken from William Anderson and Edward W. Weidner, *State and Local Government*, New York, 1951, pp. 688–689.

[13] Philip Selznick, *TVA and the Grass Roots*, Berkeley: University of California, 1949.

educational and crop-payment activities be funneled through the extension system.[14]

As a result of such varying power conflicts, there sometimes develops in counties a dual grouping of officials. One grouping would include the governing body and elected administrative officials. Another grouping would include professionalized appointive department heads and many members of the special-function boards and commissions. It is likely that informal intragroup relations are much more frequent within each of these groups than they are between the two groups, and that inter-group relations are high potential sources of jurisdictional and operational conflict, requiring the eventual subordination of one group to another.

The Michigan data provide some interesting cues on this problem, which was touched upon earlier in this chapter. The 74 supervisors were asked whether they had any comments to make on the general area of local government. The following is a summary of these responses: 15 supervisors stated that more political participation by the people is necessary; 7 that local government is losing power generally; 5 that there was too much "high level" government; 3 that local government must be protected; and 2 that supervisors should not be assessors.

Since only about one-third of the supervisors interviewed commented at this opportunity, we can only conjecture as to what the others thought. However, not one of the categories listed expressed optimism or confidence in present or future conditions. It would seem logical that if those who gave no comment were pleased with current trends they would certainly say so, at least with the same candor that the others expressed criticisms.

It is significant to note that in most instances the supervisors were *not* referring to federal centralization in voicing their alarms. To them, "high-level" government was personified by state, and even county agencies. Some supervisors resented the granting of road maintenance functions to their counties as a usurpation of democracy. It mattered not that many townships are simply unable to cope with all of their financial responsibilities without imposing high taxes and assessments on local property. Yet the determination of such taxes and assessments is probably the major task of the supervisors, and the one which creates most of their distress and problems. Practically none of the supervisors showed an awareness of this dilemma. In general, they held the traditional view of grass-roots democracy, in which things could usually be handled on a man-to-man basis. The idea that changes in role and function on the part of supervisors and other local officials might under modern, more complex conditions be necessary for efficiency, or even survival, is a concept foreign to their minds. For them, democracy meant the preservation and defense of established forms of behavior from the encroachments of external forces. Nevertheless, as has been indicated elsewhere in this chapter, there is evidence that

[14] *Ibid.*, pp. 157–164.

an informal, perhaps *sub-rosa*, power structure is operative in the decision-making processes of local officials which is somewhat at variance with their own verbalized "principles."

The significance of all this for adult education is that an extremely variable kind of reception will be given to proposals for adult education in the three fields central to this study, depending upon the kind of official (such as professional or political) who is contacted, and upon the existing power structure in which he is functioning.

COUNTY OFFICIALS AS CONSUMERS OF ADULT EDUCATION

Having now described some of the background and atmosphere in which local officials carry on their work, the more concrete methods and arrangements by which governmental units influence, and are in turn influenced by, their constituents may be discussed. County and township officials are constant consumers of adult education. Their jobs require the availability of a tremendous amount of technical information which is often obtained by the officials in the following ways:

1. State government agencies carry out as a regular part of their activities an extensive program of technical advice and assistance to local governments. Some national government agencies likewise have such programs, but in most instances they funnel their information programs through the appropriate state agencies. Thus a state department of health, for example, publishes pamphlets and brochures that aid local health officials in carrying out their job. Some of this material is original with the state, some of it is provided the state by voluntary associations or national agencies. Many state departments, such as those of welfare, highways, agriculture, education, and taxation, publish bulletins, and often sponsor state-wide and regional conferences at which county and state officials meet together for the discussion of programs for which they have joint responsibility. State agencies also have extensive field staffs which visit county officials from time to time. This on-the-job consultation provides a continuing personal contact between state and county and builds up the confidence of county officials in the several state agencies. The effectiveness of the education job that state agencies do is evident in the attitudes that county government officials have toward state agencies. It is often true, for example, that the more experienced public official has a warmer regard for state agencies than the less experienced county official. He tends to turn to the state agency for the answer when any problem arises on which he needs advice. It is also true that the more professionalized county official tends to look toward the state for the answers to his problems—at least to a greater extent than the amateur or purely partisan county official.

2. Largely independent of state sponsored conferences but sometimes also in conjunction with them, there exists a large number of state-wide associations of local government officials. In a typical state, associations of such officials

as sheriffs, county clerks, registrar of deeds, county engineers, health officers, welfare executives, county comissioners, and others may be found. These associations carry on a number of adult education activities besides annual conferences and occasionally regional conferences. Sometimes they publish monthly periodicals that contain valuable information for the officials concerned. They may have people on their staff who consult with local government officials as the demand for such consultation is made evident. They sometimes publish pamphlets. Whatever their formal activities in the adult education field, they frequently have an important effect upon legislative and administrative decisions.

3. A few state colleges and universities provide regular non-credit adult education programs for county officials. This development is fairly recent, although not confined to any one geographical area. Michigan State College's new program can be used as an example. Through the cooperation of the Michigan Institute of Local Government, an organization of county officials, various academic departments of the college, and the Department of Continuing Education, short course training programs are regularly held for newly elected county officers, and many other groups such as county health officers. These programs try to give a county official a broad prospective of his job as well as detailed training to help him perform specific tasks better. Another program at Michigan State College centers around the publication of a series of public information pamphlets. These pamphlets are published by the Governmental Research Bureau, and are on such topics as state and local finance, political parties and elections in Michigan, United Nations, and democracy. The object of these pamphlets is to present an elementary descriptive account of the subject in question together with some critical analysis. Mention should also be made of the extensive consulting service that is available to Virginia county governments through the University of Virginia's Bureau of Public Administration. This service is rather unique, but has proved extremely valuable in making county government more effective in that state.

Returning once more to the empirical data obtained in the preliminary study in Michigan, it has already been pointed out that the supervisors conception of their job and its formal requirements was inclined to be fuzzy and incomplete. When these supervisors were asked what matters they would like more information about, their answers showed further divergence, as illustrated in Table 4.

While a considerable number of respondents desired more knowledge about assessment problems, an even larger group was either unable to pinpoint their needs, or else felt satisfied with the *status quo*. It is possible that some respondents might have felt embarrassed to admit ignorance in the content and procedures of their work, and so preferred to proclaim satisfaction even though they did not possess it. Yet it is conversely possible that years of lonely grappling with their problems has given them a high degree of confidence and self-sufficiency.

When asked what sources of outside information they did use, the ones most frequently mentioned were State Supervisors Association reports, radio, newspapers, and State Tax Commission bulletins, plus a scattering of magazines. There was almost a complete absence of specialized clinics or handbooks, and nearly ten percent stated they used no sources whatever. From this data it appears that widespread formal aids to the education of local officials is almost universally lacking, and that they derive information rather haphazardly.

In connection with possible improvement of their job knowledge, the supervisors were further queried as to what sorts of educational programs would be desirable for themselves. Table 5 shows the response to this question. From this Table, it would seem that the school and clinic idea has become popular through its use at various colleges and universities throughout Michigan. There were no data on how many supervisors attended such meetings, but most of those

TABLE 4
Subjects and Topics Which Supervisors Would Like More Information About, 74 Michigan Township Supervisors, 1952

Category	Frequency of mention
Assessment and equalization	28
Legal problems	4
Road problems	4
Welfare and hospitals	2
Zoning	2
Drainage	2
Much information needed, but no specific suggestions	16
Information presently available when needed	15
No further information necessary	11

who mentioned personal attendance remarked that they paid part or all of their expenses. One unexpected manifestation of the study was a rather vociferous opposition to educational programs as a whole by several of the officials. Some of the reactions were that schools ridiculed current society and customs too much, that they increased socialist tendencies and centralization of power, and that they were political rather than educational. Whether or not these criticisms were reflections of deep-seated personal opinions, or class biases or whether they represented more recent distrust of the conduct of educational institutions, as expressed all over the country in the past few years, is difficult to determine. However, the general tenor of this negativism in the context of the interviews makes the latter assumption more probable.

In general, it is probable that many of the attitudes of local officials are still influenced rather heavily by the state agencies and associations of county officials and by the activities of state colleges and universities. However, most of these programs do not go beyond the narrowly vocational. This is understandable because of the limitation of funds that all these groups encounter. However, even the vocational emphasis in the field of county government has much to do with democracy and the nation's economy. As a result there are frequent conversations, speeches, articles, or pamphlets on such points as how to make democracy more effective, the relation of government activity to the economy, the impact of the tax structure of the economy, and the impact of world conflict on local government.

What are the possibilities of improving non-credit, non-vocational adult education of which local officials are consumers? In order to answer this question, one must first have clearly in mind the objectives that are to be achieved. Is the objective one of awareness of all the many aspects of democracy, peace, and the economy? Is the objective to encourage a certain point of view in regard to these matters? If the objective be to broaden understanding of each of these subject matter areas, much remains to be accomplished both in terms of experiments with new programs and the extension of existing pro-

TABLE 5
Educational Programs Which Supervisors Felt Desirable, 74 Michigan Township Supervisors, 1952

Category	Frequency of mention
Short "schools" and "clinics"	28
Courses in assessment and taxation	18
Courses in zoning and roads	5
Programs to explain government to the public	3
Methods of getting people to meetings	2
Explanation of duties to township officers	2
No opinion, nothing specific	12
Active opposition to formal programs (meetings not needed, waste of time, etc.)	7

grams that have proved to be valuable to more communities and individuals. Many groups of officials have rather limited appreciation of the problems of peace, democracy, and the economy. Some of them look upon democracy as meaning primarily the direct election of many local administrative officials. Others look upon democracy as meaning true town meeting government. Still others equate it with powerful local self-government. Their ideas on the nation's economy are similarly limited. For example, they have little appreciation of how their activities affect the economy or even what role the property tax plays in our economic life. International conflict and world peace often seem remote questions to them.

What can be done to stimulate a broad approach to the questions concerned with democracy, the economy, and peace? (1) State agency and professional association programs need to be broadened. Cooperation to accomplish this objective would probably be forthcoming from state and local groups if money were available to them. Speakers could be secured on background subjects and brochures published, for example. (2) There is considerable need for broadening the approach of the bureaus of governmental research of the state colleges and universities. Particularly there is need for more consultation between college personnel and local officials so that through frequent contacts a mutual confidence can develop. There is need for more broadly conceived public information pamphlets. (3) There is a need for basic research to be undertaken to test the effectiveness and validity of the principal programs in this field. Such a basic research program might be carried out in conjunction with new experiments in adult education. Whatever may be the courses of action chosen, the basic need for a vigorous program is no longer in doubt.

COUNTY OFFICERS AS PRODUCERS OF ADULT EDUCATION

Some indications of the adult education activities carried on by county officials can be gained from an analysis of the activities of local government. It should be reiterated at this point, however, that the functions of county government vary widely from state to state and county to county. For example, in a number of counties there are no county health officers. In many states, welfare is a state, not a county, function. Sometimes counties have very little or nothing to do with education, and in other places they are the principal education authorities.

One of the most common functions of county government is that of law enforcement. The county sheriff is almost a universal phenomenon. He may either carry on his activities virtually alone in a very sparsely populated county, or he may supervise a large number of deputies. In a few instances, county police forces, much like municipal police forces, are to be found. In terms of adult education for democracy, there probably is no more important official than the sheriff in most counties. There is a great potential in this respect. Problems of tolerance and inter-group relations confront law enforcement officials continually. Problems of free speech, freedom of assembly, and freedom of the press are everywhere present.

Unfortunately, almost no county sheriffs sponsor adult education programs in fields such as these. There are a number of reasons for this. First of all, there is the problem of inadequate funds. But more than that, there is a lack of training on the part of county sheriffs that results in their performing the law enforcement function in a rather routine fashion, and in some instances in an anti-civil liberty fashion. Most of the sheriffs are elected officials, and some of them think mainly of partisan considerations rather than worrying about general law enforcement problems.

A second official who is in a rather strategic position to carry on adult education activities is the county assessor. He is one person with whom almost everyone in the county becomes acquainted—if not personally, at least through one of his staff members. The property tax is probably the major source of local government revenue in the country. It has important economic effects upon individual families as well as business. Furthermore, there is a vital relationship between local governmental services and the ability to pay for them by means of the property tax. The assessor is in a position to shape the attitudes toward government of the taxpayers of the county. Yet, many assessors appear to avoid this part of their work. Because of the uncertain (and sometimes negative) conception of their own job by numerous assessors, there tends to be less tolerance and comprehension on the part of the public with respect to the property tax as a source of revenue. Many citizens automatically assume that government is getting "more than its share."

The Michigan supervisors included in the probing study offers empirical confirmation of these attitudes. As has already been shown, many of these supervisors regarded assessment as their main task which it is by law. However, many of them felt a lack of technical competence for such work, as well as believing that their constituents exhibited a lack of interest and understanding of the problems involved. The officials often expressed their opinions with a flavor of resignation, and occasionally a touch of bitterness. They suffered the headaches with but little sympathy from their fellows.

Table 6 summarizes data from the Michigan probing study describing the connecting links between the supervisors and the public. Obviously, the informal personal contacts are preponderent. However, further study is necessary to accurately describe each set of relationships under consideration in detail before its importance can be accurately weighed. Under present conditions, the routine yearly assessment visits are unlikely to have much over-all influence on either the assessor or the assessed. In fact, much property valuation is done "from the road" without any face-to-face visit at all. The supervisor merely scans the property externally and is guided by precedent and past calculations. In a broad sense, quite a few officials did not, as they put it, "go looking for trouble." They waited for people to come to them, and if they were left alone they regarded this as a sign of public satisfaction. Although public meetings were mentioned as frequent contact points, the inattendance of the citizenry at these gatherings impaired their scope and effectiveness. One conclusion suggested is that local officials do not initiate much educational activity in their communities.

Besides law enforcement and assessment, the welfare and health functions of county government intimately touch the lives of citizens, in part because of the direct contact that the county administrators have with the people in carrying out these programs. There has been some excellent educational work done by welfare and health workers. While heavy case loads and poor salaries hamper them in their attempt to be of general help to their clients, they are frequently well ahead of other county officials in breadth of approach. Health officials have carried out excellent adult education programs in preventive and public health areas. The very success of their programs depends upon such an approach. Here again, county health staffs are for the most part understaffed and inadequately paid.

The county highway field has fewer implications for adult education than most other functions of county government. However, highways play a vital role in the economic life of rural communities. Probably more attention needs to be paid to this aspect of the highway problem. Some studies were made during the depression years, and as a result a great stimulus was forthcoming for the establishment of county planning and zoning agencies. These agencies zoned the rural land so that future settlers could not establish homes in isolated areas and thus uneconomically increase county costs for highways and other services. At the same time, programs were developed to try to persuade other isolated settlers to move to better locations. Since the 1930's zoning has been extended and now may include recreation land and regular farm land as well as land just coming into use. In the highway, planning and zoning fields, therefore, there are important economic implications and these could well afford to be studied in more detail.

TABLE 6
Ways in Which Supervisors Contact Constituents, 74 Michigan Township Supervisors, 1952

Category	Frequency of mention
Personal contact and visiting in general	42
Visiting at assessment time (once a year)	26
Public meetings	22
People come with problems	15
Farm organization meetings	9
Through the township board	7
Telephone	9
Lodge or civic organization meetings	4
Regard meetings as generally ineffective	8
Used own judgment primarily	4
Few contacts with constituents	3

One may conclude from the preceding discussion that effective administration is itself an educational process. If an administrator carries out his task properly, he is constantly educating those with whom he comes in contact with regard to the subject matter under his jurisdiction. At the same time, the general public helps to educate him. This mutual education process could be formalized in some instances more than it has been. That is to say, there could be conscious attempts to increase understanding of particular governmental programs through conferences, group meetings, publications, etc. Certainly the individual county administrator could be made more aware of the possibilities in those directions. It might be valuable to have an investigation of the extent of participation by the general public in county government activities and its satisfaction with them.

There are many other adult education activities that county governments could sponsor that they do not at the present time. There are both monetary and leadership reasons that explain the present situation. An adult education program aimed at demonstrating to county government officials the wide variety of possibilities available to them at relatively small expense might prove fruitful.

It should be noted that there are still other functions of county and local government which are important in the political aspects of adult education. These include the Cooperative Extension Service, the education field in general, and libraries. Since these have been reported on elsewhere in this volume, no further treatment will be given them here.

RURAL POLITICAL OFFICIALS AND ADULT EDUCATION

Political party organization and activity in county governments is extremely varied. There is no one system of parties.[15] There are one party counties, two party counties, three, four, and more party counties and there are probably even no party counties. The roles of community political officials, as distinguished from county officials, may be quite different in adult education in these varying circumstances.

While the dominant impression one gains about political parties from the national scene is that we have a two party system in this country, it is probable that only a minority of the counties have two vigorous, actively organized parties. The most common occurrence on rural town and county levels is a one party system. In part, this is due to the homogeneity of the population of many rural areas. Thus in the South, most counties are organized only by the Democrats while throughout much of the North and West many counties are organized only by the Republicans. Two party areas are often found in more densely populated counties. But there are at least some counties that would probably qualify as no party areas; for example, some counties elect all of their officials on a non-partisan basis. There are relatively few counties having more than two organized political parties.

Within this variety of no party, one party, two party, or more party areas there is a like variation in the extent of party organization. Here again, the facts belie the usual impression, which tends to be that parties are organized down to the last precinct or election district. This is not characteristic of cities in the United States, and it is much less so of rural areas. For example, there are some state party organizations that do not even have a county chairman in each county, much less a systematic county organization presided over by the county chairman. Rural political organizations tend to be highly informal. It is not uncommon in some rural counties to have a county-wide party convention of the dominant party which only two or three people attend. Variations in political party organizations do not follow neat geographical patterns. In general, however, the Eastern half of the United States tends to have somewhat more formal party organization than the Western half.

In part, the importance of these differences in party organization for adult education is that in many cases it would not be possible to contact both Re-

[15] See Anderson and Weidner, *op. cit.*, Chapter 10.

publican and Democratic county organizations for bi-partisan support of or representation on a program. There is no sure way of knowing ahead of time who are the key party organization people in a particular county. These key people are often not the elected county officers, and their influence is expressed in unpretentious, and even casual fashion. The importance of being an official has become secondary to being able to use him as a buffer and a weapon.[16]

Among the Michigan supervisors, included in the probing study, it was revealing to discover that ascension to office was gained by default in many cases. In 16 instances, the supervisor's name was put forth by others in a caucus where the candidate was often not present. Previous experience in other town offices led to nomination in 14 cases. Pressure from friends was cited by 11 as a reason for running, and 10 indicated that they had been appointed to fill a vacancy and continued as a regular candidate. Only six actively sought office, wishing either to be of service or to reduce the inefficiency of the predecessor. Informal pressures, "drafting," and initial nonelection (appointment) seem to be the rule. This is due, in part at least, to the aforementioned one party nature of most rural town and county political structures. Therefore, choosing a candidate is usually tantamount to election. The indications are that this choice is not accomplished by the electorate at large, the latter merely legitimizing the choice by voting.

The paradox illustrated by the Michigan data is that the officials themselves exhibit the same kind of reluctance to serve and participate in local government which they complain about in their constituents. Whether this dislike for the job, or at least a stoic acceptance of it, is a *result* of public apathy, or simply an unwitting *reflection* of it, is difficult to ascertain from the present data. However, the conclusion seems inescapable that a large number of supervisors are not in office for any idealistic or programmatic reasons.

Adult Education Activities.—The adult education activities carried on by rural political officials vary quite as much as the party organizations themselves.[17] In many instances, political officials are influential members of the community, and are the source of much of the information that politically active people receive. In this sense they are constantly engaging in adult education. Perhaps more relevant to this study, however, is the question: What formal education activities do, or could, politicians engage in? There are some political clubs, particularly in a few Eastern states, that have as their objective not only a social good time, but the distribution of information on a wide variety of subjects. Although political clubs are much more frequent in cities than in rural areas, a number of counties have party organizations that hold conventions or conferences from time to time. For example, the women's branch of a party might hold a political institute, or the young Republicans or

---

[16] For more evidence on this point, see Max Weber, "Politics as a Vocation" in Gerth and Mills, *From Max Weber*, New York: Oxford University Press, 1946.

[17] In this section, "political official" and "party official" are used synonymously.

young Democrats might publish a brochure on some political issue of the day. While there is no general pattern, the most active county organizations do a considerable amount of this kind of work. Not all of these conferences or publications are of a narrowly partisan variety, although naturally they lean in that direction.

Local political officials might well be eager supporters and participants of a number of adult education projects. Certainly they seek information about more effective party organization and about the major political issues of the day even though this may not always be the center of their interest. They would support many adult education efforts aside from their desire to be consumers of adult education. The question is not so much one of their support of such adult education activities as it is whether their support would be advantageous for the objectives sought in a particular adult education activity. In some instances political officials might obstruct a particular adult education program because of its nature and in other instances they may not have sufficient prestige in the community to do the adult education program any good. Lacking case studies, it is difficult to be more precise than this.

By and large, local officials have few specific recommendations for improving contacts with their constituents or for educating the public in governmental matters. The Michigan supervisors in the probing study, when presented with this problem, could merely wish for ways and means to get people to meetings, although about fifteen percent did think that radio and television might be the answer for slack attendance. On the other hand, many respondents felt that no improvement was necesary at all, despite their pessimistic and disparaging view of citizen interest in local government. About one-third of the supervisors gave no answers when asked how local government could be improved. As indicated again and again we need better research than is available if effective adult education programs are to be effectively planned and executed.

SUMMARY

In the course of the chapter, several aspects of the relationship between rural local government and adult education have been considered.

After pointing out the paucity of recent data in this field, a brief review of some of the structural characteristics of local government was given. One of the important findings here was that the political atmosphere in the communities reflected apathy rather than vigor, and that the heterogeneity of units and personnel made analysis difficult. A sample of Michigan supervisors exhibited marked lack of clarity in their conception of the job they were filling.

Evidence was then presented to suggest that informal relationships among governors and governed might be decisive in policy-making at the community level, although such evidence certainly requires further substantiation. A composite image of the "typical" official was formulated, and an actual instance (TVA) of the problems created in a power situation was briefly described.

It was further suggested that as consumers of adult education, local officials were often eager for technical assistance, but the means for receiving help were under-developed. Short "clinics" and up-to-date printed material on specific topics seemed to be the most promising aids under present conditions.

As producers of education, officials were rather unproductive. Lacking specialized information on many problems, they tried to meet each situation as it arose, and were inclined to be passive rather than aggressive in contacting their electorate.

All of these factors created a good deal of pessimism among the officials. This was illustrated both through an articulated fear of the encroachments of higher levels of government, and by a feeling of not being appreciated or aided by the public. Data were offered to show that only a small fraction of supervisors interviewed in Michigan were active seekers of their jobs, and that most of them gained office without competition, rather than by political contests.

It is clear from the preceding that any formal adult education programs for either local officials or the rural public in general will have to receive its impetus from outside sources. These sources may be colleges and universities, private foundations, or governmental agencies. It is unlikely that the communities can carry on sustained educational activities by themselves.

Two areas of adult education stand out as virgin fields for experiments. These are the fields of law enforcement and political parties. Very little has been accomplished in this country in training local law enforcement officers in the area of civil liberties, intergroup relations, and democracy. These areas of training are not strictly vocational, and they may well pay large dividends in terms of greater individual freedom and the strengthening of democracy in general. Such a training program could be coupled with a basic research program so that the educational program could be directed at the most important points, and also so that the effect of the training program could be measured over a period of years.

Adult education in the political party area might have the effect of changing the nature of political party organization and activity. Members might become more concerned with issues and with knowing more about them. Some political parties in other countries, such as Great Britain, have carried on much more research, held many more conferences, and sponsored many more informative publications than have parties in the United States. As a result, perhaps parties in these countries have been more active and more concerned with issues than have our own. If an intelligent and alert citizenry is desirable in a democracy, and if live political organizations are means to that end, the furthering of adult education activities by political parties would help accomplish the objective.

However, it must be recognized that some resistance to externally sponsored programs will be forthcoming in many cases. Old preconceptions and suspicions would almost certainly be aroused. Any kind of educational planning, even excluding that centered upon government and politics, would not automatically find enthusiasm and support. The dividing line between acceptance and rejection of an educational program is often extremely fine, requiring delicate handling. In some instances, political officials might obstruct a particular program because of its goals or methods. In other instances, the officials may not have sufficient prestige in the community to do an adult education program any good, even though they may personally support it.

In spite of the apparent need for improvements in the working relationship between politics and education, more empirical research on present trends and conditions is necessary before large scale reforms are inaugurated. Irreparable harm and waste may otherwise result. The research itself might even prove fruitless unless the objectives of any proposed adult education are kept in mind. Generalized "good intentions" will assuredly not be adequate to do the job.

Edward W. Weidner, Director
Governmental Research Bureau
Michigan State College
East Lansing, Michigan
and
Jack J. Preiss
Department of Sociology and Anthropology
Michigan State College
East Lansing, Michigan

BIBLIOGRAPHY

A Selected Bibliography on County Government

Anderson, William, and Edward W. Weidner, *State and Local Government in the United States*, New York, Henry Holt and Company, 1951.

—— and ——, a series of ten monographs on intergovernmental relations, University of Minnesota Press, 1950–1953.

Anderson, William, *The Units of Government in the United States*, 1949 revision, Chicago, Public Administration Service, 1949.

Andrews, Columbus, *Administrative County Government in South Carolina*, Chapel Hill, University of North Carolina Press, 1933.

Bollens, John C., P. W. Langdell, and R. W. Binkley, Jr., *County Government Organization in California*, Berkeley, University of California, 1947.

Bosworth, Karl A., *Black Belt County*, University, Ala., University of Alabama, 1941.

Duncan, John P., a series of three studies on County Government prepared for the Oklahoma Constitutional Survey Committee, Nos. 12, 13, 14, Oklahoma City, 1948.

Ford, Robert S., and Claude R. Tharp, *Reorganization of Michigan's County Government*, Ann Arbor, University of Michigan Bureau of Government, 1946.

Kilpatrick, Wylie, *Problems in Contemporary County Government*, New York, The Century Company, 1930.

U. S. Bureau of the Census, *Governments in the United States in 1951*, State and Local Government Special Studies No. 29, Washington, 1952.

Millspaugh, Arthur C., *Local Democracy and Crime Control*, Washington, The Brookings Institution, 1936.
Overman, Edward S., *Manager Government in Albemarle County*, Virginia, University, Va., University of Virginia, 1940.
Snider, Clyde F., *County Government is Illinois*, Illinois Tax Commission, Springfield, 1943.
U. S. Bureau of the Census, *County Boards and Commissions*, Washington, Government Printing Office, 1947.
Lancaster, Lane W., *Government in Rural America*, New York, D. Van Nostrand Company, revised edition, 1952.
Wager, Paul W. (ed), *County Government across the Nation*, University of North Carolina Press, Chapel Hill, 1950.
Weidner, Edward W., *The American County, Patchwork of Boards*, New York, National Municipal League, 1946.

Chapter 13:
MASS MEDIA OF COMMUNICATION

Introduction

Few inventions in history have had as profound effect upon the social order as those concerning mass means of communication. The mass media—radio, television, movies, newspapers, magazines and other printed matter—have received widespread attention, both from scholars and laymen. The literature dealing with various aspects of mass media problems is gigantic and ranges from scientific treatises to elementary reviews of the latest film showing in the community theater. On the one hand, for example, the mass media may be viewed as mammoth educational tools, to be feared and respected due to an imperfect knowledge of the consequence of their use. On the other hand, they may be viewed as tools for pure gratification and enjoyment. The combinations of means and ends that different individuals and groups in society may have in the mass media unquestionably account for the vast literature in this field.

While the term "mass media" has been in widespread usage for a number of years, especially by sociologists, psychologists and journalists, it may be wise to clarify its meaning. As used here, mass media includes all means of communication in which the speaker and the audience are separated by some artificial mechanism. Characteristic of mass means of communication is that the audience is large and uncontrolled. The mass media, therefore, represent a form of communication that is impersonal, since they lack the face-to-face contact of individuals in group discussion, of the public speaker, or of the legitimate stage.

The general focus of this chapter is the impact of the mass media of communication in rural parts of the United States. Thus, we are interested in examining the channels of communication used by rural people, and specifically we wish to know the extent and nature of their use in adult education activities. The examination is being made under the viewpoint of adult educational activities in three broad areas: (1) international understanding for peace, (2) strengthening of democracy, and (3) understanding and strengthening of the economy. Special attention will be given the weekly newspaper, rural magazines, the radio, and the mass media of college and university information services departments. Lesser consideration will be given television and movies.

THE PRESENT STATUS OF THE MASS MEDIA

The overwhelming presence of newspapers, radios and magazines in America often leads us to forget that these media of communication are differentially available to different segments of our population. Lazarsfeld and Merton[1] supply the following indication of the enormous audiences reached by the mass media: "Approximately seventy million Americans attend the movies every week; our daily newspaper circulation is about forty-six million, and some thirty-four million American homes are equipped with radio, and in these homes the average American listens to the radio for about three hours a day." In view of this enormous mass media audience, let us examine the position of the rural resident in this regard.

The Press.—In 1945, 56 percent of all farm operators reported receiving a daily paper. The proportion rose to 78 percent in the more urbanized North and dropped to only 38 percent in the more rural South. Nearly one-sixth of all farm operators depended upon a weekly newspaper only for their news. Seventy-one percent of all farm operators reported receiving one or more magazines. Farm operators in the North reported the largest percentage (89 percent) and southern farm operators the smallest (55 percent).[2]

The rural weekly, an almost exclusively rural medium of communication, is unique in the intimacy it may achieve. "The position of the country weekly newspaper," according to one writer, "is that of a pulsing, throbbing institution which reaches to the grass roots of the community social structure, reflecting its life, customs and civilization."[3] In 1940 there were nearly 11,000 weekly newspapers in the United States but by 1944 the number had dropped under 10,000. The pattern of distribution of weekly newspapers is interesting. While the Middle West and Great Plains have a large number of weeklies per 10,000 rural population, the southern and southwestern states have relatively few.[4]

---

[1] Paul F. Lazarsfeld and Robert K. Merton, "Mass Communication, Popular Taste and Organized Social Action" in Lyman Bryson, *Communication of Ideas*, New York: Harper and Brothers, 1948, pp. 98–99.

[2] Edgar A. Schuler and Rachel R. Swiger, *Trends in Farm Family Levels and Standards of Living*, Washington: U.S.D.A., August 1947, p. 30.

[3] Thomas F. Barnhart, "Weekly Newspaper Management" in George L. Bird and Frederic E. Merwin, *The Newspaper and Society*, New York: Prentice-Hall, Inc., 1942, pp. 355–356.

[4] Charles P. Loomis and J. Allan Beegle, *Rural Social Systems*, New York: Prentice-Hall, Inc., 1950 pp. 550–551; for an analysis of the trend toward one-publisher communities, see

Rural magazines and periodicals are frequently overlooked since mass media of communication are predominantly urban-centered. In 1940, 86 general agricultural magazines had a combined circulation of over 16 million, or 2.63 per farm.[5] In 1950, the *Farm Journal* which described itself as "The Most Influential Farm Magazine" had a circulation exceeding 2,250,000 copies. Its influence was confirmed, for example, in Lazarfeld's famous study of how voters make up their minds in a presidential campaign.[6] In spite of the fact that the area studied, Erie County, Ohio, was less than half rural and located between the large cities of Cleveland and Toledo, the *Farm Journal* was mentioned as a concrete influence upon change in vote intention as often as *Collier's*, despite great difference in circulation.

The special characteristics of the magazine reading audience have been surveyed by Smith. His summary shows that more women than men read magazines; that the average age of magazine readers is approximately 10 years younger than the average age of non-readers; and that urban residents read magazines much more than farm or village residents. With regard to magazine reading, farmers and farm managers are similar to semi-skilled workers in the proportion of readers. Such occupational categories as "Craftsmen," "Skilled workers," "Service workers, including Domestics" and "Unemployed" all report higher proportions of magazine readers than do "Farmers and farm managers."[7]

Although comparable work has not been done for rural areas, Lazarsfeld found that "the amount of magazine reading in a city may be approximated from the number of inhabitants forty-five years old and over, the percent of industrial workers, number of taxable incomes, the number of movies, geographical location, and the size of a city.[8] Thus, he found magazine reading to increase with age, to decrease with percentage of industrial workers, to increase with income and number of motion picture theaters per 100,000 population. He found magazine reading to be high in the West, low in the South and North, and to be highest in cities between 60,000 and 100,000 population.

Radio.—The radio, like other level of living items, came to rural considerably later than to the urban people. Differences in level of living between rural and

---

Paul Neurath, "One-Publisher Communities: Factors Influencing Trend," *Journalism Quarterly*, Vol. XXI, No. 3, Sept. 1944.

[5] Loomis and Beegle, *Ibid.*, p. 552.

[6] Paul F. Lazarsfeld, Bernard Berelson and Hazel Gaudet, *The People's Choice*, New York: Duell, Sloan and Pearce, 1944, p. 136.

[7] Joel Smith, *The Characteristics of Magazine Audiences—A Survey of the Literature*, New York: Columbia University Masters thesis, 1950, Chap. 5. Cf. the following: Henry C. Link and Harry A. Hopf, *People and Books:* A *Study of Reading and Book-Buying Habits*, New York: Book Industry Committee of the Book Manufacturers' Institute, 1946, p. 112; Paul F. Lazarsfeld and Patricia L. Kendall, *Radio Listening in America*, New York: Prentice-Hall 1948, p. 115; and Louis R. Wilson, *The Geography of Reading*, Chicago: American Library Association and the University of Chicago Press, 1938.

[8] Paul F. Lazarsfeld and Rowena Wyant, "Magazines in 90 Cities—Who Reads What?" *The Public Opinion Quarterly*, October 1937, p. 35.

urban families today is not great. "Consumption patterns of farm families," according to Monroe, "have changed more than those of urban families, lessening the differences that existed between the two groups 40 years ago."[9] More than three-fourths of the farmers in the United States now own radio sets but great differences exist according to degree of rurality, between sections of the country, between those with low and high incomes, between the races, and between those with high and low education. Figure 1 shows that the percentage of radio owners decreases with increasing rurality. It also indicates the rapidity with which the radio came to farmers since 1930. In a sample of 2,535 rural families throughout the nation, it was found that only 40 percent of those with cash farm incomes under $750 per year owned a radio while 93 percent of

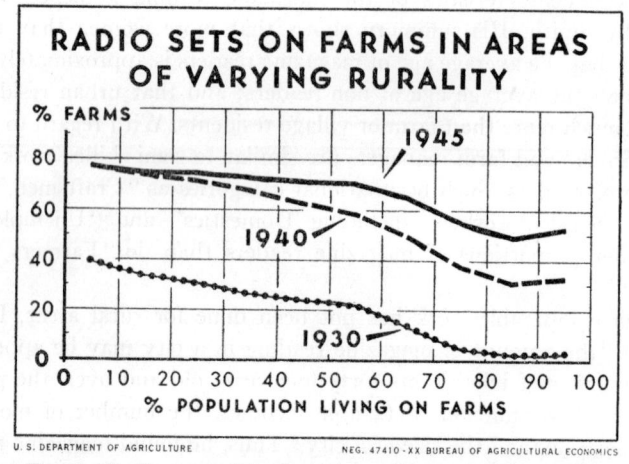

FIG. 1. Radio ownership decreases with increasing rurality.

those with cash farm incomes of $3000 and over per year owned a radio. This same study showed 79 percent of the whites and 20 percent of the Negroes to be radio owners. While 91 percent of the college graduates owned a radio, only 52 percent of those with some grammar school owned a radio. That rural people depend greatly upon the radio for news, undoubtedly associated with their relatively low subscription to dailies, is indicated in the study. Nearly 80 percent indicated "news" when responding to the question "what kind of program would you miss most if your radio gave out."[10]

Television.—Of all the mass media, television at this stage of its growth is

[9] Day Monroe, "Patterns of Living of Farm Families," *Farmers in a Changing World* 1940 Yearbook of Agriculture, Washington: Government Printing Office, 1940, pp. 848–849. For recent data on radio ownership, by place of residence, see *Radio Families—USA* 1948, New York: Broadcast Measurement Bureau, 1948. This report gives the following percentages of radio families: urban 94.2 percent; rural-nonfarm 94.4 and rural-farm 88.7 percent.
[10] *Attitude of Rural People toward Radio Service*, Washington, U.S.D.A. January 1946, p. 12 and 57; for other program preferences of rural people see Edgar A. Schuler, *Survey of Radio Listeners in Louisiana*, Baton Rouge: Louisiana State University, 1943, chap. 5.

the most urban-centered. According to recent estimates 33 percent of all U.S. families owned television receivers. A year ago the percentage was 21. Of the estimated 14½ million sets in the country, more than one-third are found in three cities, New York, Chicago and Los Angeles.[11] Television departments are now in the process of developing programs of an educational nature for primarily rural audiences at at least two land-grant colleges, Iowa State College and Michigan State College.

A recent survey of television[12] shows that middle socio-economic groups most commonly own television sets. This study indicates that only 11 percent of professional persons, only 16 percent of those having an income of $6,000 or more, and only 20 percent of college graduates own television sets.

The decision of the Federal Communications Commission in 1952 to set aside 242 channel assignments for noncommercial, educational television stations represents a milestone in American education. This decision was brought about in no small measure by the Joint Committee on Educational Television, set up by the American Council on Education, the Association for Education by Radio-Television, the Association of Land-Grant Colleges and Universities, the National Association of Educational Broadcasters, National Association of State Universities, National Council of Chief State School Officers and the National Education Association of the United States. The educational implications of this decision are profound, both for the youth and the adults of the nation.[13]

Movies.—With respect to the position of motion pictures as a medium of communication, the Public Library Inquiry of the Social Science Research Council confirms the previous estimate of movie attendance given by Lazarsfeld and Merton. This report indicates that from 45 to 50 percent of the adult population goes to a motion picture once every two weeks or oftener.[14] Authorities agree, however, that rural people go to movies considerably less often than urban people. This fact is obviously related to the availability of movie houses.[15] It is also probably related to a lesser dependence upon a cash economy on the part of the rural person. Many Cooperative Extension Service specialists observe that showing a film is a good way to assure attendance at rural meetings.

Special Characteristics of the Various Media.[16]—Social scientists and special-

[11] AP Dispatch from New York, December 19, 1951. For development of television abroad see *World Communications: Press, Radio, Film*, Paris: UNESCO 1950, pp. 28–29.

[12] Eleanor E. Maccoby, "Television: Its Impact on School Children," *Public Opinion Quarterly*, Vol. XV, No. 3, Fall 1951, pp. 421–441.

[13] Address by Paul A. Walker, "Education's Year of Decision," at the Fifth Annual Radio and Television Institute, Pennsylvania State College, July 9, 1952.

[14] Bernard Berelson, *The Library's Public*, New York: Columbia University Press, 1949.

[15] Paul F. Lazarsfeld, "Audience Research in the Movie Field," *The Annals*, Vol. 254, Nov. 1947, p. 163.

[16] Cf. Joseph T. Klapper, *The Effects of Mass Media*, New York: Bureau of Applied Social Research, Columbia University, 1949, pp. 11–17 and 11–29; for evidence of the prestige of printed matter, see Bernard Berelson, "What 'Missing the Newspaper' Means," in *Communications Research 1948–1949*, New York: Harper and Brothers, 1949, p. 123.

ists in mass media of communication have reached a high degree of consensus on the unique attributes or characteristics of the major media. The purpose of this section is to summarize the current consensus.

Among the unique advantages of printed matter one may list the following: (1) The reader may control the length of exposure. Both radio and motion pictures compel the audience to follow a set pace. Printed matter, on the other hand, allows the reader to proceed at a pace decided by himself. (2) Printed matter permits the reader to make use of the material as frequently as he chooses; radio programs and films, on the other hand, are rarely seen or heard twice by the same person. Hence the accessibility of printed matter is a unique attribute. (3) Printed matter may be written in whatever length seems advisable considering the subject to be covered. Radio and film programs ordinarily have a predetermined length and are relatively short in duration. The latter two media rarely lend themselves to detailed and complex presentation. (4) Printed matter, in general, is unique in that content is less standardized than it is in other media. Specialized and minority opinions may be expressed more readily through print than in radio or on the screen. (5) Although consensus is not complete on this point, many experts feel that printed matter possesses greater prestige than either radio or motion pictures. Perhaps the fact that print is the oldest of the mass media explains in part its high prestige value.

In summary, printed matter permits the reader to gauge his own speed and frequency of reading. It permits repeated exposure and sets no time limits. The printed media appear to be the most willing of the mass media to give representation to minority viewpoints, despite the public service demand involved in public control of the air waves. Radio, on the other hand, reaches an audience that is not often contacted by mass media. This audience tends to be less well educated and more suggestible than other audiences. Radio affords the audience at least some feeling of participation in the actual events because of the personal nature of voice and for this reason it approaches face-to-face contact. Unlike the other media, the motion picture is felt by many authorities to enjoy unique persuasive advantages by virtue of its visual material. That films are capable of "emotional possession" of the audience appears to be its special advantage. All of the mass media of communication, however, appear to be less effective in education than face-to-face discussion. The personal element involved in face-to-face discourse has not been duplicated by mass media. However, it would seem that television with its direct visual and aural appeals, is best adapted to intimate, face-to-face presentations.

THE RURAL PRESS

In an attempt to appraise the role of printed matter in the field of adult education for primarily rural people, it was decided that the most rewarding specific areas to probe would be those of country weeklies, rural magazines and college information services. Admittedly, numerous other approaches might have been made of this problem but our decision seemed best adapted to the limitations of time and budget. Consequently, a questionnaire was prepared and mailed to two samples of weekly newspaper editors, the first, a ten percent cross-section of all weekly newspaper editors in centers of 5,000 or less, and the second, all weekly newspaper editors in 263 sample counties. The details of the procedure are outlined in Appendix C.

The Weekly Newspaper Sample.—A total of 336 weekly newspaper editors throughout the country responded to the questionnaire. Responses were slightly greater than expectation (based upon rural population distribution) for the Corn belt and Range-Livestock areas and slightly under the expected returns for the Cotton belt and the General and Self-sufficing areas. As a whole, however, the regional representation of the respondents is good.

The average newspaper respondent in this study is a small town editor who has between 1,000 and 3,000 subscribers and about three times this number of readers, three-fourths of whom are rural residents. More than three-fourths of all the editors indicated that they had less than 3,000 subscribers. The number of readers reported by this sample of newspaper editors was between two and three times the number of subscribers. More than two-fifths of the editors reported that they had more than 5,000 readers. The weekly newspaper audience is thoroughly rural, with only 15 percent of the newspaper editors reporting their readers to be more urban than rural. Three-fifths indicate that their readers were more than 75 percent rural.

Non-Advertising Space Given Local Groups.—In an effort to obtain a picture of the use made of the country weekly by local groups, the editors were asked to indicate the local groups using non-advertising space. They were requested to indicate the frequency of use of space as well as to indicate whether or not such local groups had prepared articles in the three fields of interest, (1—international understanding for peace; 2—strengthening of democracy; and 3—understanding and strengthening of the economy).

Figure 2 shows variations in allotment of space to local groups reported by the editors. The weekly newspaper editors report the space is given in their newspapers to a great variety of local groups in the community. "Churches and religious organizations" was checked most frequently by the weekly newspaper editors. In order of frequency of mention are the following local groups: schools, women's clubs, patriotic and veterans' organizations, and civic and service groups.

The frequency with which non-advertising space is given to various local groups, and whether or not these groups contribute articles in the three fields of interest were reported by the newspaper editors. Such local groups as the Cooperative Extension Service, churches and religious organizations, and schools, were given local newspaper space "every week" in more than three-fifths of the cases. On the other hand, such local groups as Farmers Union, welfare councils, political parties and/or organizations, professional organizations, labor unions, and UNESCO organizations were given space "every week" by less than one-fifth of the editors. The largest consumers of weekly newspaper space, as reported by editors, are churches and religious organizations, schools, Cooperative Extension Service, women's clubs, civic and service clubs, the Grange, fraternal organizations, and patriotic and veterans' organizations, in the order named.

Local Group	Number of Times Mentioned
Churches and Religious Organizations	290
Schools	282
Patriotic and Veterans' Organizations	250
Women's Clubs	250
Civic and Service Clubs	247
Cooperative Extension Service	233
Parents' Organizations	225
Farm Bureau	225
Colleges and Universities	223
Fraternal Organizations	215
Libraries	200
Government Bureaus	192

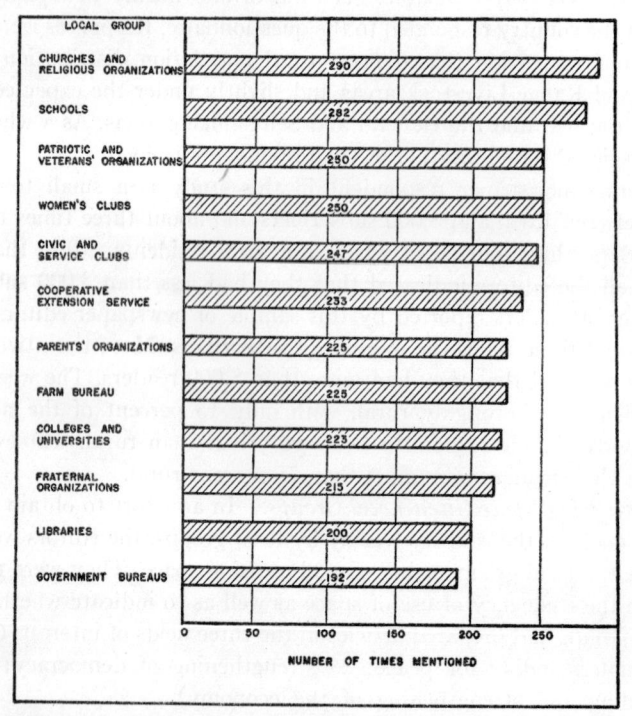

FIG. 2. The number of times newspaper respondents selected specified organizations as the ones with which they work most frequently in educational work with adults.

Very interesting results were obtained to the question concerning whether or not local groups had prepared articles in the three fields of interest in the last year. The Cooperative Extension Service received the largest proportion of "yes" answers. High proportions of "yes" answers were also received by churches and religious organizations, by government bureaus, by patriotic and veterans' organizations, and by colleges and universities. The largest percentage of "no" answers were given Farmers' Union, labor unions, welfare councils and the Grange.

Editorials and Articles in the Three Fields of Interest.—Country editors report writing a considerable number of editorials for their papers in the three fields of interest. It would appear from the comments of weekly editors that they feel the editorial page is still very important in the formation of public opinion. Approximately two-fifths of the number responding indicated that they had written one or more *editorials* in the three fields of interest in the last year. Slightly larger percentages of editorials were concerned with "strengthening of democracy" than with the other fields of interest. Only approximately one-fifth, however, indicated that they carried one or more *articles* in these fields. In an estimate of the total amount of non-advertising space devoted to the three fields, approximately one-eighth of the editors reported none. Nearly one-tenth, however, indicate that they had given more than 10 percent of their non-advertising space to these three areas. Both articles and editorials classified as "strengthening of democracy" were given more space than those concerned with "international understanding for peace."

Contributions by Local Groups.—In view of the fact that many local groups have adult education as an objective, the editors were queried about contributions of local groups to the newspaper in the three fields of interest. Although some notable contributions were reported, between 60 and 70 percent of the editors reported no articles from local groups in any of the three fields. Judging from editors' responses, local groups do not habitually submit articles in any of the three fields. There were slightly more contributions from local groups in the fields of "international understanding for peace" and "strengthening of democracy," however, than in the field of "understanding and strengthening of the economy."

The American Legion, other patriotic and veteran organizations together with the P.T.A. and school groups are mentioned most frequently as sources of articles in each of the three fields of interest. Only rarely do the editors indicate other local groups as sources of articles in the three fields.

Special Efforts of Editors to Promote the Three Fields.—The weekly newspaper editors were asked to indicate any special efforts in the past year to promote international understanding, democracy, and an understanding of the economy. They were also asked to indicate the local groups, if any, involved in this effort. The American Legion received by far the largest number of mentions in connection with special efforts made by the newspaper in these three fields. Patriotic and veterans' organizations other than the American Legion also received frequent mention. Along with such groups, the P.T.A., the Cooperative Extension Service, the Rotary, Lions Clubs, churches, the Farm Bureau and Chambers of Commerce were mentioned as cooperators in more than five instances.

An example, written by a Florida newspaper editor, illustrates one type of special effort in the fields of interest. She writes: "I organized a Community Forum backed by churches, bringing in speakers and preparing groundwork for a study group this winter. Speakers represented Florida universities, patriotic groups, various religions. International understanding was the main theme I tried to promote, but patriotic groups caused dissension."

Opinions of Editors on Most Effective Means of Promoting the Three Fields.— The responses of rural editors yield a number of recurrent themes. These may be enumerated as follows: First, the responses reveal renewed confidence in the potency of the rural weekly as an instrument of public opinion in rural America; second, the replies show confidence in the editorial, often as a slow but nonetheless powerful device to reach and influence people; third, the responses bear testimony to the handicaps, chiefly in terms of time and money, under which the weekly editor attempts to function; and fourth, the replies indicate an attitude of humility concerning past efforts in these fields and a willingness to accept suggestions and help. But let the editors speak for themselves.

From a Pennsylvania editor comes the following comment:

> It is our opinion that every newspaper in the country could use one more 'writing man,' but even the most financially able papers now find it nearly impossible to add another 'unproductive' man to their staff and payroll. Only those who earn their keep with money-making work can any longer be justified. The things you are talking about are the 'free' things—and only the bare minimum of time can be devoted to these.
>
> When I say impossible, I mean impossible—the government is now extracting from my business enough money for me to pay one more employee a very good salary. This is over and above what I figure 'normal' taxes should be, and which as a citizen I am perfectly willing to pay—for essential services. Now my business could very well use one more extra man—if I could pay him, but I can't. He could either do some of the business 'work' and allow me time for writing or be editor and allow me some time to run the business. I now do both in 80 to 90 hours per week.
>
> As a result, not more than 40 man hours goes into the writing and editing of the news content of my paper, approximately half of which I do myself. By way of comparison, to show that larger papers are not better off, I believe the N. Y. *Times* has two mechanical employees, one business office, to every writer. My proportion is approximately 3:1:1. I well know that 40 hours time is not sufficient to produce the news and other items which should go into my paper, nor to allow for the thought and research which stands behind it—but in such inflation times these things cannot possibly be paid for. Neither the small weekly nor the big daily can do the job traditionally required of it—along the lines of your three topics. The chance of so doing is now further out of reach than it was 20 years ago. But in relation to size, the weekly is still doing a better job for its hundreds of readers than the big paper is doing for its thousands.
>
> Enough of this—you get the idea.

Another editor expresses confidence in the editorial as the most effective means of promoting the three fields. He says:

> Easiest way is through editorials. However, most editors and publishers of country newspapers are too busy to write such editorials and have no time to have them set in type. Indeed, some lack the space. The thought usually is that such matters should be left up to the big city daily newspapers—and we'll concentrate on the local grass-roots issues.

Others from Kansas, Massachusetts, Illinois, and Nebraska express a willingness to cooperate in promoting the three fields but suffer from overwork. One says:

> would use suggested or pattern editorials if available.

Another writes:

> ... we will be glad to cooperate with your promotion of all three (fields of interest).

Another expresses his feelings as follows:

> I believe we editors need to be awakened to the need for promoting these fields; that local editorials would be good; that republication of articles from other media would be good. Until filling out this paper I did not realize how little I have done to further these worthwhile causes. I would be glad to publish a short article every week on the subjects if your group intends to prepare a series. We need it! Just don't make them too long—people won't read long articles.

The Nebraska editor, concerned about short articles, adapted to local readers, says:

> We find the articles which we read and would like to reprint are too long for our space limitations. We do not have the time to cut them down to size. In order to present any of the three subjects, too many words are involved. Perhaps brief articles could be submitted to the weekly press, to be run in series. We could use such a series.

In addition to regular editorials and articles, two practical suggestions as to how weekly newspapers can most effectively promote international understanding, strengthening of democracy and the economy, come from editors in New York and Colorado. One says:

> Many weekly newspapers would be glad to offer space to get the ball rolling. For use in this space I would suggest a series of articles designed to stimulate formation of local study groups, preferably one to a community for greater effectiveness and interest. Logically this could be set up in the program of adult evening education now sponsored by most of the Central School systems. Among the nation's 10,000 plus weeklies, there are few which would have the time or knowledge to promote this unassisted. Likewise a local group would certainly need continued supporting material for study and discussion. Whether this would be interesting and stimulating enough to hold this group together, who knows? It could not originate locally, except in a few instances; and in any event should be the entertaining and painless type of education such as is now popular in our school systems.

The other has this to say:

> Thanks for asking! I spent a year (1944–45) as a Nieman Fellow at Harvard and this helped me so much that I have wanted other editors to be similarly brought up to date. I think there is room for three or four other Nieman-type foundations, say in Chicago, U. of N.C. and perhaps U. of Colorado or U. of California. But instead of training reporters, I would help the man who makes policy on the papers. Radio and TV could be included. Rural editors, unfortunately, are not studious, as they are primarily business men. But they will accept knowledge in easy doses.

RURAL MAGAZINES

The Content of Selected Rural Magazines.—In an effort to gauge the amount and nature of the comment relating to the three fields of interest, six selected rural magazines were examined. The inquiry proceeded along carefully defined lines and consisted of appraising all non-advertising space. This space was classified according to whether or not it falls into: (1) international understanding for peace; (2) strengthening of democracy; (3) understanding and strengthening the economy; or (4) combinations of these three. The space was also categorized as editorials, features, signed columns, and all others. The length of each article was also determined and a percentage of the total space given the three fields for each issue was ascertained. Each issue for 1950 of the following rural periodicals was examined: *Hoards Dairyman, Successful Farming, National Livestock Producer, Cappers Farmer, Prairie Farmer,* and *Farm Journal.* Each of these magazines has a circulation of more than 200,000 and the *Farm Journal* has a circulation of slightly under 3,000,000.

On the basis of the criteria of judgment used, considerable space is being devoted to the three fields of interest. The following percentages of non-advertising space devoted to the three fields in 1950 is as follows:

Hoards Dairyman and *National Livestock Producer* ..... under 5%
Cappers Farmer, Prairie Farmer, and *Successful Farmer* .. 5–10%
Farm Journal .... over 10%

Although these represent averages, the range in the percentage of space devoted to these three fields from issue to issue is very great. In the *Prairie Farmer,* for example, the range is from 1 percent to 22 percent.

Although the total space given the three fields by the more specialized trade magazine, *Hoards Dairyman,* is relatively small, some excellent feature articles falling directly in the fields of international understanding and strengthening of democracy, have appeared. "Let's Visit Pakistan," an 800 word feature dealing with agriculture in Pakistan and a comparison with the American situation, is an example. Other examples are "Emily Richter, D. P. Dairymaid" and "Farming in Socialist England." The first tells of a displaced person from Moravia learning the American way; the latter is a first-hand account of agriculture in a socialistic economy.

Two signed columns in *Successful Farming* are regularly devoted to the three fields, directly or indirectly. "The Farmers Washington" by Richard Wilson and "Friend to Friend" by Kirk Fox (the Editor) regularly devote columns, particularly to democracy and understanding and strengthening the economy. In addition, a number of feature articles, usually with an economic flavor, are included. Two examples may serve to illustrate. "Farmers Will Feel the Blow When We Stop Helping Europe" by Nathan Koenig, shows the effect upon farm markets of the cuts in European assistance. "An Open Letter to American Farmers" by Jim Roe, a 3200 word feature, has as its aim the strengthening of the economic system.

Much of the space falling in the three fields of interest that appear in the *National Livestock Producer* is devoted to short articles concerned with government regulations as they affect farmers. The following articles are suggestive: "How Much is 42 Billion?" an article concerned with the national debt; "Decay from Within," a 250 word feature devoted to capitalism as the best way of life; and "Plan Broader Controls After Election," a 500 word feature showing the changes in our economy and the role of price control.

Two signed columns appearing in *Capper's Farmer*, one called "Between Thee and Me" by Ray Yarnell and another by Arthur Capper, are generally concerned with one or all of the three fields of interest. The average issue consistently devotes approximately 5 percent of its non-advertising space to the three fields. Representative titles include: "International Wheat Agreement," 600 words; "A County Insures Its Future," a 700 word article concerning a county improvement program, including school needs, roads, drainage, fire protection, weed control, rural health and zoning; "Foreign Youth Learn Our Ways," 400 words; "A Boy's-Eye View of Danish Agriculture," 1000 words; and "How to Avoid Paying Tax You Don't Owe," 450 words.

One issue of *Prairie Farmer* devoted more than one-fifth of its non-advertising space to our three fields of interest. This issue included two features and two editorials. "What My Citizenship Means to Me" is a 300 word essay written by a farm girl about what living in America means to her. "Collective Farming," by R. S. Yohe is a 1100 word feature concerning Israel. "Dinner Bell Rings" by Arthur Page is a 400 word editorial concerning rural and urban differences, how they are disappearing and the need for unity of town and country. "Faith, Hope and Charity," a 300 word editorial emphasizing the return to these principles, completes the space devoted to the three fields in this particular issue.

Of all the periodicals examined for this analysis, the *Farm Journal* had the largest percentage of space devoted to the three fields. According to the criteria used for this study, approximately one-eighth of each issue was devoted to the fields of interest. As we found in connection with many of the other rural magazines, the *Farm Journal* carried considerable comment on international understanding, strengthening of democracy, and the economic system in its editorials and regular signed columns. Wheeler McMillen's, the "Editor-in-Chief's Column," falls in this category. A wide range of feature articles was also found in this publication. Among the features of special note we may single out two for comment. The first is entitled "See Here, Mr. President" by Vernon Vine. This article is a 950 word feature dealing with how farmers practice democracy in Belmont County, Ohio. This is a feature concerning democracy at work. The other feature article falls clearly into the areas of international understanding. It contains more than 2000 words and is entitled "We Met the British," by Cameron Harvey. The lot of the British farmer, his tax load compared with that of the American farmer, and farming in a socialistic regime are presented.

COLLEGE AND UNIVERSITY INFORMATION SERVICES

In an effort to obtain a view of mass media from a different perspective it was decided to examine them from the vantage point of the college and university information services. For this reason, a sample of colleges and universities,[17] and a complete sample of land-grant colleges[18] was prepared. A questionnaire was mailed to the information services departments or to Experiment Station and Extension Service editors. Two hundred and thirty-one questionnaires were mailed and 92 were returned.

It seemed important to obtain responses from the information services departments relating to the time spent on various media, the relation of college media to local group usage, and especially to obtain expressions of opinions from this group of professionals actively engaged in the utilization of the media of communication.

Time Spent on Various Mass Media.—College and university information services, as might be expected, reported that they spend a large proportion of their time with printed matter and especially with press releases. Radio follows, with visual aids and television accounting for the least amount of time. Two-fifths of those reporting on television reported that some time was being devoted to this medium.

In addition to these broad categories of mass media, the information service personnel were asked to check specific classes of media handled by their departments. New releases, feature articles, and radio news releases led, each receiving nearly one-sixth of all the mentions. In addition, more than 25 mentions each were given periodicals, radio scripts, exhibits, film strips, Agricultural Experiment Station publications, and Agricultural Extension publications. The fact that television is only now entering the college mass media picture is confirmed by only 19 mentions out of more than 500.

College Media and Local Groups.—The information specialists were asked to designate local groups for which special printed materials had been prepared. The schools led in frequency of mentions, accounting for slightly more than one-tenth of all groups checked for which special materials had been prepared. The next most frequently mentioned groups, in order, are as follows: colleges and universities, civic and service organizations, professional organiza-

[17] This sample represents 20 percent of the "Institutional primary memberships" listed in the 1951 membership roster of the American College Public Relations Association. See Appendix C.

[18] This sample was a mailing to all Agricultural Experiment Station and Agricultural Extension Service editors at Land-Grant Colleges. See Appendix C.

tions, Cooperative Extension Service, federal and/or state government bureaus, and farm organizations. It is notable that the especially rural groups are frequently mentioned in the selected audiences for printed materials. Discussion group materials were reported a total of 55 times. These materials were designed for use most frequently by the schools, the Cooperative Extension Service, farm organizations, women's clubs, civic and service organizations, and professional organizations, each of which received at least five mentions.

Evaluation of the Various Media.—Two questions were asked of the college information specialist: "Which of the media ... do you believe is most effective in getting the public to *adopt new practices?*" and "which of the media ... do you believe is most effective in *changing of attitudes?*" In general, the respondents were wary about placing their confidence in any single medium. In reply to both questions, however, news releases and feature articles were mentioned most frequently as being the most effective. Rarely were there unqualified responses, as the following quotations indicates:

Frankly, I have become more than a little pessimistic about changing attitudes of people. None of the mass media has any appreciably effect unless you are telling them something they want to know. The only effective way we have found to get them to want something that will lead to a change of attitude in the adoption of a new practice is through personal contact, or in groups through a dynamic speaker."

We are now rating periodicals and TV very high, but it takes a combination of media tailored to fit the task to accomplish a job. All are most important to do a balanced job."

Possibly No. 4 (Agricultural Experiment Station publications). Despite all the work put on them, these media are relatively ineffective. New practices are adopted as a result of personal contacts with someone in whom the person making the change has trust. Experience leads me to believe that this is a basic premise.

Examples of "Best" Mass Media.—Finally, the college information specialists were asked to describe their "best" examples of mass media primarily concerned with international understanding, strengthening of democracy, or understanding the economy. One hundred and forty items were cited, of which 83 items were printed matter; 42 were radio and television programs; and 15 items fell in the category of visual aids. Out of 93 programs for which a special audience was designated, one-third were for farm groups.

Among the interesting examples reported, only a few may be selected for mention and description. The University of New Hampshire reported a series of articles published in its Alumni Magazine. The articles, called "The Alert American Series," were written by professors in the University. Sample individual articles were entitled, "Skepticism and Democracy," "Two Problems in Asia," and "Economists and Businessmen."

The University of Kansas reported very large audiences reached through a monthly leaflet entitled "Your Government." This leaflet is sent to schools and libraries in the state and is often used as supplementary reading in social science classes.

Four radio scripts falling directly into the three fields of concern in our inquiry were selected by U.C.L.A. as its "best" examples of mass media. "Pattern for Peace," "World Government—Hope or Illusion?" "The Negro's Chance" and "The Small Investor," all were broadcast over CBS, Western Division.

Cornell University chose its Tape Recording Center as one of its "best" examples of what is being done to provide information in the three fields. The introduction to the Spring 1951 catalogue of the Cornell Tape Recording Center cites its uses and purposes as follows:

The use of radio programs as a supplement to classroom instruction in schools and to Extension work in both rural and urban areas has proved highly satisfactory where the time of broadcast and the subject are practicable. Naturally, many suitable programs are broadcast at inconvenient times, and other conditions make it difficult or impossible for teachers and county Extension agents to use this method of instruction.

The same techniques might, however, be useful to convey information and to stimulate discussion in the classroom and at group meetings, as well as for Extension activities, if the teachers or individuals in charge had access to suitable material in recorded form.

The Department of Extension Training and Information at Cornell University has, therefore, inaugurated a Tape Recording Center which provides such a service to teachers, Extension agents, parent-teacher groups, and similar organizations who have tape-recording equipment. Programs of a varied nature and of different lengths are available on plastic tape. Copies of these recordings will be made for teachers, county Extension agents, PTA program chairmen, and other persons on receipt of a tape for the purpose. The only charge is the postage, both ways.[19]

Among the listings falling into our fields of interest are the following:

ECA, A Tremendous Undertaking, by Richard Bissell...... 55 min.
The Homemaker in the World Crisis, by Dean E. Lee Vincent.. 45 min.
Revolution in Asia, by Knight Biggerstaff................. 45 min.
Food and Farming Behind the Iron Curtain, by Horrell De Graff.. 50 min.
Farm Life in Formosa and Japan, by W. A. Anderson..... 50 min.
This is Life in Norway, by Halfon Wennewold, a Student.. 15 min.
The American Way (Democratic and kindly way of handling questions which arise in a club).................. 8 min.

Of special interest in view of the link between printed matter and local dicussion groups are the examples of mass media from Ohio State University. "Let's Discuss: The Citizen and His Government" and "Let's Discuss: Four Ways of Doing Business" are short leaflets designed for rural discussion group helps on these topics. "Aids to Group Discussion" is a 25-page manual for community leaders. According to the Foreword, "This bulletin aims at those who work with groups—in committee, meetings, conferences and workshops.

[19] Catalogue of the Cornell Tape Recording Center, Ithaca: Cornell University, Spring, 1951.

It is a discussion for discussion leaders of, practices, arts and skills, and group methods."

Finally, Montana State University cites its efforts to promote local drama as an activity in promoting democracy and understanding and strengthening the economy. The Public Service Division of the College supplies to the communities of the state expert help and guidance in developing dramatic programs dealing with local historical backgrounds but to be organized, written and produced by the people of the community. Emphasis is placed upon three forms: local historical pageant-dramas, dramas based on local backgrounds, and people's extemporaneous dramas (or sociodramas).

RADIO AND TELEVISION

As indicated earlier, radio came to the farmer more recently and less completely than to the urbanite. Now that television is coming of age, it too is reaching the farmer, due to his relative isolation, more slowly than the urban person. Although television has great possibilities for educational purposes, it does not as yet reach into the more ruralized sections of the nation.[20] The eventual appropriateness of TV for rural audiences must await future development in this area.

Numerous studies show that the influence of radio on farm families has been significant.[21] The study reported in *Radio Research 1941* showed that when rural electrification made radio possible in two rural counties, farmers' interest in national affairs increased, farm life became more enjoyable for both young and old, and cohesiveness of the farm family increased. Among the interesting conclusions of this study is that rural listeners avoid opinion conflicts on the air. Obviously, the farmer is more interested in farm talks, markets, and weather reports than the urban person. He also shows a greater preference for religious programs, oldtime music and religious music than the urbanite. The farm family listens to the radio earlier in the morning, more at noon, and less in the late evening than the urban family.

Of special interest to any examination of adult education programs by radio are the findings of Berelson, namely, that audiences classified by age and education are polarized according to type of program. He found that those who "like to listen to popular and dance music" decreased with increasing age and education. He also found that those who "like to listen to talks and discussions

[20] A notable exception in the development of TV for a primarily rural audience is WOI-TV, owned and operated by Iowa State College. In May 1951, the station inaugurated a book program called "Book on Trial," a weekly half-hour program featuring a panel discussion of well-known books. Plans are also in progress for a children's story hour. Another program is called "How to think about Mankind." See Robert W. Orr, "Libraries and Educational Television," *ALA BULLETIN*, Vol. 45, No. 8, September 1951, pp. 282–284.

[21] See for example, *Attitudes of Rural People toward Radio Service, op. cit.;* William S. Robinson, "Radio Comes to the Farmer" in *Radio Research 1941*, New York: Duell, Sloan and Pearce, 1941, pp. 224–295, and Kenneth S. Bartlett, "Social Impact of the Radio," *Annals*, Vol. 250, March 1947, pp. 89–97.

about public issues" increased with increasing age and education.[22] That radio audiences, in general, are stratified also by economic status is abundantly documented. Of income groups A—(5,000 and over), B—(3,000 to 5,000), C—(2,000 to 3,000), and D—(under 2,000), Group A is uniformly below average in radio listening; Group B is nearest to average; Group C is uniformly highest in listening, with relatively higher usage in daytime than evening; Group D uses the radio less than B but more than A.[23]

Characteristics of the Sample.—The present inquiry concerning adult education programs in rural areas led to a sampling of radio stations in the United States. The total sample is made up of two components, namely, 10 percent sample of the total all radio stations, and complete coverage of radio stations in the 263 sample counties. Thus, the sample includes 560 cases, including AM, FM and TV stations. See Appendix C for additional details.

An examination of the respondents to the radio questionnaire, classified by rurality of the audience and type of farming area, revealed good regional distribution. The regional representation by type of farming area was in line with expectation, based upon rural population distribution. With regard to rurality, nearly half of the radio respondents reported an audience containing more than 50 per cent rural population. Approximately half of the radio stations reporting have a primary audience within a radius of 50 to 100 miles. Twenty-seven of the stations report a radius under 50 miles while 24 indicate a radius of 100 miles or more. With regard to the population within this radius, nearly half (45) indicate a population of half a million or more; only 17 stations report less than 100,000 population. A vast majority of the stations report being on the air 15 hours or more per day.

Local Group Interest in Station.—The respondents were requested to supply information concerning local groups showing an interest in the station, as indicated by use and participation. They were also requested to indicate those groups that had "planned and presented their own radio programs over your station." These questions were designed to appraise the activity of local groups in the radio field.

Table 1 shows the frequency with which various local groups "use and participate" and "plan and present" their own programs, as reported by radio station program directors. Of all local groups mentioned as using and participating in programs over the radio stations, churches are indicated most frequently. Other organizations, including schools, civic and service organization, government bureaus, patriotic and veterans' organizations are mentioned frequently. Ninety-eight percent of all stations checked churches as having

---

[22] Bernard Berelson, "Communication and Youth," in Frances Henne, Alice Brooks and Ruth Ersted, *Youth Communication and Libraries*, Chicago: American Library Association, 1949, pp. 14–30.

[23] See H. M. Beville, Jr., *Social Stratification of the Radio Audience*, Office of Radio Research: Princeton University, 1940 and H. M. Beville, Jr., "The ABCD's of Radio Audiences," *The Public Opinion Quarterly*, June 1940, pp. 195–206.

used and participated in programs. Such groups as labor unions, UNESCO organizations, and inter-agency councils are mentioned least often. Schools, churches, and colleges and universities, were listed most frequently as local groups that had planned and presented their own radio programs.

Great differences are shown when the analysis is separated according to

TABLE 1
Number and Percent of Local Groups "Using and Participating" and "Planning and Presenting Their Own Programs," Classified by Local Groups

| Local groups | Stations reporting ||||
| | Using and participating || Planning and presenting ||
	Number	Percent	Number	Percent
Churches and religious organizations...	97	98	21	21
Schools...........................	91	92	21	21
Civic and service clubs..............	87	88	17	17
Government bureaus................	85	86	17	17
Patriotic and veterans' organizations..	81	82	13	13
Colleges and universities............	77	78	20	20
Women's clubs.....................	71	72	16	16
Farm organizations.................	69	70	13	13
Cooperative Agricultural Extension Service.........................	68	69	10	10
Political parties and/or organizations..	68	69	11	11
Welfare councils....................	68	69	11	11
Parents' organizations...............	67	68	12	12
Community councils.................	57	58	9	9
Elected or appointed government bodies	52	53	7	7
Libraries..........................	52	53	7	7
Professional organizations...........	52	53	6	6
Fraternal organizations.............	50	51	9	9
Labor unions......................	38	38	10	10
Inter-agency councils................	32	32	4	4
UNESCO organizations.............	29	29	5	5
Other.............................	20	20	3	3

rurality of the radio audience. Radio program directors for the more rural audiences report higher percentages of use for nearly all organizations. Especially is this true for farm organizations, the Cooperative Extension Service, and colleges and universities. The more urban stations report higher percentages of station use on the part of government bureaus, political parties, and welfare councils.

Of the specific farm organizations mentioned by radio program directors as having used and participated in radio programs, 4-H clubs, Home Demonstration clubs, the Cooperative Extension Service, and other organizations are checked most often. These groups are checked as having used the radio station 32 times for stations having more than 50 per cent rural audiences and only 17 times for stations having less than 50 percent rural audiences. The Farm Bureau (33 mentions) and FFA and vocational agricultural groups (18 mentions) are also checked most frequently by the more rural stations. The Grange, Soil Conservation Service and Farmers Union are the only other groups mentioned more than three times.

Other community groups receiving frequent mention as interested in the radio station include the following:

	Number of mentions
Parent Teacher Association	60
American Legion	58
Armed Forces	55
V.F.W.	50
Kiwanis	39
Rotary	36
Lions	36
Medical associations	30
Chambers of commerce	29
Federated women's clubs	26
Treasury Department	22
League of Women Voters	21

Adult Education Programs in the Three Fields.—The activity of radio stations in international understanding, strengthening democracy and the economy in the past month was requested. It must be remembered that the results of the questions concerning programming are samplings and tell us nothing concerning over-all activities in the three fields.

Table 2 serves to summarize the results of the following request: "We are interested in the programs and activities carried on in rural areas for adults in three fields, namely: (1) international understanding for peace, (2) strengthening of democracy and (3) understanding and strengthening of the economy. Kindly give us the following information regarding any program or programs your station may have broadcast in these three fields in the past month." Of the total number of radio program directors reporting, 47 failed to indicate a program falling in any of the three fields of interest. Twenty-eight, or more than one-fourth, however, listed between 2 and 5 programs. As indicated later many of the program directors had difficulty in classifying their programs as definitely falling in the three areas of interest, as suggested in the following quotation from a smaller station in Ohio:

Our local energies are directed at local programming and local problems. While these in many cases touch on the three points you have enumerated, they do not consistently deal with them. These problems are handled better than we could handle them by the network with its larger budget and greater influence in gathering material and well informed speakers. The 'America's Town Meeting of the Air' program listed is the longest sustained program which threshes out problems of all types that we have on the air.

Another similar theme comes from a Kentucky station:

We do not schedule a regular program dealing with any of these subjects specifically, other than UN ON THE RECORD. However, each of these fields forms the basis for many of our regular discussion programs both on AM and TV. We draw on a large number of citizens from both the local community and from the region at large, and where possible utilize visitors from other parts of the United States and

TABLE 2

Number of Programs, Field, Time of Day, Frequency, and Groups Cooperating in Programs Falling in the Three Fields of Interest Reported by Radio Station Program Directors, by Rurality of the Station Audiences

Number, fields, time, frequency, and groups cooperating	Total	Audience under 50% rural	Audience 50% rural and over	Rurality N.A.
Number of programs				
Total stations	107	50	49	8
None	47	23	19	5
One	21	9	9	3
Two to five	28	12	16	—
Five or more	11	6	5	—
Fields of programs				
Total programs*	151	77	72	2
International understanding	21	11	10	—
Strengthening democracy	34	14	18	—
Understanding and strengthening economy	24	20	4	2
Combination	72	32	40	—
Time of day				
Total reporting*	162	88	73	1
Morning	30	17	13	—
12–2 P.M.	23	12	11	—
2–6 P.M.	35	15	20	—
6–8 P.M.	28	14	14	—
8–12 P.M	46	30	15	1
Frequency of program				
Total reporting*	147	76	69	2
Once per month	28	11	17	—
Two to five	82	42	40	—
Five or more	37	23	12	2
Groups cooperating				
Total reporting*	175	89	84	2
Local	81	45	36	—
National or state	65	33	32	—
None (station staff)	29	11	16	2

* Total numbers reporting vary due to incomplete response to the questions.

foreign countries. These are unscripted and unrehearsed, and except in special instances are not, so far as I know, used as the basis for regular study or follow-up discussions. They do, however, have a rather large audience as audiences go for this type of program.

Our feeling in general is that it is better to bring this kind of material into established programs where possible, insuring a large and loyal audience, rather than segregating it in a slot which might be shunned by the very people who should be the listeners.

Still another poses the problem clearly:

It is very hard in covering anything as widespread as programming on radio to get a clear cut answer without minimizing the field. It might be better if you want to follow this up to ask some of the stations for a typical week or typical month of what we log as public service programming.

Even this is very comprehensive and includes everything from canned fifteen minute programs from the American Red Cross, the American Legion, Adventure in Science and Research, Army and Navy Recruiting, Bond Selling, and all of the other government activities. It includes local talks by agricultural extension agents, FFA, and 4-H groups, at least fifteen minutes a day of religious programming, and scores of other things that are touched on every day in American life which need expression and communication to the public.

I do not want to try to infer that we have some better way of doing the job, but only that it is very difficult for small stations operating with a small staff to make any kind of comprehensive report that means anything.

For example, we might say that the second of the three groups, 'The Strengthening of Democracy' might cover everything from all of the programs we carried last year for the Boy Scouts of America under the heading 'Strengthen The Arm of Liberty,' or even to the Jaycees annual campaign of 'Speak Up For Democracy.'

Among the most successful programs reported in the three fields, a number should be mentioned. Station KOMO, Seattle, reported:

"UN Defenders," an interview (10:00 to 10:15 A.M.) with servicemen now fighting in Korea with the purpose of (1) indicating unity of UN forces (2) increasing defense productions (3) donating blood and (4) buying defense bonds.

It also listed:

"Declaration of Independence" a great books discussion from 6:00 to 6:30 P.M. sponsored by the Seattle Public Library.

Another falling in the area of interest is:

"Youth Views the News," 6:30 to 7:00 P.M. It consists of student views on three major news items of the day. The program travels from high school to high school in Washington. It is a town-meeting type program and received First Award from the Institute for Education by Radio-Television in 1951 for a program presenting public issues.

As its most successful program, Station KGPH in Flagstaff, Arizona reported on:

"Voice of the People" a community roundtable, (8:00 to 9:00 P.M.) four times per month. The school system, civil defense, city employees, armed forces, PTA, church groups, Health Department, etc., cooperate. Citizens participate.

Station KRON-FM in San Francisco listed:

"Orchestras of the World" a packaged program from the Economic Cooperation Administration in Washington as highly successful. This program consisted of 55 minutes of symphonic music and a five minute talk on ECA and its purposes.

Opinions Concerning Effective Procedures in Radio.—Responses to the question concerning ways and means of increasing audience participation in the fields of interest are interesting and valuable. The question is phrased as follows:

The mass media are often thought of as a one-way type of communication. That is, the listener has little opportunity to participate or respond. Various procedures have been developed to increase the participation of radio audiences.

In your judgment, which of the procedures to increase audience participation would be most effective in programs designed to promote: (1) International understanding for peace, (2) Strengthening of democracy and (3) Understanding and strengthening of the economy?

From an AM-FM station having a large audience comes the following suggestion:

Direct question sent in by phone on any subject that is being discussed in regard to International Understanding for Peace—democracy—and world economy.

Later in our program schedule (January) we will have a 45 minute program entitled 'Let's Talk It Over' covering a number of civil and civic questions. In this, telephone questions are invited.

Emphasis upon local participation comes as a suggestion from a small radio station (about 275,000 listeners) in Kentucky. The informant says:

It occurs to me that programs designed to aid these three aforementioned causes ... must involve the sagacious use of local leaders in a round table type of radio forum. Undoubtedly, all community stalwarts have decided views on the matters in question. Perhaps a clearer insight into these problems can be effected right here in the grass roots. Give local people a chance to speak up!

From another Kentucky station we have the following comments:

"Town-Meeting-of-the-Air-Type." Another suggestion, which has been used to advantage, is an invitation to listeners to send in or 'phone in' questions for a specific group of pre-announced participants. For instance, two weeks in advance of their appearance, listeners are invited to send in questions for the mayor, the chairman of the city council, the police chief, etc. This type program requires a lot of production and advance preparation, however, is effective.

The response from a small radio station in Wyoming is worthy of inclusion. To quote:

We don't think that the average station big or small, unless located in a university town, and getting assistance from the university, finds much interest among its listeners in this type of thing and we know from experience it is difficult to develop a program of this kind. *Town-Meeting* does the best job we believe—and it's a business with them. The public is as a rule pretty apathetic. Every now and then some organization becomes pretty concerned about something, advises its membership to seek avenues of expression on the topic and we get into the picture. If some one objects to the view expressed we grant equal time—if requests come from responsible sources. We won't let anyone come in and use our services just because he feels he should—we investigate it beforehand.

We feel that educators should express more of a spirit of cooperation with existing broadcast facilities. We feel too that they should review their requests in a more practical light than some of them seem to be doing.

The respondents to this questionnaire mentioned a total of 151 different programs. Thirty-four were classified as falling in the field of "Strengthening of democracy;" twenty-four were listed as "Understanding and strengthening of the economy, and twenty-one were listed as falling in the area of "International understanding for peace." The remainder, or 72 programs, were assigned to two or more of these fields. Eighty-one programs were checked as having had local cooperation; 65 had the cooperation of national or state groups; and the remainder were put on by stations, staffs.

SUMMARY

In summary, it would appear from the questionnaire evidence, that few mass media leaders—whether they be weekly newspaper editors, radio program directors, or information specialists at colleges and universities—are now concentrating their efforts in the three fields of interest. The efforts in the three broad areas appear to be incidental and not consciously directed to especially rural audiences. Although much work is now in progress in the field of rural adult education and while the channels of communication appear clear-cut, a major emphasis upon the three fields of concern is not discernible.

Weekly newspaper editors exhibit great interest in promoting international understanding, democracy, and an understanding of the economy. Many express a desire to do more than they are now doing and would welcome assistance. They frequently mention a willingness to use feature articles, the source of which is known, and they suggest more complete use of editorials and local tie-in appeals. Program directors of radio stations suggest town-meeting-of-the-air-type programs and local write-in programs as most effective in promoting the three fields. Although placing some confidence in written materials, college information specialists emphasize a "balanced program" in which all media are utilized.

Experts suggest that effective use of mass media to promote social objectives is contingent upon one or a combination of three conditions. First, the mass media must be monopolized and counter social objectives must be neutralized; second, the mass media must be used to canalize basic attitudes; and third, mass media must be supplemented through face-to-face contacts. Lazarsfeld and Merton say:

... These three conditions are rarely satisfied cojointly in propaganda for social objectives, to the degree that monopolization of attention is rare, opposing propagandas have free play in a democracy. And, by and large, basic social issues involve more than a mere canalizing of pre-existent basic attitudes; they call rather, for substantial changes in attitude and behavior. Finally, for the most obvious of reasons, the close collaboration of mass media and locally organized centers for face-to-face contact has seldom been achieved by groups striving for planned social change.[24]

In view of such conditions, it appears abundantly evident from our data that there is no monopolization of the mass media in rural areas to promote the three fields of interest. Although these areas may be and often are touched upon, there is no concerted, organized program to further the social objectives embraced by the three fields.

Our evidence, especially that deriving from weekly editors and college information specialists, shows that mass media in the three fields are being adapted to rural audiences. Such efforts serve unquestionably to canalize existing opinion. However, nothing approaching consensus exists among rural people as to international understanding, democracy, and strengthening the economy.

Our data supply little evidence of large scale supplementation of mass media with face-to-face discussion. While this technique is being used, especially by extension service and Farm Bureau groups, it is not commonly used in connection with the three fields of interest.

J. Allan Beegle
Department of Sociology and Anthropology
Michigan State College
East Lansing, Michigan

BIBLIOGRAPHY

A Selected List

Attitude of Rural People Toward Radio Service, Washington: U.S.D.A., January, 1946.
Barnhart, Thomas F., "Weekly Newspaper Management" in George L. Bird and Frederic E. Merwin, *The Newspaper and Society*, New York: Prentice-Hall, Inc., 1942.
Bartlett, Kenneth S., "Social Impact of the Radio," *ANNALS*, Vol. 250, March 1947, pp. 89–97.
Berelson, Bernard in Frances Henne, Alice Brooks and Ruth Ersted, *Youth, Communication and Libraries*, Chicago: American Library Association, 1949, pp. 14–54.
Beville, H. M., Jr., *Social Stratification of the Radio Audience*, Princeton University: Office of Radio Research, 1940.
Klapper, Joseph T., *The Effects of Mass Media*, New York: Bureau of Applied Social Research, 1949.
Lazarsfeld, Paul F., "Audience Research in the Movie Field," *ANNALS*, Vol. 254, November, 1947.

---

[24] Lazarsfeld and Merton, *op. cit.*, p. 117.

Lazarsfeld, Paul F., Berelson, Bernard and Gaudet Hazel, *The People's Choice*, New York: Duell, Sloan and Pearce, 1944.
Lazarsfeld, Paul F. and Kendall, Patricia L., *Radio Listening in America*, New York: Prentice-Hall, Inc., 1948.
Lazarsfeld, Paul F. and Merton, Robert K., "Mass Communication, Popular Taste and Organized Social Action" in Lyman Bryson, *Communication of Ideas*, New York: Harper and Brothers, 1948.
Lazarsfeld, Paul F. and Stanton, Frank N., *Radio Research 1941*, New York: Duell, Sloan and Pearce, 1941.
Lazarsfeld, Paul F. and Wyant, Rowena, "Magazines in 90 cities—Who Reads What?," *The Public Opinion Quarterly*, October, 1937.
Radio Families—USA, New York: Broadcast Measurement Bureau, 1948.
Report of the Public Library Inquiry, *The Library's Public*, New York: Columbia University Press, 1949.
Smith, Joel, *The Characteristics of Magazine Audiences—A Survey of the Literature*, New York: Columbia University Masters Thesis, 1950.
Wilson, Louis R., *The Geography of Reading*, Chicago: American Library Association and the University of Chicago Press, 1938.

Chapter 14:

RURAL ADULT EDUCATION—THE OVER-ALL PICTURE

Most of the social systems and organizations contacted in this study not only have adult educational programs and activities but most of them have programs in at least one of the three fields: (1) international understanding for peace, (2) strengthening of democracy, and (3) understanding and strengthening of the economy. This fact is shown in Table 1. Since the figures presented in this Table were based upon returns from mailed questionnaires and the percentage of replies was not great, we may assume that the percentages are somewhat too high to represent the country. However, the data are useful in studying the nature of existing programs and activities of adult education.

Systems and Channels of Communication.—Throughout this report we have stressed the fact that educational and action programs designed for communities must, in most cases, be carried on within the existing formal and informal organizational structure and in accordance with the value systems of the people using these systems. In all communities and particularly in rural communities the informal groupings of friends, relatives and associates form the basis of the more formal systems and organizations. Unfortunately, we do not know just how the informal relationships become articulate through the formal structure. We have our own general knowledge based upon research and experience but our information in this area is inadequate. In the study, for example, it was not uncommon for a service club leader to indicate that his organi-

TABLE 1

Number and Percentage of Organizations Responding Affirmatively That They Have General Educational Programs or Activities for Adults, and Affirmatively That Such Programs or Activities in the Three Fields of Interest Were Sponsored in the Past Year

Organization	General educational programs or activities for adults — Number responding	Percent yes	Educational program or activity for adults in three fields in past year — Number responding	Percent yes
Schools	813	63	569	40
Cooperative Extension Service	590	100	578	89
Farm organizations	949	87	805	76
Farm Bureau	404	96	366	79
Grange	307	92	258	72
Farmers' Union	120	98	121	91
Cooperatives	78	49	60	45
Civic and service clubs	1599	65	1400	66
Lions	217	45	183	51
Rotary	145	57	128	86
Kiwanis	101	48	78	74
Optimist	9	44	8	63
Civitan	7	29	3	67
Altrusa	7	71	5	80
Quota	4	50	3	67
General Federated Women's Clubs	283	76	234	80
Business and professional women's clubs	65	69	52	87
American Association of University Women	35	97	35	100
League of Women Voters	29	100	28	100
Parent-Teachers Association	533	76	522	57
Chamber of Commerce	91	41	65	49
National Association for the Advancement of Colored People	12	67	12	83
County Medical Society	61	41	44	41
Government bureaus	241	88	212	57
Farmers Home Administration	89	88	78	62
Soil Conservation Service	99	96	92	54
Production and Marketing Association	53	72	42	52
Libraries	238	43	102	59
Churches	211	45	179	80
Diocesan rural life leaders	36	53	29	86
Protestant ministers	175	43	150	79
Continuation Education Departments	986	68	592	73

zation worked most with or through the local school. Frequently these civic club officials are school staff members. Also many of the same leaders gave a local church as the organization with which their civic clubs worked most, and we know that frequently this leader is an officer in the church on which he is reporting. However, the nature of the present study did not permit investigating these phenomena, and we know very little about the interrelationships of friendship and other informal groupings as structured into the formal groups we have been describing. We do not know precisely how to implement a given program of education falling in the three fields. Recent studies such as those presently being conducted by the Social Research Service of Michigan State College demonstrate that the organizational programs whereby rural communities obtain hospitals are very different from programs which result in communities obtaining public health services. But no one knows precisely the best organizational procedure with which to carry on a given community project, whether of an educational or activity nature.

If democracy is to be strengthened and our other objectives attained, such blind spots must be eliminated. We cannot use the know-how of the Communists because our goals are totally different. But one cannot read objective reports of their operations without believing they have fewer blind spots than we. So much space is given to our lack of knowledge because it is crucial for the program of the Fund for Adult Education. The author does not believe effective programs to attain the objectives of the Fund can be designed without further community research and experimentation carried on under carefully and intelligently designed programs.

INTER-SYSTEM COMMUNICATION

As Figure 1 indicates, the study staff has attempted to increase the knowledge available on inter-agency communication. All informants were requested to answer the following question: "What other organizations do you work with, or through, in your educational work with adults?" This question was followed by the request: "Check as many as apply," and a list of 20 organizational categories plus an "others (specify)" category. Figure 1 illustrates how the principal systems or organizations in rural America work together to achieve their objectives.

Core Groupings of Agencies in Communication.—As in the case of individuals, organizations vary in the frequency and intensity with which they work together in obtaining their objectives or meeting their respective needs. Figure 1 indicates that the category "farm organizations" was mentioned most frequently as cooperating by nine organizations, "schools" by five organizations and "churches and religious organizations," by four. Those three organizations were mentioned second most frequently by a total of ten organizations. Thus, the importance of these three organizations in the adult educational network in rural areas is crucial. In addition, frequent mention was made of the Cooperative Extension Service, and civic and service clubs. Figure 1 must be interpreted with caution, however. The chart is designed to show only those organizations which work together most frequently and intensively, as judged by the frequency of mention by leaders. Thus the "Big 5" organizational categories mentioned above received eight out of every ten "most frequent" mentions whereas the remaining categories received only two out of ten of the mentions of leaders requested to indicate "names of three organizations with which you

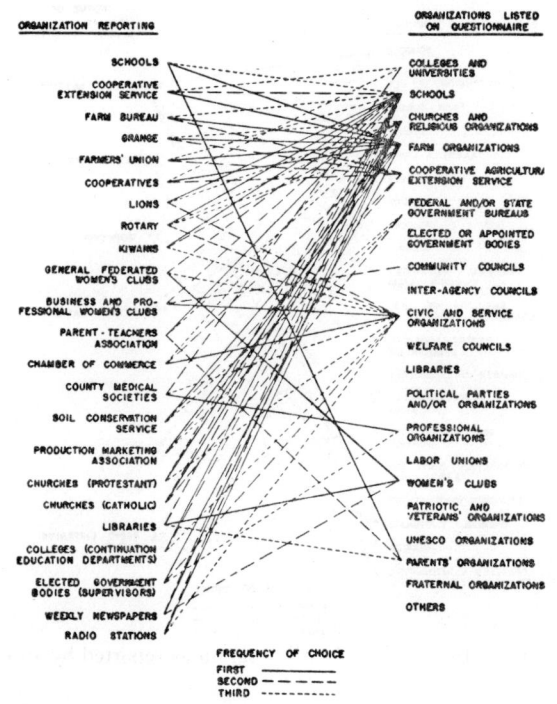

Fig. 1.—Ranking of groups through which specified organizations work in their adult education activities.

work most." Some of the less frequently mentioned organizations such as labor unions are not prevalent in rural areas; whereas the church, for example, is everywhere.

Other organizations than the "Big 5" play relatively insignificant roles in the cooperative communication system whereby rural people may be reached across organizational lines. This is not to infer that systems such as fraternal organizations and community councils, which were listed on the schedule sent to the leaders, do not participate actively in the adult educational process. However, the "Big 5" organizations are the ones the propagandist or expert in psychological warfare would, other things being equal, want to get control over or access to.

Although it is common knowledge that professional organizations and farmers' organizations, attempt to influence legislation through their lobbies, only a few organizations mentioned government bodies as a type of organization with or through which it worked in adult education. Apparently, applying political pressure is not considered "working with or through" government bodies. This and many similar shortcomings of the present study might have been surmounted if a series of community studies based on field interviews

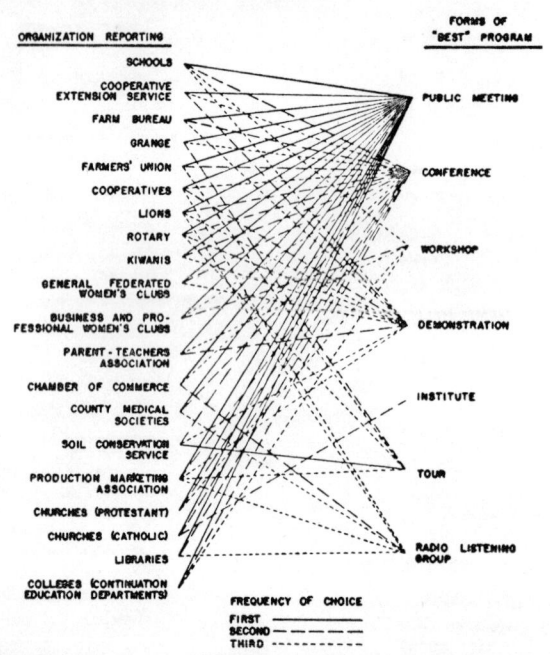

Fig. 2.—Ranking of the form of "best" program as reported by specified organizations.

had been possible. Such studies would have enabled the investigators to describe the relationship and importance of family, friendship and organizational groups for the communication system in general. Also the function of such factors as social stratification, demography and ecology could have been studied more effectively.

FORMS AND PROCEDURES USED

BEST PROGRAMS AND ACTIVITIES IN THE THREE FIELDS

Forms of Best Programs.—Figure 2 and Table 2 present a summarization of the data collected from the request on the questionnaire: "Please check the form or forms which your best program or activity in the three fields took." The following categories were available to be checked: "Conference, Workshop,

TABLE 2

Number and Percentage of Organizations Responding on the Form or Forms of the Best Program or Activity in the Three Fields of Interest

Organization	Number responding	Percent responding							
		Public meeting	Conference	Work shop	Demonstration	Tour	Radio listening group	Institute	Other
Schools	370	68	31	28	28	4	6	4	12
Cooperative Extension Service	531	82	31	17	53	28	22	11	7
Farm organizations	673	84	31	11	19	14	11	6	—
Farm Bureau	324	84	32	9	18	17	10	6	—
Grange	202	80	21	10	25	5	5	4	—
Farmers' Union	115	93	46	20	10	25	21	10	—
Cooperatives	32	84	19	6	22	9	19	6	—
Civic and service clubs	924	78	17	12	14	5	8	4	12
Lions	93	84	22	8	9	2	9	5	15
Rotary	110	53	19	4	7	7	5	2	23
Kiwanis	58	64	16	3	19	7	10	2	16
Optimist	5	60	—	20	—	—	20	—	—
Civitan	2	100	—	—	—	—	—	—	—
Altrusa	4	—	—	—	—	—	—	—	—
Quota	2	—	—	—	—	—	—	—	50
General Federated Women's Clubs	186	67	13	10	12	5	7	5	14
Business and professional women's clubs	45	76	20	22	13	2	9	2	9
American Association of University Women	35	60	9	31	—	9	11	—	34
League of Women Voters	28	75	21	46	—	4	14	7	11
Parent-Teachers Association	296	100	15	13	24	4	3	2	5
Chamber of Commerce	32	88	38	3	6	19	41	12	—
National Association for the Advancement of Colored People	10	100	50	30	20	10	20	10	—
County Medical Society	18	61	22	11	6	6	17	—	28
Government bureaus	165	59	42	2	42	45	10	2	12
Farmers Home Administration	62	48	53	2	34	34	5	2	19
Soil Conservation Service	68	65	32	3	62	69	12	1	7
Production and Marketing Association	35	69	40	3	17	17	17	3	9
Libraries*	—	—	—	—	—	—	—	—	—
Churches	144	73	39	17	12	3	7	21	10
Diocesan rural life leaders	23	57	39	13	13	4	9	39	—
Protestant ministers	121	76	39	18	12	3	7	17	12
Continuation Education Departments	402	49	38	27	12	7	14	20	22

* Rank order mentioned and not percentages are available for librarians, namely, 1—public meetings, 2—conferences, 3—radio listening groups, 4—workshops, 5—demonstrations, 6—institutes, and 7—tours.

Public meeting, Demonstration, Institute, Tour, Radio Listening groups, and Others (Specify)." All of the organizations except the Soil Conservation Service mentioned public meetings most frequently as the form of their "best" program in the three fields of interest. The Soil Conservation Service mentioned tours most often. As indicated by Figure 2, conferences were given many second-place mentions. Of special interest are radio listening groups, mentioned second most frequently by Cooperatives and third most often by the Farmers'

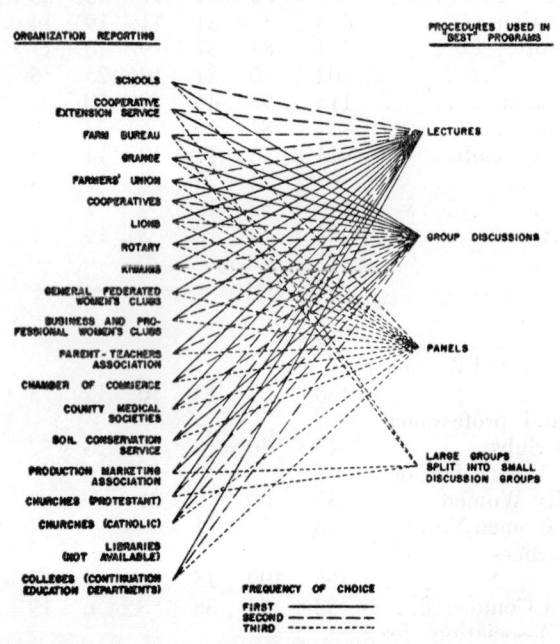

Fig. 3.—Ranking of procedure used in "best" program as reported by specified organizations.

Union, Libraries, the American Association of University Women and County Medical Societies.

Procedures Used in Best Programs.—Figure 3 and Table 3 present a summarization of the data gathered from the question: "In conducting the program or activity what procedures were used?" The following categories were listed: "Lectures, Group discussion panels, Large groups split into small discussion groups, and Others (Specify)." The organizations or systems reported lectures and group discussion equally often. These two types of procedures were given either first or second place in order of frequency of mention. Panels were mentioned often but ranked third for all except three of the organizations reporting. The three remaining organizations mentioned large groups split into small discussion groups as the procedure used in their best programs in the three fields.

TABLE 3
Number and Percentage of Organizations Responding on the Procedures Used in the Best Program or Activity in the Three Fields of Interest

		Percent responding			
Organization	Number responding	Lecture	Group discussion	Panel	Small group	Other
Schools	387	70	74	28	14	14
Cooperative Extension Service	509	70	83	24	26	24
Farm organizations	755	64	83	21	18	1
Farm Bureau	360	55	88	17	20	1
Grange	249	72	73	21	17	1
Farmers' Union	117	68	92	32	15	1
Cooperatives	29	76	62	31	7	3
Civic and service clubs	924	86	62	32	9	10
Lions	93	100	56	9	2	15
Rotary	110	90	39	15	4	10
Kiwanis	58	86	34	10	—	12
Optimist	5	80	60	—	—	—
Civitan	2	100	—	—	—	—
Altrusa	4	—	—	—	—	—
Quota	2	50	—	—	—	—
General Federated Women's Clubs	186	88	58	32	6	8
Business and professional women's clubs	45	82	56	40	11	9
American Association of University Women	35	74	63	43	29	9
League of Women Voters	28	64	82	54	32	18
Parent-Teachers Association	296	86	80	45	12	10
Chamber of Commerce	32	81	78	56	16	12
National Association for the Advancement of Colored People	10	80	80	40	20	10
County Medical Society	18	100	67	22	—	6
Government bureaus	172	45	85	17	12	33
Farmers' Home Administration	65	29	86	20	9	37
Soil Conservation Service	71	65	87	18	10	39
Production and Marketing Association	36	36	81	11	19	14
Libraries*	—	—	—	—	—	—
Churches	147	86	67	19	18	10
Diocesan rural life leaders	25	80	60	36	16	4
Protestant ministers	122	91	69	16	19	11
Continuation Education Departments	430	86	80	44	24	17

* Not available.

MASS MEDIA AS CHANNELS OF COMMUNICATION OF SOCIAL SYSTEMS

Figure 4 and Table 4 summarize the results of the analysis of the responses to the request: "Indicate mass media used in your programs or activities." The organizations reported using newspapers most frequently, but motion pictures received mention nearly as frequently. Agencies can, generally, more easily get space in newspapers than they can get radio time on the air. Also films can be rented or purchased and notices may be placed in local movie houses.

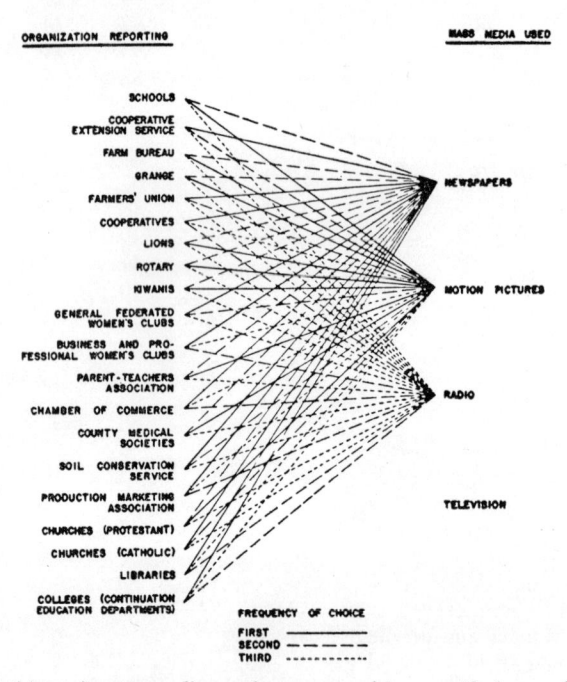

FIG. 4.—Ranking of mass media used as reported by specified organizations.

Only the leaders of the National Association for the Advancement of Colored People mentioned the radio more frequently than any other mass media. It is interesting to note that the League of Women Voters uses television to a greater extent than motion pictures.

As indicated by Figure 4, when the radio station directors and weekly newspaper editors were requested to indicate the organizations they worked with or through most, churches and religious organizations and schools were mentioned most frequently. Here again we find choice within the "Big 5" organizations mentioned above. An interesting exception is found for radio stations with less than one-half rural audience, where the otherwise seldom-mentioned category, government bureaus, receives frequent mention.

TABLE 4
Number and Percentage of Organizations Responding on Mass Media Used in Programs or Activities

Organization	Number responding	Movies	Newspaper	Radio	TV	Other
Schools	469	62	51	21	2	52
Cooperative Extension Service	585	68	99	70	4	2
Farm organizations	677	75	68	28	1	12
Farm Bureau	309	72	65	30	2	14
Grange	235	85	63	16	1	6
Farmers' Union	99	76	90	45	—	8
Cooperatives	34	44	74	50	6	35
Civic and service clubs	1349	39	34	17	3	7
Lions	121	50	25	12	1	12
Rotary	100	46	30	10	2	12
Kiwanis	80	36	34	23	1	6
Optimist	7	57	29	14	—	—
Civitan	4	50	25	25	—	—
Altrusa	4	50	50	—	—	—
Quota	4	100	—	—	—	—
General Federated Women's Clubs	214	30	44	14	3	9
Business and professional women's clubs	105	19	40	30	4	7
American Association of University Women	45	25	42	25	4	4
League of Women Voters	42	7	50	31	12	—
Parent-Teachers Association	505	50	30	14	3	3
Chamber of Commerce	73	16	36	32	1	15
National Association for the Advancement of Colored People	10	10	40	50	—	—
County Medical Society	35	37	31	14	6	12
Government bureaus	183	47	87	38	1	21
Farmers' Home Administration	57	25	86	33	2	21
Soil Conservation Service	93	69	95	41	1	4
Production and Marketing Association	33	24	70	39	—	70
Libraries	53	38	70	42	4	58
Churches	157	65	57	27	1	1
Diocesan rural life leaders	22	55	86	41	—	—
Protestant ministers	135	67	53	24	1	1
Continuation Education Departments	530	37	51	45	7	60

PARTICIPATION OF FOREIGN PERSONS ON PROGRAMS

The first hand contact which rural areas now have with other nations and peoples is one of the greatest and most impressive differences in rural life in

TABLE 5

Number and Percentage of Organizations Responding That a Foreign Person Appeared on a Program in the Past Year

Organization	Number responding	Percent responding YES
Schools	542	20
Cooperative Extension Service	563	52
Farm organizations	620	20
Farm Bureau	361	18
Grange	179	27
Farmers' Union	16	25
Cooperatives	64	13
Civic and service organizations	1346	37
Lions	164	34
Rotary	125	89
Kiwanis	85	64
Optimist	7	100
Civitan	4	0
Altrusa	5	63
Quota	3	100
General Federated Women's Clubs	258	36
Business and professional women's clubs	59	54
American Association of University Women	31	87
League of Women Voters	26	50
Parent-Teachers Association	479	17
Chamber of Commerce	53	19
National Association for the Advancement of Colored People	10	20
County Medical Society	37	5
Government bureaus	214	7
Farmers' Home Administration	78	9
Soil Conservation Service	93	4
Production and Marketing Association	43	7
Libraries*	—	—
Churches	176	47
Diocesan rural life leaders	25	25
Protestant ministers	151	48
Continuation Education Departments*	—	—

* Data not available.

the last two decades. Not only have sons and daughters fought in the armed forces abroad but Americans are travelling more abroad, and foreigners frequent rural communities much more than ever before. Table 5 summarizes the data gathered from responses of leaders to the question, "during the past year did any foreign person appear on your program?" Certainly the data presented in this table will impress those who are accustomed to think of rural people as provincial and anxious to avoid anyone foreign. The tremendous effort of civic, farm, and women's organizations in their efforts to understand and befriend foreign peoples, is indicated in this table.

ORGANIZATIONAL LEVELS SUITABLE TO THE ADVANCEMENT OF ADULT EDUCATION IN THE THREE FIELDS

Every organization of any size must determine the extent and principal directions of its activities as well as relevant administrative arrangements. Sometimes the nature of the agency itself and the institutional nature of its program determine its level of operation. Thus the school district is the chief stage upon which the drama of the individual school unit is played. The Soil Conservation District is the most important local unit of the Soil Conservation Service but this service has very strong national and regional administrative units. Also the district varies in size and nature.

After the staff had finished with the field work on the project and as a part of a questionnaire completed by the staff, members were requested to indicate percentage-wise the expenditures they would make for different levels if they had ample funds to advance adult education through social systems and organizations in the three fields of interest.[1]

All categories listed received some allocation of funds by staff members and there was considerable agreement concerning the organizational levels which should receive the most. Allocations were made for two categories, namely, (1) organization programs involving no mass media and, (2) such programs as involved mass media used with discussion groups. For both categories of organization, the levels or organization to which the staff allocated the highest proportions of funds were the following, in order of highest allocations to lowest: (1) local community or neighborhood, (2) state, (3) county, and (4) multi-county. Other organizational levels which received relatively small allocations were (5) national, (6) school district, (7) several communities combined and (8) the region. If the study staff's judgment is correct, these data support the thesis that adult education specialists, to be more effective, must learn more about the operation of social forces in the community, state and county.

OVERALL GENERALIZATIONS CONCERNING ADULT EDUCATION AGREED TO BY THE STAFF

The fieldwork finished and having filled out the questionnaire on the day preceeding, the staff spent the whole day attempting to arrive at basic generali-

[1] The reader is reminded that the staff would place most stress on carrying the programs through the organization categories, Farmers' Organizations, Schools, the Cooperative Extension Service, the Parent Teachers Association, Colleges and Universities, Civic and Service Organizations and Inter-Agency councils.

zations concerning adult education in the three fields of interest in rural areas. The following assumptions, in line with the work manual, were agreed upon: (1) participation in adult education programs is largely voluntary and (2) groups carrying on adult education programs are relatively autonomous.

The following are the generalizations agreed upon: There is on the part of all the organizations studied a very great need expressed for reliable and accurate information in the three fields and there was a strong desire indicated for critical evaluation by impartial agencies of the material available. Both the subject matter and the techniques by which it is employed should be adapted to the special needs and requirements of the agencies and organizations using it.

Adult education in general and in the three fields in particular will be made more effective if those who are responsible for it have training in appropriate organization skills and educational methods. All leaders involved in adult education in rural America need professional training and experience in rural life, the social sciences and adult education. Such training should be of professional level and coupled with in-service training. Relatively few leaders are sufficiently trained in these fields.

Although not all needs are met by the existing systems and organizations, more immediate progress can be made by working through existing organizations rather than by launching new ones. To be effective, adult education programs must begin with the interests and felt needs of both individuals and groups. Greater achievements in the three fields of special interest could be made if they were incorporated in meaningful and practical terms as organizational objectives of the agencies involved. There is a general and expressed need for improvement in organization; i.e., in making organizations more effective in attaining their present objectives in adult education. However, if agencies are to be continually effective, individuals and groups must be assisted in recognizing all their needs and relating their objectives to these.

For many rural agencies, participation of families as units is preferable to participation or training of individuals separately. In rural areas the family is a relatively important social system. Furthermore, the effectiveness of any mass media may be greatly increased by relating it to the system of interpersonal relationships. Pertinent to this generalization is the organization of discussion groups, radio listening groups, and many other groupings which use mass media.

In general, the more rural the area, the more disadvantaged it will be in non-vocational adult education facilities. This is true of resources, accessibility, and utilization of mass media and other facilities. Related to this generalization is the fact that local units require a minimum population and economic base in order to have an adequate service. Local areas with less than this minimum population and economic base cannot service the areas in which they operate adequately, except through cooperative relations with larger units.

Charles P. Loomis, Director of the Study
Social Research Service
Michigan State College
East Lansing, Michigan

APPENDIX A

The Contributors

Two major objectives are sought in presenting this section. The first is that of introducing and identifying the contributors of individual chapters to the study of adult education in rural areas. The second objective is that of suggesting the nature and varieties of the channels of communication in a number of the types of farming areas of the United States. In pursuing this objective, each of the contributors was requested to reconstruct from memory, the organizational affiliations and level of participation of his father and mother. Each was asked to recall the period when a youth of 15 to 20 years, still in the parental household. The assignment required each contributor to recall his parents' group affiliations and to estimate the extent of participation and interaction at the local, trade-center, county, and state or regional levels. The results were then portrayed graphically according to a standardized scheme. The contributors, arranged alphabetically, appear on the following pages.

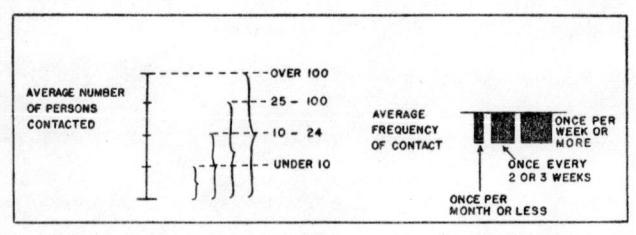

KEY

J. ALLAN BEEGLE

Allan Beegle, author of *The Mass Media of Communication*, Chapter 13, was born and reared on a farm near Bedford, Pennsylvania, in the general and self-sufficing type of farming area. He attended the local high school and was graduated from Penn State in 1939. He then took a Master's degree in rural sociology at Iowa State College in 1941. His Ph.D. degree, awarded in 1946,

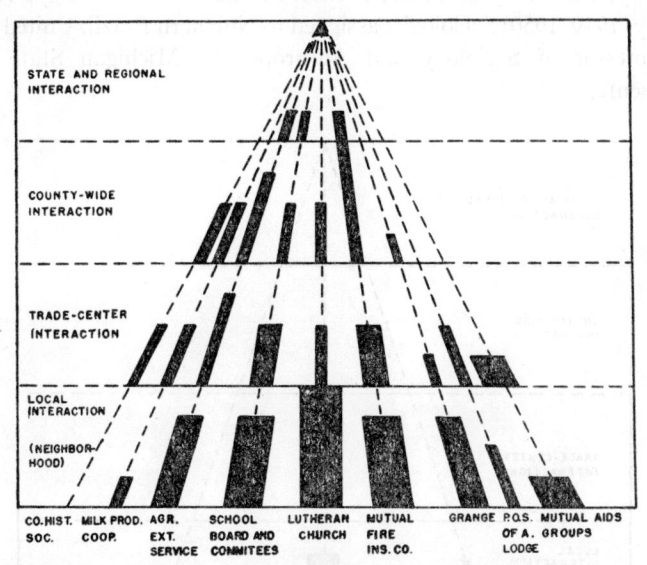

GROUP INTERACTIONS AT VARIOUS LEVELS—BEEGLE'S PARENTS
(Bedford County, Pennsylvania)

is from Louisiana State University where he specialized in rural sociology, demography and agricultural economics. He is now professor of Sociology and Anthropology at Michigan State College. Among his publications are *Rural Social Systems*, a textbook written in collaboration with Dr. C. P. Loomis, and numerous Experiment Station bulletins and journal articles.

OLEN LEONARD

Olen Leonard was born on a small farm and ranch in Wise County, Texas. After completing local primary and high schools he attended Texas A. and M. College for three years, transferring then to Fredericksburg State Teachers College in Virginia where he received a B.S. degree in 1931, with majors in mathematics and education. During 1937–39 he attended George Washington and American Universities in Washington, D.C. fulfilling all requirements for the Master's degree in sociology and anthropology with the exception of a thesis. From 1940–1943 he was a graduate student in sociology and anthropology at Louisiana State University where he received the Ph.D. degree in 1943.

His employment record includes the following: Teacher in Public Schools at Leesburg, Virginia, 1932–35; Social Scientist, Bureau of Agricultural Economics, U.S.D.A., 1936–43; Extension Specialist and Assistant Chief, Division of Training and Extension, Office of Foreign Agricultural Relations, U.S.D.A., 1944–46; Director, Cooperative Agricultural Experiment Stations in Bolivia, Office of Foreign Agricultural Relations, U.S.D.A., 1946–48; Associate Professor of Sociology, University of Texas, 1948–49; Professor of Sociology, Vanderbilt University, 1949–1950; Sociologist assigned to Northern Brazil, United Nations, 1951; Professor of Sociology and Anthropology, Michigan State College, 1951–present.

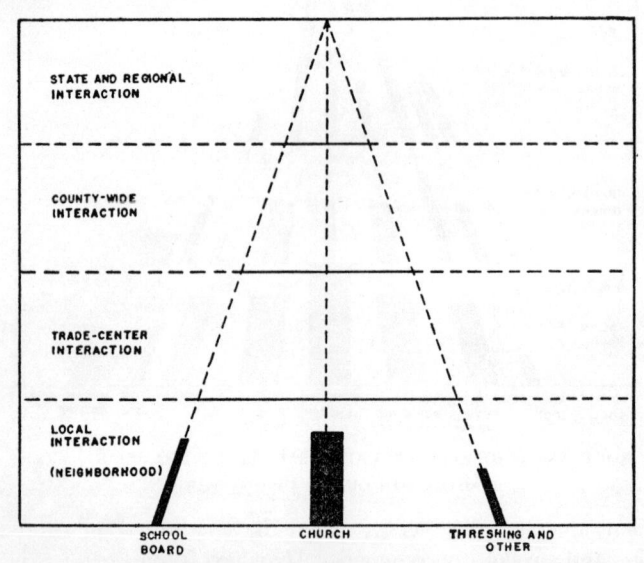

GROUP INTERACTION AT VARIOUS LEVELS—LEONARD'S PARENTS
(Wise County, Texas)

Major publications include: *Santa Cruz, Bolivia*. La Paz (Bolivia) Prensa Universal, 1947; *Canton Chullpas, Bolivia*. La Paz (Bolivia), Prensa Universal, 1948; *Role of the Spanish Land Grant in Social Organization and Processes of Spanish American Village*, Ann Arbor: Edward Brothers, Inc., 1946; Monographs for U.S. Department of Agriculture and United Nations Articles in Journals.

T. WILSON LONGMORE

T. Wilson Longmore, author of Chapter 7 and co-author of Chapter 6 of this report, was born in Louisville, Colorado, a rural mining town. His father was at various times farm owner, postmaster, merchant and billiard parlor operator. He attended small-town public elementary and parochial schools. The family moved from Colorado to Ohio and back again to Fort Collins where he attended high school and was graduated from Colorado A and M College in 1933. From 1933 through 1936, he taught in a 4-teacher rural consolidated high school located in a sugar beet farming area. Later he worked in the Colorado State Lands Use Planning Office on the campus at Fort Collins. Graduate study was taken at the University of Southern California and Colorado A and M College and the Master's degree was received from Louisiana State University in 1942. His Ph.D. was awarded in 1950 by Michigan State College, specializing in rural sociology. He is now social scientist in charge of standards and levels of living research in the United States Department of Agriculture. His major

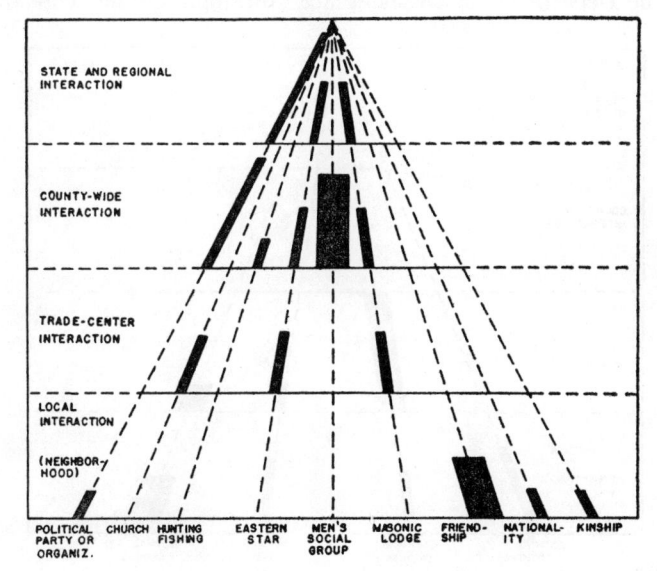

GROUP INTERACTIONS AT VARIOUS LEVELS—LONGMORE'S PARENTS
(Larimer County, Colorado)

publications include: co-author of *Rural Life in the United States, Experimental Health Program of the U.S. Department of Agriculture*, and a number of bulletins and articles.

CHARLES P. LOOMIS

Charles P. Loomis, author of the introductory and concluding chapters of this report and director of this study, was born on a farm near Brownfield, Colorado in 1905. In 1907 his family moved to Nebraska where he grew up on a 160-acre irrigated farm in school district # 8 near Gering in western Nebraska, between the Range-Livestock and the northern part of the southern Wheat Area. He attended the two-room country school in District # 8 and high school in the trade center of the area in Gering, three miles from the farm and business college in Scottsbluff, two miles beyond Gering. When 19 years of age his family sold the Nebraska property and moved to an irrigated farm near Las Cruces, New Mexico. He graduated from New Mexico College of Agriculture and Mechanic Arts in 1928, took his Master's degree in rural sociology, agricultural economics and psychology in 1929 at North Carolina State College, and his Ph.D. in sociology and agricultural economics in 1932 at Harvard University. He has held teaching positions in Las Cruces, New Mexico, North Carolina State College and Harvard University and research and administrative positions in the Bureau of Agricultural Economics and the Office of Foreign Agricultural Relations in the United States Department of Agriculture. He is now head of the Department of Sociology and Anthropology and Director of the

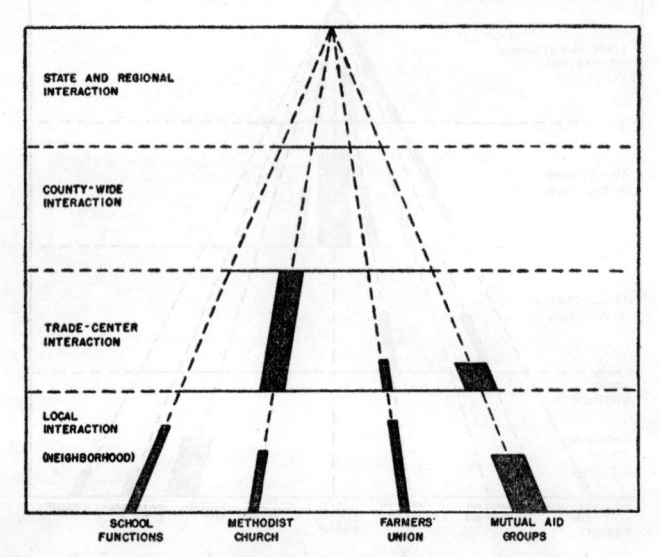

GROUP INTERACTION AT VARIOUS LEVELS—LOOMIS' PARENTS
(Scotts Bluff County, Nebraska)

Social Research Service and Area Research Center at Michigan State College. Among his publications are *Rural Social Systems*, a textbook written in collaboration with J. Allan Beegle, *Studies in Applied and Theoretical Social Science*, *Studies of Rural Social Organization*, and *Fundamentals of Sociology*, a translation of Ferdinand Tönnies' *Gemeinschaft and Gesellschaft*.

SHELDON G. LOWRY

Sheldon G. Lowry, co-author of the chapters on Foreign Student Exchange and Continuation Education, was born in Cardston, Alberta, Canada. He lived on his father's adjoining farms in Alberta and Montana, and he attended a two-room country school 3½ miles from home. This region borders the range-livestock and wheat (dry farming) areas. At the age of eleven he moved with his parents and two immediately older brothers to Kalispell, Montana. Three years later they moved to Provo, Utah where he attended high school and college. He graduated from Brigham Young University in 1946. He taught in the public schools in Pocatello, Idaho in 1946–47 and took his Master's degree in sociology and anthropology from Michigan State College in 1950. During the summer of 1950 he worked with the National Child Labor Committee on their study of Migrant Labor in Colorado. He was a graduate assistant in the Department of Sociology and Anthropology at Michigan State College four successive years, two teaching and two research. From January to

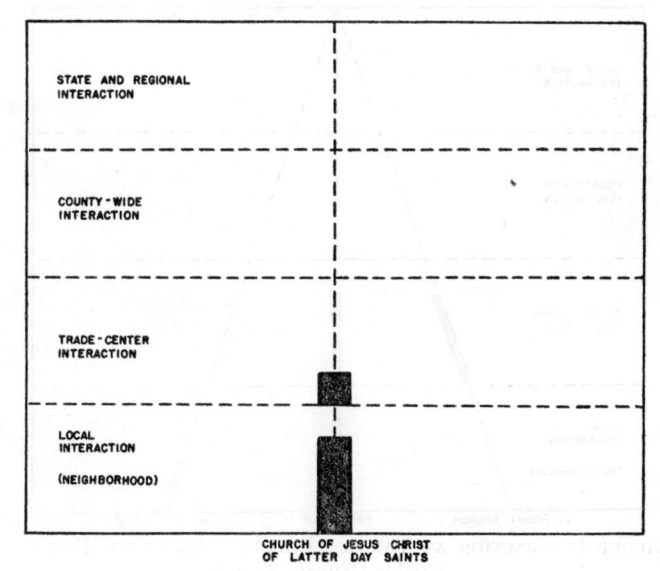

GROUP INTERACTION AT VARIOUS LEVELS—LOWRY'S PARENTS
(Utah County, Utah)

June 1952 he worked as a Research Associate with the Health Information Foundation where he was engaged in a study of health plans in industry. At the present time he is an assistant professor in the Department of Rural Sociology at North Carolina State College.

JOSEPH L. MATTHEWS

Joseph L. Matthews, author of Chapter 3 on the Cooperative Extension Service, was born in Sabinal, Texas in 1908, and was reared on a cattle ranch in the South Texas range-livestock area. He graduated from high school in Sabinal, and attended the University of Texas for two years. He was a professional agricultural worker for a number of years, including a period as county agricultural agent, then attended the Agricultural and Mechanical College of Texas, graduating with a B.S. degree in Agriculture in 1940. After graduation he was employed first as an agricultural planning specialist on the State Extension staff and later as county agricultural agent. During 1942–1944 he served in the Armed Forces, after which he returned to the State staff as planning specialist. In 1947 he received his M.S. degree from Texas A. and M. After a year's study at the University of Chicago in 1947–1948, he returned to the Texas Extension State staff where he was responsible for personnel training and evaluation of programs. He received his Ph.D. degree from the University of Chicago in 1951. In the same year he was appointed to his present position with the Extension Service, United States Department of Agriculture, in charge of the Educational

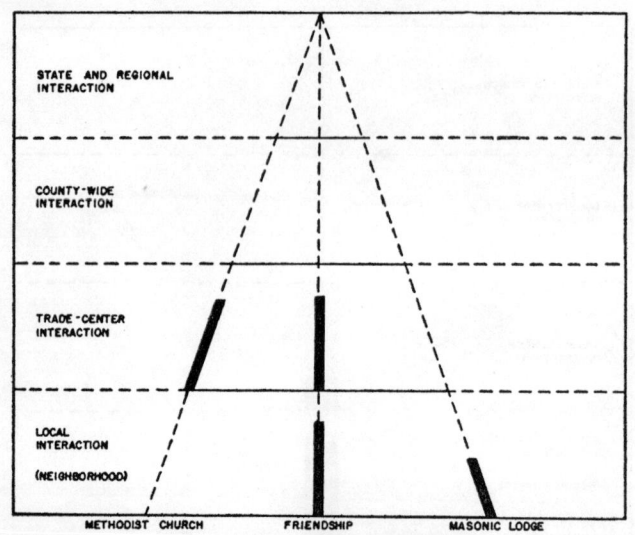

GROUP INTERACTION AT VARIOUS LEVELS—MATTHEWS' PARENTS
(Uvalde County, Texas)

Research Section, Division of Field Studies and Training. He has made or contributed to a wide range of research and field studies, the most recent of which is published as Extension Service Circular No. 477, "National Inventory of Extension Methods of Program Development."

FRANK C. NALL

Frank C. Nall was born and reared in Detroit, Michigan. He attended one of the city's public high schools, after which he spent two years in the United States Navy. Upon finishing his naval service he entered Michigan State College where he received his Bachelor's degree in sociology and anthropology in 1951, and his Master's degree in 1953. He has pursued studies in France at the Sorbonne and the Institute d' Ethnologie as well as at the French National

Demographic Institute. He now holds an assistantship in the Area Research Service at Michigan State College.

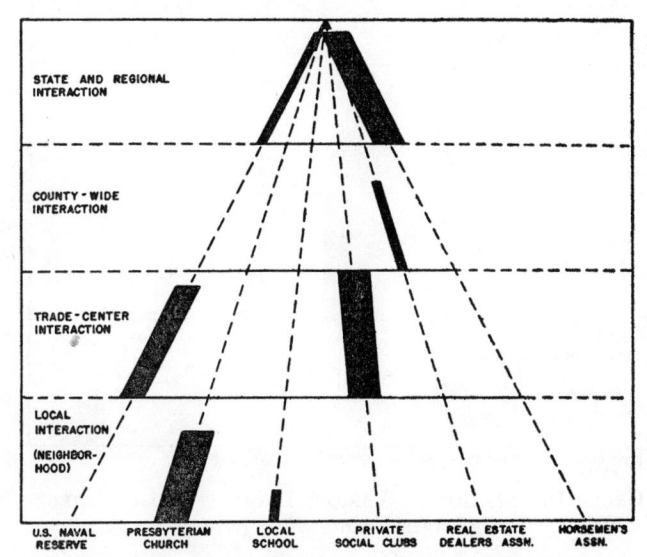

GROUP INTERACTION AT VARIOUS LEVELS—NALL'S PARENTS
(Wayne County, Michigan)

JACK J. PREISS

Jack J. Preiss, co-author of Chapter 12, on Local Government and Politics was born in New York City in 1919. His family moved to Hackensack, New Jersey, about six miles from New York, in 1929, and he attended public schools there. He graduated from Dartmouth College in 1940, with an A.B. in sociology.

Before entering the Army Air Corps in 1941, he worked on farms in Vermont, and was instrumental in setting up an experimental work camp operated by the U.S. Dept. of Agriculture. After a medical discharge from the Service, he worked in Washington for the War Production Board, and later for the Sikorsky Aircraft Corporation in Bridgeport, Connecticut.

In 1945 he attended Stewart Technical School in New York, and became a licensed aircraft and engine mechanic, as well as pilot. For the following four years he operated an airport business in Lebanon, New Hampshire, near Dartmouth.

He returned to academic work in 1950, and received his M.A. in sociology from Columbia University in 1951. For the past two years he has been a graduate teaching assistant in the Department of Sociology and Anthropology at Michigan State College.

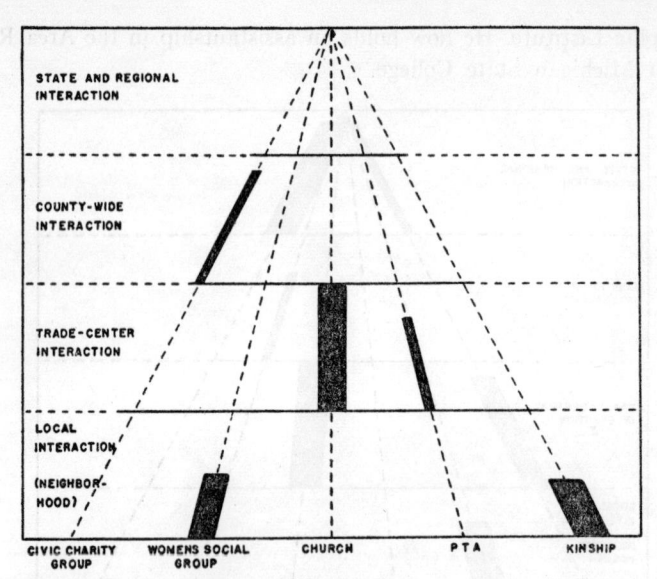

GROUP INTERACTION AT VARIOUS LEVELS—PREISS' PARENTS
(Bergen County, New Jersey)

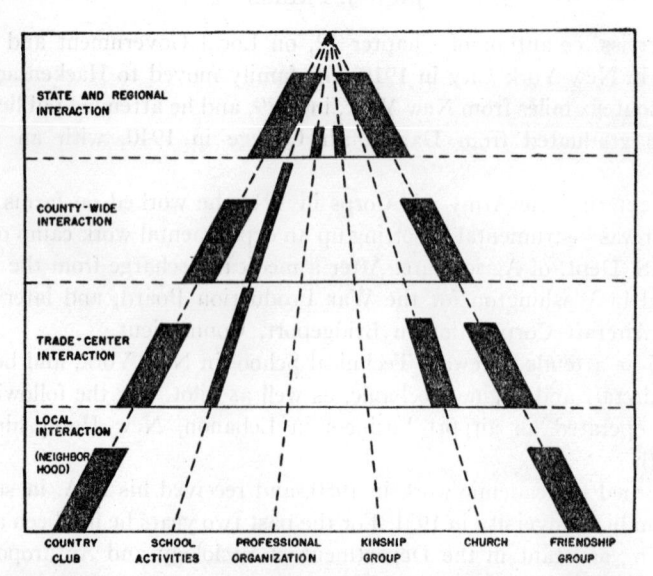

GROUP INTERACTION AT VARIOUS LEVELS—ROHRER'S PARENTS
(Green Lake County, Wisconsin)

WAYNE C. ROHRER

Wayne C. Rohrer was born in Milwaukee, Wisconsin. Both his parents had urban backgrounds. For the period 1924–1933, he lived in Green Lake County, Wisconsin in the diary type of farming area. Because of his fathers occupation the family was more located in, than a part of the rural culture of this area. His father is a professional golfer which occupation demands that the family move quite regularly "following the sun." The overriding consideration in the decision to settle in a permanent job in a warm climate was determined by the son's nearing high school age. After 1933, he lived in Galveston, Texas. High school was completed in 1937, and he attended Texas A. and M. College from 1938–1942. He completed his B.S. in rural sociology in 1946. After working for a regional farmers consumers' cooperative he returned to Texas A. and M. for graduate work, taking an M.S. degree in rural sociology in 1948. For the following year he worked as assistant professor (research) in the Texas Agricultural Experiment Station in rural sociology and land economics. He came to Michigan State College in 1949 to work toward the Ph.D. degree.

ORDEN C. SMUCKER

Orden C. Smucker, author of *Adult Education in the Rural Church*, Chapter 9, was born in the town of Goshen, Indiana in 1909 where his father was an in-

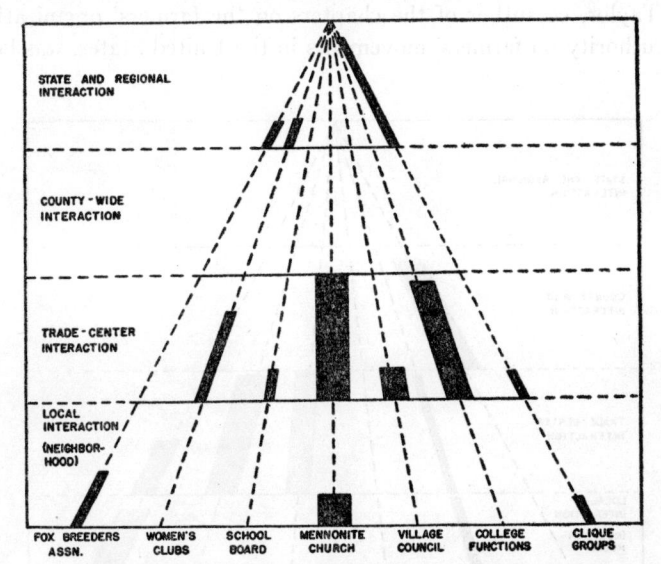

GROUP INTERACTION AT VARIOUS LEVELS—SMUCKER'S PARENTS
(Allen County, Ohio)

structor in speech at Goshen College, a Mennonite institution with a rural constituency. In 1912, his family and he moved to Phoenix, Arizona and in 1915

the family moved to Bluffton, Ohio where his father was a professor of speech
at Bluffton College, also a Mennonite institution with a rural constituency.
This is in the general and self-sufficing type of farming area. Here he attended
the grade school, high school and college, graduating with an A.B. degree in 1931.
He received the M.A. degree from the University of Chicago in 1933. His major
work was with the late Dr. Arthur E. Holt, nationally known leader in the
rural church and Dr. E. W. Burgess of the sociology department. After teaching for several years in a rural high school he entered the Ohio State University
from which he graduated in 1945 with the Ph.D. degree in sociology and a
minor in education. He has held teaching positions at Bluffton High School,
Bluffton College, the Ohio State University, Bowling Green (Ohio) State
University, Stephens College, San Francisco State College. He is now associate
professor of Social Science and a staff member of the Department of Sociology
and Anthropology at Michigan State College. He is also active in the adult
education work of the college, giving numerous courses off-campus in various
parts of the state. In research he has specialized in friendship groups, clique
structure and religious organization. He has published twelve articles in various
social science and education journals.

CARL C. TAYLOR

Carl C. Taylor, co-author of the chapters on the farmers' organizations and
leading authority on farmers' movements in the United States, was born on a

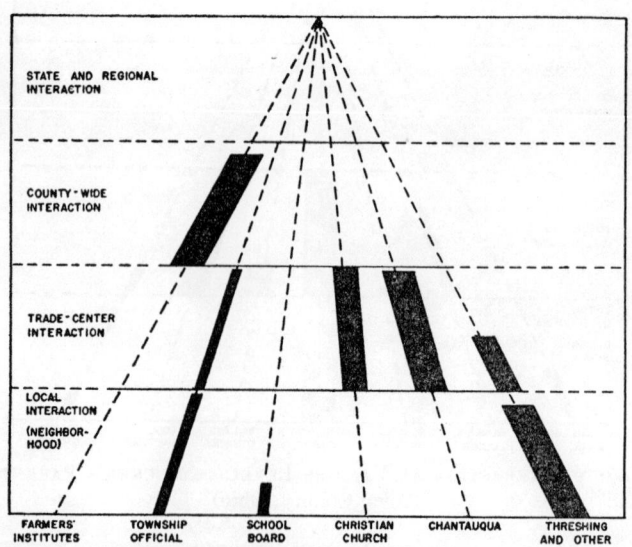

GROUP INTERACTION AT VARIOUS LEVELS—TAYLOR'S PARENTS
(Shelby County, Iowa)

farm in Shelby County, Iowa in 1884. He attended the local schools in Shelby County and operated the parental farm before proceeding to preparatory school and college at Drake University. His father, Capt. Taylor, was an outstanding farm leader in the county. Carl Taylor obtained his M.A. degree at the University of Texas and his Ph.D. at the University of Missouri. He was head of the Department of Sociology and Dean of the Graduate School at North Carolina State College. He also taught at the University of Texas, Mount Holyoke, Missouri, and North Carolina.

He was successively employed in research and administration in various government bureaus concerned with agriculture, including the Subsistence Homestead Division in the Department of the Interior, Regional Director of the Land Policy Section of the Agricultural Adjustment Administration, Assistant Administrator of the Resettlement Administration, and Head of the Division of Farm Population and Rural Life of the Bureau of Agricultural Economics in the United States Department of Agriculture. He has served as president of the American Sociological Society and the Rural Sociological Society.

He is author of numerous books and professional publications, including *The Social Survey: Its History and Methods, Rural Sociology, Human Relations, Rural Life in the United States,* and *Rural Life in Argentina.* A two-volume work on the farmers' movements in the United States is in the process of preparation.

JOHN F. THADEN

John F. Thaden, author of the chapter, "Adult Education in Public Schools," was born on a farm near Monticello, Iowa, in 1894. In 1900 his family and he moved to northeastern Nebraska where he grew up on a 320-acre farm near Randolph, in the Corn Belt. He attended a one-room country school in School District # 38 and later taught in one of the four schools in this district. He was one of 14 to graduate from Randolph High School in the class of 1914. Randolph was then a village with a population of about 1400. He was graduated from the College of Agriculture, University of Nebraska in 1920 with a major in agricultural economics. He completed his work for the Master's degree at Iowa State College in 1922. Work toward the doctorate was pursued at Columbia University in 1922–1923. He completed the doctorate in sociology and economics at Michigan State College in 1930. He held teaching positions at the School of Agriculture, University of Nebraska and teaching and research position at Iowa State College and Michigan State College. He is now associate professor of Sociology and Anthropology at Michigan State College and Research Associate with the Agricultural Experiment Station. Among his publications is a chapter titled, "Adult Education" in *Sociological Foundations of Education—A Textbook in Educational Sociology,* edited by Joseph S. Roucek in 1942, a chapter on "Leadership" in a textbook in introductory sociology, titled *Society Under Analysis*, published in 1942, and numerous research articles pertaining to demography and school district organization.

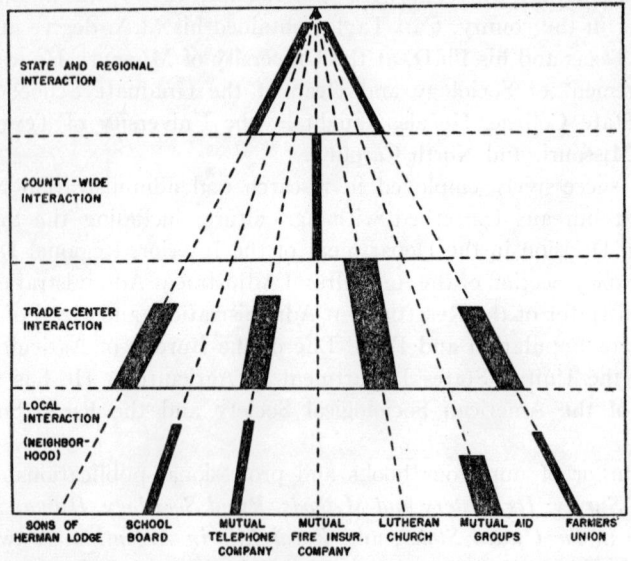

GROUP INTERACTION AT VARIOUS LEVELS—THADEN'S PARENTS
(Cedar County, Nebraska)

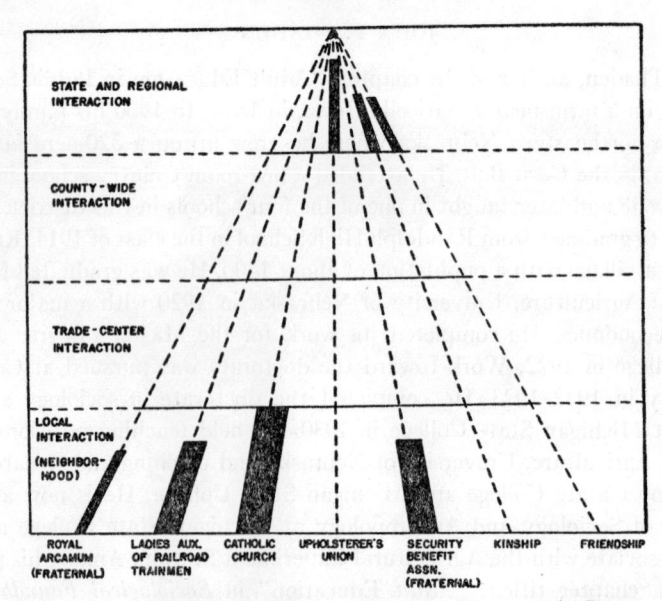

GROUP INTERACTION AT VARIOUS LEVELS—WARNEKE'S PARENTS
(Cook County, Illinois)

RUTH WARNCKE

Ruth Warncke, author of Chapter 8, was born and reared on the southwest side of Chicago. She attended Lindblon High School, and Crane Junior College (city college). She received a B.S. in education from the University of Illinois in 1931, and an M.A. in English literature from the University of Chicago in 1932. Miss Warncke studied in the graduate school of education at Northwestern University at intervals from 1935–1939 and took a B.S. in library service from Columbia University in 1942.

She taught upper grades and served as teacher-librarian, Glenview, Illinois, 1933–1941. (Suburban community—2,000 population) Her other positions include: Head of young adult department, Schenectady, New York, 1942–1944; Reader's Advisor, Grand Rapids Public Library, 1944–1945; Director of Adult Education, Kent County, under Michigan Experimental Program in Adult Education, 1944–1947; Kent County librarian, 1947 to the present time.

EDWARD W. WEIDNER

Edward W. Weidner, was born in Minneapolis, Minnesota, 1921. He has spent all of his time in urban communities with the exception of a number of summers

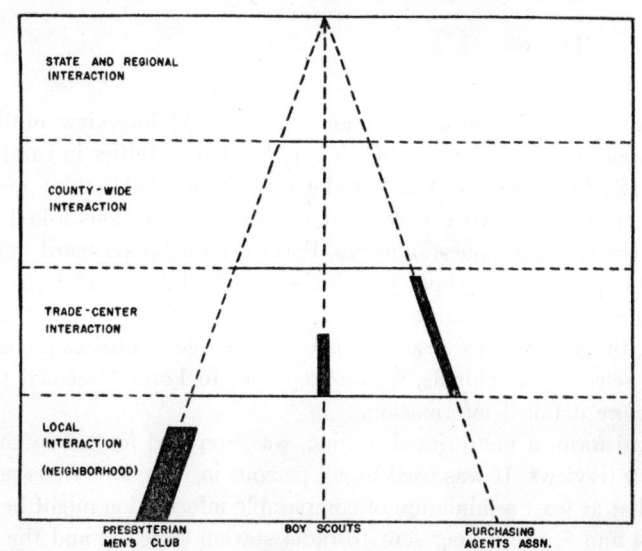

GROUP INTERACTION AT VARIOUS LEVELS—WEIDNER'S PARENTS
(Hennepin County, Minnesota)

during which he lived in rural areas, and except for a very large number of field trips which were to the rural areas. He received his B.A. in 1942 from the University of Minnesota, and his M.A. in 1943 from the same institution.

After a year's graduate work at the University of Wisconsin, a year's employment with the National Municipal League in New York City, he received his Ph.D. from the University of Minnesota in political science in 1946. He had held teaching positions at the University of Wisconsin, the University of Minnesota and the University of California at Los Angeles and Michigan State College. He is presently Director of the Governmental Research Bureau at Michigan State College, and professor of Political Science. Among his publications are *American State Government*, a textbook written in collaboration with William Anderson; *State and Local Government*, a textbook written in collaboration with William Anderson; co-editor of a series of 10 monographs on *Inter-Governmental Relations, County Boards and Commissions*, and *The American County-Patchwork of Boards*.

APPENDIX B

Schedules Used in Study of Adult Education in Rural Areas

Eight printed questionnaire forms and one dittoed interview outline were prepared and used in our study of adult education activities in rural areas of the United States. A sample of each of the forms is included in this appendix.

Form 1, printed in two versions but identical in questions asked, was the most widely-used of the questionnaires. Form 1, a double postcard, was mailed to such groups as high school principals, rural ministers, civic and service organizational personnel, and to county agents and home demonstration agents.

Form 2, the most extensive and detailed of the questionnaires prepared, was mailed to selected individuals, whose responses to Form 1 seemed to justify securing more detailed information.

The third form, a non-printed outline, was prepared for use in connection with field interviews. It was used by all persons in their interviews as a guide in order that at least a minimum of comparable information might be secured.

Forms 4 and 5, the former sent to radio station directors and the latter to weekly newspaper editors, provided the basic information contained in the chapter dealing with the mass media.

Form 6, a double-postcard questionnaire was mailed to a sample of librarians in the United States. This form was utilized exclusively in the study of the library's activities in the field of adult education in rural areas.

Form 7 was prepared to obtain a picture of the foreign-student program in our colleges and universities. Foreign student advisers and others acquainted with the foreign student programs were requested to provide information relating to adult education on this form.

Form 8, designed for information services departments in our colleges and universities, yielded information contributing to the mass media chapter. Among others, this questionnaire was mailed to all Experiment Station and Extension Service editors at the Land-Grant institutions.

Form 9 was prepared to assess the adult educational activities of the farm organizations. This form was mailed to samples of the Grange, Farm Bureau, Farmers' Union and Farmers' Cooperative Organizations.

In addition, the questionnaire entitled, "Opinions, Attitudes, Judgments and General Thinking of the Staff of the Study of Adult Education in Rural Areas," is included.

Form 1

The Fund for Adult Education of the Ford Foundation has asked us to find out what types of educational programs are being carried on among rural people in the United States. Will you please help us by answering this brief questionnaire and returning it promptly? Thank you.

Organization for which you are reporting..

A. Does your organization have any educational programs or activities for adults?

YES ☐   NO ☐

    1. If yes, about how many different people were reached last year?................
Of these, how many live in the open country or in centers of less than 2,500 people?
Check one: Almost none ☐   About ¼ ☐   About ½ ☐   About ¾ ☐   Almost all ☐

B. Indicate mass media used in your programs or activities: ☐ Radio   ☐ Television

    ☐ Newspapers   ☐ Motion pictures   ☐ Other (Specify)................   ☐ None

C. During the past year did any foreign person appear on your program?   YES ☐   NO ☐

D. What other organizations do you work with, or through, in your educational work with adults? (Check as many as apply)

    1-☐ Colleges & universities
    2-☐ Schools
    3-☐ Churches and religious organizations
    4-☐ Farm organizations
    5-☐ Cooperative Agricultural Extension Service
    6-☐ Federal and/or state gov't. bureaus
    7-☐ Elected or appointed gov't. bodies
    8-☐ Community councils
    9-☐ Inter-agency councils
    10-☐ Civic and service organizations
    11-☐ Welfare councils
    12-☐ Libraries
    13-☐ Political parties and/or organizations
    14-☐ Professional organizations
    15-☐ Labor unions
    16-☐ Women's clubs
    17-☐ Patriotic and veterans' organizations
    18-☐ UNESCO organizations
    19-☐ Parents' organizations
    21-☐ Fraternal organizations
    20-☐ Others (Specify)................

Of the above GENERAL TYPES of organizations which you have checked, list here the SPECIFIC NAMES of the three with which you work most. (List FIRST the ONE you work with most.)

1.................. 2....................... 3.........................

We are particularly interested in any programs or activities for adults which deal with the following three fields:

    1—INTERNATIONAL UNDERSTANDING FOR PEACE
    2—STRENGTHENING OF DEMOCRACY
    3—UNDERSTANDING AND STRENGTHENING OF THE ECONOMY

These programs or activities may have taken the form of conferences, workshops, demonstrations, meetings, contests, exhibitions, radio programs, institutes, organizing of councils, etc.

E. Was any program or activity for adults that included (1) international understanding for peace, (2) strengthening of democracy, or (3) understanding and strengthening of the economy, carried on within or by your organization during the past year?   YES ☐   NO ☐

    1. If YES, give name or brief description of your best program or activity................

    2. In your best program or activity, about how many different people were reached last year?...

—over—

Form 1—*Reverse*

Of these, how many live in the open country or in centers of less than 2,500 people?
Check one: Almost none ☐   About ¼ ☐   About ½ ☐   About ¾ ☐   Almost all ☐

3. Please check the form or forms which your best program or activity in the three fields took:
   ☐ Conference   ☐ Public meeting   ☐ Institute   ☐ Radio listening groups
   ☐ Workshop   ☐ Demonstration   ☐ Tour   ☐ Other (Specify)............

4. In conducting the program or activity what procedures were used?
   ☐ Lectures   ☐ Large groups split into small discussion
   ☐ Group discussions   groups
   ☐ Panels   ☐ Other (Specify)...................

Please go back to No. 4 and DOUBLE CHECK the procedure used most extensively.

F. If you know of any other outstanding programs or activities in these three fields, please give names, and addresses of persons who can give the most information about them.

              Name   Mailing Address   Organization
   ....
   ....

G. YOUR NAME........................... OCCUPATION.........................
MAILING ADDRESS..
October 29, 1951

SRS
Form 1

FIRST CLASS
PERMIT NO. 941
Sec. 34.9, P. L. & R.
East Lansing, Mich.

BUSINESS REPLY ENVELOPE
No Postage Stamp Necessary If Mailed in The United States

—POSTAGE WILL BE PAID BY—

Social Research Service
Michigan State College
East Lansing, Michigan

Form 2

Form 2, an amplification of Form 1, is a 15-page printed booklet and has not been reproduced here due to its length and complexity. Those interested may obtain a copy of it upon request to the Director of the Social Research Service, Michigan State College, East Lansing.

Form 3

Personal Interview

1. Origin and history of organization.
    a. When first began.
    b. Person or persons responsible for initiating work.
    c. Most important events in shaping direction of organization's work (i.e. any clashes with other and similar phases of work, association with development of other organizational work in locality or center, etc.).
2. Objectives of the organization.
    a. Original objectives and purposes.
    b. What respondent considers as present most important objectives.
3. Importance of and nature of program planning.
    a. Is it geared to the needs and desires of the local people or is it designed by experts and technicians at higher levels.
    b. How is it done, i.e., dictated from above, decided through staff conferences, or through meetings and contacts with local leaders, groups, requests, surveys, etc.
4. How policy is made in the organization.
    a. Interviewer probes for recent example.
    b. Interviewer probes to get composition of policy forming group or groups.
    c. Interviewer probes to determine how group or groups function in policy formation.
    d. Interviewer probes to ascertain whether policy sessions are (a) group centered, (b) leader centered, or (c) both.
    e. Interviewer probes to see how action is initiated when new policies are made.
    f. Interviewer probes to ascertain the nature of pressures exerted in policy formation.
5. In developing policies for adult education probe on same points as in question 4.
6. If not already revealed, probe to ascertain whether procedures in policy formation as stated are actually followed.
7. What is the spatial distribution of offices and personnel of organization? If possible show on a map (try to get a copy of the map).
8. If you could, would you do more in these three fields?

9. If yes, what are the obstacles (i.e. why they are not doing more).
    a. Attitudes of policy makers (boards, administration, etc.).
    b. Limitations on space and other facilities.
    c. Lack of tehnical guidance.
    d. Attitudes of local people.
10. Do the people in your organization have adequate training to handle these fields?   YES( )   NO( )

    If YES, what do they have?

    If NO, what do they need?
    Training in what skills? (Indicate fields, examples: sociology, psychology, economics, education, etc.)............................
    ....
    ....
    What attitudes or motivation?...............................
    ....

February 27, 1952

FORM 4

A STUDY OF ADULT EDUCATION

Sponsored by

The Association of Land-Grant Colleges and Universities

and

Fund for Adult Education of the Ford Foundation

Your name.................................Your street address................................

Radio station call letters..................City and State..................................

1. Please give us the following information concerning the coverage of your radio station.
    a. Approximately what radius does your station cover?................miles.
    b. Approximately what is the population within this radius?................persons.
    c. Approximately what percent of this number is rural (i.e., open country and centers under 2,500 population). Please check.

    1-[ ] 0–24%
    2-[ ] 25–49%
    3-[ ] 50–74%
    4-[ ] 75–100%

    d. How many hours per day on the average is your station on the air?...............................
    e. Has any study been made of your station's listening audience? Yes............... No...............
    f. If yes, are results available? Yes............... No...............
    g. If yes, would you please send me a copy of any such report?
    h. Approximately what percentage of the population of your area of coverage listens to your station? Please check.

    1-[ ] 0–24%
    2-[ ] 25–49%
    3-[ ] 50–74%
    4-[ ] 75–100%

2. Please check any of the following local groups that show an interest in your station (as indicated by use and participation):

    1-[ ] Colleges and universities

    2-[ ] Schools

    3-[ ] Churches

    4-[ ] Farm organizations (Specify)...

    5-[ ] Cooperative Agricultural Extension Service

    6-[ ] Government bureaus (Specify)..
    ....

    7-[ ] Elected or appointed government bodies..
    ....

FORM 4—*Continued*

8–[ ] Community councils

9–[ ] Inter-agency councils (Specify)..

10–[ ] Welfare councils

11–[ ] Civic and service clubs (Specify)...

....

12–[ ] Libraries

13–[ ] Political parties and/or organizations

14–[ ] Professional organizations (Specify)..

15–[ ] Women's clubs (Specify)...

16–[ ] Labor Unions

17–[ ] Patriotic and veterans organizations (Specify).........................

18–[ ] UNESCO organizations (Specify)...

19–[ ] Parents' organizations (Specify)...

....

20–[ ] Fraternal organizations

21–[ ] Other (Specify)..

   a. Please go back and **double check** the local groups which have **planned and presented their own** radio programs over your station.

3. We are interested in the programs and activities carried on in rural areas for adults in three fields, namely: (1) INTERNATIONAL UNDERSTANDING FOR PEACE, (2) STRENGTHENING OF DEMOCRACY and (3) UNDERSTANDING AND STRENGTHENING OF THE ECONOMY.
Kindly give us the following information regarding any program or programs your station may have broadcast in these three fields in the past month.

(1) Name of Program	(2) In which of the fields (1, 2, or 3 above) does it fall?	(3) Time of day and length of program	(4) Frequency of program last month (listed in col. 1)	(5) Check groups cooperating in program			(6) If local groups cooperated, give their names
				Local groups	National or State groups	None (Station Staff only)	
Example: Our foreign policy	1, 2	8:00–8:30 A.M.	4	X			Farm Bureau and P.T.A.
1.							
2.							
3.							
4.							
5.							

FORM 4—*Continued*

4. We are interested in some details concerning your most successful regular program in any of the three fields: (1) International understanding for peace, (2) Strengthening of democracy and (3) Understanding and strengthening of the economy. Kindly give us the following information regarding your most successful program:

   a. Name of program..

   b. What **local** group or groups were most responsible for suggesting, planning, or presenting some of the broadcasts?...

   ....

   c. What **non-local** group or groups were most responsible for suggesting, planning, or presenting some of the broadcasts?...

   ....

   d. Please describe the form that the broadcasts usually take: (Examples: speech, interview, round table, dramatization, music, etc.)...

   ....

   ....

   e. Do any groups use the information from these broadcasts as the basis for local group discussions?

   Yes............ No............ Comments:...

   ....

   f. If yes, what groups use it for discussion?...

   g. Do you send out scripts of this program to your audience? Yes.................... No....................

5. The mass media are often thought of as a one-way type of communication. That is, the listener has little opportunity to participate or respond. Various procedures have been developed to increase the participation of radio audiences.

   In your judgment, which of the procedures to increase audience participation would be most effective in programs designed to promote: (1) International understanding for peace, (2) Strengthening of democracy and (3) Understanding and strengthening of the economy?

   ....

   ....

   ....

   ....

SRS Form 4
October 22, 1951

FORM 5

A STUDY OF ADULT EDUCATION

Sponsored by

The Association of Land-Grant Colleges and Universities

and

Fund for Adult Education of the Ford Foundation

Your name ....

Mailing address ....

Name of weekly newspaper ....

1. Please give us the following information concerning the coverage of your newspaper.
    a. Approximately how many **subscribers** does your newspaper have? ....
    b. Approximately how many **readers** does your newspaper have? ....
    c. Approximately what percentage of your reader is rural (i.e., open country and centers under 2,500 population) .... percent.
    d. Has any study been made of your newspaper readers? Yes............ No............
    e. If yes, are results available? Yes............ No............
    f. If these are available for circulation, please enclose a copy.

2. We are interested in the programs and activities carried on in rural areas for adults in three fields, namely: (1) INTERNATIONAL UNDERSTANDING FOR PEACE, (2) STRENGTHENING OF DEMOCRACY, AND (3) UNDERSTANDING AND STRENGTHENING OF THE ECONOMY. We would appreciate your indicating the frequency with which you give local groups non-advertising space in your newspaper and whether or not they have prepared articles in these three fields in the last year.

LOCAL GROUPS	Every week	Every two or three weeks	Once per month	Less often	Not at all	Have they prepared articles in any of the 3 fields mentioned above in the last year?	
						Yes	No
Libraries............................							
Cooperative Agricultural Extension Service............................							
Churches and Religious Organizations..							
Schools...............................							
Farm Bureau.........................							
Grange...............................							
Farmers' Union......................							
Patriotic and Veterans' Organizations..							
Community Councils.................							
Civic and Service Clubs..............							
Welfare Councils....................							
Political Parties and/or Organizations..							
Professional Organizations...........							
Government Bureaus.................							
Colleges or Universities..............							
Women's Clubs......................							
Labor Unions........................							
UNESCO Organizations..............							
Parents' Organizations...............							
Fraternal Organizations..............							
Other (Specify)......................							

(OVER)

FORM 5—*Continued*

3. Kindly give us the following information regarding any space given in your newspaper to the three fields of interest in the past year.

FIELDS OF INTEREST	Estimated number of editorials and articles in the last year		Check approximate percent of non-advertising space devoted to each of the three fields				In general, how were these articles received by your readers?			
	Editorials	Articles (excluding news articles)	None	Less than 5%	5 to 10%	More than 10%	Well	Average	Poor	Don't know
(1) International Understanding for Peace										
(2) Strengthening of Democracy										
(3) Understanding and Strengthening of the Economy										

4. We would appreciate knowing something concerning the interest of local groups in promoting or preparing articles in the three fields of interest.

FIELDS OF INTEREST	About what proportion of these articles were offered or suggested by your readers?			Indicate some of the sources of these offerings or suggestions (Example: PTA, American Legion, etc.)	Indicate any other sources of articles in the 3 fields (Examples: AP, Bell Syndicate, etc.)
	None	Less than half	More than half		
(1) International Understanding for Peace					
(2) Strengthening of Democracy					
(3) Understanding and Strengthening of the Economy					

5. During the past year, did you make any special effort through your newspaper to promote (1) International Understanding for Peace, (2) Strengthening of Democracy, and (3) Understanding and Strengthening of the Economy? Yes [ ] No [ ]

   a. If yes, what did you do?..
   ....

   b. Were any local groups involved in your effort? Yes [ ] No [ ]

   c. If yes, please name the local groups involved..
   ....

6. It is generally believed that newspaper editors such as yourself are extremely important in the formation of public opinion. Please describe how, in your opinion, weekly newspapers can most effectively promote (1) International Understanding for Peace, (2) Strengthening of Democracy and (3) Understanding and Strengthening of the Economy?..
   ....
   ....

SRS Form 5
October 22, 1951

Form 6

BOOKS AND PAMPHLETS MOST USED

Author	Title	B—Book P—Pamphlet	Circulated	Reviewed by Librarian for Group(s)	Used as Material for Group Discussion
		Circle one B P	Circle one Yes No	Circle one Yes No	Circle one Yes No
		B P	Yes No	Yes No	Yes No
		B P	Yes No	Yes No	Yes No
		B P	Yes No	Yes No	Yes No
		B P	Yes No	Yes No	Yes No
		B P	Yes No	Yes No	Yes No
		B P	Yes No	Yes No	Yes No
		B P	Yes No	Yes No	Yes No
		B P	Yes No	Yes No	Yes No
		B P	Yes No	Yes No	Yes No

FILMS MOST USED

Title	Circulated	Showed to Group(s)	Used as Material for Group Discussion
	Circle one Yes No	Circle one Yes No	Circle one Yes No
	Yes No	Yes No	Yes No
	Yes No	Yes No	Yes No
	Yes No	Yes No	Yes No
	Yes No	Yes No	Yes No

Your name.................................... Library..

Address...

We shall appreciate your returning this card promptly. If you wish to enlarge on the use of these materials, will you follow the card with a letter? Thank you.

O-740

FORM 6—*Reverse*

DIRECTOR
C. P. Loomis
Social Research Service
East Lansing, Michigan

STUDY OF ADULT EDUCATION
IN RURAL AREAS

October 19, 1951

SPONSORS:
Assn. of Land Grant
Colleges and Universities
and
Fund for Adult Education
of the Ford Foundation

Dear Librarian:

The Fund for Adult Education of the Ford Foundation has asked us to make a survey of the extent and nature of education for adults in the rural areas of the United States. We are primarily interested in three subject matter fields:

    I. INTERNATIONAL UNDERSTANDING FOR PEACE.

    II. STRENGTHENING OF DEMOCRACY.

    III. UNDERSTANDING AND STRENGTHENING OF THE ECONOMY.

It is important to know what books (non-fiction, fiction, juvenile or adult), pamphlets and films in these fields probably have been most used by adults from the rural areas in the past year. Will you list such titles on the other side of this card and check the ways in which they have been used? Please return the card promptly. Thank you.

                Yours sincerely,
                Ruth Warncke
                Section on Public Libraries

FORM 6

FIRST CLASS
PERMIT NO. 941
SEC. 34.9, P. L. & R.
East Lansing, Mich.

BUSINESS REPLY ENVELOPE
No Postage Stamp Necessary If Mailed in The United States

—POSTAGE WILL BE PAID BY—

Social Research Service
Michigan State College
East Lansing, Michigan

FORM 7

Foreign Student Section
STUDY OF ADULT EDUCATION

DIRECTOR
Charles P. Loomis
Social Research Service
Michigan State College
East Lansing, Michigan

SPONSORS
Association of Land-Grant
Colleges and Universities
and the
Fund for Adult Education
of the Ford Foundation

October—1951

We would appreciate having your answers promptly. For your convenience return address and postage are included.

Your name.................................Position....................................

Mailing address...

1. How many foreign students are enrolled at your institution at the present time?.................

2. Indicate how these foreign students participate **ON CAMPUS** to increase the knowledge of students and faculty about people from other countries. Check as many as apply.
    1-[ ] Lectures
    2-[ ] Folk or costume dances, festivals, etc.
    3-[ ] Parties, teas, banquets, etc.
    4-[ ] Intergroup discussions and meetings
    5-[ ] Rooming with American students
    6-[ ] International House affairs
    7-[ ] Other (Specify)...........................
    ....
    a. **Double check** items above which contribute most to the knowledge of students and faculty.

3. Indicate how these foreign students participate **OFF CAMPUS** to increase the knowledge of U.S. citizens about people from other countries. Check as may as apply.
    1-[ ] Lectures
    2-[ ] Folk or costume dances, festivals, etc.
    3-[ ] Parties, teas, banquets, etc.
    4-[ ] Planned visits to homes
    5-[ ] Rooming with U. S. students
    6-[ ] Intergroup discussions, meetings
    7-[ ] Rooming in U. S. homes
    8-[ ] Other (Specify)...........................
    a. **Double check** those which contribute most to increase knowledge of U. S. citizens.
    b. Indicate approximate number of your foreign students participating in **OFF CAMPUS** activities during the past year.................................

4. What planned means do you use to acquaint your foreign students with our life? Please check as many as apply.
    1-[ ] Tours to visit places of interest
    2-[ ] Visits, for day or more, with families
    3-[ ] Visits to farms
    4-[ ] Visits to businesses
    5-[ ] Participating in discussions, etc.
    6-[ ] Rooming with U. S. students
    7-[ ] Special courses in English for Foreign students
    8-[ ] Special courses (other than language)
    9-[ ] Other (Specify)..
    ....
    a. **Double check** those you consider of most importance.

5. Indicate the organizations having programs or activities in which your foreign students participate.
    1-[ ] Colleges and universities
    2-[ ] Schools
    3-[ ] Churches and religious organizations
    4-[ ] Farm organizations (Specify)..
    5-[ ] Cooperative Agricultural Extension Service
    6-[ ] Government Bureaus (Specify)...
    ....
    7-[ ] Elected or appointed government bodies (Specify).............................
    ....

(OVER)

Form 7—Continued

8-[ ] Community councils
9-[ ] Inter-agency councils (Specify)...
....
10-[ ] Welfare councils
11-[ ] Civic and service organizations (Specify)...
....
12-[ ] Libraries
13-[ ] Political parties and/or organizations
14-[ ] Professional organizations (Specify)...

15-[ ] Labor Unions
16-[ ] Women's clubs (Specify)..
17-[ ] Patriotic and veterans organizations (Specify)..

18-[ ] UNESCO organizations (Specify)...
19-[ ] Parents' organizations (Specify)...
20-[ ] Fraternal organizations (Specify)..

21-[ ] Other (Specify)..
....

   a. List in order, the 4 organizations under No. 5 above in which your foreign students participated most in the past year.
     1... 3...
     2... 4...

6. Indicate the proportion of all your foreign students who spent time **off** campus in rural areas (i.e., open country and centers of less than 2,500 population) last year.

    1-[ ] Almost none
    2-[ ] About ¼
    3-[ ] About ½
    4-[ ] About ¾
    5-[ ] Almost all

7. If your foreign students participated in none of the programs or activities mentioned in the previous questions would you please briefly state why?

8. In your opinion what 3 institutions, other than your own, are doing most to help foreign students and U. S citizens become acquainted with one another?
    1..
    2..
    3..

9. Do you find special difficulties in having foreign students on campus? Yes [ ] No [ ]
   a. **If yes,** specify major difficulties. If there are nationality differences please indicate opposite each difficulty the nationality groups most involved.

Type of Difficulty	Nationality Group Most Involved
1.	
2.	
3.	
4.	

Please return this questionnaire even though you have no program which you care to report upon.

October 25, 1951

FORM 8

A STUDY OF ADULT EDUCATION

Sponsored by

The Association of Land-Grant Colleges and Universities

and

Fund for Adult Education Established by the Ford Foundation

> This Survey is approved by the
> **AMERICAN COLLEGE PUBLIC RELATIONS ASSOCIATION**

FORM 8—*Continued*

Your Name.................................... Your Title....................................

Name of College or University.. City & State........................

1. Please give us the following information concerning the organization of information services at your institution:

   a. Name of information services department..

   b. Indicate the school, division or college in which this department is located.........................
      ....

   c. Indicate to whom (Department head, Dean, President, etc.) the director of information services is responsible? ....

   d. Indicate the number of full-time employees (or the equivalent) in the information services department
      ....

   e. Indicate the titles of these positions together with the special functions performed.

TITLE OF POSITION	SPECIAL FUNCTION
1....................................	....
2....................................	....
3....................................	....
4....................................	....

   f. Are all information services at your institution under the direction of this department? Yes-[ ] No-[ ]

   g. If no, please name the other services and give their special functions:

NAME OF SERVICE	SPECIAL FUNCTION	INDICATE SCHOOL OR DIVISION IN WHICH IT FALLS
1....................................	....	....
2....................................	....	....
3....................................	....	....
4....................................	....	....

2. Please check the kinds of mass media handled by or through your department and the approximate percentage of the total time spent on each.

MEDIA	Handled by or through your Department		Approximate percentage of total time spent				
	Yes	No	None	Less than 25%	25–50%	50–75%	75% and over
Radio							
Television							
Printed Matter							
Press							
Visual Aids							
Other (Specify)							

FORM 8—*Continued*

3. Which of the following classes of media are handled by or through your department? **Please check.**
    1-[ ] News releases
    2-[ ] Feature articles
    3-[ ] Periodicals
    4-[ ] Agricultural Experiment Station publications
    5-[ ] Agricultural Extension publications
    6-[ ] Film strips
    7-[ ] Radio scripts
    8-[ ] Radio news releases
    9-[ ] Filmed programs (TV)
    10-[ ] Exhibits
    11-[ ] Other (Specify)..

4. Which **one** of the media checked in question 3 do you believe is most effective in getting the public to **adopt new practices?**..
    Comment:..
    ....

5. Which **one** of the media checked in question 3 do you believe is most effective in **changing of attitudes?**
    ....
    Comment:..
    ....

6. Please check any of the following groups for which you have prepared special printed materials.
    1-[ ] Colleges and universities   13-[ ] Political parties and/or organizations
    2-[ ] Schools   14-[ ] Professional organizations
    3-[ ] Churches and religious organizations 15-[ ] Labor unions
    4-[ ] Farm organizations   16-[ ] Women's clubs
    5-[ ] Cooperative Agricultural Extension Service 17-[ ] Patriotic and veterans' organizations
    6-[ ] Federal and/or state gov't bureaus 18-[ ] UNESCO organizations
    7-[ ] Elected or appointed gov't bodies 19-[ ] Parents' organizations
    8-[ ] Community councils   20-[ ] Fraternal organizations
    9-[ ] Inter-agency councils   21-[ ] Others (Specify)
    10-[ ] Civic and service organizations   ....
    11-[ ] Welfare councils   ....
    12-[ ] Libraries

    a. Please **double check** any of the groups above for which you have prepared **discussion group** materials.

7. We are interested in mass media originating from educational institutions that concern three fields, namely: (1) International Understanding for Peace, (2) Strengthening of Democracy and (3) Understanding and Strengthening of the Economy.
    Kindly give us the following information regarding not more than five of your "best" examples of mass media from these three fields handled by or through your department in the past year.

Title or Description of examples of Mass Media*	Check Type			For what special audience was it designed, if any? (Example: farmers, young adults, etc.)	Estimated number of persons reached			
	Radio-TV	Printed Matter	Visual Aids		less than 1,000	1,000 to 10,000	10,000 to 25,000	25,000 or over
1.								
2.								
3.								
4.								
5.								

* Please enclose examples, if available.

November 10, 1951
SRS form 8

FORM 9

A STUDY OF ADULT EDUCATION

Sponsored by

The Association of Land-Grant Colleges and Universities

and

Fund for Adult Education Established by the Ford Foundation

Form 9—Continued

The Fund for Adult Education established by the Ford Foundation has asked us to find out what types of educational programs are being carried on among rural people in the United States. Will you please help us by answering this brief questionnaire and returning it promptly? Thank you.

Organization for which you are reporting..

A. Does your organization have any educational programs or activities for adults?   Yes [ ]   No [ ]
   1. If yes, about how many different people were reached last year?.......................
      Of these, how many live in the open country or in centers of less than 2,500 people?
      Check one: Almost none [ ]   Almost ¼ [ ]   About ½ [ ]
                   About ¾   [ ]   Almost all [ ]

B. Indicate mass media used in your programs or activities: [ ] Radio   [ ] Television
   [ ] Newspapers   [ ] Motion pictures   [ ] Other (Specify)..........................
   [ ] None

C. What other organizations do you work with, or through, in your educational work with adults?
   (Check as many as apply)   12-[ ] Libraries
   1-[ ] Colleges and Universities   13-[ ] Political parties and/or organizations
   2-[ ] Schools   14-[ ] Professional organizations
   3-[ ] Churches and religious organizations   15-[ ] Labor unions
   4-[ ] Farm organizations   16-[ ] Women's clubs
   5-[ ] Cooperative Agricultural Extension Service   17-[ ] Patriotic and veterans' organizations
   6-[ ] Federal and/or state gov't bureaus   18-[ ] UNESCO organizations
   7-[ ] Elected or appointed gov't bodies   19-[ ] Parents' organizations
   8-[ ] Community councils   20-[ ] Fraternal organizations
   9-[ ] Inter-agency councils   21-[ ] Others (Specify)..........................
   10-[ ] Civic and service organizations
   11-[ ] Welfare councils   ....

   Of the above GENERAL TYPES of organizations which you have checked, list here the SPECIFIC NAMES of the three with which you work most. (List FIRST the ONE you work with most.)
   1...................... 2...................... 3......................

   We are particularly interested in any programs or activities for adults which deal with the following three fields:
   1.—INTERNATIONAL UNDERSTANDING FOR PEACE
   2.—STRENGTHENING OF DEMOCRACY
   3.—UNDERSTANDING AND STRENGTHENING OF THE ECONOMY

   These programs or activities may have taken the form of conferences, workshops, demonstrations, meetings, contests, exhibitions, radio programs, institutes, organizing of councils, etc.

D. Was any program or activity for adults that included (1) international understanding for peace, (2) strengthening of democracy, or (3) understanding and strengthening of the economy, carried on within or by your organization during the past year?   Yes [ ]   No [ ]
   1. If YES, give name or brief description of your best program or activity ....
      ....
   2. In your best program or activity, about how many different people were reached last year?..........
      ....
      Of these, how many live in the open country or in centers of less than 2,500 people?
      Check one: Almost none [ ]   About ¼ [ ]   About ½ [ ]   About ¾ [ ]
                   Almost all [ ]
   3. Please check the form or forms which your best program or activity in the three fields took:
      [ ] Conference   [ ] Public meeting   [ ] Institute
      [ ] Workshop   [ ] Demonstration   [ ] Tour
      [ ] Radio listening groups   [ ] Other (Specify).......................

Form 9—*Continued*

4. In conducting the program or activity what procedures were used?
   [ ] Lectures   [ ] Large groups split into small discussion groups
   [ ] Group discussions   [ ] Other (Specify)..
   [ ] Panels
   Please go back to No. 4 and DOUBLE CHECK the procedure used most extensively.

E. International Understanding For Peace

   1. During the past year did any foreign person appear on your program?   Yes [ ]   No [ ]
   2. During this period has your local group discussed or had a speaker on any international problem?
      Yes [ ]   No [ ]
   3. Do you have a committee which deals with international problems?   Yes [ ]   No [ ]
      If yes, what is the name of the committee?
   4. Do you receive any printed materials from your State or National Organizations on international problems?   Yes [ ]   No [ ]

F. Strengthening of Democracy

   1. During the past year did you have programs on the following topics? (Check as many as apply)
      a-[ ] Citizenship issues
      b-[ ] Stimulating citizens to vote
      c-[ ] Other (Specify)...
      ....

   2. Has your local sponsored any special community betterment programs or projects? Yes [ ] No [ ]
      If yes, describe and indicate what was accomplished..
      ....

   3. How does your local group attempt to improve participation in meetings? (Check as many as apply)
      a-[ ] Having open discussions
      b-[ ] Stimulating youth participation
      c-[ ] Training local leaders
      d-[ ] Training discussion leaders
      e-[ ] Other (Specify)...
      ....

G. Understanding and Strengthening the Economy

   1. During the past year has your local discussed any of the following? (Check as many as apply)
      a-[ ] Government agricultural policies
      b-[ ] Inflation and/or price controls
      c-[ ] The family farm
      d-[ ] Cooperatives
      e-[ ] Labor problems
      f-[ ] Other (Specify)...

   2. Have you had speakers from business men's groups or organized labor? (Check as many as apply)
      a-[ ] Business men's groups
      b-[ ] Organized labor

   3. When you discuss economic problems, from what sources do you get information or discussion materials?
      ....
      ....

H. YOUR NAME..OCCUPATION................................

MAILING ADDRESS..

November 13, 1951
SRS Form 9

Form 10

December 26, 1951

Opinions, Attitudes, Judgments and General Thinking of the Staff of the Study of Adult Education in Rural Areas

Staff member's name....................

Each of us has been striving during the last months to increase his knowledge and understanding of adult education as it is carried on in rural America, particularly as related to the three fields (1) INTERNATIONAL UNDERSTANDING FOR PEACE, (2) STRENGTHENING OF DEMOCRACY, (3) UNDERSTANDING AND STRENGTHENING OF THE ECONOMY, and particularly as carried on by the organizations and activities on which we are each reporting. We have attempted to appraise the need for adult education as reported by leaders in the organizations we have been studying and to report these leaders' use and evaluation of the effectiveness of certain forms or patterns of programs or activities and methods or procedures. In so far as possible we have as a group defined our working objectives and definitions and developed our instruments and study procedures.

Now as director of the study I have prepared the following questionnaire for the staff to fill out. This instrument is designed to get some general and tentative recordings of the staff's individual reactions to certain propositions before concerted group discussion of the findings has taken place. Of course, the following assumptions you are asked to make are unrealistic and any contemplative answering of the questions will require more situational facts than are presented. Nevertheless it may be useful to try to answer the questions.

QUESTIONNAIRE FOR STAFF

Over-all Assumptions:

Assume that you are a foundation director with one million dollars to spend on Adult Education in rural United States during the next five years and that your objectives are to achieve the greatest possible progress in:
  1—INTERNATIONAL UNDERSTANDING FOR PEACE
  2—STRENGTHENING OF DEMOCRACY
  3—UNDERSTANDING AND STRENGTHENING OF THE ECONOMY

In considering the relative emphasis to place on short time as versus long time attainments use your own ideals and standards. Throughout, *use your own* values and judgment. This is not a study of what your informants think but of what *you think* at this stage of the study. Remember the above assumption, namely, that you are a foundation director. We should step out of our research roles if these answers are to be useful in the conclusions.

Question 1

Assuming that the programs and activities you would organize can be broken into two components: (1) Action including evaluation and administrative research, and (2) Fundamental research, indicate the approximate percentage you would assign to fundamental research. (Use your own definitions.) ...... %

Question 2

What part, if any, of the amount above under Question 1 is not used for fundamental research should be used for evaluation and administrative research? .... %

Question 3

Assuming that your programs and activities could be broken into three categories of adult education: (1) mostly mass media alone, (2) programs or activities involving little mass media and (3), programs and activities designed to use mass media in conjunction with face-to-face discussion and other similar situations, indicate the approximate allocations of funds you would make:

Assistance in programs or activities including evaluation and administrative research	(1) Mostly mass media only	(2) Programs and activities with little mass media	(3) Mass media used with face-to-face discussion and similar activities and programs	Total
	%	%	%	
Fundamental research.........				
Total..................				100%

Question 4

If you allocated any percentages above in Question 3 for mostly mass media, indicate below the approximate percentage you would expend for the following:

Schedules Used in Adult Education Study 371

	Radio	Television	Printed Matter	Motion pictures	Total
	%	%	%	%	
Assistance in programs or activities including evaluation and administrative research................					
Fundamental research.............					
Total......................					100%

Question 5

Assume that all programs or activities involving little emphasis on mass media mentioned previously can be broken into two categories (1) preparing materials of all kinds and (2) organization and training, indicate the percentages of total expenditures you would make for preparing of materials %......
What part of this latter amount should go for fundamental research %......

Question 6

Assume that the whole adult education program can be broken into the three categories we have used, indicate approximate percentages you would spend for each:
   1—INTERNATIONAL UNDERSTANDING FOR PEACE ......%
   2—STRENGTHENING OF DEMOCRACY ......%
   3—UNDERSTANDING AND STRENGTHENING OF THE ECONOMY ......%
                                     TOTAL   100%

Question 7

Assuming that the entire expenditures you are to make for adult education using the above mentioned one million dollars can be broken into the following two categories: (1) Employment of and assistance to foreign students, scientists and technicians in the United States to advance the three fields of interest covered in this study and (2) Other expenditures, indicate the approximate proportion of the total expenditure you would give to (1) above ......%

Question 8

For your programs and activities involving little mass media, indicate percentages of the total expenditures which would be made in the adult education program to be developed for rural United States by the following levels.

	Percentages expended at different levels for programs and activities	
	Non mass media	Mass media used with discussion, etc.
1-( ) School district		
2-( ) Township		
3-( ) Local community or neighborhood		
4-( ) Several communities		
5-( ) County		
6-( ) Multi-county		
7-( ) State		
8-( ) Region		
9-( ) Nation		
10-( ) Other (specify)..........................		
Total	100%	100%

Question 9

For your efforts at the state level, indicate which of the following agencies you would involve in your program:
(Check as many as apply)
    1-( ) Colleges and universities
    2-( ) Schools
    3-( ) Churches and religious organizations
    4-( ) Farm organizations
    5-( ) Cooperative Agricultural Extension Service
    6-( ) Federal and/or state government bureaus
    7-( ) Elected or appointed government bodies
    8-( ) Community councils
    9-( ) Inter-agency councils
    10-( ) Civic and service organizations
    11-( ) Welfare councils

12-( ) Libraries
13-( ) Political parties and/or organizations
14-( ) Professional organizations
15-( ) Labor unions
16-( ) Women's clubs
17-( ) Patriotic and veterans' organizations
18-( ) UNESCO organizations
19-( ) Parents' organizations
20-( ) Fraternal organizations
21-( ) Others (specify) ....

Of the above GENERAL TYPES of organizations which you have checked, list here the SPECIFIC NAMES of the three state agencies with which you work most. (List FIRST the ONE you work with most, e.g., State Department of Public Instruction, Farm Bureau, CIO.)

1. .... 2. .... 3. ....

Question 10

For your efforts at the community and neighborhood level indicate which of the following you would involve in your programs:
(Check as many apply)
1-( ) Colleges and universities
2-( ) Schools
3-( ) Churches and religious organizations
4-( ) Farm organizations
5-( ) Cooperative Agricultural Extension Service
6-( ) Federal and/or state government bureaus
7-( ) Elected or appointed government bodies
8-( ) Community councils
9-( ) Inter-agency councils
10-( ) Civic and service organizations
11-( ) Welfare councils
12-( ) Libraries
13-( ) Political parties and/or organizations
14-( ) Professional organizations
15-( ) Labor unions
16-( ) Women's clubs
17-( ) Patriotic and veterans' organizations
18-( ) UNESCO organizations
19-( ) Parents' organizations
20-( ) Fraternal organizations
21-( ) Others (specify) ....

Of the above GENERAL TYPES of organizations which you have checked, list here the SPECIFIC NAMES of the three community agencies with which you would work most. (List FIRST the ONE you work with most, e.g., High School, Local Rotary Club, 4-H.)

1. ....   2. ....   3. ....

Question 11

In your programs on the community level indicate by placing numbers before the following categories the forms of program for which you would make the largest expenditure of money and effort. Place 1 before the category you would expend the most for, 2 before the one you would spend next most for, and 3 before the category you would spend least for.

( ) Conference   ( ) Public meeting   ( ) Institute
( ) Workshop   ( ) Demonstration   ( ) Tour
         ( ) Radio listening groups
         ( ) Others (specify) ....

Question 12

In the programs you sponsor on the community level indicate the procedures you would use:

( ) Lectures   ( ) Large groups split into small discussion groups
( ) Group discussions   ( ) Others (specify) ....
( ) Panels

Please go back to No. 12 and DOUBLE CHECK the procedure to be used most extensively.

Question 13

If you had money available for adult education and all other types of education what proportion of this would you allocate for adult education? ...... %

Question 14

Please indicate by checking what you believe to be the most important factors in developing in the individual the tendency to make decisions on the basis of objective criteria:

1–( ) Influence of individuals
2–( ) Influence of material from formal course work
3–( ) Influence of instructors in formal course work
4–( ) Influence of discussion in formal courses
5–( ) Influence of other organized discussion groups

6–( ) Influence of mass media
7–( ) Increased leisure time
8–( ) Deep personal experience
9–( ) Others (specify) ....

Double check the three items above in Question 14 which you consider to be most important. Place 1 before the most important, 2 before the 2nd most important, 3 before the 3rd.

Question 15

Please indicate what you believe to be the most important factors in increasing the individual's basic knowledge in the three fields we have been studying:
1–( ) Influence of individuals
2–( ) Influence of material from formal course work
3–( ) Influence of instructors in formal course work
4–( ) Influence of discussion in formal courses
5–( ) Influence of other organized discussion groups
6–( ) Influence of mass media
7–( ) Increased leisure time
8–( ) Deep personal experience
9–( ) Others (specify) ....

Double check the three items above in Question 15 which you consider to be most important. Place 1 before the most important, 2 before the 2nd most important, 3 before the 3rd.

APPENDIX C

Sampling Procedures Utilized

Since special sampling problems were encountered by each section leader, the details of the procedures utilized in the individual chapters will be included separately in this Appendix. The decision to use sample counties in order to obtain regional representation is common to most of the chapters of the report. Therefore a description of this sample is necessary prior to a discussion of procedures used in the several chapters. After considerable discussion by the committee, it was decided that two previously-drawn series of sample counties, one including 196 counties and the other 71 counties, would be used. A general description of these samples, together with a listing of the counties included, follow:

THE BUREAU OF AGRICULTURAL ECONOMICS GENERAL-PURPOSE SAMPLE

A national sample of 101, 196, 301, and 391 counties has been developed for use in enumerative surveys of the Bureau. The sample was planned to meet the following objectives:

(1) To provide an efficient national sample;

(2) To be representative with respect to the major type-of-farming regions of the United States;

(3) Within each major type-of-farming region, to be representative with respect to a number of important items relating to the agriculture and farm population of that region;

(4) To make possible two-way summarization at lower than the national level—by 8 major type-of-farming regions and/or by 4 major group-of-States regions;

(5) To provide a flexible method of expansion of the basic 101-county sample into a general-purpose national sample twice, three times or four times as large;

(6) To provide a flexible method of expansion of the basic 101–county sample into special purpose samples and/or into samples permitting estimates by major type-of-farming regions or by major group-of-States regions.

The method of stratification used was planned in accordance with these objectives. All counties of the United States were grouped into 101 strata and one county from each stratum was selected for the national sample. The grouping of counties into 101 strata was done as follows:

(1) All counties were grouped into the following major type-of-farming regions adapted from a revision by the Division of Farm Management and Costs of its latest published map:

Corn belt	Range-livestock region
Cotton belt	Western specialty crop areas
Dairy region	Wheat region
General and self-sufficing region	Residual group (all counties not falling in the 7 regions listed)

(2) Within each major type-of-farming region, the counties were next grouped according to the major group-of-States region in which they fell—Northeast, North Central, South, and West. (These 4 regions are combinations of the 9 Census geographic divisions.) This gave 20 groups of counties, with each group falling wholly within a major type-of-farming region and a major group-of-States region.

(3) These 20 groups of counties were further subdivided into 101 strata, with approximately 60,000 farms in each stratum.
   (a) The 10 largest groups of counties (containing 2,405 counties) were subdivided into 81 strata, each containing approximately 60,000 farms by the use of component indexes. For each major type-of-farming region 12 Census items relating to agriculture and the farm population were combined into 2 or 3 indexes for each county. (The indexes are called "component" indexes because the formulas for weighting together the Census information were obtained by component analysis of the intercorrelations of the 12 items in each major type-of-farming region.) Counties were then classified into strata according to the counties' values on these indexes. This is the method used to achieve the third objective listed above, namely to assure representativeness of the sample with respect to the agricultural and farm population characteristics deemed important in a given region.
   (b) The 6 smallest groups (of the 20 groups of counties mentioned) were not further subdivided, each group being used as a single stratum.
   (c) The 4 groups of "residual" counties (one group in each group-of-States region) were subdivided into 14 strata on the basis of geographic location and type-of-farming criteria.

After all counties were grouped into the 101 strata, one county was drawn for the sample from each stratum. The drawing was done by the use of random numbers in such a way that the probability of a county's being included in the sample was proportional to the number of farms in the county. In a stratum, the counties were arranged in alphabetical order, the number of farms was recorded for each county, and these were added, with a subtotal made after each county's number of farms was added in. A list was prepared of 101 random numbers within the range from 1 to about 60,000. Each of these numbers was used to determine for one stratum which county was to be chosen. In a given stratum, the particular county was chosen which had a subtotal of farms nearest to the random number and larger than the random number. The attached list shows the 101 counties selected in this way.

Objectives (5) and (6) were met by further stratification. The 101 strata described were each further subdivided into 2, 3, and 4 strata. By the same method of selection, a 196-county, a 301-county, and a 391-county sample were drawn, each sample including all the counties of each smaller sample. When it is desirable to supplement the 101-county sample in certain type-of-farming areas or in certain regions, additional counties from the larger samples can be combined with the 101 counties. Somewhat similar procedures were used in the developing of the 71 Sociological Laboratory Counties which contained 4 counties included in the 196-county sample.

LIST OF 196 SAMPLE COUNTIES

Corn Belt

Illinois
Greene
Grundy
McLean
Mason
Pike
Wabash

Indiana
De Kalb
Elkhart
Newton
Vermillion

Iowa
Boone
Bremer
Fremont
Lucas
Mahaska

Kansas
Brown
Doniphan

Minnesota
Pipestone
Sibley

Missouri
Adair
Howard

Johnson

Nebraska
Holt
Sarpy
Saunders
Sherman
York

Ohio
Clark
Crawford
Shelby
Williams
Wood

Cotton Belt

Alabama
Colbert
Dallas
Elmore
Marshall
Sumter

Arkansas
Clark
Crawford
Desha
Drew
Mississippi
Prairie

Florida
Jefferson

Georgia
Chattooga
Hart

Montgomery
Pulaski
Warren
Washington

Louisiana
Allen
East Carroll

Mississippi
Carroll
Claiborne
Jasper
Lawrence
Leflore
Lincoln
Monroe
Quitman
Walthall
Warren

Missouri
Mississippi

North Carolina
Anson
Nash
Richmond
Union
Wake
Wayne

Oklahoma
Lincoln

South Carolina
Florence
Lancaster

Texas
Brazoria
Coleman

Fayette
McLennan
Milan

San Jacinto
Stonewall (Kent*)
Travis

Williamson
Wilson
Wise

Dairy Region

Michigan

Genesee
Gratiot
St. Joseph
Washtenaw

New York

Albany
Columbia
Lewis
Orange
Oswego

Virginia

Fairfax

Wisconsin

Barron
Dane
Green Lake
Juneau
Shawano
Waukesha
Winnebago

Minnesota

Otter Tail

New Hampshire

Strafford

Ohio

Ashland
Summit

Pennsylvania

Crawford
Lancaster

General and Self-Sufficing Region

Arkansas

Searcy

Connecticut

Windham

Illinois

Bond

Indiana

Jackson
Perry

Kentucky

Russell

Maine

Kennebec

Missouri

Carter
Christian

Perry

New York

Chenango

North Carolina

Alamance
Iredell
Randolph
Watauga

Ohio

Hamilton
Jackson
Knox
Noble

Oklahoma

Ottawa
Pittsburg

Pennsylvania

Juniata
Schuylkill
Somerset

Tennessee

Fontress
Franklin
Humphreys
Jackson
Scott
Sumner

Virginia

Smyth

West Virginia

Doddridge
Lewis
Marion
Nicholas
Summers

* Pseudo-county

Range-Livestock Region

Colorado	New Mexico	Texas
Arapahoe	Bernalillo	Gillespie
	San Miguel	Kendall
Kansas		
Coffey		*Wyoming*
	South Dakota	Crook
Nevada		Natrona (Hot
Washoe	Lawrence	Springs*)

Western Specialty Crop Areas

California	San Joaquin	Idaho
Mendocino	Tehama	Jerome (Lincoln*)
Orange		*Utah*
Sacramento	Tulare	Sanpete

Wheat Belt

Idaho	Stevens	Griggs
Fremont		Stark
	Nebraska	
Kansas	Deuel	*Oklahoma*
Cloud		Garfield
	North Dakota	
Minnesota	Barnes	*Washington*
Polk	Grand Forks	Douglas

Residual

California	Louisiana	Minnesota
Humboldt	Jefferson Davis	Carlton
Florida	*Maine*	*Mississippi*
Okaloosa	Aroostook	Pearl River
Volusia		
	Massachusetts	*New Jersey*
Kentucky	Hampden	Cumberland
Lyon		
Fayette	*Michigan*	*North Carolina*
Nelson	Van Buren	Beaufort

* Pseudo-county

Forsyth
Granville

South Carolina

Horry

Oregon

Tennessee

Clackamas
Coos

Montgomery

Pennsylvania

Virginia

Erie

Frederick

Washington

King
Thurston

Wisconsin

Bayfield
Langlade

LIST OF 71 BUREAU OF AGRICULTURAL ECONOMICS SOCIOLOGICAL LABORATORY COUNTIES

Corn Belt

Illinois

Minnesota

Nebraska

Jasper

Indiana

Nobles

Seward

Henry

Iowa

Missouri

Ohio

Crawford
Hamilton

Randolph

Wyandot

Cotton Belt

Alabama

Louisiana

Oklahoma

Dallas
Tuscaloosa

Avoyelles

Pottawatomie

Arkansas

Mississippi

South Carolina

Desha
Izard

Calhoun
Coahoma

Union

Georgia

North Carolina

Texas

Oconee

Harnett

Ball
Fisher

Dairy Region

Connecticut

Michigan

New York

Litchfield

Eaton

Oneida

Maryland

Vermont

Frederick

Minnesota

Rutland

Massachusetts

Wisconsin

Hampshire

Goodhue

Monroe

General and Self-Sufficing Region

Georgia	New Hampshire	Tennessee
Rabun	Belknap	
	North Carolina	Humphreys
Kentucky	Haywood	Wilson
Magoffin	Pennsylvania	West Virginia
Missouri	Bradford	
Dent	Huntingdon	Greenbrier

Range-Livestock Region

Arizona	Sweet Grass	Texas
Coconino	New Mexico	Val Verde
Kansas	Santa Fe	Utah
Morris	South Dakota	Summit
Montana		Washington
Custer	Lyman	Franklin

Western Specialty Crop Areas

California	Imperial	Idaho
	Santa Barbara	Ada
Butte	Tulare	Bingham

Wheat Belt

Kansas	North Dakota	Oklahoma
Ellis	Ward	
Haskell	Wells	Woods

Residual

Colorado	Louisiana	North Carolina
Bent	La Fourche	Columbus
Florida		Virginia
Polk	Maine	Pittsylvania
Taylor	Piscataquis	Washington
Kentucky	New Jersey	Clark
Graves		Wisconsin
Scott	Camden	Sawyer

ADDITIONAL SAMPLE AND METHODOLOGICAL NOTES

Chapter 2.—The basic data for this chapter were secured primarily through mailed questionnaires and selected personal interviews with leaders in the field of adult education.

Form 1 (see Appendix B) was mailed to all administrators of 12-grade public school systems in the 263 sample counties (see description in Appendix C). This questionnaire was sent to 2340 school administrators and was filled out and returned by 837. Thus, 36 percent of the total number responded to the questionnaire. The 837 usable returns were the result of two successive mailings.

In addition to Form 1, Form 2 was used to secure additional, more detailed information concerning programs judged to be of special interest. These data were used qualitatively and were not subjected to statistical analysis.

Personal interviews were conducted with state adult educational personnel in New York, New Jersey, Wisconsin, Pennsylvania, and Michigan.

While the responses given on Form 1 by the public school administrators are of great value, the author is aware of varied interpretations of apparently simple questions. For examples, 510 answered "Yes," 303 answered "No," and 24 failed to answer the question: "Does your organization (high school) have any educational programs or activities for adults?" It is probable that some did not include an out-of-school youth or adult program in vocational education or an on-the-farm training program for Veterans as adult education. Others probably answered affirmatively on the basis of the existence of a parent-teacher or other parent organizations in the community. This question probably would have yielded more accurate responses from school administrators if the terms "classes," or "adult evening classes," had been used in lieu of "programs or activities."

Chapter 3.—Three major sources form the basic data presented relative to adult education programs of the Cooperative Extension Service. These include the records of the Federal Extension Service, Form 1, a mailed questionnaire (see Appendix B), and selected personal interviews.

Form 1 was mailed to all Cooperative Extension Service personnel in the 263 sample counties. This questionnaire was sent to a toal of 735 persons and replies were received from 618, making a return of 84 percent of the individual workers surveyed. Completed questionnaires were received from one or more county extension workers in 260 of the 263 counties. All 46 states with sample counties were represented in the replies received and 23 of these states have 100 percent representation.

Some of the completed questionnaires contained answers for an entire county staff. The county extension staff organization in some states is such that one person is responsible for the entire county program. Therefore only one completed questionnaire should be expected from such a county.

In certain states the county agricultural agent is responsible for all agricultural extension work and the home demonstration agent is responsible for all home economics extension work regardless of the size of the county extension staff. This may in part account for the low percent of returns from assistant county agricultural agents and assistant county home demonstration agents. The following table summarizes the returns from the various kinds of county extension workers:

Type of extension worker	Total*	Questionnaires mailed	Percent of U.S. total	Questionnaires returned	Percent returned
Counties with agents	3,042	261	9	260	100
County agricultural agents	3,339	285	9	265	93
Assistant county agricultural agents	1,845	124	7	93	75
Home demonstration agents	2,840	234	8	192	82
Assistant home demonstration agents	728	46	6	28	60
4-H club agents	656	46	7	39	82

* Continental United States only.

The percentage of returns is very good for county agricultural agents, for home demonstration agents, and 4-H club agents. Lower percentage returns came from assistant agricultural and home demonstration agents, due in part to wide variation among the states in the number employed in proportion to the number of county agricultural and home demonstration agents. Eighty percent of the 4-H Club agents are employed in the Middle West and the Northeastern States with none in the South. The concentration of 4-H Club agents in states with small area may account for the smaller sample.

Chapters 4 and 5.—Personal interviews with farm organizational personnel, observation of local meetings, and mailed questionnaires constitute the basic sources of information concerning the farmers' organizations.

Personal interviews were held by the authors with the national officers and headquarters staffs of the four major farmers' organizations. Ten state headquarters were visited and at least one local meeting of each of the farm organizations was attended.

The quantitative data consists of the responses from mailed questionnaires sent to two samples: first, to all local units of farm organizations and cooperatives in the 263 sample counties, and second, to a general 5 percent of local, county, and state farm organizational units.

Forms 1 and 9 (see Appendix B) were used to obtain the quantitative data for Chapter 5. The tables used in the chapter combine the results from the two samples.

A summary of the numbers of questionnaires mailed and returned for the farm organizations and farmers' cooperatives follows:

Questionnaires mailed and returned	Farm organizations									
	Total		Farm Bureau		Farmers' Union		Grange		Cooperatives	
	Number	Percent	Number	Percent	Number	Percent	Number	Percent	Number	Percent
Questionnaires mailed	4495*	100	1379*	100	341	100	1364	100	1411	100
Completed questionnaire returns	1054	23	465	34	128	38	349	26	112	8

* Continental United States only.

Chapter 6.—The primary data forming the basis of this chapter are derived from mailed questionnaires and from personal interviews with selected service and civic club leaders.

Form 1 (see Appendix B) was mailed to representatives of civic, service and professional clubs throughout the United States. The number of questionnaires ranged from only 15 in the case of Quota to 4,350 in the case of the PTA. The numbers of questionnaire mailed, and the numbers and percentages returned, are shown in the following summary:

	Number of cards sent	Number returned	Percent returned
Service clubs (men)			
Lions	720	223	31
Rotary	370	153	41
Kiwanis	273	106	39
Optimist	51	10	20
Civitan	34	8	24
Service clubs (women)			
Altrusa	31	8	26
Quota	15	5	33
Parent-Teachers Association (PTA)	4350	551	13
General Federated Women's Clubs (GFWC)	827	293	35
Chamber of Commerce of the U.S.	282	98	35
County medical societies	236	67	28
National Federation of Business and Professional Women's Clubs (B. & P.W.)	142	69	49
Association of American University Women (AAUW)	98	35	36
National Association for the Advancement of Colored People (NAACP)	94	14	15
League of Women Voters	67	29	43

Chapter 7.—The basic data for the chapter concerned with the special agencies within the Department of Agriculture came from official documents and personal interviews with the agency representatives. Only secondary use was made of the mailed questionnaire. However, in the case of the Farmers Home Administration and the Soil Conservation Service, representatives of these agencies in the 263 sample counties were requested to fill out a mailed questionnaire, namely Form 1 (see Appendix B). As a result of two successive mailings, 89 questionnaires were returned on the part of Farmers Home Administration personnel, and 103 were returned by Soil Conservationists.

Chapter 8.—The findings contained in this chapter are based primarily upon personal interviews with professional librarians and upon the responses from two mailed questionnaires.

Forms 1 and 6 (see Appendix B) were mailed to 1,383 libraries located in the 263 sample counties (see description in Appendix C). After preliminary analysis of the first returns, a sample second-mailing was sent to the libraries. Two hundred and thirty-eight responses, or a 16 percent return, was obtained as a result of two mailings.

In interviews with librarians and in letters from them, the most frequent reason given for not returning the questionnaire was that the librarian did not consider that he carried on any adult education activities. Significantly, 74 percent of the questionnaires received from the second mailing reported no activities. Another reason given was that the small staffs do not have time to answer the many questionnaires which reach them. A postcard asking why the original questionnaire was not answered was sent to a sample of 100 libraries. Thirty libraries answered. Of this number, 15 said they had no program in adult education, 3 added that the staff had little time for answering questionnaires, 6 other libraries gave lack of time as their reason for not answering, 6 did not recall receiving the questionnaire, and 2 knew no reason for not having answered.

A large difference in the percentage of returns is evident among the various types of libraries. Nearly 48 percent of the state agencies returned the questionnaires or wrote letters concerning their services. Eighteen percent of the better supported county or regional libraries answered the questionnaire. Ten percent of the less well supported county or regional libraries, and nearly 9 percent of the village and city libraries responded.

It seems evident that the poor response from libraries is owing largely to the fact that few libraries serving rural areas are able to conduct activities for the education of adults. The larger units of service respond more frequently, probably indicating that more of them conduct activities, and that their staffs have more time and professional interest than the staffs of the smaller and less well supported units.

Chapter 9.—The findings in this chapter are based largely on information secured from interviews with leaders in the religious rural life organizations of

Jewish, Catholic and Protestant religious groups. Each of the leaders made available to the writer pertinent literature describing in detail the activities of his respective organization.

For the Catholic and Protestant groups mailed questionnaires were sent to ministers and church leaders in order to secure supplementary information. This was not done for the Jewish Agricultural Society, the principal agency of rural adult education among the Jews, because this organization is neither operated nor controlled by Jewish church officials or rabbis. There is no local organization having contact with the rural Jews. Instead the local work is done by a representative from a central office and two regional offices.

Form 1 (see Appendix B) was used as a questionnaire for the Catholic and Protestant groups. For the Catholic group we were fortunate in securing a list of the 70 Diocesan rural life directors to whom the questionnaire was mailed. These leaders, for the most part rural parish priests, direct rural life activities in the Diocese under the direction of the national executive secretary, Msgr. Luigi Ligutti. After a second mailing there were 36 responses or 51 percent of the total on the mailing list. In the second mailing there were numerous letters returning the questionnaire with the statement made by the Diocesan leader to the effect that he did not consider that he carried on any adult education activities.

640 questionnaires were mailed to Baptist, Methodist and Lutheran ministers in the 263 sample counties. (See description in Appendix C.) We were handicapped by not having a mailing list of Methodist and Baptist pastors. Each of the many Methodist and Baptist bodies maintains its separate list of pastors and with time limitations we were unable to contact the nearly 40 separate denominational headquarters for the lists. Consequently the letters were addressed to "The Pastor of the Methodist Church" and "The Pastor of the Baptist Church" in various rural communities selected from the 263 sample counties. In the southern communities of the sample, letters were also mailed to the colored Methodist and Baptist pastors.

Many of these communities had neither Baptist nor Methodist churches and 97 of the 580 letters mailed to these two denominations were returned undelivered. We were fortunate in obtaining a list of Lutheran ministers and 60 letters were mailed to these ministers addressed by name in the communities of the sample. After a second mailing to the three denominations we received a total of 175 responses from 543 ministers on the mailing list, or approximately 32 percent.

The churches in the sample were village and town churches in communities of the sample counties with a population range of 1,000 to 6,000. In selecting the sample we chose the county seats of the 263 sample counties. If the county seat did not come within this population range designated, we selected as an alternate the first community alphabetically listed in the county within the range.

In the second mailing inquiring as to reasons for not responding the first time, a considerable number of letters were received stating that there was no formal adult education program other than usual Sunday school and church activities. This would not come within the scope of our concern in reference to adult education. In view of the fact that most of our church questionnaires were not addressed to specific names, 32 percent could be considered as an adequate response.

Chapter 10.—The results of a mailed questionnaire and personal interviews with selected leaders in the field of continuation education constitute the basic data for this chapter. Form 1 (see Appendix B) was mailed to all colleges and universities in the United States in November 1951. Approximately 2800 questionnaires were mailed and 1021 were returned, 986 of which were usable in whole or in part. As a result of two mailings, approximately 56 percent of all colleges and universities responded.

Although no check was made of the representatives of the returns, the authors have reason to believe that colleges and universities with programs were more likely to return the questionnaire.

Chapter 11.—Two primary sources of data are utilized in the chapter dealing with the international exchange of persons. These are personal interviews with selected foreign student advisors and other persons interested in the exchange of persons, and a mailed questionnaire, Form 7 (see Appendix B).

Form 7 was mailed to approximately 1800 colleges and universities throughout the United States and its possessions. Two successive mailings resulted in 945 usable schedules, or 53 percent of the total number mailed.

Chapter 12.—Due to the time schedule and shortage of funds, no attempt was made to sample local government officials in the 263 counties. However, a special investigation of county supervisors in five counties of Michigan was made. A total of 86 supervisors in a sample of five Michigan counties was interviewed personally, the results of which are given in the text of this chapter.

The specific aims of this field study, conducted in the Spring of 1952, may be enumerated as follows:

1) to ascertain the officials' conception of his job and its requirements.

2) to learn something of the manner in which the official duties were performed.

3) to learn how the officials were selected for office.

4) to ascertain the avenues of contact between officials and constituents.

5) to learn existing beliefs of officials as to the meaning and substance of local government itself.

Chapter 13.—Three specially prepared questionnaires form the basic data for the chapter concerning mass communication. Form 4 was mailed to radio station program directors; Form 5 to weekly newspaper editors; and Form 8 to college and university information services departments (see Appendix B).

Additional data were secured from a content analysis of selected rural magazines and periodicals.

Two samples of radio station program directors were mailed a specially prepared questionnaire, Form 4. The first consisted of a 10 percent sample of all AM, FM and TV stations throughout the country. The second consisted of complete coverage of all stations in the 263 sample counties (see Appendix C). In the first instance 307 radio stations were contacted; in the second, 253 were contacted. Thus, the total sample consists of 563 cases. After a second mailing, 107 completed questionnaires, or 19 percent of the total, were returned.

Two samples of editors were sent copies of Form 5. The first consisted of a 10 percent cross-section of all weekly newspaper editors in places of 5,000 or less population in the United States. The second consisted of all weekly newspaper editors in the 263 sample counties (see Appendix C). In the first instance, 657 questionnaires were mailed; in the second, 967 were mailed. From both the general sample and the sample counties, 21 percent of the questionnaires were returned after two mailings. A total of 336 weekly newspaper editors returned the questionnaire, 136 of which came from the general sample and 200 came from the sample counties. In addition to the mailed questionnaires, a content analysis was made of selected rural magazines or periodicals. All non-advertising space for 1950 issues was appraised according to whether or not it fell into the following three fields: (1) international understanding for peace; (2) strengthening of democracy; (3) understanding and strengthening the economy; or (4) combination of any of these three. The length of each article so classified was determined and a proportion of the total non-advertising space was computed. The periodicals selected for this analysis were: *Hoards Dairyman, Successful Farming, National Livestock Producer, Cappers Farmer, Prairie Farmer,* and *Farm Journal.*

One aspect of the mass media question to which access was desired was adult educational programs originating in the colleges and universities. Form 8 was prepared and mailed to 20 percent, or 160 "Institutional primary memberships" listed in the 1951 membership roster of the American College Public Relations Association, and to all, or 71 Agricultural Experiment Station and Agricultural Extension Service editors. Thus, a total of 231 questionnaires was mailed and 92, or 40 percent were returned as a result of a first mailing.

APPENDIX D

Sub-Committee Document

ORIENTATION
MANUAL
FOR
STUDY OF ADULT EDUCATION IN
RURAL AREAS

September 14, 1951

OBJECTIVES OF STUDY

1. To determine the nature and magnitude of existent programs of adult education in rural areas in the fields of (a) international understanding for world peace, (b) understanding and strengthening of the economic order, and (c) the understanding of democracy, its functioning and structure.

2. To appraise current practices and methods in the three fields specified under 1 and to determine the amount of time, effort and expenditure devoted to the fields listed in number 1 above.

3. To make recommendations to the Fund for Adult Education as to programs or activities which might be encouraged and supported.

SCOPE OF STUDY

Since time and funds are not immediately available for an exhaustive initial investigation of adult education, as defined in a broad sense, rather arbitrary limitations are established for the area of study to include such programs as are being conducted by the land grant Colleges, the U. S. Department of Agriculture and related agencies, state and private universities and colleges, the various farmers organizations, special commodity organizations, the public school system, churches and related or affiliated organizations, public libraries, civic service and local community organizations, local government, and selected autonomous organizations reaching into the smaller units of areas and communities. The part played by mass media of communication in programs of adult education will also be included. Despite its relationship to certain of these fields, vocational and avocational education is arbitrarily excluded from consideration here.

DEFINITION OF TERMS

1. *Adult Education*, as interpreted in this study, includes non-formalized, non-credit bearing and non-vocational education directed to persons who have finished their formal education.

2. Programs or activities will be considered rural in which people living in the open country or in places of less than 2500 population participate.

3. Fields of study:

a. *International understanding for world peace.* (1). The mitigation of tensions which now threaten world peace; (2). The development among the peoples of the world of the understanding and conditions essential to permanent peace; (3). The improvement and strengthening of the United Nations and its associated international agencies; (4). The improvement of the structure and procedures by which the United States Government, and private groups in the United States, participate in world affairs.

b. *Understanding and strengthening of the economic system.* (1). The elimination of restrictions on freedom of thought, inquiry, and expression in the United States, and the development of policies and procedures best adapted to protect these rights in the face of persistent international tension; (2). The maintenance of democratic control over concentrations of public and private power, while at the same time preserving freedom for scientific and technological endeavor, economic initiative, and cultural development; (3). The strengthening of the political processes through which public officers are chosen and policies determined, and the improvement of the organizations and administrative procedures by which governmental affairs are conducted; (4). The strengthening of the organization and procedures involved in the adjudication of private rights and the interpretation and enforcement of law.

c. *The understanding of democracy, its functioning and structure.* (1). The achievement of a growing economy characterized by high output, the highest possible level of constructive employment, and a minimum of destructive instability; (2). The achievement of a greater degree of equality of economic opportunity for individuals; (3). The improvement of the structure, procedures, and administration of our economic organizations: business firms, industries, labor unions, and others; (4). The achievement of more satisfactory labor-management relations; (5). The attainment of that balance between freedom and control in our economic life which will most effectively serve the well-being of our entire society; (6). The improvement of the standard of living and the economic status of peoples throughout the world; (7). Raising the level of economic understanding of the citizens of the nation.

PROCEDURE

The sources of data for the study will vary from one organization to another and from one area to another. Organizations which exist at the National, Regional and State levels will have numerous files, records, studies and evaluations which will provide valuable sources for pertinent information in the three fields. In so far as time and funds will permit this information will be checked against similar and supplementary data secured from participants at community and local levels. Study will be made of all procedures utilized in realizing the objectives of the various programs with special emphasis upon learning why special or particular methods were adopted for a certain program or programs, and what were considered as their advantages. Special effort will be made to determine the extent to which particular media have been and are being used in various types of programs, what the advantages and disadvantages of each seems to be in the various types of programs. Attention will also be given to determining the manner in which such educational devices as face-to-face contacts, discussion groups, cliques, friendship, and other similar groups are being used as follow-up or as supplementary techniques to the various mass media employed.

A questionnaire will be developed which will be mailed to all State leaders through which information on existing programs or activities will be secured. Detailed information will be secured on selected programs and activities. Section leaders of the study will visit selected states or areas for intensive personal interviews and collection of data.

Correspondence regarding any of the schedules used in this study should be directed to Charles P. Loomis, Director of the Study of Adult Education in Rural Areas, Michigan State College, East Lansing.

DISCHARGED
DISCHARGED DEC 4 '69
DISCHARGED 1972
DISCHARGED
DISCHARGED